STORIES
MY FOLKS
TOLD ME

STORIES
MY FOLKS
TOLD ME

STORIES MY FOLKS TOLD ME

SUSANNE KELLER

Library of Congress Control Number:		2016908951
ISBN:	Hardcover	978-1-5245-0656-8
	Softcover	978-1-5245-0655-1
	eBook	978-1-5245-0654-4

Print information available on the last page.

Rev. date: 06/21/2016

To order additional copies of this book, contact:
Xlibris
1-888-795-4274
www.Xlibris.com
Orders@Xlibris.com
742433

With deep and abiding love, I dedicate this book to all who have already led and all who will follow this line.

Susanne Keller

CONTENTS

CONTENTS

CHAPTER 1

The Good Earth

LONG, LONG AGO, in the time when the last glacier was receding from what is today central Illinois, a wonderful almost magical substance which would forever affect the land was being deposited with the melt water of the dissolving giant of ice. This gift of the ice was a very special soil, made from all the sedimentary rock which the glacier, like a giant scraper, had pulverized and with its caterpillar-like, forward-moving action had laid atop the ice and carried along down to today's central Illinois. There, finally, after ten thousand years and at its southern-most reach, the glacier melted and endowed the underlying basalt rock with a wonderful rich and loamy soil, ideal for future agricultural crops, so deep it could be tilled and turned over and replanted for twenty generations or more before its vitality was ever so slightly diminished. Geologists call this glacial till. Agronomists call it about the most fertile soil in the whole world. And there the inexhaustible depth of rich Midwestern soils, those sixty inches of miraculous earth, lay year after year, century after century, increasing in vigor, just waiting for the first farmer to appear.

Gradually over the eons of time, plant life took hold to eventually become, in today's Illinois, the Tall Grass Prairie, lost to us now except for the many restorations around the Middle West. Fierce winds were the only thresher of those prairie grasses so long ago, like a double-edged winnower scattering the seeds aloft to spread and reproduce; fire was the only fertilizer to add the carbon so necessary to life; bees and insects were the only living pollinator, plentiful, thorough, and gentle.

Amazingly, even before the glacier advanced down today's North America, human beings had appeared on its northwestern shore. For millennia, as early as 40,000 to 25,000 years ago, as temperatures grew colder and water was absorbed from oceans to form glacial ice, a land bridge was created where formerly there had been ocean water. Known today as the Bering Strait at the northwestern corner of today's Alaska, it became a connection between Siberia and North America along which hunters, following big game such as mammoth, bison, and mastodons, wandered and often remained. Slowly over time men spread out over the whole continent. Then between 23,000 and 16,000 BC, the ice grew to such a formidable size that it actually impeded the access of early people's movement into North America. Finally, by 13,500 to 12,000 years ago, the melting of the glaciers returned the water to the strait and closed that land bridge completely to migration into North America.

Between 10,000 and 8,000 BC, shortly after the final retreat of the ice, those few small bands of Early Archaic people, profiting from the warmer temperatures, began following the receding glacier. Their movement across the stark and inhospitable landscape, bare of edible grasses, berries, or vegetation, in the immediate postglacial period resulted in slow progress, but over thousands of years as the climate became warmer there was gradual improvement in the environment. Wildlife began to thrive and prairie grasses took hold. Mankind responded by increasing in number, strength, and vitality.

These small bands of Stone Age people traveled continuously. They needed to follow the herds of buffalo, the rabbits, the turkeys, the squirrels which provided the meat for their diet. While the capture of this game was actually infrequent, they could usually count on finding berries, nuts, seeds, edible leaves and bark to sustain them until a large animal could be brought down with their Stone Age tools. It never occurred to these people to stop wandering, to dig a hole in the soil, drop a seed into it, water it, let it grow, collect and eat the ripened grain, for they were following the instincts and habits of earliest man. The earth waited.

Over thousands of years these peoples, slowly and imperceptibly, advanced over all of what is now North America including of course today's central Illinois, but they left the land essentially undisturbed. Inconspicuous footpaths were worn down as generations of human feet walked, where animals before them had walked, the same routes along river banks and inland to certain locations which were part of their seasonal routine. These paths later gave white settlers from Europe their first system of trails, and eventually those trails became some of the roads assumed in modern times.

Once the Native Americans began to plant their seeds of corn, squash, and beans, it was only possible in narrow strips of the alluvial plain, the silty sediment deposited by the flowing waters along rivers and streams. Inland, away from the waters' edge, the soil was too densely covered by the tall grass prairie with bulbous roots a foot thick, tightly crammed together and tangled, completely impenetrable to their Stone Age tools. Even those early sowers didn't stay in one place for many years, however, so essentially the earth, only occasionally disturbed by a primitive stone hoe, continued to lie fallow. The earth continued its wait for the first man with a tool sharp enough to penetrate the prairie grasses.

By eight thousand years ago the soil was home to prairie grasses like Switch grass, Lead Plant, Indian grass, and blossoms such as Big Bluestem, Prairie Rosin weed, and Coneflowers. All the plant life flourished in a dense tangle of roots and bulbs known today as the Tall Grass Prairie covering not only Illinois but west of the Mississippi River in today's Iowa and Missouri, until the grasslands of Kansas and Oklahoma assumed dominance. Every spring new growth of these tall grasses appeared, drank in the sunshine and rain, grew to five feet tall or more with an average height of six to eight feet, gently swayed in the summer breezes, began to dry in the heat and drought of fall, and finally fell dead with the frigid frost and deep snows of winter.

Although unseen by the eyes of man, over and over, year after year, this cycle was repeated, each time layering a thin, new, rich topsoil of decaying leaves, blossoms, and stems onto the glacial enrichment below. Beneath the ground level, in each yearly cycle, some of the fibrous roots of the wild prairie grasses would also die, decompose, and become the humus or organic matter that made the resulting soil so fertile. Together the grasses and deep tangle of roots are called sod, a mass of thick, tight soil so dense it could not be cut with a stone utensil, pervious only to rainwater by the drop, yet ideal to check the leeching of calcium and other minerals so necessary for plant nutrition. This slow but regular action over the millennia produced the deepest topsoil, as much as five feet, ever recorded. Still the earth waited.

The ecosystem of the Tall Grass Prairie included animals as well as plants. There were rabbit, opossum, coyote, bat, fox, skunk, prairie dog, weasel, mink, badger, raccoon, mole, squirrel, woodchuck, gopher, mouse, rat, and deer, as well as the relic of the mastodon: the bison or buffalo. Birds filled the air in flocks of painted buntings, meadowlarks, sparrows, vireos, woodpeckers, piping plovers, owls, grouses, kites, and hundreds more.

Then, slowly but surely toward the end of the 15th Century, Europeans who had been venturing farther and farther west in their search for a route to the riches of the Far East or who had simply been following their fishing prey as far as the Grand Banks in the north Atlantic and off the coast of today's Canada, happened to sight landfall, today's America. This was a new kind of man who appeared on the scene. He and his kind approached from the east. They were not Stone Age men but were modern men, Europeans skilled in celestial navigation who had been sailing the Atlantic Ocean in the new caravels since the Portuguese Prince Henry the Navigator in the early 1400s. Traveling by river and stream after they had penetrated the landmass through the great waters now known as the St. Lawrence Seaway, the earliest of those men were searching for a route to the Orient. Later their kind came looking for furs and feathers, minerals and iron. They enriched themselves through trade with the Native Americans, but they were not farmers, so still the earth waited.

The Spanish were the first Europeans to lay claim to lands in the New World through the explorations of Christopher Columbus in 1492. He discovered islands off the coast of today's Florida although he believed that he had arrived in the West Indies or today's India. Spaniards, Juan Ponce de Leon in 1512 and Alvero Nunez Cabeza de Vaca in 1527, explored today's Florida, and Hernando De Soto explored the southeastern landmass of America in 1539. By 1565 the Spanish had established their first settlement of St. Augustine at today's north Florida coast of the Atlantic Ocean. This was indeed the first successful European settlement in North America.

Not to be left out of the exploration for riches, Queen Elizabeth I of England encouraged the seafaring adventurer and intellectual, Walter Raleigh, by knighting him and commissioning him to establish a settlement for her in today's Virginia. This he accomplished in 1585, but it did not survive due to conflicts with the Native Americans and the difficulty of supplying a colony so far from the motherland.

James I, successor to Elizabeth, too was keen on riches and colonization. As in Elizabethan times, the method was for the crown to issue charters to "companies of adventurers," who risked their own money as an investment on future returns. This time the Londoners traveled to the former Raleigh settlement by entering the Chesapeake Bay in 1607 and marking out a town they called Jamestown after their sovereign. Twice it nearly failed and population shrank drastically, but by 1610 it could be said that the first enduring English settlement was on the map.

Ten years later saw the now famous landing of the "Mayflower" at New Plymouth in what was to become Massachusetts. Captained by Miles Standish and led by William Bradford and William Brewster, were forty-one families who came to America not primarily for gain but to create God's kingdom on earth. They were zealots, idealists, utopians, and they were Calvinists, all English, and mostly from London. They were going to America to pursue religious freedom, unified in their Puritan Christian convictions.

Dutch explorers such as Henry Hudson and Adrian Block, not to be surpassed by the Spanish and English, also played a key role in colonizing the continent. Initially in 1602, they too traveled west from their homeland aiming for the West Indies, landing instead in the mouth of the river which today bears Hudson's name and sailing on into Long Island Sound. In 1626 having established lucrative ties with the Native Americans on the lower Hudson River, the Dutch convinced those Indians to sell them an island at the mouth of the river. The Dutch named the island Manhattan, and the settlement they called New Amsterdam.

It was the French, however, who first explored today's Illinois. Though he never made it to Illinois or even to the Great Lakes, the purview of his compatriots, Jacques Cartier was the first French explorer to venture along the eastern seaboard of today's Canada, even into the opening which led to today's St. Lawrence River. Soon after, in 1598, another Frenchman, Samuel de Champlain, voyaged deeper into the area of the St. Lawrence Seaway where his friendly relations with the Native Americans enabled him to establish settlements, attracting 300 citizens from France to brave the hardships of the northerly wilderness. The culminating success of Champlain was when he secured the first enduring French settlement in America at Quebec in 1608.

Frenchman, Robert Cavalier de LaSalle, followed in 1682. With fifty-four Frenchmen and Indian guides, he explored farther on into the Great lakes of Lake Ontario, Lake Erie, Lake Huron, and Lake Michigan all by canoe and finally by rivers to the great Mississippi River. In time he claimed the entire valley of the Mississippi River for King Louis XIV of France and named the enormous land mass Louisiana in honor of his king. All the land including the Great Lakes in the north to the Gulf of Mexico in the south, from the Allegheny Mountains in the east to the Mississippi River in the west was encompassed in this gigantic, unknown vastness, now claimed by France. Subsequently, the French culture went deep into Illinois in the 17th and 18th centuries, establishing forts, posts, trading villages, and farms but only along navigable waters, the sole roads of that day. In the many river junctions and portages, settlements sprouted. The bluffs overlooking waterways, especially, were ideal for military posts, providing natural sentry points.

Often the early French sojourners were representatives of the Catholic Church. Such a man, Jacques Marquette, had studied for twelve years at Jesuit universities back in France before he was sent, in 1666, to work in the Indian missions in Canada. There he endeavored to learn the Native American languages and eventually could converse fluently in six different dialects. Thus thoroughly prepared he was sent by his religious order to Sault Saint Marie to work with the Ottawa Indians. Tribal warfare there later forced Marquette to abandon his Lake Superior mission, however, so he traveled to the north shore of the Straits of Mackinac, between Lake Michigan and Lake Huron, where he founded the St. Ignace mission in 1671.

One day the trader Louis Joliet came to the mission. He said that he had heard about a great river that flowed so far to the south that no one knew where it ended. Father Marquette had also heard Indians speak of the endless river, so he decided to accompany Joliet as chaplain for the expedition, intending to do missionary work with the tribes along its shores. Together then, Father Jacques Marquette and Louis Joliet, set out in spring of 1673 from their base on Mackinac Island and the mission at nearby St. Ignace where several of the Great Lakes converge. In two birchbark canoes, accompanied by six voyageurs, with some parched corn and dried meat for sustenance, and with the intent to map the region, establish friendly relations with the native people whom they encountered, convert when possible the Indians to Christianity, document plant and animal life, and generally acquaint themselves with the wonders of the virgin world so unknown to their sovereign back in France, the two embarked on their historical journey.

Down the west coast of Lake Michigan they paddled deep into the land no European had ever seen. Southwest of today's Green Bay, Wisconsin, the explorers entered the Fox River and from there into the Wisconsin River and by easy portages on to the Mississippi River. Mid-July found the expedition as far as the mouth of the Arkansas River where they met with Spaniards who based on the discovery of the area by their compatriot, Herman de Soto, claimed the Mississippi for themselves and were willing to go to battle for it. Guided instead by peaceful, scientific purposes, the two leaders, running low on provisions and abused by voracious mosquitos, returned north via the Illinois and Kankakee Rivers to their base on Lake Michigan. Joliet continued on east to Montreal, but Marquette stayed until late 1674 when he led another excursion to the Chicago portage.

At that time the principal Indian nations in today's Illinois were the Algonquin and Iroquois. Tribes within the Illinois Confederacy were names: Tamaroas, Michigans, Kaskaskians, Cahokias, Peorias, Illinois, Miamis, and Delawares among others. All are names which today are commonly known place names in today's Illinois. Though the Indians had to eventually yield control of the land, give up their basic culture, and withdraw physically from Illinois, the names they gave to places have endured to the present day throughout the state. Kaskaskia, located on the Mississippi River seven miles south of present-day Ottawa, was the principle town of their confederacy. There Marquette and Joliet met the Indian leaders in 1673 and reported receiving the greatest possible hospitality.

The year after this trip on the Mississippi River, Marquette set out on a return visit to work with the Illinois people, but plagued by bad health and unable to travel, he spent the winter of 1674-75 with two French companions in what is now Chicago. By spring though his health was deteriorating and despite cold, wet weather, he attempted to travel along the eastern shore of Lake Michigan to his home base, his St. Ignace mission farther north. En route, he felt so poorly that he asked to be taken ashore where there he died, shortly before his thirty-eighth birthday. Today two Michigan communities, Frankfort and Luddington, vie for the designation of Father Marquette's death site.

Word had reached Louis XIV, ruler of France, of the vast, open, empty tracts of land in his possession far away across the ocean in New France. Settlers, he knew, would be essential to keeping the huge possession for himself, so notices throughout France appeared to announce free grants of land to any man who would seize the opportunity. Such an unheard of prospect of land of one's own was commensurate with a freedom such as no common man in Europe had ever hoped for! To sweeten the package, King Louis even threw in a cow, pig, farm implements, and a wagon, ensuring the immediate departure of thousands of his subjects for the New World. America held vast riches but the real magnet drawing men to her shores was the promise of land, simply unattainable back in Europe with its centuries old class system set in stone.

Relations between the Native Americans and those French settlers who followed the early explorers actually were peaceable. The French families endeavored to get along with their Indian neighbors in the spirit of cooperation and mutual agreement as opposed to the British settlers who generally held the Indians in contempt as inferiors. To be sure, both European groups exploited the natives in order to get what they wanted. Though very small in population (the French population of all Louisiana never exceeded 10,000) five villages were established in present day Illinois: at Cahokia (5 miles south of present St. Louis), St. Philip near Cahokia, Kaskaskia on the Kaskaskia River Fort, Fort Chartres (12 miles north of Kaskaskia), and Prairie du Rocher near Fort Chartres. These were trading centers, not farming communities requiring seizure of Indian lands though, so the good earth still lay fallow.

In 1765 this land of the Illinois Indian Confederacy fell from French into English hands according to the Treaty of Paris of 1763 which ended the Seven Years War (1755 – 1760) in America. Although France and England had been at peace in Europe, General George Washington's 1754 clash with French troops, in today's upstate New York, created a virtual state of war in North America. In response, the British sent troops to assist Washington. The combined American and British forces expected to make short work of the war but many Indian tribes joined with the French and Canadian troops, making it difficult for either side to win. The tide was finally turned when the British announced they would wave all expenses of the war if the Americans would supply more troops. This they did in unexpected numbers which resulted in the fall of fort after fort to the British. By the end of those "French and Indian Wars" won by the British, France ceded to England all her territories on the North American mainland and as a result, several thousand French colonists, stretching from Quebec to Illinois to Louisiana, became British subjects. France gave Britain all of its lands east of the Mississippi River and transferred claim to all its possessions west of the river, including New Orleans, to Spain. But still the land awaited the first tiller.

Britain was now the world's most powerful nation. It felt justified in centralizing its imperial authority and to forcing the colonies to contribute more revenue to the British treasury. In Britain's view, the colonies existed solely to sustain the Fatherland. Across the Atlantic, however, their colonial officials were confronted with the ambitions and attitudes of Americans who increasingly felt themselves equal in every way to the Britons and not bound at all to a subservient role.

Society was indeed advancing along the colonial Atlantic seaboard where a continuous wave of Europeans, primarily Englishmen, was settling towns and farms after their first arrival in the early 17th century. Cities such as New York, Philadelphia, Charleston, Providence, and Boston were founded. Schools and universities such as Harvard, Yale, and William and Mary were established. Colonial governments were established incorporating representative governments, elected assemblies, freedom of religion and speech, and jury trials. Among the early American settlers were farmers who gradually advanced west as far as today's Pennsylvania and West Virginia, but until this point in history they could not yet seek land as far west as Illinois because the land belonged to the British crown. The earth was still waiting.

By the mid-1770s the restrictions and taxes imposed by the British to their colonies in North America were so egregious that representatives of the thirteen colonies gathered to find a way to defend their rights against British edicts. Fifty-six delegates attended the first Continental Congress in Philadelphia on September 5, 1774. The delegates summarized their principles and demands in a petition to King George III, who immediately and correctly surmised rebellion in the minds of the colonists. Still, most colonists clung to hopes of reconciliation until the last barrier to accepting independence finally crumbled in January 1776 with the publication of Thomas Paine's "Common Sense." It was printed in both English and German and sold more than 100,000 copies within three months or one copy for every four or five adult colonial males.

From that point, the movement toward independence took possession of the citizens, stimulating local gatherings of colonists to pass resolutions favoring American independence. Allegiance to George III had dissolved and it was now time for a formal statement of separation. That job fell to a committee including John Adams, Benjamin Franklin, and Thomas Jefferson, who as principal writer obliged with his "Declaration of Independence" of July 4, 1776.

Securing Independence was of course a long, laborious, never certain endeavor. For five years from 1776, the revolutionary army under the leadership of General George Washington conducted war to secure true autonomy and separation from England. Through many failures and successes his troops with the help of the French leader, Lafayette, finally achieved the pivotal success over Cornwallis at Yorktown which ended the fighting. With the signing of the Peace of Paris in 1783 which officially concluded the Revolutionary War, America now gained all the formerly British lands west to the Mississippi River. Those new lands still awaited the first farmers.

Six years between the end of the revolutionary war and the election of George Washington to the presidency of the United States in 1789 were vital ones in which a fragile nation began to take shape. In May 1787 fifty-five delegates from every state but Rhode Island gathered in Philadelphia's Independence Hall to write the Constitution for the new nation. A Congress was established, courts were set-up, a judicial system appointed, a banking system organized, and a Bill of Rights was written, among many essential efforts necessary for a functioning democracy. As always, progress was uneven as opposing arguments had to be heard and consensus established.

By 1800, even before the fighting had ceased, more virgin land was available to pioneers. Spain had become a weak and declining power in the world to the extent that she lost her American territory to Napoleon Bonaparte of France in the Treaty of San Ildefonso in Europe. Then in 1803, the same Napoleon of France declared that he wished to sell his lands in America in order to pay for his wars of aggression in Europe. Happily, President Thomas Jefferson paid $15 million to acquire all the land from the Mississippi River in the east to the Rocky Mountains in the west, from the forty-ninth parallel in the north to the Gulf of Mexico in the south. This was the famous Louisiana Purchase, still more land to await the first farmers.

With so much land now in the possession of the United States federal government, ways were sought by the authorities to secure the orderly settlement of the public lands. The Ordinance of 1785 divided public lands into townships of six miles square each and then subdivided each township into one-mile-square lots, called sections, of 640 acres each. The sale of these extremely large parcels would generate income for the federal government, but few immigrant farmers could afford to buy them, resulting by default in purchases by speculators.

Believing that the small farmer was the backbone of the nation, Vice-president Thomas Jefferson and the Republicans began in 1800 to ease the transfer of the public domain to farmers by passing new federal land laws. These land laws dropped the minimum purchase to 320 acres and allowed up to four years for full payment. The price was $2.00 an acre. In 1832 the minimum was further reduced to 40 acres and the price was down to $1.25 an acre.

Whether sold by speculators or the government, most of the public lands eventually found its way into the hands of small farmers. Finally, families who wished to possess their own farm, to till their own soil, to support themselves by their own sweat and toil were able to migrate west to that very special farmland. And so they did! Between 1790 and 1860 five million people, including our folks, migrated from Europe. The good earth was ready and waiting and its new masters were coming in droves.

There was a big obstacle however: the Native Americans who naturally were determined to obstruct the usurpation of their ancestral lands by the white settlers. Their resistance to the arrival of organized parties of white settlers has been recorded in countless books and movies until it is the basis of American folklore, and so we know that although they were experienced fighters among themselves they generally lacked the organization and modern tools of warfare to be consistently successful against the formidable weapons of the white men.

The superior methods provided by the U.S. government also included the many fortified enclosures or forts which were built and staffed by U.S. soldiers. Each fort could house one hundred or more soldiers and consisted of a strong timber or stone palisade or wall with a blockhouse made of logs at each corner. These United States Army posts were established for the protection of the settlers at the upper Mississippi at Fort Snelling, today's Minneapolis where the Minnesota River enters the Mississippi, at Fort Crawford where the Wisconsin River enters, at Fort Armstrong where the Rock River enters, at Fort Madison where the DesMoines River enters, and at Jefferson Barracks where the Missouri River enters. Between these soldiers and the Indians, skirmishes as well as famous battles were waged over a period of many years even into the late 1830s. By that time, though, the army could, through intimidation, prevent the Indians from attacking whites.

Yes, the United States government had made preparations for the migration of new settlers to its new western lands by systematically eliminating the Indians who had been fighting to prevent the encroachment of the white settlers. At first the Indians were persuaded or bribed to relinquish some lands by signing a treaty, receiving cash or guns, and agreeing to move farther west. But in reality, Mother Earth was considered sacred to these people. They believed that the land belonged to the Great Spirit, not to man. Though the tribes in which they lived fought neighboring tribes very frequently, their disputes were not over property rights or ownership of land but hunting rights and later grazing rights. The treaties which the United States Government signed with the Indians became the death knell to the Stone Age people.

The white men had a different set of values, however. Foremost in their minds was to own property on which they could farm. Because the Indian believed all land belonged to the Great Spirit, they could not understand the meaning of the agreements they signed. Furthermore, the Indians didn't always understand the European language. They were at a huge disadvantage; they were persuaded to sell their land to the white man, in effect, doing business in a foreign language and dealing with a foreign topic, the selling of land. There was no way they could possibly have made wise business decisions under such circumstances. The treaties, nevertheless, took the land and gave it to the Federal Government, who in turn sold it to railroad companies and to white settlers. Then, the land belonged to humans, not to the Great Spirit. Everyone benefited except the Indians!

The final guillotine drop came when it became apparent to the U.S. Government in Washington DC that acquiring the land piecemeal by treaty was neither efficient nor speedy enough. More desperate and cruel measures were undertaken. President Andrew Jackson secured passage in 1830 of the Indian Removal Act, which authorized him to exchange public lands west of the Mississippi River for Indian territories to the east. Congress appropriated $500,000 to cover the expenses of the removal. But the real costs of removal, human and monetary, were vastly greater. During Jackson's eight years in office, the federal government exchanged 100 million acres of Indian land for 32 million acres of public lands at a cost of $68 million. Notable as an exception to the peaceful march of Indians westward was the case of the Sac and Fox chef, Black Hawk, who resisted removal from today's Illinois until 1831. He and his band fought an uprising after moving west of the Mississippi only to return east again the following year. It took federal troops and Illinois militia to virtually annihilate Black Hawk's followers before their remnant again crossed westward of the river. Black Hawk's downfall was the final inducement for other tribes to cede their lands. The land was still waiting.

With the Native American no longer an impediment to land acquisition in today's Illinois, practical obstacles did remain. The transportation system linking the eastern seaboard to Illinois had severe weaknesses. Roads, called turnpikes, were expensive to maintain, and horse-drawn wagons could carry only limited load of people and produce. To facilitate westward migration, Congress had authorized funds in 1816 for construction of the National Road, a highway begun in 1811 that reached Vandalia, Illinois, by 1838. A broad, hard-packed dirt road, it could accommodate the large wagons pulled by oxen which became a part of our folk history and known as the Conestoga wagon train. Though the Illinois landscape lacked the craggy mountains, bold ocean coasts, and fast plunging rivers to suggest awesome forces of nature, it still took a strength of great magnitude in that day to traverse her.

The tall grass prairie lands of Illinois were themselves an impediment to settlement making them the last acres to be chosen there. The tangle of small but dense roots could not be penetrated by the plow of the day leading to rumors that the grasses were actually floating on bodies of water and would swallow any travelers attempting to venture over it. Scarce timber furthered the myth and indicated to those folks insufficient water and poor soils. Very real though were the voracious flies, the wind-whipped prairie fires of orange flames shimmering against an inky night sky and blackening miles of prairie overnight, and the steep contrast of intense summer heat and humidity with winter's blast of freezing ice and snow. Such impediments combined with the imperviousness of the soil kept the farmer at bay until the 1830s. But the land was silently waiting.

Often, it was even faster to travel by water. Keelboats, just a raft or flatboat with a rudder for underwater steering, could navigate the waterways upstream only and at a snail's pace. Significantly, the great rivers between the Mississippi River and the Appalachian Mountains ran north to south, with the exception of the Ohio River, and hence could not serve settlers wishing to move from east to west.

Therefore, the first improvement in transportation stimulated an unprecedented migration from the eastern seaboard westward. This was the completion of the Erie Canal in 1825 which was the most famous of many canals built by back-breaking labor, linking the Hudson River with Lakes Ontario and Erie in the west. From there it was possible to access other canals which joined the Ohio River with the Mississippi and with the Great Lakes. Not only were the canals used by people moving themselves and their possessions toward the west but they were, like the rivers of the day, the highways on which they shipped their agricultural produce to port cities and then on to larger markets. Canal boats were powerless, pulled by a horse or donkey tethered to it walking the tow path on both sides of the water, pulling the boat and its contents forward. Canal construction, paid by state governments, was considered mind bogglingly expensive yet the networks of them reduced the cost of shipping from 20 to 30 cents a ton per mile in 1815 to 2 to 3 cents a ton per mile by 1830.

Next, in the mid-1820s came the advent of the steamboat to the Mississippi-Ohio Rivers system. They were vastly superior to flatboats, whether on river or canal, for they offered relative speed. Especially for those, such as our Buehrigs, wishing to travel from New Orleans north to Louisville or St. Louis, the travel time could be reduced from four months to twenty-five days. They offered the privacy and comfort of cabins as well.

But the possibility for travel really exploded with the coming of the railroads to today's Illinois in 1850. Cheaper to build, faster, and able to reach more places, railroads had an obvious advantage over canals and rivers and also contributed to the growth of communities located far from waterways. They were built by private corporations not governments.

Yes, improved transportation had made possible a great migration. By 1840, one-third of all Americans lived between the Appalachian Mountains and the Mississippi River. Between 1816 and 1821, six states including Illinois had entered the Union.

Each of the eager farmers heading to Illinois had a certificate of ownership which he had purchased from a U.S. government land agent, located in cities of the east coast and also in Illinois towns like Kaskaskia, Shawneetown, or Edwardsville, for a specific section of land which was composed of one square mile or 640 acres. The land agent surveyed, then registered, documented, and recorded each section in an official government ledger so that when a parcel was sold the deed or title of ownership was given to the purchaser, each step of the transaction faithful to the law. If a pioneer lacked the going price of $1.25 per acre in 1830, he could also purchase half a section, a quarter, or even a sixteenth. In those days, with technology still primitive, one man with one horse or mule could actually only handle forty acres, of which there are sixteen in a section of a township.

Many of the first land owners were Revolutionary War or War of 1812 soldiers who had been paid for fighting with land, instead of dollars, which the government didn't have. Payment in land instead of currency was a common scheme of governments since ancient times. Marseilles, France, for example, was settled by Greek warriors after their service in the Greco-Persian Wars of the mid-Sixth Century BC. Roman soldiers, likewise, were given land in Britain and France as compensation for their military service there. Of course, many soldiers had no intention of farming, so they sold the land to eager men who did desire to till the rich soil of Illinois. The land brought a price of $1.25 per acre in 1830. Finally, the land of rich alluvial till, as the gift of the glacier is called in geological terms, was going to be turned over, seeded, cared for, and

STORIES MY FOLKS TOLD ME

harvested. The long-waiting earth was ready—and the pioneers, our ancestors among them, were on their way to claim it!

A number, given to each pioneer family name, will be added to subsequent descendant's stories so that the reader can trace the lineage of that person.

STORIES MY FOLKS TOLD ME

Immigrants

1. Peine from Hofgeismar, Hessen

2. Buehrig from Lesse, Lower Saxony

3. L.H. Buehrig from Lesse, LS
    Caroline Austmann from Detmold,
    North Rhine Westphalia

4. Imig from Pfalzdorf, North Rhine
    Westphalia

5. Graff from Pfalzdorf, North Rhine
    Westphalia

6. Peter and Elizabeth Graff from
    Louisendorf, North Rhine Westphalia

7. Wilhelm Oehler from Weisweil, Baden
    Marie Mueller from Altmersbaden, today's
    Prussia

8. G.T. Rost from Ruedersdorf, Brandenburg
    Anke Wilken from Etzel, Lower Saxony

CHAPTER 2

The Pioneers

Stephen Henry Peine and Anna Margaret Davin Peine arrive 1845
—1—

O NE OF THE earliest settlers to Tazewell County, in the center of Illinois and the area with perhaps the richest soil of all, were Stephen and Margaret Davin Peine. They arrived in 1845 from their home in Hofgeismar just north of Kassel in the state of Hessen in north central Germany with their children, three year old Mary and baby Henry A., born just one year earlier on April 3, 1844. They had been married five years prior to emigration. The motivation which they themselves gave for their particular emigration was to escape the difficult times caused by forced conscription into the army and widespread hunger which was ubiquitous under the profligate ruler of Hessen, Elector Wilhelm II.

Margaret and Stephen came to a country where a revolution had already taken place while their birthplace, Germany, still a patchwork of small principalities, duchies, grand duchies, free city-states, and a couple of large kingdoms, such as Prussia and Bavaria, would not be politically unified until 1871. Those regal entities had all been part of the Holy Roman Empire established by Charlemagne in the year 800. The sovereigns each held supreme authority over the common people, made the laws, led the wars, directed the life of state. Under them were the nobles who held office through a hereditary right and the priests. Next, civil servants handled the flood of reports, dispatches, petitions, and finally at the lowest level were the peasants or farmers and the village merchants. Society was locked into that system for more than a thousand years until the Prussian prime minister, Count Adolph von Bismarck led his kingdom into many wars with the lesser states, defeating them so that they all agreed to join the new Germany, an entity which had never before been more than a geographical fantasy. But when that occurred Stephen and Margaret were long gone from Hofgeismar.

The title "Elector" referred to the seven most powerful rulers in the Holy Roman Empire who together formed an Electoral College to appoint the emperor of the Empire. The rulers of Hesse-Kassel held one of these electoral seats. Elector Wilhelm II, 1777—1847, ruler of Hesse-Kassel, from where Stephen and Margaret hailed, continued the tradition of his line to keep a very large standing army. Seven percent of the population was under arms, in fact. Because of the excess number of his soldiers, the ruler was constantly hiring out contingents of the army as mercenaries. Most famously Hesse-Kassel rented soldiers to King George III of Great Britain during the American War of Independence. "Hessian" became American slang word for all the Germans deployed by the British in that war. It was expensive to maintain so many men in arms so taxation was confiscatory, causing much deprivation and hunger even for those like the Peines who were tenant farmers and could grow their own food. But even by working harder and harder they could not keep up with taxes and rent.

There actually is a town, Peine, located in Rhineland Westpfalia. Perhaps earlier ancestors of Stephen Peine came from there though genealogy searches affirm that Stephen and Margaret Peine were not from there but from Hofgeismar. Even so, the town of Peine has a coat of arms, a copy of which is in the possession of Peine descendants today.

Besides the impetus of forced conscription, taxes, and hunger impelling Germans to emigrate to the United States, there was a history of people leaving German lands to better themselves. In 1763—67 when Catherine the Great of Russia, a German princess of Prussia who married Paul who became the czar of Russia and survived him as ruler, needed people to settle lands along the Volga River as a buffer against invading Mongol horde, she reached back to her former homeland advertising land, autonomy, exemption from military service, and the right to speak their German tongue. Population pressure in the German states of Bavaria, Baden, Rheinland-Palatinate, and Hesse led to the emigration of enough Germans to fill one hundred and four villages along the Volga River, hence the name Volga Germans. Another example were the Banat Germans who were enticed from the Schwabian folk living along the Danube River in southern Germany into the Hungarian state of Banat in order to regrow a population which had been decimated by a series of wars with Turkey in the 18th Century. Those same Germans, the Volga Germans and Banat Germans after World War II were persecuted in the land where they had put down roots, were robbed of their citizenship, and expelled, forcing them to return to a war torn Germany.

Today's state of Hesse where the Peines lived was even then known as the origin of the Grimm Fairy Tales. The brothers Grimm, Jacob and Wilhelm, had traveled to the villages of Hesse and farther afield throughout Germany in the late 18th Century interviewing village story tellers, listening to the folk stories, writing them down, and finally first publishing them in 1812. Margaret and Stephen surely knew the beloved fairy tales like Cinderella, Hansel and Gretel, and Little Red Riding Hood, all with a little lesson or moral woven in, and so enchanted little Mary and Henry with their telling.

Agriculture was underdeveloped at the time with scarcely any advances since pre-historic times and increasingly unable to support a population undergoing rapid growth. Still Hesse boasts one of the earliest wine producing districts of Germany, the Rheingau, where the famous German Riesling is produced. Overpopulation was arguably the principal cause of emigration. Europe was the first continent on earth where death rates fell substantially faster than birth rates. The population of Germany more than doubled from 1800 to 1870 in spite of all the emigration. Many of those leaving the overcrowded countryside knew they had little hope of making a living in the cities and preferred to risk emigration to America.

Stephen and Margaret likely traveled by train from Hofgeismar to Bremerhaven where they boarded a steamship to Baltimore, Maryland. Or perhaps they availed themselves of the new emigrant boat service which plied on many of the European rivers traveling from Kassel north to a German seaport to board their transoceanic steamship. Just five years prior to the Peines' journey, travel by steam power had been introduced affording the traveler greater speed and comfort and cheaper fare over the wooden sailing ships. Their passage likely lasted three weeks and cost ten dollars per adult.

Margaret had carefully sewn their gold coins into their clothing for safe-keeping, and she had brought along satchels of food for the passage, seeds for their future farm, and the barest minimum of clothing. Steerage passengers in the new iron ships were expected to cook their own food. The shipping company provided weekly: two and a half pounds of bread, one pound of wheat flour, five pounds of oatmeal, two pounds of rice or five pounds of potatoes, half a pound of sugar, half a pound of molasses, two ounces of tea, and straw to sleep on. In addition, the Peines were entitled to three quarts of water per day for drinking and for hygiene.

At the time of their voyage, conditions below in steerage were still considered deplorable, and it wasn't until 1848 that the American Passenger Act was passed to require a minimum measure of space per person, a ventilation system to allow air to circulate below despite the weather conditions above.

Presumably, Margaret and Stephen had heard of the health risks of confinement aboard ship and so they attempted to spend as much time up on deck as possible especially for the sake of their small children. They were familiar with stories of "Ship Fever" or typhus which was highly contagious and often fatal. It was common knowledge that it was carried by lice, so they were constantly on the lookout for the pesky little worms, frequently sifting through each other's hair and clothing.

Still, upon boarding the ship they already were infused with a feeling of freedom and optimism. There they were without passport or papers, health certificate or any other documentation because these were not then required, practically without luggage in fact; if they were lucky, in due course they would go ashore in Baltimore, no one asking them who they were or where they were going, and they would just vanish into the body of the New World. The famous Ellis Island immigration procedures were not even created until 1878 long after our ancestors arrived!

The Peines had heard wonderful things about America from letters written to friends back in Hofgeismar—letters which were read aloud to rapt gatherings 'round the fireside and told of a wonderful place where there was no crushing tax burden, no customs duties every time one turned around, no tithes because there was no state church, no conscription because the army was one-fiftieth the size of Prussia's, no political police, no censorship, no legalized class distinctions. All classes wore the same clothes! Employers and their hands ate at the same table! No one called anyone "master!" Yes, Stephen and Margaret were excited and full of hope about their decision to emigrate. He was forty years old and she was thirty.

Left behind in Germany were Stephen's parents, Johannes, born in 1783, and his French-born wife, Henrietta Lizetta Albrecht, his brothers and sisters, grandparents, friends and relatives. Stephen's grandfather was George Heinrich Peine born around 1760 in Hesse. Stephen was born November 29, 1806, in Hofgeismar, Hesse.

The Peines of Stephen's childhood were a bilingual family with mother speaking French and father speaking both French and German. The Napoleonic wars of 1803--25 had wreaked havoc and depravation on life in Hesse-Kassel. Soldiers were constantly marching through, confiscating foodstuffs and clothing, killing with impunity, causing the border between Germany and France to be constantly in flux during those years, filling the people with fear and dread. After Napoleon's victory over most of Europe, the Peine family found their home in Hofgeismar was suddenly in French occupied territory. Created arbitrarily by Napolean as the Kingdom of Westphalia with its capital in nearby Kassel, it was part of the makeover of the entire Rhineland and North Germany, ruled by one of his incompetent relatives, filled with French soldiers, and governed with tyranny. That one French man could wipe out so much history, reorganize states at will, make up new names for them, give them to relatives to rule, fill with French troops certainly bred a hate for the French in our folks! As a boy during the occupation Johannes had been exposed to the French language spoken all around him, and he was even forced to learn it. For awhile during his childhood he was even called upon to act as an enforced interpreter for the French during the Napoleonic occupation. Because

French citizens were lured across the Rhine River to the occupied lands in former Germany in order to turn them as quickly as possible into French dominated lands, the woman he fell in love with and married was a woman originally from France, Henrietta Lizetta Albrecht. But of course he didn't consider her as the enemy. Her family were Huguenots or French Protestants, which in that time of zero tolerance for those of a different religion, was important to the Protestant Peines.

Margaret left a full compliment of Davin family members too, of course. In fact, her family can be traced back to 1660 with the birth of Michael Davin in the village of Fenestrelle, in the northern state of Torino, Italy. Michael Davin married Susanne Roux in Fenestrelle but they left Italy at some point, and he died while they were living in France. Susanne 1664—1738 was also born in Fenestrelle, but she died in Hofgeismar, Hesse, Germany. Their son Jean Davin 1685—1745 was born in Mentoulles, near Fenestrelle, Italy and married Marguerite Ray who was born in France. They too with his mother, Susanne, settled in Germany where their son, Jean Johannes Davin 1733—1792 was born. His wife, Marie Catherine Bollen, was German born as well and bore him a son, Johannes H. Davin in 1774. Anne Gertrude Holmann, born in 1786 in Germany, was his wife. Anna Margaret Davin, born March 3, 1816, was their daughter who married Stephen Peine in 1840 and emigrated with him five years later to the United States.

Once settled in America, she found that it took months for letters written back to Germany to be answered. Though she knew she was fortunate to live in a German community where she could understand the language and be understood, could be supported in her homesick moments which did come, ever so often she would look at a common household item and be reminded of her family in Hofgeismar and the tears would surely come. Even a date on the calendar would remind her of her mother's birthday or a friend's illness. Of course, Christmas was a particularly emotional time. Busy as Margaret was in her new life, there were moments when her mind would turn to those she had left behind, to conversations or events they would never again share. When she learned by letter of the death of a loved one or birth of a friend's baby it was months after the event had transpired; she was thousands of miles from all she had known in her former life and sometimes it hurt her profoundly because a little part of her had not wanted to leave. She probably instinctively knew that as Michel de Montaigne wrote: "The easy, gentle, and sloping path…. is not the path of true virtue. That demands a rough and thorny road." Margaret never expected her life to be easy. The easy stuff doesn't teach us much. Only what is difficult and challenging enhances our growth!

Once the Peines disembarked from the ship, "Louise," in Baltimore, they must have stepped into a scene of utter pandemonium where many languages were shouted offering rooms, food, cart transportation of baggage to the new arrivals. Shocked and fearful, they clung to the nearest man voicing German and followed him to a rooming house operated by Germans where they found accommodation for a few days rest, got back their "land legs," and ate some wholesome meals prepared by the proprietor's wife and daughter. Stephen soon sought the land office where he could view the lists of lands for sale in Illinois, his desired destination based on letters written by earlier immigrants back to Hofgeismar. Those letters had extolled the richness of the soil in today's central Illinois, its availability, and its low cost.

Now, it was necessary to unstitch the pockets of their clothing, to remove the larger pieces of gold to lay down at the land office to purchase specific acreage in Illinois. With trembling hands, Stephen received the title of ownership to his very own land, his future home, and the beginning of the Peine heritage in America. It was the turning point of his life, the opening of a new chapter, a true milestone, and was every bit as much so for Margaret now pregnant with her third child yet forced to embark on yet another arduous journey still westward.

America's network of rivers and canals were the highways of the day. Flatboats handled loads like the Peine family with their meager possessions, active toddlers, and heads full of dreams. Meals were purchased at reasonable intervals from vendors on shore who came aboard to display their wares to the non-English speaking Peines. Most tasted strange to Stephen and Margaret and especially to their toddlers but hunger was their companion, and the children were not spoiled or picky eaters. The meals had been prepared by an enterprising housewife who lived on the shores of the Ohio River.

The landscape passing before their eyes was the beautiful Ohio River valley, as the major segment of the journey was spent on the Ohio River. Smaller streams and canals afforded the Peines access to and from it, and finally after several weeks they stopped in Dayton, Ohio. There Margaret was delivered of baby Sophina. As soon as Margaret was strong enough, though, Stephen and Margaret continued on to central Illinois where the remainder of their family was born. Hettie and Stephen came to the family while at their first home in Hittle Township in central Illinois; George, named for his great-grandfather back in Germany, was born May 2, 1856 on the Peine family homestead located five miles southwest of Minier, Illinois. It is his line which we shall follow.

From history books we read that the tall grass prairie sod around Pekin, Illinois, like that purchased by Stephen and Margaret had only recently, by 1837, been "broken," a term used to describe the painstaking job of preparing the dense mat of roots and plants for tilling and planting of seeds. Though the prairie grasses had existed since the last glacial age and had created their own sustaining ecosystem, a gnarl of small but dense, tough roots up to two feet deep, no seed dropped into it by man could ever take root. A team of three or four oxen, yoked together, was required slowly dragging an enormous, special plow across the unbroken prairie grasses to lift the sod, turn a furrow of 20 or thirty inches wide completely over to expose the underlying "gift of the glacier," rich, black, loamy soil. The plow consisted of a beam of straight timber seven to ten feet long to which a team of oxen was tethered. The forward end of the beam was carried by a pair of wheels, into whose axle were framed two stout upright pieces just far enough apart to allow the forward end of the plow beam to fit between them. To that end of the beam and on top of it was fastened by a link, a long lever or rod running between the two standards in the axle and fastened to them by a strong bolt running through both standards and axle. This bolt acting as a fulcrum for the lever was in easy reach of the man steering the plow. By raising or lowering the rear end of the lever rod he could increase or decrease the depth of the furrow which optimally was only two inches deep. One wheel ran in the furrow and was two to four inches larger than the other one running up on the sod so that the machine could run level. Just forward of the moldboard which did the turning over of the sod was the "shear," a disk of the very best steel fresh from the anvil and file, polished to a keen razor sharpness, slicing a four inch cut in the tangle of tall grass roots. The moldboard followed, usually made of wood that had to be constantly cleaned with a wooden paddle, and turned the loosened sod completely upside down. The driver needed his whip at all times to control the oxen, of course. When the turf was well broken, the strips of sod lay in furrows upside down so the vegetation now on the bottom decayed and roots below that would die out by next spring's planting. Thereafter, the mellow, soft, unobstructed soil with inexhaustible fertility three to six or even nine feet deep of the richest black loam could be cultivated,.

Two men, three yokes of oxen, drawing a 24 inch plow could manage to break two acres in a day. Spring or early summer were the preferred time for the work. Price per acre was $2.50 to $4.50, the former applied when the men were boarded by the farmer, the latter when the men provided their own bed and board via their "prairie schooner" or wagon. The animals were on their own in that department, allowed to graze at their will on the prairie once the work day was completed.

Once this heavy work of the oxen was accomplished those oxen, too slow, too plodding, and prodigious eaters, really were of little use to the farmer. Instead, he valued the horse as his most valuable stock. Even before a barn for the horse could be built, the animal showed resourcefulness, surviving even when exposed to the elements, lacking shelter or proper care.

By the time of the Peine family's arrival in Tazewell County, all danger of conflict with the Indians was also past. The Kickapoo, under the leadership of Machina (Great Turtle) and the Pottawatomie had already left the area with the final exodus of the Indians in 1832. At the time of the Peine's appearance in 1845 just a few buildings stood where the town of Minier is today located. Incorporation didn't occur till July of 1872. The fledgling village stood on a low flat prairie with ponds of water which hardly went dry during the entire year, so proper drainage was one of the first demands on the village residents. To that end, open ditches were dug in the early days to be replaced in 1880 with underground drainage tiles.

Cases of "claim jumping," a big problem to pioneers in the mid 1830s, were fortunately all adjudicated by the time our folks arrived fifteen years later. In a typical case, a man would fill out the necessary papers and pay for the acres at an official land claim office, go with aid of a map to his acres, stake a claim to his land by planting a claim notice on a pole at the four corners of his property, return east to pick up his family, and return as fast as he could to the acreage only to find a "claim jumper" farming his land without authorization. Naturally, a dispute ensued, and could only be settled at one of the informal courts which the settlers themselves established to insure justice. Each side of the dispute had to appear to answer questions, were grilled, witnesses were called, likewise grilled, and a final, irrevocable decision declared by the judge. Best of all, the system worked! Early pioneers were generous to each other with their tools, their teams of animals, their help putting out fires, and their cooperation in the settlement of newcomers. But a man's land was his own not to be given up for anything!

An attempt in 1846 to establish grain standards measuring moisture, weight, quality, and color led to the establishment in 1850 of the Board of Trade in Chicago. Though hotly debated and initially criticized by farmers as a tactic to lower the price of wheat and other commodities, they eventually saw that a system with inspectors grading wheat as it entered and left Chicago, with warehouses to hold the grain while there, and with liability established for defects in the grain shipped out, was a good and profitable arrangement for them. Quality soared; prices garnered top dollar. This birth of the "futures market" was the natural progression of the system, just in time to meet the demand from Europe, where the Crimean War caused food shortages, for Illinois grain and meat. For Stephen Peine this was another step forward, an improvement in the business part of agriculture, a source of security and prosperity after his yields left his wagon. He might still light his cabin by candle or with or an oil lamp burning whale oil, replaced by kerosene in 1850, might still heat by wood in a fireplace, but incrementally his life was improving.

At that time in Logan County just south of Tazewell County people were recorded to believe that liquor mitigated the physical aches and pains of life, eased the pain of rotten teeth, sore gums, arthritic joints, and accidental breaks and scrapes, so they took whiskey as a cure. For decades, at thirty cents a gallon, liquor enlivened "house raisings," hog slaughters, dances, and merry-making. By 1850 fermented cider began to displace whiskey as the common drink and laws were passed to limit the quantity to one quart and the age to seventeen and above. Just twenty years later, the temperance movement was in full sway, indicating that liquor consumption had become a social problem. For the German immigrants, whose beer was their national drink like water was to Americans, the movement was abhorrent, enough to cause them to leave the Republican party to which they had long given their full allegiance. The temperance law passed in 1872 was quickly abandoned as unenforceable and the Germans breathed with deep relief.

The Peine family in America was complete by mid-century with six children: Mary, Henry, Sophina, Hettie, Stephen, and George. The youngest, George, was tiny as well as fragile, and family lore noted that his newborn head would fit neatly into a tea cup!

Though the Peine family existence may sound romantic from this distance of time and place, life on the farm in the middle of the twentieth century was very hard work. Physical labor for Stephen from sun-up to sundown with the help of his wife and six sons and daughters was unrelenting. Chores were accomplished with no mechanized help or electricity. The horse and mule were truly the farmer's source of power but one which required daily care and effort. First the farmer was faced with the backbreaking work of clearing the field of sod, the tightly growing tangle of grasses. Then seeds were sown, fields were weeded, seedlings were nourished with a mix of manure and straw, and the heavens were beseeched for rain. Each morning cows were led to the grassy field and back to the barn again in the evening, garbage called "slops" was carried in a bucket out to the pigpen for the nourishment of those ravenous animals, the free-range chickens pecked about the farmyard all day looking for their diet of ground corn. Even a little child could be put to work and trusted with the hand grinder with which they ground corn for the chickens or still finer for their own baking use. In America, the Peines learned that corn flour was more plentiful and cheaper than wheat flour, so that's what they ate!

Still, the belief survives that farming is a good thing in itself. More than a way of making a living, it is a superior way of life, a paragon. The farm keeps a place in America's regard that the factory-filled city has never managed to achieve. Folks feel that better morals as well as purer air are to be found in the country than in the city. True or not, it was definitely the opinion in the mid-1800s when it was the prime American occupation. Manufacturing, hand trades, and construction were sources of employment but far less than farming. The typical American worked on a farm and any look at the economic basis of our culture must start with farming. The luckiest ones were in central Illinois' Tazewell County. There German immigrants were recorded observing that the land could be planted twenty-five years without augmenting with fertilizer, so rich was the soil. Not entirely gone, though, were the manure pits, a cornerstone of the farmstead in Germany!

Caring for the animals was actually a pleasant job for little Henry, Mary, Stephen, Sophina, Hettie, and George. They gave names to the various cows, pigs, and chickens, they cared for them by carrying food and water, cleaning their hides, replenishing their bedding straw, and even talking to them. Children of that day loved their dog as much as those of today do. The beloved animal was not permitted in the house, however, for he was a helpmeet as well as a companion and pet with duties like corralling the other animals to the property or serving as guard should a chicken thief, or more likely a fox, slip into the barnyard at night. But cutting wood to store beside the house, slaughtering an animal when the larder was empty, or pickling the meat in order to preserve it was work which required an adult's strength.

The Peines felt attracted to the area around the village of Minier in Tazewell County because many families from Germany were settling there. With so many new customs in a new country to adjust to, it was comforting to be able to make themselves understood, at least, with their fellow Germans. One big adjustment they encountered in rural life in America was the isolation of the farm family. Back in Germany, the farm families resided in a home in the village, walked out to their fields each morning, and returned to the community of farm homes at sundown. The barn with all the animals and farm tools was attached to the house back in the Old Country, but in America because of the larger size of the farms each farm home was out in the middle of a field, apart from the village and its supportive life.

How lonely this must have been at times to these settlers so newly separated from all they knew and loved! A ride in a horse drawn cart to town must have been a very special and much anticipated event for parent and child, alike. The occasions for doing so were likely to attend their Protestant church services, taking the harvest to market, or attending one of the famous pioneer get-togethers such as a barn raising or church suppers. How often roads clogged with mud or snow prevented any socialization outside of the farm home can only be imagined, though. German, alone, was the language in the home as well as church and all social events involving the Peine family.

Even the rainstorms in America were different, more dramatic, accompanied by more frightful thunder and lightning than that of the continental weather of central Germany where bounded by the Black Forest, Vosges, Taunus, Harz, and Thueringen forests, and of course the Alps mountains, winds were prevented from gathering force and blowing for thousands of miles as they did on the plains of Illinois. Prevailing weather in Hofgeismar came from the north Atlantic; rain was frequent enough but often came in the form of an endless days-long mist. To the Peines' shock and awe, in Illinois the rainstorms came with blinding lightning that scored the sky from zenith to horizon, then after a fearsome silence came great earth-shaking claps of thunder so loud folks thought they would jump right out of their skins! A moment later a few drops like bullets would strike the ground! All the excitement passed in about twenty minuets, but they could hear the thunder as it passed afar off usually to the east. Frightening as the fury of nature was, the Peines surely rejoiced in the life-giving drops, relished like every growing thing on the farm the delicious refreshment of the rain, and marveled in it all, once tranquility was restored.

Summer brought fun times for the family. Out of frugality as well as preference, the children were allowed to kick off their shoes and run about barefoot in the hot weather. Days were longer which permitted more time for games and fun. Family picnics to a nearby stream with its cooling waters for bare feet, its rich banks wooded with black walnut, graceful elm, and shading cottonwood, its wild strawberries or grapes for the picking were idylls in an otherwise laborious life. There in the quiet current-less nooks of the stream, myriads of wild fowl had prepared for their eggs to hatch year after year since time immemorial. It was peaceful nature at her best, Margaret undoubtedly thought. Long walks to neighboring farmsteads to play with other children while the mothers chatted nearby probably provided a much needed respite from the constant farm chores too!

With the formation in the mid-1800s of County and State Agricultural Societies, information was disseminated to help farmers improve their skills, use new advances in mechanization, or learn about new agricultural science. Simultaneously, came county fairs with displays, contests, prizes, and fun social events for the whole family.

The country school which all the Peine children attended, under the direction of one schoolmarm, closed for three months in the summer so that the students could help their parents in the fields, thus establishing a custom which never changed to this day. Even during the remainder of the year attendance at the one room school house could be spasmodic for the older children whose help on the farm was essential. As a rule though, German immigrants insisted on schooling for their children to teach them English and arithmetic. The virtues of honesty, candor, reliability, order and discipline they would learn at home.

While digging in the earth, Stephen or the children occasionally found bones so large they could only be those of buffaloes, skulls and horns attached. Perhaps their homestead had earlier been a watering place for the immense creatures. Then surely, if they looked closely enough, they would find arrowheads from the native hunter, who passed by not so long ago when Peine land was native hunting ground.

Most of the clothing of the family was sewn at home by hand. Sweaters and socks, caps, and mittens were knitted by mother and sisters. A vegetable garden near the house provided essentials for their diet and was the work of all the family members, although the cooking and preserving of it was under mother's supervision. Meals in those days were pretty simple and wanting in variety, but they were as nutritious as possible and filling which was then the prime consideration over taste. Margaret's fuel was wood for a cook stove, and her cooler was a deep hole in the ground. All the water she used had to be carried from the pump at the well outside the kitchen door. When nature called, one walked to the "outhouse" conveniently located behind the house.

Fence-building to keep the barnyard animals corralled, to convey the size of his holdings to all who would look, to fill him with pride whenever he himself surveyed them, would have been one of the early demands on Stephen's schedule. But as most chores in the early 19th Century, the job was not as simple as stringing barbed wire around some posts. In fact, barbed wire did not even exist until 1873. Instead, Stephen would have cut rails or slices of whatever timber was available on his land, and like Abe Lincoln he would have woven them into a haphazard looking line about four feet high along his property line. Stones would have served admirably but were scantily deposited by the glacier in Illinois. Where trees too were scarce, farmers would have cut bricks of sod and stacked them high to form a barrier.

The planting of trees around their home would also have been an early project for the Peines. As a windbreak out on the open prairie where winds blew strong and long unencumbered, as lovely ornamentation, and as a magnet to nesting birds, there was nothing like a tree! Rapid growing trees such as locust, cottonwood, or aspen were popular choices of the day but the slower ones like oak, chestnut or elm were chosen too for their majesty and endurance. Fruit trees too, especially cherry or apple, were desired by the German immigrants. Whatever the species of tree, though, perhaps the greatest joy gained from them was the arrival of songbirds come to make their home in the branches, endlessly cheering the Peines with their song: bobolink, brown thrasher, robin, finches, whippoorwill, nuthatch, turkey.

Much of the Peine diet, in those days when a farmer was a hunter as well, consisted of wild game. Quail, turkey, grouse, bobwhite, rabbit, and squirrel nested and flourished in the prairie; deer throve in a grove of trees; hawks, crows, woodpeckers, red-winged blackbirds soared above. Not all found their way to the Peine table but presumably, like most early settlers, they ate more of the abundant game than they did

STORIES MY FOLKS TOLD ME

of their own domestic animals. Margaret, erasing from her mind the recollection of the cheerful little beings so abundant just outside her door, which had so recently accompanied her on a summer walk or cheerfully warbled to her as she passed by the nest, nevertheless prepared the quail boiled, roasted, fricasseed or fried, always an incomparably tasty morsel. The fabled panther lived in the woods but never strayed on to the prairie to hunt. Stephen needed his rifle, though, to protect his family and livestock from the red and grey foxes and the wolves, ruthlessly hunting, prowling marauders, working in large troops, trotting continuously, growling, barking, yelping, whining in the night as they searched for flesh to fill their bellies. Slaughter in the sheep fold could take just minutes to be complete!

During the summer and fall of 1858, all Illinoisans were consumed with the political race for the U.S. Senate seat between the incumbent, democrat Stephen A. Douglas, and the young challenger from Springfield, IL, republican Abraham Lincoln. Traveling throughout the state, challenging each other in formal debates attended by vast crowds in each of the cities of Ottawa, Freeport, Jonesboro, Charleston, Galesburg, Quincy, and Alton, the two men garnered prodigious attention. Slavery, the topic most on the minds of the listeners and on the lips of the contenders, shaped the dialogue to a national level, questioning if the territories in the west could choose slavery if the citizens voted for it as Douglas persuaded or as Lincoln decried. Denying he was an abolitionist, Lincoln called slavery a monstrous injustice which should be condemned as wrong and kept from growing to the territories. In Lincoln's famous "Nation Divided" speech, he implored that the nation could not survive half slave and half free. But still, due to political maneuvers he lost the race. But he won the war: the national presidential election two years later! Slavery was the issue which drove a wedge between the north and south arms of the democratic party causing Douglas' support to be splintered and as a result Lincoln won the presidency. Surely, Stephen Peine, like all Illinoisans, was caught up in the powerful contests and part played by fellow Illinoisan, Abe Lincoln.

Occasionally, in those brighter, slower days of summer, Margaret would perhaps look high into the bright air of a morning and be struck by a premonition, a sense of future prosperity for her children growing up, thanks to her and Stephen, in the New World where unlike in the Old World personal development was not stymied, where the children were exposed to the expectation that they could be all that they wanted to be. She had such grand hopes for her six children, and to them she dedicated her life! Yet, when her youngest, George, was only two years old, Margaret, possibly in childbirth, unexpectedly died. It was December 7, 1858; she was only forty-two years old.

Little George had been born prematurely, but Margaret had nursed him through to health. Now, the motherless children were to be raised by their older sister, Mary Catherine. Young though she was at sixteen, Mary did her very best to substitute for her mother to the small grieving children and her forlorn father. Though it was unbelievably sad out on the isolated Peine farm, the family somehow survived, were fed, clothed, schooled, and made do. Many household responsibilities fell to Henry's youthful shoulders as well.

For Stephen, who had been married to Margaret nearly twenty years when she, his wife, his lover, his confidant was suddenly gone, the loss was a terrible blow. Theirs had been a marriage based on love not arrangement for those began to pass from custom in Renaissance days and were fully superseded by love in 1800. Back in Germany, they had likely lain in bed nights talking over the pros and cons of making such a bold move to become emigrants. Mary could trace her family back many generations to 1660. Should they leave forever the home and everything they knew in the world? When one would waver, the other would encourage, though each would assume both sides of the question at different times. Finally, Stephen could make the big decision to leave only because Margaret supported him, bolstering him and giving him the necessary courage.

Once in America, she had worked by his side to make their land bountiful. She had made a home from the most rudimentary of supplies. She had born him six children, clothed and nourished their bodies and minds. Still, they all knew that death was ever lurking near in their day. It seemed almost natural, even expected because death came more frequently, stole quietly into each home to gather away especially the

STORIES MY FOLKS TOLD ME

baby, the woman in childbirth, and the one past forty. In the 1850s, male life expectancy was thirty-eight years, the female forty years. A baby had more than one chance in ten of dying before its first birthday. No, death in the mid-1850s was not a surprise, but it was always a blow with consequences.

Now, Stephen wondered how he could go one without her. It was, of course, his faith in God's will and the mitigating power of nature, experienced as he worked the land, which gave him the strength to continue. Renewal came before his eyes everyday as he watched the crops ripening, the animals develop, his own children maturing. The lesson of nature was, as always, that life goes on. Soon enough he realized that he had to go on living; he had to return to the demands of his family and farm, so slowly life came back to him as it comes back to frozen limbs with the sensation of a pain and a discouragement that was unspeakable.

The family sustained one another, the demands of life on the farm imposed themselves, and the Peines simply submerged their pain and disappointment and got on with life as best they could. Through the difficult years, Mary was doing an admirable job serving in her mother's stead but, of course, she couldn't be expected to give up her own life entirely. When she was nineteen Jonas Friend swept her off her feet and into married life on his farm in nearby Hittle Grove, Illinois, but motherhood eluded her as baby after baby died and was buried at the Hittle Grove cemetery, today a national landmark site near Minier. What an ironic plight for a young woman who as a child had proved her worth as a mother in the raising of her brothers and sisters.

Henry, their oldest son, though underage, enlisted in the Union Army 7th Illinois Cavalry in 1864 and served till the end of the war. He fought in the great battle at Nashville in which fierce campaign his horse was shot from under him. Quick reaction enabled him to seize the horse of a dead rider and make his escape! Much hard service ensued causing physical disabilities from which he suffered the rest of his life, but he was grateful to survive and like his comrades never tired of relating his war experiences. Hard tack, bean soup, and bacon were the standard fare except at Christmas when soldiers received boxes from home filled with delicacies of roast turkey, pies, cakes, and such for a grand feast. Throughout his life, Henry kept long-lasting camaraderie, produced by hardships in war, with his fellow Grand Army of the Republic veterans association. The Civil War was such a life changing event in Henry's life that he never tired of talking about it when gathered with others on the front porch, around the table, or at the store. At his funeral in November, 1917, last honors were accorded him as the remnant of the Grand Army of the Republic marched beneath the stars and stripes. There were no flowers but a soft blanket of green and white beneath the starry flag he loved and fought for. He was buried in Minier cemetery.

Henry was one among six thousand German immigrants living in Illinois who served in the Union Army. The 43rd Infantry composed wholly of Germans was led by men experienced in fighting back in the Old World. Fifteen mile per day marches were normal in that day before transport vehicles existed and trains were rarely available for troop transport. Illinois volunteers, as a whole, mustered in numbers far in excess of the quota for the state. The draft was instituted in March, 1863, but was not used because of the great number already volunteering. In all, 250,000 served from Illinois which was considered a noble number in that day. General jubilation erupted when the Union Army was victorious. Yet six days after the war was won, the American President was assassinated. Abraham Lincoln's goal was achieved but in an almost Christlike manner he had to give his life. Then general desolation reigned over the land!

Economic depression also followed closely on the Civil War, motivating farmers to organize social economic organizations such as the Grange movement and the Farmer's Alliance which called for regulation of the railroads and grain elevators, elimination of price fixings and monopoly of farm machinery, especially of plow manufacturing. By 1883, however, conditions had improved for the farmer.

A very happy time for the Peine family came January 31, 1871, when the eldest son, Henry, married Caroline Buehrig of Fort Madison, Iowa, who coincidentally like Henry had been born in Germany in the same month and year as he, 1844, in the neighboring state of North Rhine Westphalia. Her family had also immigrated to America in

1845 but, of course, the two families did not know each other back in Germany despite the coincidental dates of birth and emigration year. The wedding took place in Ft. Madison, Iowa, where Caroline's brother, Ludwig Heinrich or Louis Henry, was a minister of the Gospel.

Henry moved with his bride to the village of Minier where he embarked on a business partnership with William Buehrig, Caroline's brother, to sell dry goods from a store on the commercial street at the center of the village. This business partnership continued until 1883 when it was formally dissolved and William sold his interest in the business to Henry's younger brother, George Peine. Henry dedicated his career to the successful business till his retirement in 1903 when the management succeeded to his son, William Willis Peine.

Henry and Caroline spent their married life in Minier where they raised seven children: Flora who died young; Alfred C. of Muskegon, Michigan; Edward Henry of Oklahoma; Arthur F; William, Lena and Emma, of Minier.

Henry Peine became one of the few immigrants to journey back to the Old World when he returned to visit his place of birth in 1890 and traveled extensively in Germany, France and England. He had left Hofgeismar when he was only one year old, completely without memories but having heard all his life about people and places there, and speaking fluent German, he was curious. Upon his return he helped to launch the Minier Milling Company, one of the most ambitious enterprises ever begun in Minier but destined for failure. He continued his position as chief executive of the store which bore his name until 1903 when he retired and passed his interest to his son, William Willis, in association with George.

Always interested in politics, Henry was frequently a delegate to Republican county and state conventions. A member of the Methodist Evangelical Church in Minier, he served as its treasurer for many years. Still a proud patriot, he was a founder and supporter of the area veterans association, Post 168 of the Grand Army of the Republic and a charter member of the local association of the insurance company, Modern Woodmen of America. Community leadership was exemplified in the

Peine family from their earliest years in America. How proud Margaret and Stephen could be! As his children grew up and only son Stephen was left to take over the farm, the pioneer Peine moved out to the farm in Hittle Grove to Mary's care. His and Margaret's aspirations for their children were realized!

It was there, at Mary's and Jonas' that he passed away at the age of sixty-six and was buried in the Hittle Grove or Little Mackinaw cemetery beside his wife. While the family was still in the mourning period, scarcely four months later, Jonas Friend led another sorrowful cortege to the same cemetery to bury his beloved Mary and their two sons who had died within five days of each other. That sad day was August 31, 1872.

In retrospect we see those twenty-seven years in America had altered forever the destiny of the Peine name. No longer was their orientation back in Germany but looking forward in the new land where Stephen and Margaret had reset the family compass. All the Peines were now proud American citizens, landowners, tax-payers, and were represented in the ranks of the military. Now at Stephen's death the land had to pass to the next generation. That land, the prolific gift of the glacier, now fell to the three young sons of Stephen. Since son Stephen was the one most interested and since his brothers were engaged in the eponymous store in Minier, the stewardship of the Peine homestead fell to him and stayed with his line of the family.

At the time of the farm succession to the second generation, Sophina was married to John Liese and farmed near Marshalltown, Iowa. They were the parents of eight children: Henry, Bertha, Wilfred, Grace, Charles, Edna, Ethel, and George. Hettie, never married, resided on the family farm with her brother Stephen and his family.

The lives of Stephen and Margaret Davin Peine prove the social scientists' general laws of migration which hold that as the distance of migration increases, the greater the obstacles will be and therefore the greater the ambition of the immigrants must be. Any migration takes courage, planning, forethought, and energy. But desire to change ones situation in life is not enough. The immigrant must display the willingness and ability to act on that desire in order to achieve one's goal. Only the most motivated of the immigrants, like Stephen and Margaret Peine, those who in sociologist's words had the "migrant advantage" of internal resolve, optimism, tenacity, and resilience, could hope to succeed.

Pioneers Johann Friedrich Hennig "Henry" Buehrig and Sophie Christine "Caroline" Bank Buehrig arrived 1845
—2—

Coincidentally, just as the Peine family was departing Hessen in north-central Germany, in the very same year, 1845, Henry and Caroline Buehrig with their six children also left for the New World. The families didn't know each other nor did they travel on the same ship, but unbeknown to them then their paths would eventually merge on a future wedding day and again later on still another wedding day! Henry was 43 years old when they set sail; Caroline, 40; Henrietta, 15; Ludwig Heinrich, 13; Johann Daniel Friederich (Fred), 9 or 11; Johann Heinrich Christian Carl (Charles), 6; Heinrich Friederich Wilhelm (Will), 4; and Henrietta Christine Caroline (Caroline), 1 ½. A daughter, Sophie, was born in West Point Township, Lee County, Iowa, two years after their arrival to complete the family.

The Buehrigs could trace their lineage back to the birth of Caroline's father, Johann Hennig Bank whose birth on February 28, 1774, was recorded in church records in Lesse, near Braunschweig, in the state of today's Lower Saxony, Germany. Henry's parents, Johann Andreas Buehrig born in 1754 and Anne Dorothea Caroline Hofmeister Buehrig born 1760 are also listed in Lesse. The pioneer immigrant to America, Johann Friedrich Hennig Buehrig, was born August 10, 1802 when his mother was forty-two and his father forty-eight, and is further recorded in the church records of Lesse as is the birth of Sophie Christine Caroline Bank, born May 25, 1805. Both Hennig and Caroline are inscribed on the obelisk monument in the Minier, Illinois, cemetery and on a commemorative window in the Evangelical Church of Minier.

Germany at the time of these births was not a unified country under one ruler but was a league of cities and small states, each ruled by a nobleman king, prince, duke or count. The most prominent of the German rulers was Frederick the Great, King of Prussia; his brother-in-law, Karl I,

Duke of Braunschweig ruled the Duchy of Braunschweig, today's Lower Saxony from where the Buehrigs hailed.

In 1754, the year of Johann Andreas' birth, the French and Indian War broke out in America as a struggle between France and England in the New World. It started when the twenty-one year old surveyor, George Washington, was sent by Virginia to force the French out of the Ohio Valley. The British colonial forces of Virginia under his command fired on a small detachment of French soldiers near Fort Duquesne, today's Pittsburg, killing their commander and capturing the rest. In retaliation, the French sent their entire force against Washington, overwhelmed him and caused him to surrender at the Battle of Great Meadows. After disarming his command, they allowed it to march back to Virginia.

This initial encounter between the French and English in the New World grew into a war which by 1745 spread to Europe and lasted until 1763. Known as the Seven Years' War, it involved all the great powers and many of the lesser states as well including the Duchy of Braunschweig where young men were conscripted to fight with the forces of Frederick the Great, an ally of England. They were led by Karl Wilhelm Frederick, son of the ruling Duke of Braunschweig, who became a military commander of unusual ability as befitted the nephew of Frederick the Great. Though victorious in the field, the cost of the war brought the Duchy to bankruptcy.

In the year following the birth of Hennig Buehrig, the largest land treaty in history, the Louisiana Purchase, was signed on April 30, 1803, by Napoleon's Finance Minister and the emissaries of Thomas Jefferson, President of the United States. Needing money to continue his campaigns in Europe, Napoleon sold the Louisiana Territory, an area of 875 thousand square miles for $15M or less than five cents an acre. This deal, which went almost unnoticed in Europe, would by the end of the century have affected the lives of millions of European emigrants like Hennig and Caroline Buehrig who in 1846 bought a farm in the Territory of Iowa which would become one of the dozen states created out of the Louisiana Purchase.

With Napoleon controlling much of the continent of Europe, Karl Wilhelm Frederick, now the ruling Duke of Braunschweig, accepted command of the Prussian armies that were still fighting "the little corporal." The Duke was defeated and killed at the battle of Auerstadt on November 4, 1806. Subsequently, Napoleon began rearranging the German states, attaching the Duchy of Braunschweig to Westfalen and making his brother, Jerome, king of the combined states, thereby bringing the Buehrig family and the Banks, like the Peines already described, under the rule of a Bonaparte.

The Duchy of Braunschweig, about the size of the present state of Rhode Island, was situated on the southern edge of the fertile plain of northern Germany where cereal grains, sugar beets, potatoes, garden produce of all kinds, and fruits of every variety were easily grown.

Braunschweig, the capital of the duchy of the same name, was founded around AD 861. By the 13th century it had become one of the most important commercial cities in northern Germany and a member of the Hanseatic League, a world-wide shipping and trading association. Its location on the Oker River which flowed north to empty into the Aller River and on northward to Bremerhaven, a merchant marine city on the North Sea, satisfied the criteria to be in the League. For centuries Braunschweig existed as five separate villages each with its own walls and gates within which were built fine examples of Romanesque, Gothic, and Renaissance architecture.

Ten miles southwest of the city of Braunschweig was the village of Lesse where the births of two known generations of the Buehrigs were recorded. Hennig and Caroline Buehrig established their home in the nearby village of Osterlinde where six of their children were born, but had recorded the births in a church in Westerlinde. Today, these villages of Lesse, Osterlinde, and Westerlinde are suburbs of the city of Salzgitter, all with the same zip code, in the state of Lower Saxony.

The years 1840 through 1845 saw a great exodus of German farm families like Hennig and Caroline Buehrig and their six children. Overpopulation was forcing many out as was unfavorable weather; plus, news from the New World was very positive and alluring. Henry and

Caroline must have been very determined, courageous, and united in their plan yet somewhat desperate, at the same time, for overpopulation was forcing many families out of Germany. A father could no longer pass on to each son a farm large enough to support a family nor could he find available land to buy. To avoid the option of sending his sons out to work as day laborers which paid very little, he sold the land he himself had inherited and embarked for America where the proceeds of his German holdings, after paying transport for his entire family, would buy five times as much land as he had owned in Germany.

Weather, too, was a factor encouraging emigration. Throughout Europe during the early 1840s, there had been too much rain, then too little rain with extremes of heat and cold during the growing season. The potato crop failed completely in 1842 and since not only humans but cows, sheep, and pigs ate potatoes, the absence of food to feed them meant the animals had to be butchered and eaten. All crops were miserably poor in 1843. Though the harvest was satisfactory in 1844, the summer of 1845 was disastrous. Those who could afford to leave did so by the thousands; emigration took on the aspect of a flight. By the fall of 1846 when pastures again dried up, rye had suffered from the heat, fruit had withered on the trees, and potatoes had been afflicted by rot, Hennig Buehrig had already reaped his first harvest in Iowa.

That immigrant was neither a dreamer nor an adventurer tearing his family from the civilized world only to deposit them in the American wilderness. He would have known of the literary societies where men gathered to read aloud the latest emigrant's handbook printed in German, informing them of most aspects of making the move to America. Suggestions on the best seasons to make the trip, what to take with them, the price of land in various, states, territories or settlements, soil and climatic conditions throughout the United States, cost of building a cabin, house or barn with instructions for doing so, and a list of implements necessary to start farming would be included in the handbook. Hennig was a master blacksmith by trade but intended to assume the entry-level position in America: farmer.

Hennig would have known that the shipping lines out of Bremen and Hamburg in Germany and French lines out of LeHavre had offices in major cities where their representatives provided advice to the prospective emigrant, quoted the Atlantic fares, and provided a contract for space on a sailing vessel at an approximate date with guides at intervals across Europe to speed the emigrant to his chosen wharf.

Letters, received by neighbors from friends or relatives who had already settled in the New World, were occasion for gathering and learning how the writer had fared in America. Most of them told of unbelievable plenty, no tax collectors, no tithes to the church, no army conscription, no great contrast between the rank of men, and no sharp class distinctions.

Hennig began to see hope, freedom from want and hunger, and a future for his children in a daring plan to emigrate. He was truly excited and enthusiastic until inevitably this spirit became infectious and attached first to his teen-agers, Henrietta and Ludwig Heinrich, and perhaps last to his wife, Caroline. She, like most women of the day, felt a strong attachment to relatives, her village, her things, her friends, all that was familiar; and above all she had a genuine fear of the sea. Stories and letters of shipwrecks abounded as well to her hearing. Besides, traveling with the needs of small children of six, four, and one and a half years was definitely daunting!

Nevertheless, by late summer 1845 all preparations for the departure of the family were made: property and belongings sold, children inoculated against smallpox, bundles of clothing and bedding packed to take, hampers of food prepared for the entire journey, a contract acquired for space aboard a ship, a permit obtained to exit the Duchy of Braunschweig, and the proceeds of Hennig's worldly wealth exchanged for gold and silver coins, the only negotiable currency he could use in the New World. Travel for the Buehrig family was by sailing vessel.

Typically, the emigrants would join a few thousand others who milled around their hampers of food and bundles of bedding, many sleeping on the pier, afraid to leave it until they were advised they could mount the gangplank and board the ship. Some, looking at the sailing vessels and the swell of the sea, lost heart and turned back. The more confident waited patiently among their restless youngsters and crying babies while their ship unloaded American cotton from the hold, mended sails and rigging, and took kegs of water aboard. If, due to wind and weather the ship had arrived late, six weeks might be spent on the pier!

When all was finally in readiness, Hennig would have urged Caroline and the excitedly scampering children aboard with their hampers of food, the trunk, and bundles of bedding. Their provisions probably included oatmeal, flour, bacon, biscuits, tea, and coffee to be cooked in one cooking area with all the other emigrants. The all important bag of gold he himself guarded by carrying it sewn into his very clothing!

Although most emigrants to the United States sailed directly to the New England coast, specifically to New York City, Hennig knew that their final destination was to be far inland near the Mississippi River and that would mean difficult overland travel. He favored more time at sea to the most distant port in America, New Orleans, and river travel thereafter. Had they landed in New York, Boston, or Philadelphia, they would have had to cross the Allegheny Mountains and creep long distances by wagon, a more cumbersome journey, considering their baggage and the size of their group, and a more expensive way than utilizing waterways.

It is likely that the family sailed from the French port of Le Havre because their destination was not New York but New Orleans. Le Havre carried on a lively commerce with New Orleans at that time principally to pick up cotton. It was not so long ago that New Orleans was a major city of New France and was still a destination of many French emigrants and commerce. Thousands of Germans also landed there annually where they found passage up the Mississippi River was cheap and a convenient access to the many tributary rivers which together formed the great highway that took them deep into the Promised Land. From New Orleans to St. Louis cost two dollars, perhaps two fifty.

The voyage across the Atlantic Ocean likely took six to eight weeks, but from their departure from their home in Osterlinde, Braunschweig, Germany, to their final destination of Ft. Madison, Iowa, travel time likely was around four months. This was a time of forced inactivity new to folks who had known only a life of toil. Likely they relished that time to enjoy the magnificent spectacle of a full moon rising over the horizon; the stars at night which seemed so close they could almost reach out and touch them; the impromptu music of a shepherd's pipe, tambourine, or accordion; the fellow passengers who cracked jokes or told stories about their forsaken village life; the community life which evolved as various families shared the cooking fire and even combined their provisions into one pot for more interesting dishes; and the great camaraderie as they dipped their tin cups into the common fresh water barrel.

Baby Caroline quickly became the "darling" of all on board. At first she insisted on being held only by Mama or Henrietta, but there were so many friendly hands and smiling faces which reached out to her, often with a shiny penny or bon-bon, that soon her out-going, social personality exhibited itself, and she had quite a retinue of caregivers whenever she toddled away from her mama. Women, long past the years of holding a baby, delighted in engaging Caroline for some "baby talk" while Mama found in this a little relief for herself. Little Charles and Will, too, at the age of six and four were little charmers as they tried to learn the word for all the new objects of mariner life about them; German or English it didn't matter for all were new words to them!

Wistful, longing looks were often cast at the Buehrig family by fellow travelers who mostly were traveling alone, having left wife and children back in the Old Country while they traveled ahead to establish themselves before sending money back for transport of their loved ones and eventual happy reunion in America.

By the 1840s, ships were built to be more seaworthy than they had been in the previous century. The chronometer, a device that determined longitude, allowing a sailing vessel to proceed at night without fear of drifting off course, had been perfected. Previously, ships had been obliged to pull their sails at sunset and lay out at sea until morning, a great loss in sailing time. Charts had been devised to allow for magnetic fields which affected compasses. Thus, a ship no longer ended up south and east of its reckoning. Only if a storm pushed it far off its course and damaged the sails, masts and riggings would a ship have loitered longer than necessary in the Atlantic, for food and water aboard were limited.

The first sight of land ahead was the mouth of the Mississippi River pouring its muddy waters into the deep blue of the Gulf of Mexico. Frances Trollope, an English woman and mother of Anthony, arriving on Christmas day, 1827, after seven weeks at sea, gives us in her book, "Domestic Manners of the Americans," the best description of the sights and impressions that entry to New Orleans via the Mississippi River made on a traveler:

"The shores of this river are so utterly flat, that no object upon them is perceptible at sea. Large flocks of pelicans were seen standing upon the long masses of mud which rose above the surface of the waters, and a pilot came to guide us over the bar long before any other indication of land was visible. I never beheld a scene so utterly desolate as this entrance of the Mississippi. Only one object rears itself above the eddying waters; this is the mast of a vessel long since wrecked in attempting to cross the bar. By degrees bulrushes of enormous growth become visible, and a few more miles of mud brought us in sight of a cluster of huts called the Balize, by far the most miserable station that I ever saw made the dwelling of man, but I was told that many families of pilots and fishermen lived there. For several miles above its mouth, the Mississippi presents no object more interesting than mud banks, monstrous bulrushes, and now and then a huge alligator luxuriating in the slime. Another circumstance that gives to this dreary scene an aspect of desolation, is the incessant appearance of vast quantities of driftwood, which is ever finding its way to the different mouths of the Mississippi. Trees of enormous length, still bearing their branches, and still oftener their up torn roots entire, the victims of the frequent hurricane, come floating down the stream. Sometimes several of these, entangled together, collect among their boughs a quantity of floating rubbish, that gives the mass the appearance of a floating island bearing a forest, with its roots mocking the heavens, while branches lash the tide in idle vengeance: this as it approaches the vessel, and glides swiftly by, looks like a fragment of a world in ruins.

"As we advanced we were cheered by the bright tints of vegetation. The banks continue invariably flat, but a succession of plan-less villas, sometimes merely a residence, and sometimes surrounded by their sugar fields and Negro huts varied the scene, and for a length of one hundred and twenty miles, from the Balize to New Orleans, the land is defended from encroachments of the river by a high embankment which is called the levee, without which the dwellings would speedily disappear. When we arrived, there had been constant rains. She (the Mississippi) was looking so mighty and so unsubdued all the time, that I could not help fancying she would someday take the matter into her own hands again, and if so, farewell to New Orleans."

With such desolation greeting him, Hennig Buehrig must have felt the guide books to be wrong; Caroline must have withdrawn to weep. Only the children, fascinated by pelicans and alligators, would have reacted happily to the passing scene. When their ship entered the mouth of the Mississippi, a river pilot was rowed out by four black sailors, the first colored people the Buehrigs had ever seen in their lives, who came alongside their ship and then aboard to take management of their ship. Their special knowledge of the conditions necessary to navigate a sailing ship against the rapid current of the river as it poured into the ocean was essential.

In the territory claimed by Robert La Salle for the French king in April of 1692, New Orleans at the time of the Buehrig arrival was the lone city of the Louisiana Purchase of 1803. Appearing in the descriptions of that day to be a large, glittering city, lighted by gaslights seemingly without care of cost, the city surely assaulted the Buehrigs with a multitude of new sights, sounds, and aromas. Slaves, linked together by chains and driven through the streets like oxen under yoke, were surely a sorry, sullied sight to the Buehrigs! Merchants and tradesmen hurried over cobblestoned streets to their offices and shops; ladies in dainty leather boots picked their way through the muddy lanes. Vessels of all sizes were docked beside their sailing ship so the family was entertained watching goods, unloaded from flatboats which brought goods down river from the north, being reloaded onto the ocean going craft which would soon depart for LeHavre. This was truly a world trading center! They were warned, though, that the low marshy position of the city gave rise to unhealthy airs and vapors so were hopeful to continue northward soon.

The family did not, in fact, remain longer than necessary in New Orleans. The place, with its slave markets, Creole atmosphere, and loud and raunchy wharf area did not appeal to the German temperament. Crowded with immigrants, the city was happy to see them go for they would not then become a public burden if they had misjudged their financial condition. Soon after procuring food for the trip and buying tickets for their conveyance northward at the wharf, they meandered past the toiling, sweaty, chanting, herculean, black stevedores to their packet boat room and settled in for the next stage of their journey.

Soon the family was proceeding fourteen hundred miles up the Mississippi River, twelve days by stern wheeler steamship, traveling against the current, and requiring four feet of water depth for navigation to St. Louis where they spent the winter of 1845-46. Frequent stops, required to take on wood that fueled the steam engines, goods, and the all important mail, offered the Buehrigs a chance to walk on solid ground, exercise their legs, and generally have a closer look at this land they had chosen to adopt as their own. From what they could observe of the first days, it was a pretty level terrain without mountains or valleys. Upriver country appeared less cultivated; virgin forests appeared huge and dark reminding them of those back in Germany.

St. Louis was a thriving river town, yet still small and built all of wood. Perhaps Hennig and Ludwig found temporary employment there. As was customary then, they boarded in a private home sharing the kitchen and outhouse with the owner, presumably a German. They did encounter their first struggles with the English language there on this interval, though. The children would surpass the parents in the mastery of it but the large German population of St. Louis eased everyone's linguistic problems. Hennig also took advantage of the idle time to consult land companies and the Federal Land Agency there, happily learning that his options were great; there was plenty of land available in nearby states or territories bordering the Mississippi River where they were headed.

Once on board their northbound packet boat, fueled by steam again, the family soon passed today's Alton, Illinois, where high palisades dwarfed the little boat and they stood on deck transfixed by the amazing cliffs which overhung the river. Before their very eyes they could see a commanding view of the Missouri River which was entering the

Mississippi from the west. Those limestone sedimentary rocks, bold and towering, extend for fifty miles along the river and display an escarpment where the mighty river cut through for eons on it way to the ocean. A little town was already in appearance as the Buehrigs passed, built in three layers up the stone wall. Some of the homes were even built into the wall of stone, others of stone so abundant at the river's shore. Later, high rolling ridges divided by deep valleys, where bright phlox and wild geraniums dancing in the sun caused Caroline to yearn to go ashore and pick them, could be seen from deck. So close were they to shore, she could even hear birds singing!

The waters of the Mississippi, in that day before locks and dams, were really roiling now. Standing on deck at dusk, they tried to imagine where all that water came from and concluded it was surely from a far off land. Back in Germany they had heard of the mighty, majestic waters, and now here they were looking down right at the fabled waters, dark brown with its load of sediment, speeding beneath their boat! Not so long ago, they didn't even dream of plying their way northward on the famous Mississippi River, now there they were, deeply affected by the scenic grandeur passing before their eyes.

French place names as well as Indian names along the river caught their attention, impressing yet again the message that they were in a foreign land: Baton Rouge, Beaumont, Oceola, Bayou, Natchez, Pointe Coupee, Black Hawk, Keokuk. Such words refused to just roll off the German tongue!

The family was soon impressed as well by the magnitude, the vastness of the land which stretched away from the water's edge, without obstruction, all the way to the horizon. There they saw millions of acres lying silent, tenanted only by wild animals of a myriad size and shape but hidden by the tall grasses. So bountiful, compared to the crowded Old World from whence they came, was that virgin earth. They couldn't help but love this new nature; their hearts swelled with it, knowing they would soon be a part of it. Although unknown to them, the earth had long awaited their arrival, was ready to offer them the gift of the glacier.

The territory of Iowa on the west side of the Mississippi River where the Buehrigs then found themselves had been opened up to settlers just twelve years before, in 1833, as a result of the annihilation of the Sac and Fox led by Chief Blackhawk in 1832. Black Hawk's last despairing effort to drive the White man away so that Indian life could go on as it always had, failed, and the downfall induced the other Northwest tribes to cede their lands. Between 1832 and 1837, the United States acquired nearly 190 million acres of Indian land in the north and east of the Mississippi for millions of dollars in gifts and annuities to the natives. Germans, never known to be true frontier folk who might contend with the Indians, tended to choose their settlement sites in areas free of Indian threat and already inhabited by the white man.

Hennig Buehrig was no exception. He chose the settled area at Fort Madison, a village of 1600 people on the Mississippi in Iowa Territory. In March 1846, Hennig and Caroline and the six children left St. Louis aboard a stern wheeler of the type used in the deeper waters of the river. It took them 200 miles upstream to the village of Keokuk where the Des Moines River flows into the Mississippi. There they were obliged to transfer to an Upper Mississippi steamer designed for use in shallower water and capable of being navigated through the treacherous passage of the fifteen mile Des Moines Rapids between Keokuk and the hamlet of Montrose, the last stop before Fort Madison.

The upper river boats were of shallow draft, merely sitting on the water and gliding over it. The steam machinery, instead of being placed in the shallow holds of the boat, was up on the deck along with the pilot's cabin and the superstructure. Set side by side were the towering smoke stacks. Travelers and merchandise occupied the deck because there was no "below" on those boats in shallow water. Canvas sheeting offered occasional protection from the elements, but generally passengers learned to huddle together and spread their own tarps over themselves in bad weather. It was a windy and chilly journey to be taking in March especially with small children.

The entire river with snags, shifting sandbars, rocks, and seasonal variance from flood stage to periods of low water, was no easy river to navigate, requiring at all times a pilot who knew every mile of the channel. Mark Twain's 1883 "Life on the Mississippi" clearly describes the mysteries and the dangers which lay below the surface of the water. In order to pass safely through the Des Moines Rapids above Keokuk called for a special rapids pilot, skillful navigators who were the highest paid pilots on the river.

The arrival on board of the special rapids pilot was a sight the travelers never forgot! Dressed as befitted the king of the river, he wore a hand-tailored Prince Albert style suit made in St. Louis, a lavender shirt, a ruffled shirt bosom, a diamond stickpin, a tall silk hat, kid gloves, silk stockings, and leather shoes of finest quality, all of which gave assurance to the passengers that the steam wheeler would safely reach Montrose on the other side of the rapids. For years after, Ludwig Heinrich, the boy of the family, regaled the folks with hilarious impersonations of this river pilot!

Hennig and his sons were fascinated at the skill shown by the pilot as he seemingly slipped over or around the huge boulders of the rapids. But excitement and fear quickly changed to dismay at the sight of Montrose. It was an ugly hamlet with its front street facing the river and known to river men as "rat row." In spite of the uninviting appearance, the family went ashore just to warm themselves and eat a bite at one of the taverns while freight and mail was unloaded from the boat.

It is doubtful that their English was yet adequate to understand fully the excitement then taking place in Montrose or the American history which was there transpiring: The village was located directly across the Mississippi from the beautiful Mormon city of Nauvoo, Illinois, where just one month earlier on the fourth of February, the vanguard of Mormons, who were being expelled from Illinois, had ferried across the river and gone into hiding, camping near Montrose. Led by Brigham Young after the murder in Navoo of Joseph Smith, they were collecting supplies, training oxen and drivers, building and repairing wagons, and in the bitter cold organizing their flight into the vast unknown West. Fifteen thousand of their believers would soon join them for their trek which would eventually lead them to Salt Lake City, Utah. But the Buehrigs were oblivious to the historical event!

Proceeding up-river from Montrose, the Buehrigs were not displeased with their first sight of Fort Madison. It spread along a wide plain at the river's edge against a backdrop of stately high bluffs. Beyond them, the rolling prairie spread west offering nothing to the eye but the Tall Grass Prairie and the sky.

When the Hennig Buehrig family settled in the Territory of Iowa in 1846 it was one vast prairie of tall grasses reaching chest high on a man, mingled with beautiful geranium and moccasin wildflowers. One day the family decided to drive out of town, cross a stream, wind a bit among beautiful heights and thinly wooded stands when suddenly the country opened up before their eyes and there it was: the tall grass prairie, a stretch of rich verdure composed of grasses and blooming flowers, a clump of trees occasionally breaking the sameness of the flat countryside, seemingly going on for miles in every direction, as far as the eye could see. For Caroline and the family, their first sight of the prairie stretching out before them was one they would never forget. They were stunned and awed into silence as if they had been gripped by a force of nature!

This was virgin land which had never been turned over and seeded. The tall grasses with their tangled, matted mass of roots reaching two feet or more into the soil was not tillable with the technology of the day, the wooden plow blade. The owner had no choice but to hire a prairie breaker who came in a small covered wagon, his living quarters, with four to eight pair of oxen and a breaking plow, weighing upwards of 125 pounds of wrought iron steel constructed to cut a furrow two feet wide. So laborious was this assignment that only two acres could be broken up in a day at the cost of $2.50 to $4 per acre. In other words, it could cost twice as much to prepare the land for the first planting as the land itself had cost! Then it would take three winter freezes for the turf to rot and the fields to become fallow or a total of six to eight years to put the claim into full production.

Hennig Buehrig was well advised to buy land that had already been under cultivation for then he could reap a harvest his first season. His first purchase, eighty acres, dated February 23, 1846, was from a private landowner in West Point Township, Lee County, Territory of Iowa. He paid $500 in partnership with Christian Mumme as recorded at the Lee County Court House in Fort Madison, Iowa, Book 3, page 101. On March 30, 1846, scarcely a month later, it is recorded in Book 3, page 123, that Christian and Sophie Mumme sold their interest in the eighty acres to Hennig Buehrig for $200.

The Buehrigs could have bought virgin land from the government for $1.25 an acre but they were willing to pay $6.25 an acre for land which had already been broken and was ready and waiting to be cultivated. Spring planting time was approaching, they had been traveling for over four months, and they were anxious to get to work. There was even a dwelling on the property which surprised them because in Germany the farm family resided in a nearby village and walked or rode a horse out to the field.

Eighty acres was considered a huge parcel for one man and his teen-age son to farm in mid-century with the meager technology available to them. In fact, forty acres was about all one man could conceivably harvest in the two week window afforded him at the end of the growing season. The window of opportunity for planting was wider considering the vagaries of spring weather, but the timing for harvest was always very strict. There was no way Hennig could have managed such a large acreage by himself so he probably tilled and seeded only the drained, level, accessible portion or hired help.

The very next year, on February 6 1847, a little natural born American citizen appeared in the Buehrig household; Sophie was her name. This healthy little bundle of joy was the last baby Caroline bore, so she doted on her mightily though she often was grateful for the willing hands of older sisters and brothers to help with little Sophie's care. Days were never long enough for Caroline; chores associated with a large household were never finished; and like all good mothers she sometimes felt she didn't have enough time for each child. Still she derived a profound comfort one day when she looked out and could actually see signs of life where a neighbor was building a cabin! The light from the little house at night lent such a feeling of camaraderie as if she were not so alone under the big black, star-studded sky.

Meal preparation was dependent solely on what they could produce from their animals, harvest, or trap. Food preservation was achieved by burying such vegetables as potatoes, carrots or storing in the spring house where cool water delayed the spoilage. Every part of a butchered animal was used for their consumption. Caroline was an original recycler though she had never heard the word! Worn clothing was patched from yet older pieces of fabric. Finally what was left of an article of clothing was cut into little squares to be used to make a crazy quilt for the bed. Women of the day had no paper towels, no toilet paper, no Kleenex, no paper diapers, no sanitary napkins, no plastic bags, but she really didn't know to miss them!

Back in the old country Hennig had been a master blacksmith, a skilled craftsman who owned his own shop, in addition to farming a small plot. The blacksmith in those days was indispensable to the community, rendering all kinds of services, from shoeing horses and crafting pots, pans, and skillets, to manufacturing farm implements such as hay rakes, forks, scythes, and plows. Among the most demanded services was the furnishing of ironwork for mills, which abounded at the time. He took to farming in America as an entry-level route to prosperity. A businessman at heart, he continuously purchased more property or sold some other acres. None of his sons took to farming, for they were also businessmen. Still, his skill as a former blacksmith no doubt helped him greatly in Iowa where he needed to forge his own tools or at least modify those he could purchase. Then as now, farmers needed to constantly customize their tools to suit some variation in the soil density, slope of the field, or imperfection.

In one transaction, Hennig Buehrig bought a land certificate for a Federal Land Grant of forty acres on December 30, 1850, and granted on March 10, 1852 by the General Land Office of the United States, Department of the Interior, Washington, D.C., signed by Millard Fillmore, President of the United States. Those forty acres were located in West Point Township, Lee County, Iowa, where his previously purchased land was.

Still increasing his land ownership in Lee County at the age of fifty-one, Hennig purchased a land certificate of sixty acres in West Point

STORIES MY FOLKS TOLD ME

Township. This land was part of the section which had been reserved in the Land Grant Ordinance of 1785 as a source of income for schools. The law established as the basic unit of settlement a township six miles square. Every township would be subdivided into thirty-six sections of 640 acres each, one of which would be used as a source of income for schools. In compliance with this law, Hennig's purchase was recorded in Book 5, page 639, Land Records of Lee County Court House at Ft. Madison, Iowa, issued February 12, 1853.

Life on the farm for the nine Buehrigs was not all toil and sweat. Ft. Madison was a developing town about four miles away and right on the Mississippi River. It must have been a great treat to hitch up the wagon and venture into Fort Madison to watch the passing scene, especially what passed up and down the Father of Waters. By the time the Buehrigs arrived, sternwheelers were common on the Mississippi. Boats came down from Galena, Illinois, carrying lead, grains, hides, beef, pork, leather, and mail to St. Louis. By the 1850s the packet boats had a regular schedule and fancy side-wheelers were carrying immigrants upstream: Germans, Swedes, Norwegians, Bohemians, Welsh and Irish. Some brought their own plows and wagons; some shared their deck space with horses, cattle, pigs, and poultry.

Because of the wild, unsubdued condition of the river at that time, the life of a steamboat was only five years. A boat usually came to a violent demise with a snagged bow, water rushing in, or fire racing up from the boiler deck, or a boiler explosion hurling metal pieces up to the sky. When the famous Lansing burst her twin boilers, the clerk's body was found in Iowa and the pilot's in Illinois! Fresh stories of paddlewheel boat exploits were always making the rounds in Ft. Madison so a visiting Buehrig would bring it home and regale the family around the dinner table.

As the years went by and the children grew to adulthood fewer and fewer were gathered around that table. In fact, not one of the sons took up farming; they all attended a West Point Township public school with an eye to entering commerce. Besides learning, piety was emphasized in the home where each morning, the patriarch stood before the family assembled at the breakfast table and read the Bible aloud. A clear, correct High German learned in their Lower Saxony origin, of course, was the only language spoken in the home.

The Buehrig's undoubtedly knew of traveling ministers or "circuit riders," a minister of the Methodist denomination who traveled by horseback to serve settlers living isolated on the prairie from the mid 1780s to the Civil War, but their unfamiliarity in English and preference for Lutheranism over the riders' Methodism likely kept them at the periphery of that aspect of American society. Always on the move, rarely staying at a cabin more than overnight, covering a circuit of thirty to one hundred miles, taking five to six weeks to cover, carrying only his Bible, songbooks, and clothing in his saddlebags, the circuit rider was naturally a young, single man. Glorified in novels and song, a romantic figure in that day when everyday life could be lacking in entertainment, he found his flock in simple cabins, fields, meeting houses, or courthouses which soon gave way to established churches, boosting Methodism to the largest Protestant denomination in America.

Son Ludwig Henry, whose line we shall follow, was a peripatetic man who found work in store-keeping which took him to various towns in Illinois, perhaps representing a wholesale house, one town of which was Minier in Tazewell County near Bloomington. There he became acquainted with the Peine merchants.

He married Martha Kroehnk of Ft. Madison, Iowa, with whom he had a daughter, Lydia, born August 18, 1860, but sadly the marriage was short-lasting because Martha died at the time of Lydia's birth. Distraught and yet responsible for his baby daughter, he begged his parents and sisters to care for Lydia until he could come to his senses. He would come back for her, he assured them.

Hennig and Caroline's son, Charles, at age 27 in 1866 attended a business college in Burlington, Iowa, operated by Bryant, Stratton and Co., where he pursued a full course of instruction in bookkeeping, commercial arithmetic, commercial law, practical penmanship, correspondence, and general business. He completed his degree in seven months for which he paid $50. Charles would eventually use his business degree but first he took a test to qualify for a teaching certificate, one issued in Montrose in 1867 and one issued in Fr. Madison in 1869, signifying he had been examined in spelling, reading, writing, geography, history of the United States, and English grammar.

He then taught school from 1868–70 in Ft. Madison just before he married Rosa Weber of Nauvoo, born in Switzerland. After that he became a partner in the grocery store of Frau Abel & Co. in Ft. Madison for awhile and then formed a boot and shoe business just down the street with his brothers Frederick and William. After removal to Minier, Illinois, in 1880, he and Fred opened a general store, Buehrig Brothers, on the one shopping block of the village. Fred bought him out in 1900 so that he could accept the position of cashier at the Minier State Bank, also located on that block, a position he held until his death on February 1, 1917.

None of the Buehrig sons enlisted in the Civil War although they were of age. Perhaps their location so far west on the frontier led them to feel disconnected to national matters. Perhaps their parents, feeling they had brought them this far from the constant wars of their native land, didn't want them to risk their lives for the new homeland and pressed them to subvert any militaristic instinct. Yet, like most German immigrants, the Buehrigs with their high sense of moral principle and Christian beliefs were abolitionists. Slavery to them was the shame of a free country and since slaves were forced to work for free they were an unfair competition to those who had only their hard work to earn them prosperity.

Daughter, Henrietta, married just a few years after the family's arrival in Ft. Madison to Jacob Abel, lived out her days till 1917 in Iowa.

The baby immigrant, Caroline, worked as a domestic in the home of a dentist, Edwin Toof in Ft. Madison before she met and married Henry Adam Peine of Minier, Illinois, on January 31, 1870. The wedding was solemnized by her brother, the Reverend Ludwig Henry, in Ft. Madison. Presumably, he also introduced them having long been acquainted with the Peines of Minier. This was the first happy occasion which linked the Buehrig and Peine families even if it meant that Caroline would move so far away as Minier with her new husband. At first the newlyweds settled on the Peine farm south of Minier, but after a year they moved into town where Henry started his dry goods store which endured for over one hundred years.

By the 1870s railroads had pretty much replaced the patchwork of canal and stagecoach operations that had dominated domestic transportation before the Civil War. They were steam powered and could reach speeds of thirty to forty miles per hour. Even villages like Minier were on the line with regular scheduled stops.

Sophie Buehrig had stayed on the farm with her parents, but she too left when she married George J. Lauterbach on September 10, 1874. They farmed all their lives in the Ft. Madison area of Iowa.

In their mid-seventies, Hennig and Caroline Buehrig no longer able to maintain the farm moved into Ft. Madison. Records show they had earlier sold forty acres for $400 on April 12, 1867, to Stephen Krogmeier and in February, 1880, they sold 30 acres to Joseph Hellige in Ft. Madison. Perhaps there were other parcels sold along the years.

In every letter since she moved to Minier, Caroline had begged her parents to move to be near her. Rapt description of her new life and community endeavored to persuade them to move to her. They missed her too, her magnetic personality, her imagination, her gift for fun, and her loving ways. They visited Minier a time or two, saw that what Caroline said was true about the village, her adorable children, her likable husband, and his many Peine relatives, and so was planted the seed of their eventual move to Minier.

But what about their sons with wives and children in Ft. Madison? How could they leave them? The solution which became rapidly apparent was that they all should move to Minier! The four sons, one still single, since they were not tied to the land, deemed themselves mobile and desirous of striking out anew in Minier. The two married daughters, promising to visit them in Minier, stayed in Iowa. Besides, the family had that certain kind of bond among each other which came to all immigrants who had left all others behind in the old country, had experienced the adventure of travel together in their tightly knit group, had striven together without anyone else's help for many years to tame the land

STORIES MY FOLKS TOLD ME

to make a homestead, and had lived together out on the farm rather isolated from other people. Solidarity defined the Buehrig family. They were a firm unit and together they would stay so!

Daughter, Caroline Peine, the baby of the family when they left Germany, seems to have been the motivation for this monumental event. Pulling up the roots which they had so deliberately set down in Iowa must have been quite a physical and emotional undertaking for them, but Caroline raved about life in Minier, and she wanted them to live in her home and enjoy the family life with her brood of seven children. And so after thirty-five years in Iowa, they did. But we can only, from this distance, imagine the emotions that filled the hearts of the older couple when making the long trek. Wrenched yet again from the comfort of a known, predictable world, reduced of possessions to only what they could pack and carry, wracked by doubts about the wisdom of the move, they traveled most likely by train whose wheels repeated over and over "going to Caroline," "going to Caroline" and approached at last the door of their loved one. Then, there would be new tales to tell, old ones to retell, pleasant and painful experiences to exchange, their hearts overflowing, like a stream in spring, with love and anticipation.

Fred and Charles had previously on a visit to Carolyn in Minier explored the possibility of a business there, so right away they rented a location for a grocery store. The Minier News of July 3, 1880, stated: "Buehrig Brothers are successors to J.M. Hart at the old stand." That location was right on the main shopping street. A couple of weeks later the Minier News stated: "Mrs. Charles Buehrig (Rosa) and family and Mrs. Frederick Buehrig (Caroline) and family arrived on Thursday, July 15, from Fort Madison, Iowa, and will henceforth make their residence in this place. Mr. Frederick Buehrig will remain in Fort Madison awhile to close out the stock of boots and shoes of Buehrig Brothers when he will also come to Minier to give his attention to the grocery business of the firm here."

Charles and Rosina Buehrig brought their four children, Carl, Edward, William, and Eda to Minier (George, and twins Clara and Clarence were born in Minier). Fred and Caroline Buehrig brought their two children, Frederick Jr. and Adolph, as well. William Buehrig married Molly Blaney after moving to Minier and so raised their four children Pearl, Otella, Sadie, and La Della, there. In all, nineteen people with the name Buehrig arrived in Minier in the summer of 1880; all the adults had been born in Germany except Rosa from Switzerland.

The weekly Minier News printed numerous announcements about the various Buehrig businesses in town:

July 3, 1880 – "Fair and honest dealing is the motto of the Buehrig Brothers," "Build up your town by trading at Buehrig Brothers," "All the good people of Minier and the surrounding country are invited to try the new firm of Buehrig Brothers"

August 7, 1880 – "For choice figs, dates, lemons, oranges, fish, ham, bacon, baloney, cheese, canned goods or anything else nice and good to eat, call at Buehrig Brothers."

August 21, 1880 – "The firm of F. Buehrig and Brother shipped their stock of boots and shoes to this place this week and will consolidate it with their grocery business here. It is the largest stock of this kind ever brought to this place and the room over their store has been rented to accommodate the goods. Mr. Fred Buehrig arrived here today."

September 3, 1880 – "Buehrig Brothers display two very neat signs. The boot and shoe sign is of novel design and attracts much attention."

December 14, 1880 – "Buehrig Brothers have received a large line of toys for theHoliday trade."

The move to Minier turned out to be a very satisfying one all around and living in Caroline's big household was fulfilling as Grandmother Caroline assisted her daughter with the little ones, supervised the country girl's help in the kitchen, and held a baby, her favorite occupation, at every opportunity. Grandfather Hennig mentioned the noisiness of the children and the door banging open and shut all the time, but he too thrived in the embrace of his daughter and the male camaraderie he developed with patrons at his sons' stores.

Many an evening, after the closing hour, found the four Buehrig brothers sitting around the wood stove at the back of the store discussing subjects like the news of the day, a scientific or religious item from a big city newspaper such as the Chicago Tribune or Bloomington Pantograph, or occasionally a philosophical topic. Often the discussion turned into a spirited debate, an argument even, with outspoken sides being taken, broken only by the 10 o'clock whistle from the train station which signaled that the brothers should walk to their respective homes together. Sunday afternoon, as was the custom of the day, found them all together again at one of their homes.

Hennig was the first of the pioneer Buehrigs to leave this earth on March 8, 1882. He was just short of his eightieth birthday and went peacefully in his daughter's home surrounded by his large and loving family. Funeral services were held in the German Evangelical Church and burial was in the new Minier cemetery.

The death of Caroline followed three years later, July 13, 1885, when she was eighty. She had shown no signs of slowing down when one day she simply slipped and fell, followed by a slow recovery which folks said contributed to her demise. Services were again held at the German Evangelical Church. Ludwig Henry was unable to conduct either service because he was pastor in Fondulac, Wisconsin, but he came as soon as possible to solace his brothers and sister.

When Caroline's remains joined those of Hennig in the brand new Minier cemetery, they became the first couple to be buried there. An Obelisk stands as their monument stone with inscriptions in German still legible. To the east is the grave of their son Frederick and family. To the south is the monument for their daughter, Caroline and Henry Adam Peine. It appears that of the four male children of Hennig and Caroline only the lines of Ludwig Henry and Charles survive to carry the Buehrig name.

In the German Evangelical Church of Minier, today's Church of Christ, are the beautiful stained glass windows, in the art-deco style, which will memorialize forever the names of the pioneers Hennig and Caroline Buehrig.

Pioneers Ludwig Heinrich Buehrig and
Caroline Austmann arrived 1845
—3—

Though they were youngsters when they immigrated with their parents to the New World, they were both born in the Old World and so are counted as pioneers. Caroline Austmann was born February 28, 1845 in Detmold in today's state of North Rhine Westphalia right next to the famous Teutoburger Forest where the Romans under Emperor Caesar Augustus finally gave up their attempt to conquer the German tribes. In AD 9, the Roman general Varus lost three legions and his own life there prompting the Emperor to cry: "Varus, Varus, give me back my legions!" Thereafter the Romans were kept south of the Danube River and west of the Rhine River by the fierce German tribes. Their leader, Churusko Arminius enabled the Germans to abjure the creep of any Latin words into the German language. German was not then nor ever would be a Romance language!

Young though she was when she left Detmold, Caroline would never forget the timber-framed houses or the medieval castle of her childhood town in Germany. Her father, the Reverend Louis Austmann (10-7-1816–10-9-1897), and mother, Caroline Hummermeier (8-19-1817–1-5-1883), had brought Caroline and her brother, Paul Austmann (3-26-1843--4-11-1921) to Peru, Illinois, just north of Minier to lead a congregation of German immigrants living there.

Ludwig Heinrich, the oldest son of Hennig and Caroline Buehrig, was born January 13, 1832 in Lesse in today's state of Lower Saxony but not many miles north of Caroline's birthplace in North Rhine Westphalia. Both spoke a clear, fine, High German.

The two met when Ludwig Heinrich was at the nadir of his life. His bride of one year, Martha, had died in childbirth although baby Lydia survived. Distraught, the young man left his baby in the care of his parents in Ft. Madison, Iowa, and set out to get his bearings in life. Aimlessly, Ludwig Henry drifted into Peru, Illinois, where friends took him to their minister, the Rev. Louis Austmann, also an immigrant from Germany. Over the many hours of consolation and meditation between the two men, the minister's daughter was introduced and love was kindled, grief was stricken. Shortly afterward he married Caroline Austmann of Peru, Illinois, and with her father Rev. Louis Austmann as his mentor, Ludwig Henry prepared to become an Evangelical Lutheran minister of the Gospel and to lead congregations in many Illinois locations for the rest of his life.

The reverend helped Ludwig Henry to look to the Gospels for relief from his despair and for understanding of life's sorrows and problems. Great emergencies and crises show us how much greater our vital resources are than we had supposed; God will never ask a man to bear more than he can cope with; crises tap into a strength that one didn't know one possessed; one must be grateful for this surge of inner strength. Though sorrow oppressed his soul, Ludwig was helped to understand, as men and women of every generation must, why God allows bad things to happen to good people. Like the Biblical Job, who had suffered profoundly, Ludwig took the attitude of humility and trust in God, believed that suffering was a test of his fidelity, that he would be rewarded in the end, and that man's finite mind cannot probe the depths of the divine omniscience which governs the world and his own small lot. Ludwig took to heart Job's conviction that if we accept good things from God, should we not also accept evil? Trusting in God in spite of loss and disappointment, placing himself in God's hands was not easy yet his faith saw him through "the valley of the shadow of death." Perhaps the Reverend also quoted from Habakkuk, whose Biblical prophecy dating from 605 BC beautifully expresses the assurance that the just shall not perish in the midst of terrible calamities.

Later, the many lessons he read in the Bible and his own profound experience with disappointment and distress were an endless source of mitigating solace and understanding to draw upon when leading his flocks. He believed it was the irrefutable proof of the role of divine providence in human affairs that he should meet Caroline and her father, change the course of his life, and serve the Lord for the rest of his long life. As Sophocles first said, "One word frees us of all the weight and pain of life: That word is love."

Perhaps the act of breaking up home and traveling so far to begin anew when he was just a boy of thirteen caused Ludwig Henry to be bitten with a wanderlust which drove him to many new hometowns during his career and life. In all, he resided in: Okawville, Illinois; Sandwich, Illinois; Hollowayville, Illinois; Ft. Madison, Iowa; Minneapolis, Minnesota; and Fond du Lac, Wisconsin. Even so, he reconnected often with his family whether they were living in Ft. Madison, Iowa, or in Minier, Illinois.

Finally happiness returned to Ludwig Heinrich with his marriage to Caroline Austmann. They retrieved baby Lydia and set out on a life meandering through the Middle West where he served as pastor to a number of German Church of the Gospel congregations. In addition to Lydia, together they had ten children: Martha (named for Ludwig's first wife) born August 6, 1861 in Sandwich, Illinois; Mary, January 8, 1863 also in Sandwich and whose line we will follow; Anna, December 12, 1866 in Hollyville, Illinois; Theodore, November 17, 1868 and died a half year later, also Hollyville; and Adolph Henry, June 20, 1870 in Ft. Madison; Henry, September 2, 1872 in Ft. Madison; Amanda, June 1, 1875 in Minneapolis, Minnesota, but lived only nine years; Paul F.E., March 15, 1877 in Minneapolis but lived less than a year; Paulus, July 25, 1880 in Fond du Lac, Wisconsin, and Herbert Dan, July 27, 1882 in Fond du Lac.

Religion in America had an importance a century and a half ago which is hard to imagine today. Its functions were many and its forms--Congregationalists, Catholics, Shakers, Lutherans, Unitarians, Baptists, Methodists, Mormons, Presbyterians, and Episcopalians--were bewildering to those so recently arrived from Germany where there were but two christian beliefs: Lutheran or Catholic. But despite the many differences in doctrine and attitude, there was in American religion a common bond, not an intellectual, but an emotional one. It was love: love of God, love of Christ, love of the church which one identified with, and it was much more openly and ingenuously expressed than it would be today. The church was then truly the center of one's life, a force to explain the mysteries of life in that day of little formal education, the arbiter of social behavior, the heart of the members' social life.

STORIES MY FOLKS TOLD ME

Ministers such as the Reverend Buehrig strove to help their parishioners to find answers to life's ultimate questions such as: What is the meaning of my existence? What is a worthy way for me to spend my life? How should I treat those around me? How can I satisfy my desires yet be considerate of others? Character building and social responsibility were his aims and objectives back in that day before society became secularized. Folks freely expressed their Christian beliefs, would speak of them aloud, and firmly believed that their denomination was the one true faith even to the point of bigotry. They would instruct the next generation in their belief hoping that in so doing they would prevent a harvest of pleasure-driven, self-absorbed young Americans.

Alexis de Tocqueville said it well in his "Democracy in America" of 1835: "The greatest part of America was peopled by men who, after having shaken off the authority of the Pope, acknowledged no other religious supremacy; they brought with them into the New World a form of Christianity which I cannot better describe than by styling it a democratic and republican religion (not meaning today's political parties). This sect contributed powerfully to the establishment of a democracy and a republic, and from the earliest settlement of the emigrants politics and religion contracted an alliance which has never been dissolved."

The wayfarer Rev. Buehrig had to perform many roles under the heading of minister back in those days before marriage counselors, child rearing specialists, advice columnists, and social welfare agencies. His advice was asked the more eagerly because he spoke out of his own personal trial, out of human wisdom, and out of a close study of scripture. The Bible was his guide and he knew that book best. This meant not only the application of the Ten Commandments to domestic life but also the constant use of the entire Bible as a source for examples and precepts or guiding principles. All the answers lay in its pages which he could cite chapter and verse. For example, he would have advised rigid propriety in the behavior of women, sedulous avoidance of pampering the child, averting attempts of relatives who would interfere with the management of the family, stoicism in the face of difficulties, and turning away from gossip.

He would have reminded his flock that forgiveness is a fundamental tenant of their faith, as in "Father, forgive them, they know not what they do" or in the parable of the prodigal son, when the father runs to his son to embrace and kiss him before the son has even asked for forgiveness, or in the Lord's Prayer: "Forgive us our debts." Difficult as it is, the Reverend taught that they must forgive the repugnant, hurtful acts of spouse, child, neighbor, colleague, or parent even before he comes to them contrite and remorseful, asking for mercy. Further, in Matthew's gospel, Chapter 26, verse 31—46, Ludwig would have found guides for daily living to give his people: to feed the hungry, to clothe the poor, to welcome strangers, to care for others even prisoners for "Amen, I say to you, whatever you did for one of these least brothers of mine, you did for me."

In his day, he would have preached that the husband was the head of the family and appointed from on high to direct the life of the family. But still, as it was the right of the husband to rule, so it was his duty to rule with moderation and love—to love his wife "even as Christ loved the Church." Ephesians verse 25. So also, the obedience of the wife was not to be the reluctant offering of an ungracious spirit, but the cheerful service of a happy mind. In the reality of those times, the wife was more often the true equal of her husband as his own wife, Caroline, who bore him ten children in twenty years, ran a large household, and still found time to assist in his calling as it was then expected of preachers' wives. She was truly a partner and in no way a subservient being, a truth he would have readily acknowledged!

Back then in the second half of the 19th Century, life was particularly fragile, death was the dreaded grim reaper; male life expectancy was in the early forties, a bit more for women. Infant mortality was such that ten percent of newborns never lived until their first birthday. Diseases such as tuberculosis, typhoid fever, croup, measles, tetanus, and scarlet fever had not yet been conquered so the families of the sufferers required the council and support of ministers like the Reverend Buehrig. Long hours were spent with heads bowed over the Bible and hands clasped in prayer beseeching help from above to save a life or sustain the grieving. "For I am the Lord, your God, who grasp your right hand; it is I who say, 'Fear not, I will help you; your redeemer is the Holy One of Israel."

Isaiah 41. In the Old Testament books there are success stories such as the Exodus, but there are long, long stretches where there are great difficulties—exile, destruction of the Temple, terrible leaders, drought. But the people still managed to believe in God's promises—"Fear not … I will help you"—even in those hard times which lasted not just part of one lifetime, but the lifetime of several generations. Ludwig's parishioners needed to hear about that kind of perseverance so they too could trust in God and learn to bear hardships and setbacks over which they had no control, perhaps even for a long stretch of time. As the pastor perhaps said, "The Old Testament has a special way of teaching the value of patience in the face of trial."

"Sorrow makes us wise," said Alfred, Lord Tennyson. We're able to reevaluate what's really important in our lives when we experience loss. From that comes growth and true appreciation for what we have. The Reverend Buehrig had the experience of personal disappointment and loss himself to be helpful to others who were suffering pain while others who had not gone through such turmoil could not empathize or speak to it. Some of the toughest "crosses" we are asked to bear are the ones we didn't expect or ask for. "Why this? Why now? Why me?" his followers might have asked. Then the Reverend could have looked to Luke 23:26 where Simon, a Cyrenian, just happened to be at the right place at the right time to be pressed into service to carry the cross behind Jesus. That wasn't Simon's plan when he got up that morning, he didn't volunteer for the job, he just put his shoulder to the cross as best he could, and walked behind Jesus one step at a time, just trying to get through the day. Furthermore, it is written in Luke and likely preached by Ludwig: "If any want to become my followers, let them deny themselves and take up their cross daily and follow me." Surely, this shared experience of "carrying a cross" brought Ludwig into closer fellowship with his flock!

When death did take place, the body was prepared at home and viewed there before the church service and burial; a black wreath hung on the front door of the deceased home for months. Frequently the family held a wake, customary whether Protestant or Catholic. Once the body was buried, family and friends visited the grave often, planted flowers appropriate to the season, and generally made a little shrine to the deceased. This was especially traditional in German communities.

Black clothing, signifying mourning, was the mode worn by family members for a year or till death in the case of a widow.

Death's closest relation in that culture was to religion. In Bible and sermon, in prayer and ritual, in advice and exhortation, the representatives of the church in America strove to cope with that omnipresent fact of death. Providing the Christian consolation was thus one of Reverend Buehrig's great services and formed a fundamental aspect of his life's calling. Conceivably, he might have suggested to his parishioner facing the end that for a Christian, death is never for its own sake. It is in dying, as St. Francis said, that we are born to eternal life. Just as we know not from whence our soul came, we know not where it will go. We call that destination "heaven" and pray that is where our soul is headed, but what it will be like, how we will recognize those who have gone ahead, how we will function there, we cannot yet know. We have only the assurance of Christ himself that He will be there, He will know us, and He will make a place for us there. When a fearful sufferer pressed that he just couldn't be sure of that, the good pastor assuredly suggested that more prayer and more reading of the Bible was needed.

Poetry, literature, and music of the day echoed the mournful suffering of the griever. We love to read yet the poetry of Ralph Waldo Emerson as in "Threnody" over the loss of his five year old son, of William Cullen Bryant in his "Hymn to Death", of Walt Whitman in his "When Lilacs Last in the Dooryard Bloomed" about the death of Abraham Lincoln, of Henry Wadsworth Longfellow in his "Resignation" about the death of his wife, Fanny, or "The Wreck of the Hesperus" about the victims of a shipwreck, and of Edgar Allen Poe in his "Ulalume" and "Annabel Lee" about the death of his child-wife, Virginia.

The "Good Book" which the Reverend Buehrig followed was the one translated by Martin Luther from Greek to the German language back in 1522. Intending to bring the holy book to the common people who could not read Latin, to take the reader as close as possible to what the original text said, and to allow the reader himself to choose what he wanted to read, he created, in the process, a great work of literature, in language that is dignified, beautiful, sonorous, and elegant. As in the case of our own English King James translation, quotations from the

Luther Bible have passed into everyday German usage: "the salt of the earth," "labor of love," "root of all evil," "fell flat on his face." The words of beloved German poets Goethe and Schiller abound with quotations taken directly from their Bible. Sacred music reigns in the German language and follows the wording from their Bible: the Oratorios of Bach, chorales of Haydn, the Messiah of Handel, operas and masses of Mozart, songs and masses of Schubert, and even the "Missa Solemnis" of Beethoven takes its text from the Bible.

As de Tocqueville observed, it is difficult to underestimate the contribution, made by ministers such as Ludwig Henry Buehrig and their churches, to society as a whole. Because they were held in such respect and esteem in their circle no matter how small, their words and council were heeded, sound values were promoted, solutions to dissension were found, and temptation was resisted. Then as now and always, mere mortals were weak to the lure of alcohol, gossip, lust, swearing, laziness, spousal abuse, or brutality to children, but with the help of a dedicated pastor they could be prodded back to right living. The fatherless and the widow were among his flock as well and motivated the members to share. Feelings of guilt, genuine or imagined, even then erupted, as when the surface of the skin is scratched, for the human condition dictates it. Reverend Buehrig did his best to council for this although in his church confession to a priest was not the custom.

Then, as today, the big questions of his flock were: Is there really a God? Is evil going to win after all? Am I wasting my time trying to lead a decent life? At death do I simply dissolve into nothingness? Those folks, like us, simply couldn't go through life without facing those kinds of doubts, which with the guidance of the good reverend they'd call upon their faith with hope, just as the patient sower who entrusts his seed to the earth and sun, must do.

In all, Ludwig Henry's peregrinations led his family to many towns in the course of his ministry: Okawville, Illinois, 1860-1861; Sandwich, Illinois, 1861; Hallowayville, Illinois, 1866; Ft. Madison, Iowa, 1870; Columbia, Illinois, 1875; Minneapolis, Minnesota, 1876; Fond du lac, Wisconsin, 1882.

The first of Caroline and Ludwig Henry's children to marry was Lydia to William Baekermeier. They spent their lives in Peru, Illinois, where they raised two children Herbert and Hulda. Martha married the Reverend Simon Hoffmeister, also in Peru, where they raised Lydia, Alma, Paul, and John. With Mary's marriage to George Peine the connection of the Buehrig and Peine families further cohered in Minier. There they raised Adela, Paul, and lost baby Cyril. Anna married the Reverend Franz Boshold, lived in Belleville, Illinois, and raised Julius, Edna, and Esther. Adolph Henry married Augusta, dwelled in St. Louis and became parents of Elmer Paul and Adolph Herbert. Herbert Dan married Emma D., lived in St. Louis, but had no children.

1910 photo in St. Louis of Caroline, Ludwig Henry, Herbert Dan (front), Theodore (back), Anna, Henry, wife of Theo, Martha, Adolph and his wife Augusta.

Each wedding of their children was a joyous occasion for the Buehrigs, and of course Ludwig Henry officiated at each. Weddings in those days customarily took place in the bride's home but not under Reverend Buehrig's watch! He solemnized the weddings in his church. Also customary in the day before the concept of a honeymoon, was for the bridal couple to spend their first night in the bride's home, second night in the groom's family home, and the third night in their new home which had been in the meantime filled with food by their friends. "Shivaree" took place the first evening the bridal couple was in their own home: young friends marched to the house with a clatter of horns, tin pans, fiddles, drums, and anything to make a loud noise. Soon the groom would open the door and invite the noisemakers to troop in and wish them well.

When Ludwig Henry took sick around 1915 he and Caroline went back to Peru, Illinois, where daughters, Lydia and Martha, lived. Daughter Mary, in Minier, had died five years before. As was the custom in the days before retirement income or rest homes, they spent the Reverend's last days split between the two daughters' homes. When the patriarch bid adieu to his earthly sojourn on July 18, 1916 at the remarkable age of eighty-four, he was buried in the Peru Cemetery.

Back in the day when life expectancy was short, not many women lived to enjoy a long period as a grandmother, but to this Caroline was an exception. As she lived out the rest of her widowed life in the various homes of her children she was the doting "Oma" (German for Grandma) to the little ones in whichever home she was residing. Anthropologists tell us that grandmothers have been an underrated yet crucial source of power and sway in our evolutionary history. Their presence helps to explain why we are the way we are—slow to grow up and start breeding but remarkably fruitful once we get there, empathetic and generous as animals go, and family-focused to a degree hardly seen elsewhere in the primate order. By studying primitive peoples, anthropologists find that the presence or absence of a grandmother often spelled the difference between life and death for the grandchildren. In fact, having a grandmother around sometimes improved a child's survival prospects to a far greater extent than did the presence of a father! Furthermore, they found that when a child was weaned from mother's milk but not yet possessing strength and immune vigor of their own, the presence of a grandmother cut their chances of dying in half! While the older women were no longer using their stalwart bodies for childbearing, they were directing their considerable energies to their grandchildren, filling the gap between busy mother and vulnerable child. And all the while, she gave and received a great quantity of love which perhaps explains the mysterious mechanism of her grandmotherly role!

Caroline survived her husband fifteen years by living with her St. Louis children until January 21, 1931, when she was the age of eighty-six. Astoundingly, Caroline outlived her two older daughters, Martha and Mary, besides her children who died in childhood. It is amazing as well to consider that Caroline outlived her grown granddaughter, Adela, Mary's daughter in Minier! Bethany Memorial Park Cemetery in St. Louis is the matriarch's final resting place where also are buried her father and mother, her brother Paul and her two sons, Paulus and Henry. Living nearby and devoted to maintaining their mother's gravesite were daughter Anna and sons, Adolph Henry and Herbert Dan.

Pioneers Carl Imig and Wilhelmina Cloos Imig arrived 1859
—4—

In the middle Rhine River valley, as the great river flows northward into today's Holland and finally into the North Sea, measuring only about the size of modern Massachusetts, lay the German principality of Rhineland Pfalz, today called the state of Rhineland Palatinate and Saarland. Known even now for its exceptional fertility of soil, flat terrain, and glorious growing weather where bumper crops of wheat and corn filled the granaries year after year, this is the thriving land where vineyards and fruit orchards have dotted the landscape since Roman times and castles have been in existence since medieval times. Bordered on the west by the Rhine River and just across from France, this was the "wine cellar" of the Holy Roman Empire.

The Pfalz has a mild, sunny climate just perfect for wine culture. Today's classic white varieties, such as Liebfraumilch, Riesling, Silvaner, Mueller-Thurgau, Grauburgunder and reds such and Spaetburgunder, Dornfelder, and Portugieser have their antecedents back in the 17th Century when instead of large vineyards cultivated for export, each homestead boasted a few vines which were turned into wine for family consumption. Likewise, fruits such as apples, peaches, cherries, or apricots were distilled into "schnapps" at home for personal enjoyment.

Then as now, the fall harvest festival was a highlight of th[...] villagers with parades and markets and plenty of opportu[...] and mix with folks from nearby villages or returning dist[...] Dancing, one can imagine, was always a favorite part of a fe[...] the consumption of the local wines and beers.

The principality of Rhineland-Pfalz had much to offer its citizens. Besides the fertility of the soil, the city of Worms was a large commercial center, the city of Mainz was an important trading center, and Koblenz sits where the Mosel River enters the Rhine and where three mountain ranges intersect. Throughout the principality, underground saline springs surface to form famous cure-spas such as Bad Durkheim and Karlruhe known for their healing waters.

Appealing as the location of the principality was, it nevertheless had a distinctly negative geographic element. It lay on the eastern shore of the Rhine River with France directly across, in the major east-west transit area of Germany where invaders found it very easy to pass through on their way to France and likewise where French armies chose to pass on their conquering invasions of Germany and lands east. The relatively flat terrain enabled an army to move through swiftly while at the same time feeding itself, man and beast, from the bountiful stores of produce growing or stored along the way.

The landscape of the Pfaltz is still dotted with Celtic and Roman landmarks, the Palatinate Forest, dozens of castles, and Romanesque churches as they did back in 1620 when the Imig name is first mentioned. The earliest extant record found for the old German name, Immich, which has since evolved into Imig, is 1620. The proof is inscribed on a tombstone in the Biebern cemetery which reads, "Peter Immich" born 1620 in nearby Fronhofen, the same year, coincidentally, that the pilgrims set foot on Plymouth Rock in today's Jamestown, Massachusetts. Records in the town of Fronhofen, near Simmern in Rhineland-Pfalz, indicate that over forty generations of Imigs had worked the soil of this garden spot. Peter's wife, Gertrude, is mentioned as well on the tombstone where her year of death, 1658, is still legible.

Astoundingly, during the lifetime of this first identified Imig, the famous Thirty Years War of 1618–1640 was waged—and he survived! One of the most devastating of wars, this was fought between Catholics and Protestants throughout the European continent but mostly on German soil. In the fierce battles to determine which religion would dominate, the German population was reduced from 20,000,000 to 13,500,000; sixty-six percent of the buildings, eighty-five percent of the horses, and eighty-two percent of the cattle were destroyed. Yet, the Imig blood line remained intact for records exist of Johannes Imig born in Fronhofen in 1647, died in Biebern in 1685 and married to Eva (last name unknown) born 1652, died in Biebern 1728.

In 1674, Louis XIV of France invaded the Pfalz to burn and plunder. Again in 1680 the French invaded and again in 1688, under Napoleon Bonaparte. The misery of the people must have been unimaginable as plunder, murder, and terror complicated their attempt to till the fields. Increasing the burden on the farmers was the absence of many men who were away conscripted to bear arms for the defense of the principality. The hard field work undoubtedly fell to the women and girls, yet in some areas the inhabitants were not able to cultivate their fields for three succeeding years. Even the beautiful castle of Heidelberg with all its precious treasures was demolished, the city of Mannheim was destroyed, and starvation was the lot of all, even the Imigs. Only the strongest survived!

Still despite the turmoil of war, records in Biebern document a Peter Imig born in 1678 in nearby Nannhausen, died April 14, 1740 in Biebern and married to Anna Christina Bender, born 1678, died 1752 in Biebern. Further evidence reveals a Johann Michael Imig born in Biebern in 1701, died there in 1770, married to Susanna Christina Schmidt, born 1701 and died 1748 in Biebern. Life went on, at least for the strongest!

Into this continuing environment of terror was born Johann Christoph Imig, 1725 in Biebern. His wife Anna Catharina Thomas was born in 1729 Rheinboellen located a bit east of Biebern and closer to the great Rhine River. Both, however, ended their days in Pfalzdorf in 1798 and 1792, respectively, which means that they had fled the Palatinate region during their lifetimes to settle farther north in Germany. The Imig name was then no longer associated with the sunny Rheinland-Pfalz region but with today's state of North Rhine Westphalla.

The Imig's had moved north to a completely different state of Germany; their reasons were probably many but desperation was primary. Besides the devastation of the land overrun by conquering armies, the problem of religion arose. After the Thirty Years War, the rulers of the Pfalfz or North Rhine Westphallia had chosen Roman Catholicism and expected all their subjects to join them. Most did, except those like the Imigs, people of conscience and principle, who would not abandon their Protestant faith. Persecution of non-Catholics was systematically carried out with property confiscated and in many cases expulsion from the Duchy.

Still life went on. The Imigs built their homes in the manner of all Germans at that time of stone with thatched roofs and cobblestone or earthen floors. If stones were not available homes were built of straw or reeds woven together and plastered with clay hardened by the sun. This masonry structure, bonded when possible with wooden beams, withstood the shaking of strong winds or pelting rain. Wood was very scarce as the forests belonged to the ruler and used as his private hunting ground. If an Imig wished to enter the forest to pick up fallen limbs and deadwood to bring home for fuel, he had to ask permission of the prince's steward. The few pieces of furniture the Imigs managed to acquire were often hewn out of a dead tree that was granted by that agent. Since they lived in a grape growing area, they were also allowed to help themselves to the pruned branches from the vines which were piled high at pruning time of the year. That wood made good pegs for construction in that day when iron nails were not yet invented.

To complicate matters for the Imigs, from 1794–1815, Fronhofen, Biebern, and Pfalzdorf were briefly part of France conquered by Napoleon Bonaparte, so JoHann Jacob Imig, born 1762 and died 1831 in Pfalzdorf married to Anna Catharina Gembler born in 1763 and died 1800 in Pfalzdorf were officially French citizens. To their no doubt relief, the Congress of Vienna of 1815, held to settle the Napoleonic wars, returned the villages to Germany. Today Fronhofen is part of the town of Simmern in Rheinland-Palitinate but Biebern, first mentioned in AD 754 as a center of monastic life near the Mozelle River, stands alone.

By the time Pfalzdorf was returned to Germany, Anna Catharina had bourn seven children, died and was supplanted by JoHann Jacob Imig's second wife Maria Catharina Augustin, born 1780 and died 1853 in Pfalzdorf. She bore JoHann Jacob twelve children and survived him by twenty-two years having been eighteen years his junior. It is assumed that all these generations of Imigs were farmers, able to feed large families and attain long lives.

Life had become disappointing for the Imigs those last years in the Rheinland Palatinate region of west central Germany because of overpopulation; there were too many people for the land to support. They wanted to expand, to enlarge their farm acres, in order to support their growing family, but they were surrounded by hostile Roman Catholics who barely tolerated this group of Protestants and denied them access to new land. Besides overpopulation and segregation, taxes raised to the confiscatory point just to enrich the coffers of the Duke and support the military which had been necessary as long as anyone could remember and the difficulty of cultivating their acreage when armies were constantly marching over and plundering the fledgling crops convinced them in the year 1741 that it was time to strike out in a new direction, time to succumb to the lure of America.

Word had reached them that the British were looking for colonists to settle their lands in America. Immigrant agents were employed by shipping companies in Holland and England, who received a commission for every person they recruited. Understandably, this job attracted unscrupulous types, agents who succeeded in extracting money from the emigrants or even stealing from them the few possessions they might have. Many who arrived in New York or Pennsylvania had been so thoroughly divested of their possessions and bills had been run up against them while on shipboard that they had to be sold into indentured service for a number of years after their arrival. Desperation to escape their present lot was indeed the driver of fearless folks like the Imigs to take the risk of emigration.

Despite the primitive modes of travel in the 18th Century, the hardy Imigs loaded their belongings, seeds, and utensils onto wagons for the long trek north or perhaps onto flatboats to float on the Rhine River north to Rotterdam where they sought passage across the Atlantic Ocean to New York. Records show that about twenty families made this trip from Biebern but how long it took or how many stopovers were required to earn food and supplies is not known to us today. Following the mighty river as it flows northward, they passed Koblenz, Simmern, and Cologne, perhaps stopping in each to work or acquire supplies along the way.

Once in Rotterdam, the Imig group joined hundreds of other emigrants waiting there for space aboard a ship but then was told that ships were not available at all! England and Spain were embarked on a naval war in 1741 and needed all the vessels for the war! Of course, that meant the stream of emigrants who had been arriving from all parts of Germany was stranded and became a burden to the city. To prevent insurrection, the government of the Netherlands sent a notice to the Royal Prussian Department of Defense and the County of Kleve that from then on no German emigrant would be permitted to enter Holland who had not sufficient proof of permission to travel to England and proof of entitlement to travel on an English ship from Rotterdam. Crestfallen with disappointment, the Imig group was sequestered at Schenkenschanz, an ancient Dutch fortress built near the town of Kleve in the year 1586. There in primitive conditions they were to be detained until they had received passports from the English.

Finally, at the end of May, 1741, the despairing twenty families in the Imig group gave up the hope of receiving travel papers from the English. Instead, they sent a request to the Kleve town council asking permission to settle in the Prussian lands around the town and be given a piece of uncultivated land on which to support themselves. While still waiting for word, the twenty families were allowed to move into the city of Goch for the winter where a number died of exposure and typhus. Eventually, in May 1743, an official order came, signed by Frederick the Great of Prussia, granting the group permission to stay on the Heath, a barren, uncultivated, useless piece of land called the Heath of Goch. They never made it to the new world, but they found themselves on new land in a part of Germany completely new to them, even to the Prussian dialect spoken there.

Since the Heath of Goch was practically an island formed by the convergence of the rivers Niers and Rhine and was surrounded on all sides by a Catholic majority, the twenty families on the Heath stayed mostly among themselves. It was less than one hundred years since the religious wars of Europe, and antipathy between Catholics and Protestants was still very high. In addition the Imigs spoke a dialect called Hessisch which made them stand out in a region where the prevailing population spoke High German. Ostracized by their neighbors for these reasons, they were nevertheless impervious to ridicule through the sustaining familial bond they held among themselves.

Now a ragged band of refugees in an inhospitable land, the Imigs were faced immediately with backbreaking work to drain the heath to make it arable. Consumed by desperation but with community spirit and the help of all, they did. They had to eat, and they were entirely dependent on themselves. At first they actually sought shelter in caves until they could gather stones to build houses with roofs they thatched themselves. Not a forward step exactly but a resort to the primitive, best describes our folks at that point.

In time they cleared the swampy land for tillage, built homes, church, and school for their community. It was backbreaking work but that is all they expected out of life. Still, being human they found chances for fun and celebration. Not so many festivals were on the calendar of Protestants as were those of Catholics, but the Imigs did look forward to and enjoy some reprieve from the tedium and ennui of their lives. Such a highlight of the year was the grape festival, an all day, all night event for which they prepared for weeks. Work stopped, everyone came, mingled, gossiped, drank some wine, danced, ate too much, and generally forgot the burdens of their lives. Festivals were like a tonic which raised everyone's spirits!

The festivities began at early morning with a prayer and short religious service to thank God for the bounties they had received. When this was over, the women began preparing the foods they had brought while the younger men ran races, wrestled, and generally tried to impress the young girls who stood avidly watching. The older men sat around in groups discussing the crops, the new methods of tilling, and of course the weather which was then as now a major preoccupation of farmers. Usually, someone had brought in a bottle of something stronger than grape juice so the men would saunter over behind a tree and sample some.

For children there were always games or another favorite—the story teller. Books were scarce in the village and few people could read anyway. Even fewer had time to do so, but wonderful tales were handed down verbally from generation to generation. Every village had at least one woman or man who was the acknowledged story teller, regaling adults as well as children for a half hour or all afternoon or evening if folks desired. These stories came from way back in the distant past of these Germanic folk. Some had to do with the Niebelungen tales, some were later assembled by the brothers Grimm into their collection of fairy tales, some were romantic, many were frightening, but all had an important moral lesson woven into the story line.

At noon and all afternoon came the feasting till everyone was full and they returned to their play. Sometimes the pastor was called upon to perform a marriage ceremony or two right there out in the open! After a leisurely supper, the commencement of the evening activities began. In the center of the field was a huge pile of logs, twigs, and branches, straw and other combustibles which they had previously assembled now just begging to be ignited. Once the fire was flaring against the dark sky, folks gathered 'round. Out came the violins, accordions, harps, and simple percussion instruments. Voices of singing filled the air with beautiful folkloric and religious songs which had been passed down through the generations and absolutely everyone knew by heart. Soon couples formed to dance the "laendler," a folk dance which later evolved into the more formal dance we know as the waltz.

Of course, the young teenagers were busy too especially if there was a new girl from a neighboring village or if some young girl had blossomed into a real beauty since last year's festival. It was at sunset too that the fermented form of grape juice—wine—was introduced and enjoyed in its many varieties by women and men alike. These folks raised potatoes too and knew how to distill the fermented potato juice into a very potent drink—"Schnapps." But it was barley and hops, grown on their property, that was a source for their favorite daily drink—beer. Even today, Germans prefer beer over water, but at the Grape Festival they pretty much stuck to the drop of the vine!

Incredibly the Imigs lasted seventy-nine years in that confined, make-do place. But in 1820, they recognized that the Heath of Goth could no longer accommodate their numbers so members of the Imig family seized the opportunity to found the nearby towns of Pfalzdorf and Louisendorf. Pfalzdorf is in the present-day county of Kleve, near the city of Kalkar, in the state of North Rhine-Westphalia. Louisendorf, just a bit to the east, had been settled by French Hugenots, and is today part of the town of Bedburg-Hau. All are very near today's Holland and are at latitude 53 degrees and longitude 7.35. Imig names are still found in the Evangelical Church records and other legal papers filed in the towns; Imigs farm there even now the same plots that their ancestors dug out of the barren land so many years ago.

With the countryside under the sway of the local ruler, the Duke of Kleve, conscription to the army had been particularly heavy in the first half of the 19th Century as the rulers attempted to resist the onslaught of Napoleon. No sooner was he vanquished in 1815 but the king of Saxony in northern Germany became very aggressive in his attempt to seek lands belonging to his neighbors, Mecklenburg and Posner. In short, it seemed to the young German men that they were called time after time to bear arms at the whim of the hereditary ruler, for reasons having very little to do with their own lives. At the same time, the military life had long appealed to many young men bored with a prosaic village life or the monotony of agrarian life and looking for excitement and variety. As a result, there arose real competition for those seeking adventure, newness, the novel—the distant shore of America. Like a siren call luring the adventurous and independent young men of Germany, came word into common parlance of an awesome opportunity!

But the group of kin who set out to emigrate in 1859 was actually the third attempt of the Imigs for around 1760 a group of Imigs had already left for America. They had received word from some of the families who had migrated to the New World in previous years, reporting that one could get 160 acres of land free just by building a house on the land and farming it for five years. Such a large amount of land was unfathomable to the people in Germany. Only the Duke had that much! Folks wrote from America that one could cut down any tree on his property if he wanted without asking permission of anyone; the land there was so rich that harvest after harvest was bountiful. Why, they would be crazy not to go and grab some of that free land!

It took some time to prepare, sell what they could not take, turn the proceeds into gold, sew new clothes, and head by flatboat on the Rhine to Rotterdam to wait for a ship. There were no regular schedules for sailing ships then, so they just had to wait for one loaded with cattle to put into port, unload, and for $100 per adult, $50 for children they could board it. Someone mentioned the smell but they were used to that what with the design of their homes allowing their animals and stalls at one end of the home.

Once the Imigs were at sea, someone took count and sure enough they were short one person, a ten year old boy! He had missed the boat out of sheer fright at the noises and shunting of cattle and people, sails flapping at tall masts, lines of rope everywhere. Shocked and confused as they were, his parents could do nothing for the ship was under sail without him, and that was the last anyone heard of those Imigs—they were lost at sea! Young Johann Jakob Imig actually made it back to Pfalzdorf where he grew up and was the grandfather of the Imigs who immigrated to America in 1859, the line we are following.

He married Anna Catharina Gembler in 1789 who bore him seven children. In 1800 she died and he remarried to Maria Catherina Augustin who mothered twelve children for Jakob, seven sons and five daughters. Their son, Carl, is the family ancestor who immigrated to America in 1859. He traveled with his wife Wilhelmina Cloos in a large group of Imigs and Graffs including their eight children: Jacob, Heinrich, Carl, Friedrich, Valentine, Wilhelmina, Eva Catharina, and Maria Elizabeth Graff.

It is their daughter, Elizabeth, born 1845 in Pfalzdorf, died 1906 in Minier, Illinois, whose line we are following. She was only fourteen at the time of the crossing. Five years later when in Tazewell County she married Henry Peter Graff, born 1838 in Louisendorf, died 1911 in Minier and coincidentally was also a member of the immigrant group from North Rhine Westpfallia. His mother, Anna Catherina, was also born an Imig, so the tradition of Imigs and Graffs marrying each other continued on to their new fatherland in Illinois. Together Elizabeth and Henry had eight children.

It was a consequence of originally living practically on an island in the Heath of Goth that naturally resulted in the tendency of Imig families to intermarry with other Imigs, cousin with cousin being the closest degree. They also have long married Graff family members going back at least to 1830 in Pfalzdorf from whence the Graffs, together with the Imigs also immigrated to America. On record in Kalkar near Louisendorf is the marriage on April 29, 1830 of Heinrich Peter Graff (1795- 1865) to Anna Catherina Imig in Pfalzdorf. Both of their baptisms are recorded there in church records.

It was for the third time, then, when in late 1858, a number of the Imig families along with several Graff families were making preparations for the long journey to the New World. Clothing had to be repaired or sewn anew, belongings not needed had to be sold or given away with the assets turned into pieces of gold which the women sewed into the men's vests. These were to be worn only by the heads of the families next to their skin and not removed until they reached their destination. Everything they couldn't wear was packed into bags and sacks of all sizes, each homemade. If they couldn't wear it or carry it, it didn't go! Some bags contained small packages, wrapped in hog bladders to make them moisture-proof, holding precious seeds to plant in Illinois, the amazing soil of high repute.

Some of the Imigs were actually small landowners in the Duchy of Kleve for they had been awarded ownership of small plots over the years as reward for services rendered to the duke. The sale of these plots was easily accomplished, they found, because land was in short supply and much desired by those staying behind. The payments were quickly turned into gold for the journey.

Good-byes were said with tears and of course some misgivings for it's human to "get cold feet" before embarking on such a monumental enterprise. Some still remembered the party who left about one hundred years before and were never heard of again. This was in effect the third time that Imigs had attempted to emigrate to America, this time to succeed. Records reveal there were thirty four Imigs and Graffs who traveled together north to the sea to book passage on a steam ship.

Traveling in such a large group of relatives and fellow neighbors, like the Graff family, sustained and fortified them. They were all in this life-altering emigration together, could shore each other up, could help one another to be brave. They recognized their precarious situation but were courageous and not at all abashed by their hurtle into the great unknown. Surely they felt it a challenging, exciting journey and the surprises to come would be a part of the thrill of the unknown.

They had heard all the tales about America. Land in the new world was very cheap, even obtainable in 160 acre parcels for free just by building a house and living on it for some years. Trees could be cut down and used to build a house on your own land without even asking permission from anyone. The land was so rich you could grow almost anything. Yes, life was going to be better in their new home, they just knew it!

After a long and tiresome wait at the wharf, the cattle boat arrived and was unloaded. That done and a cursory clean up, the families shuffled on board and found refuge on a lower deck. They noticed the smell of cattle but didn't complain since they were used to it, like a little reminder of home. Still, if truth be told, they would say they found the scent of their own animals preferable to any others in all the world. The fare was still $100 per adult and $50 per child which they paid in gold.

The ship was a little smaller than they had expected and in their not so qualified opinion it didn't look very sea-worthy. But they certainly didn't want to wait who knew how long for the next ocean going ship. It was then early 1859, and they wanted to plant a crop yet that spring.

Most folks went through a siege of sea-sickness, for the small ship just rode the waves like a cork bobbing up and down on each wave as it came. The worst though was when the North Atlantic winter gales struck in full force making everyone sick all over again. They would be on top of a wave with no sky only water to be seen, and the next moment they were in the valley with water higher than the boat on every side, enough to convince even the stout-hearted that this was the end!

Eventually the storm subsided but the ship had sprung a leak causing all able-bodied men to answer the call to man the pumps to keep the ship afloat. The sea biscuits had become damp and were infested with weevils, which had to be picked out before eating the biscuits. The salted beef was losing its flavor but most of the other foodstuffs had already been consumed, so they were on short rations. Much longer than anticipated because of the storm, the trip took five weeks before they arrived at the Promised Land, at New York City.

The very first thing they did upon stepping on land was to kneel in unison and offer a prayer of thanksgiving for their safe arrival. Then heads up and they were on the next segment of their way to their new life. From New York City to Minier, the Imigs and Graffs traveled by train, a trip of many sidetracks, shifts, and transfers, but compared to life at sea, it was pretty calm. They truly enjoyed the enforced idleness spent mostly gazing in wonder out the window at the passing beautiful landscape of their new homeland.

During these quiet times on their way to Illinois they regaled each other with stories of the life they had just left. A favorite was about the visit of the tax collector: Early one morning the Duke of Kleve's emissary, the tax collector, came to make his yearly visit to the home of Peter Imig who as the head man in the village was expected to wine and dine the dignitary. Peter was surprised by the visit and consternation ensued as he discovered there was no meat anywhere on the property to serve such an important person. A quick canvas of the neighbors yielded one goose egg. No one had butchered lately so when they were out of meat, they were out of meat and nothing to do about it!

STORIES MY FOLKS TOLD ME

Peter went out to the yard and looked around. There were a few chickens but he needed each one to establish the flock for next year. Desperate, he went to the pig sty where there were four shoats, or piglets, but they were next winter's supply of meat.

Still on such an important occasion, Peter had to have meat for the dinner. Finally he thought of a solution. He didn't like it but he had to do it. He went in to the house, grabbed the butcher knife, and charged out to the pig sty. What a commotion ensued with an unbelievable squealing of pigs! It was all his wife, Margarethea, and the eight children could to do divert the dignitary's attention. Finally, he returned with eight ears and four tails, motioned to his wife to come into the kitchen and proceed with the cooking. She was a resourceful woman so by adding onions, potatoes, kale, and lots of herbs, she cooked those ears and tails into an impressive dinner, and she saved the family's winter supply of meat—and their reputation!

Eventually, the train journey of Carl and Wilhelmina Imig brought them to their final destination, Hopedale, Illinois, and in time for spring planting too. They settled on a farm which they purchased about four and one-half miles northwest of Hopedale. Using the seeds they had brought from the Old Country and with some given them by generous neighbors they actually got in a crop that year of 1859. It was not possible in that day to buy seeds from a store; the farmer had to save some of his seeds from the previous year to plant in the spring.

By this time John Deere's steel plow was available, though, and Carl was amazed to see how it cut through the rich but sticky soil, turned over the furrows in neat ridges, and left the rich alluvial earth of the Mississippi Valley on the ground not on the plow blade, called a moldboard. Unlike on the old wooden moldboards the soil didn't stick to the shiny steel plow blade and he didn't have to stop every few feet to clean it off with a paddle; this new steel blade was miraculously self-scouring! Carl could pull the plow with one horse and cover two acres in a day. That brand-new technology had cost him fifteen dollars!

When it came time to harvest their grain much of it was kept locally but any surplus commodities or livestock had to be hauled in horse-drawn wagons to either Pekin or Peoria, the river-side terminals, where they were conveyed onto barges to float down the Illinois River to the Mississippi and on down to New Orleans. There were not many roads and no bridges but some steep hills along that thirty-five mile wagon drive! Carl and his sons carried two big logs for each wagon, one strapped to each side of the rig, to block the wagon on the downhill so it wouldn't run over the horses. On the uphill the logs were used to anchor the rig while the horses rested. This was dangerous work. On one of those trips Jakob Fenner, Carl's second son, slipped under the wagon and was killed. What a sad group returned from that trip!

Another time the entire family went on a big outing with Carl to the great city of Peoria with the exception of his daughter, Wilhelmina, who was then a young lady of nineteen. She was selected to be the sacrificial lamb who had to stay home to feed the livestock, milk the cows, and generally watch the place. Late in the afternoon she saw a man slip into the barn. She didn't recognize him and waited behind the window for him to leave. When he did not, she grew uneasy with worry. All she could imagine was that he intended to wait until dark and then he would sneak into the house and steal her father's gold. Now, she alone was responsible for the homestead and all they had! What should she do, she agonized? Then she remembered what they had done back in Germany to protect their valuables from invading armies. She stole out to the garden, dug a hole as deep as she could, and buried the gold. Then she went back into the house to worry that the man had seen her in the garden. Poor Wilhelmina was in such a state of anxiety by that time that she lit a candle and retraced her steps to the garden, dug up the gold, and hid it in several places in the house. Still she felt possessed by her fear, so when she could stand it no longer she took the gold, slipped out a window on the far side of the house, and started for the home of a relative to spend the rest of the night.

Across the swamps and ditches, through the grove of trees, and along paths difficult to follow in the moonless night she staggered nearly four miles to the home of her married sister, Anna Catharina. Johann Pleines, her brother-in-law, answered her impatient knocks and drew her in to shelter and solace. Wilhelmina was very relieved but mighty embarrassed to learn the next day that the man in the barn was a neighbor! He knew the family was away and wanted to borrow a tool. He knew exactly where it was so he grabbed it and exited by the back door and returned it the next day.

In the early days only the best of the acreage was tilled. Patches of swamp or very wet land would not be attempted at first. Often the land was purchased by a very frugal Imig because the unviable spots made the acres cheaper. Later when time and cash became available these swamps or marshes were drained, drainage tile laid to take away the water, and then miraculously rich soil appeared where before undesirable land had been. But until that day, those sloughs, undrained for farmland, were the home of a vast variety of birds, water fowl like geese, ducks, cranes, curlews, snipe, plovers, rails, and herons congregating on their migrations north and south. April brought a cacophony of cries and calls, a medley of sounds and colorful scenes to entertain the isolated family on the prairie—and game galore for the eating!

Carl and his wife and children gave their all to their Illinois farm where every bit of their energy was necessary to produce a crop and provide for their sustenance. Within three years, however, the patriarch Carl died at the age of fifty-eight. He is buried at Gaines cemetery near Minier, Illinois, as is his wife, Wilhelmina, although she didn't join him for another twenty-nine years when she was seventy-six years old.

This pioneer family had survived and prospered by their own efforts which were prodigious, but they were helped as well by the larger group in which they emigrated and settled. They gave in return, and in doing so they helped to create something that would not have come into being if many people had not worked together. They were individualists who made something larger than themselves by their membership in a community of like-minded individuals. As d'Tocqueville observed, "they acted as if their whole destiny were in their own hands, but when they reached out to grasp it they found themselves joining hands with others."

Looking back, we marvel that Carl and Wilhelmina could accomplish all they did with such primitive tools, yet each person at each point in history assumed they lived at the most advanced era. They did not know the future cures, inventions, styles, or technological advances. They saw life through their own prism, content and comfortable, working within the limitations of their day, not missing a thing which would ease the lives of folks to come.

In the Evangelical Church of Minier, today's Church of Christ, are the beautiful stained glass windows, in the art-deco style, which will memorialize forever the names of the pioneers Carl and Wilhelmina Cloos Imig.

Pioneers Heinrich Peter Graff and Anna
Catherina Imig Graff--arrived 1858

—5—

Much of the history of the Graff family is the same as the Imig family for they too hailed from Louisendorf, North Rhine Westphalia, Germany. Both families had long been associated with each other, had married into each others' families, shared the Protestant faith, and had identical reasons for wanting to leave Germany. It is in the Evangelical Church in nearby Kalkar where the Graff family wedding, baptismal, and death records have been inscribed over many generations. As far back as May 12, 1737, a Heinrich Graff was baptized with Johann Bernd Bergman serving as godfather; in 1795, another Heinrich Peter Graff was baptized; in 1811, an Anna Imig was baptized; and on April 23, 1830, the two were married in Pfalzdorf, North Rhine Westphalia, Germany; and on August 22, 1838, their son Heinrich Peter, whose line we will follow, was baptized.

These families did not leave penniless or ill-equipped or disposed to be dependent. On the contrary, they had investigated the options long and hard, had read news accounts of emigrants, saved money for the trip, and chose to leave all together in a rather large group thus assuring cohesion, security, comfort, and encouragement for their journey into the unknown. The parents wanted to give their children advantages in life, a better future, opportunities which they couldn't give them back in Louisendorf, just like conscientious parents of any day wish to do.

Together the two families did indeed travel to America on the same ship, the "Ariel," out of Bremen which landed in New York City on May 5, 1858, and in the same group traveled further to Minier, Illinois, in Tazewell County. The Graffs, like the Imigs, were Protestants living in a Catholic region of Germany which caused them to suffer derision, oppression, rejection from jobs, ostracism from schooling, and general prejudice. Some succumbed and converted to the other religion but most increased in their solidarity and grew a stronger faith because of it.

The patriarch of the Graff pioneers, Heinrich Peter Graff (1795—1865) and his wife Anna Catharina Imig (1814—1877) were by the time of their immigration a mature couple of sixty-three and forty-seven, respectively, and brought their large family along: Valentin, 27; Anna Christine, 25; Maria Eva, 22; Heinrich Peter, 20; Jacob, 17; Maria Elizabeth, 14; Christine, 7; Anna, 6; and Wilhelm, 4. Members of the Wullenweber and Pleines families were part of this large group from Louisendorf and Pfalzdorf traveling to Tazewell County as well. Their names are all listed on the manifest of their ship, "Ariel," except for the wives who were simply listed as "wife" or "spouse," a telling indication of the status of women of that day. Unmarried women were listed as "frau" if at all.

By 1859 when the Imig and Graff families immigrated to America, the wood-hulled, romantic-looking sailing ships, the famous Clipper Ships, had already been displaced by steel ships powered by steam. Conditions for the immigrants berthed deep in the hull of the ship had improved over time, but still it was crowded, food was rationed, and noise and commotion prevailed. Berths were two feet wide and arranged in tiers, like shelves, at the sides of a narrow isle, twenty to a compartment. Single men slept in their own compartment as did single women. Most important of all, the steam ships cut weeks off the travel time of the sailing ships.

Life for these families on board ship was made endurable by the company of each other. Sharing a common history, the same German dialect, their Protestant faith, even the ages of the children which coincided made the trip merrier and less lonely for the parents as well as the children. When they weren't helping their mothers prepare meals or watching the smaller children, the girls would gather to talk, sing songs, and assess the many boys passing by. The boys romped with each other and generally investigated the immense ship, trying to figure out how it worked, not caring that they were told not to stray. For all, parents and children alike, it was a time of forced inactivity which they were not accustomed to but must have liked.

Back in Louisendorf, Heinrich Peter, 20, had never really noticed Elizabeth Imig, thirteen, but in the confined space of the ship he couldn't help looking at the tall, slim, dark-haired girl with the big, brown eyes. Her sisters, Wilhelmina and Catharine, were beauties too and more his age, so in the evening when the young people gathered on deck to admire the starry sky it was to the older girls and youths to whom he gravitated. Singing, story telling, and joking were always a part of those ship board evenings except when the weather was stormy which it often was in the early spring time of the year.

Although locomotive travel was deemed very expensive, as expensive as their ocean crossing had been, the large family of Graffs had prepared for this known fact and boarded in New York City, destination: Tazewell County in Illinois. They had lodged a few nights in the city in order to change some gold to dollars, replenish their food stocks, and essentially find their land legs again. It was a challenge for Anna to keep track of her large brood, but by assigning the older ones to the smaller ones she managed. Of course, theirs was neither a direct nor a non-stop train. Many a night they had to lodge in one of the many rooming houses which were located near the train stations.

To their surprise they experienced camaraderie, as they had on the ship, on this long sojourn westward. Perhaps because of the small children, it seemed that perfect strangers, where they lodged or vendors who sold them food, amiably tried to understand their German and attempted to be helpful in some small way. Already Anna and Heinrich were feeling a degree of welcome in their new chosen country!

Once in Tazewell County, they sought refuge with a farm family until they could take possession of their own land. They had already negotiated with a land agent at a United States Land Office in Bloomington,

STORIES MY FOLKS TOLD ME

Illinois, for acreage which had been surveyed and divided into eighty acre parcels. When they had their name registered to it, signed the deed, and paid $100 which was the usual cost at that time, they could begin their new life as Illinois settlers. There was no going back now! The Graffs were committed to the United States, proud they had made it this far, and optimistic about their future.

Immediately the hard work began for the men as with their indispensable axes they felled the few trees, glad for the firewood. A cow was likely their first purchase, then a mare, a couple of pigs, and a rifle to hunt venison, grouse, turkey, or rabbit which provided a good measure of their diet. If Anna had not brought an iron cooking skillet or flat iron pan, that had to be an early purchase as well, for most of their meals would have come from a large lidded skillet. For instance, Anna would bury the skillet in the cooking coals of the fireplace, remove the lid, insert the cornbread dough, cover, bury in the coals, and bake. Although in Germany she had never heard of cornmeal, she learned quickly in America that folks seemed to live on cornmeal, that it was one-third the price of wheat flour, and was readily available. There were many sorts of Indian corn, from red to white, but yellow was the most common. The family learned that it was an acquired but wholesome taste when mixed with eggs, starter yeast, and milk, so Heinrich declared that in America the Graffs would do as the Americans do—eat corn!

Corn was planted by hand in rows in Heinrich's day although he likely had a harrow, a single shovel plow for corn, a couple of hoes, rakes, forks, a scythe, a cradle, a spade, and a scoop. Before too long he probably had one of John Deere's new steel plows which were then coming on the market to replace the old wooden plows. The plow was drawn by a horse to prepare the soil for planting. Once the stalks were up, he would pass the plow between the rows first one way and then after another week the perpendicular to the first pass. Sometimes a third plowing was called for; a hoe was employed to remove the weeds that had escaped the plow. A local blacksmith likely made his harrow. Mowers were as yet unknown. Cultivation was accomplished with a hoe and double shovel plow. A combined thresher and separator with a capacity of 200 bushels of wheat or 400 bushels of oats per day did exist, but we do not know if Heinrich used one. If not, he certainly knew how to handle a scythe and a cradle, two hand implements used from time immemorial to cut the stalk. To separate the grain from the husk, or thrashing, was done in the open air on earth trampled hard by constant trudging in the vicinity where the grain was stacked.

There seemed to be no end to the uses for corn—and they had not even known of corn back in Germany! There, it was too far north to grow. Here, it was the exclusive winter feed for the animals. By April, Heinrich and his sons had planted the grains of corn just in time for the heavy rains which fell propitiously when needed for germination. As the ears ripened, they became heavy, pendant, but the sheaths protected the ears from summer rains and through the dry late summer. Sometimes cows were allowed into the field at that point but normally, Heinrich cut the corn once it was ripe. That happened in early October yielding four to five ears to a stem, 500 to 1000 grains each. One hundred ears yielded a bushel of corn. Quite a bounty, thought Heinrich, in the fabulous gift of the glacier though he probably didn't know the origin of the rich soil, could not have imagined for how many ages that plain had been spread out beneath those soft skies and radiant sun, how its flowers had bloomed and faded, its grasses grown and decayed, how many storms swept over all its wide expanse, how thunder echoed on and on, how winds had blown endlessly and raging fires had marched unrestrained from end to end, how long all that power and magnificence had displayed unseen by any human eye!

Stems and leaves of the corn stalks made excellent hay for winter use as well as bedding for the stock. The Graffs surely noticed too that the corn standing in the field, tassels wafting in the wind, seemingly growing taller right before their eyes was a beautiful sight to behold. And when the sun went down accentuating the golden cast of their broad field, they surely had to stop their toil and exclaim at the beauty of the moment just as much as they had done at sunsets over the ocean on their passage!

Protecting their stock from predator animals was always a priority for Heinrich. A small grove of trees on his property yielded enough rails to build a fence. By splitting the trees into five foot lengths, he laid the first rail down on the ground at a slight angle, and then lay the second rail with an end extended over the first like the letter X only crossing not at the center but near an end. On each side of the crossing, he drove a stake to secure the rails in place. Once he had laid the lowest rails completely to form the enclosure, other rails were placed upon these, crossing, and building up until the fence was tall enough, usually nine rails high.

At night the family heard the unceasing howl of the wolves and worried about the sheep and chickens especially. They were safe in the barn at night, but during the day the fence was their shield. The cows, however, could be left in the field to graze during the summer days. If no neighbor owned the land next to Heinrich's it was considered common pasture and he could put his stock to graze it. He didn't fear they would wander off because it was this animal's innate nature to seek the barn at night. A block of salt was helpful, he found, to lure the milk cows back to the milking station twice a day.

Corn stalks and waste were burned in the home fire in addition to wood but in the uninsulated house, warmth was always a relative sensation. Upstairs, in the bedrooms there was no heat in the winter, but the family was accustomed and didn't know any different. Mosquitoes were a terrible nuisance, though, in spring and autumn especially and tormented the Graffs lying up in their beds swatting as they slept. These they were unfamiliar with in Germany and so they were heard to complain.

Rattlesnakes lurked in the cornfields but never attacked except in self-defense. They were poisonous, though, and a bite quickly became fatal. Just to be wise, they kept on hand the antidote herb they called "rattlesnake's master." Other non-venomous snakes would occasionally wrap around someone's leg but could be removed with a stick or knife.

On the other hand there were some lovely insects like the butterflies which the Graffs deemed much more beautiful and plentiful in America than back home. Their depth of color and delicacy were remarkable. Lightning bugs or fireflies, which came in swarms like sparks of fire, mystified them for they too did not exist in Germany. Plentiful, also, were the various kinds of owls which filled the night with their sounds and the whip-poor-will, a noisy bird at night. For sheer volume, though, all were surpassed by the bull frog's loud croaking near creeks and ponds!

It would be hard to list all the wild animals known to the Graffs on the farm but surely they knew the mink, opossum, and raccoon. Delicious quail, they likely ate as well as wild turkey. Huge flocks of birds passed overhead and at planting time were complete pests requiring the little children to run shouting and waving rags of cloth to protect the seeds in the ground. Hundreds of hummingbirds, magpies, jays, goldfinches, sparrows, thrush, robin, lark, and blackbirds filled the air over the seasons with their brilliant plumage.

One very special bird filled the skies above the Graffs every spring flying northward and every fall flying southward in torrents of Biblical proportions; people could hear them coming from miles away. As they grew closer the sound of the coming tempest resembled distant thunder despite the clear and beautiful day. When the storms hit, it was utter chaos. Children screamed, women gathered their long skirts and hurried indoors, horses bolted, several people dropped on their knees and prayed. The sun was blotted out from the sky and the noise was deafening. "The sound was unimaginable like railroad trains passing at high speed or a thousand thrashing machines operating at the same time while above in the sky was a cloud so thick and huge and dense it blackened the heavens," a contemporary described in metaphors of that day. But it wasn't a cloud. The storm was not a storm. The rains that fell were feathers, the hail that fell were droppings. It was the great migration of millions of passenger pigeons!

This was a bird whose sheer numbers were virtually indescribable. Believed to be at the time of the Graffs' immigration the most numerous bird on the earth, they consisted of up to forty percent of North American bird life, as many as five billion displaying beautiful iridescent colors of blue-grey head and wings but a strikingly rosy-red breast. With a wing span of two feet and a total length of seventeen inches, they were no small bird. An extremely social bird, they traveled in huge flocks east of the Rocky Mountains estimated to be over a million when migrating, traveling at 62 miles an hour in a plume one mile wide and 300 miles long, darkening the sky for three entire days. Because Illinois was not heavily forested the birds merely passed through, perching overnight in the groves of Oak, Alder or Walnut trees strong enough to support the weight of the many birds packed tightly together. Still it was common for the branches to break under the collective weight of so many birds causing a scene of uproar and confusion as birds beneath were crushed and killed. Though they were only passing through Illinois they still required food and water and for that they had pretty easy pickings of acorns, chestnuts, beechnuts, grapes, mulberries, all berries, worms, caterpillars, and snails. Oh, and corn! Woe to the Illinois farmer whose corn was ripe in the field when that 300 mile long cloud of hungry passenger pigeons appeared!

Undoubtedly our folks dined on the passenger pigeon, perhaps as "pidgin pie" or roasted, fried, baked, stewed, boiled, smoked, salt-cured, jerked, or pickled. The meat was rich and dark, each bird yielding eight to twelve ounces of succulent meat. Squabs or year-old birds having been fed a fat and protein-rich, cheese-like secretion from the parents' crops weighed ten to twenty ounces. Even before the arrival of the white men, the passenger pigeon was a favorite food and an easily procured source of meat attainable to anyone with a club, stones or net due to their unaggressive, placid temperament. But with a shotgun it was reported that a man could bring down dozens with one shot.

Nesting areas were in the forests of the northern Great Lakes region and in the lowlands and swamps to the south of Illinois near the Gulf of Mexico, so the passage of the pigeons over Illinois was brief but magnificent. Large stands of trees were necessary for their nesting/ breeding requirements which they found in the still virgin forests of the northern United States and Canada. One sole egg in one nest was the yearly product of one breeding pair, yet the population by their sheer numbers nevertheless grew to the billions. The length of life of the individual pigeon is not known, but that the species came to a complete demise at the turn of the 19th Century after decades of wanton shooting for sport, for tables in the large cities of the eastern U.S., and for the fashion demand for feathers is unequivocal. When at the same time the northern virgin forests, the nursery of all passenger pigeons, were felled the end of the iconic birds just accelerated. Both mighty species succumbed at the same time in a world where concepts like conservation, sustainability, bio-diversity, environmental protection were unknown.

The weather of 1860, the first year the Graffs farmed in Tazewell County, was wholly favorable with excellent harvest of crops of every kind. Then the election of Abraham Lincoln the following November depressed markets and demoralized business in general because with Lincoln in the White House the south was determined to secede. Corn, that winter, sold for as low as ten cents a bushel. Much of the crop was burned for fuel.

Having just arrived in America, not speaking English, probably their orientation not yet enough focused on their new homeland to have established strong political convictions, and crucial to their father's success on the farm, the Graff sons did not engage themselves as soldiers in the Civil War. Very few recent immigrants did. Henry Peine of Minier, having arrived earlier in 1845, was an exception when he enlisted and gave five years of his life to the northern cause.

Rain was the farmer's friend then as now, but rain-saturated roads were a perilous malady to Heinrich and his sons back then as the wagon, full of produce headed to market or full of the family headed to the village, became immersed in the sticky wet earth. If the wagon was full of people, he could ask them to get out, but it was too inconvenient to unload the crops! In either case using a rail, he would try to pry up the wheels, clean them of mud, and then prod the horse to pull harder. Often success came only after several such attempts!

Summer rainstorms have always seemed louder and more frightening in the country where the blades of electricity slashing and snapping across the open sky could be seen fully in the obstruction-free rural landscape. Amplified by a strong westerly wind, and accompanied by subsequent booms of thunder, they terrified not only the youngest Graffs but full-grown adults as well. Afterward when the skies cleared and birds were again heard singing, it would be time to walk into the fields to assess the damage which most likely in those days before tiling was water standing in the field, burying the seedlings if it was spring-time or stalks of grain pounded flat to the ground if it was mid-summer.

At that point, Heinrich and his sons could still rescue the crop, but if the thunderstorms came late in the growing season when they were letting the grains dry in the field, the water could make their work a lot harder and perhaps even destroy all their work of the year. Farmers in those days became virtual meteorologists who could scan the sky for troublesome weather on its way.

Cold as it was in winter, that was a good time to stand at the cabin door to admire a starry night sky. Yes, nature was generous with her splendor and likely was appreciated by the Graffs despite their very busy lives. Their hard work surely brought them enjoyment and gratification. It was as if this pleasure they felt was a byproduct not found when it was sought but when they were fully engaged in something else, then given as a bonus. Just one of the mysteries of life, beautiful because it cannot be explained. They saw that their children had grown and developed inner resources and abilities demanded by the life in America which back in Pfalsdorf would never have been ignited. Here the demand on their faculties was far greater, their minds were stretched and utilized to a far greater degree. Here, the family had so much more land, requiring mental acuity for calculating seed requirements, cash needs, yields, or for constructing a bridge over the slough. How happy Heinrich and Anna must have been just to see their children developing their talents to the fullest extent, becoming all that they were capable of becoming!

Typical of immigrant families, the Graffs were a tight knit household. Such a bond of dependency and love was naturally formed as they toiled together in the field and home, sat at table together day after day, year after year with no interruption of telephone, television, or delivery services, and gathered around the warming embers at the end of the day. Those red, glowing coals could amplify the loving warmth in the room, could silently conjure images, evoke old tales, induce calm feelings, just as they did for earliest men in our prehistoric past and for us today, if truth be told.

Once the Graff family was firmly established on the land they eagerly sent their younger children to the nearby one-room school. As many as forty scholars might attend during the winter months each given individual instruction by the young schoolmarm as she went from child to child with her wonderful picture books and letter forming models. The same young woman boarded part of the school year with the Graffs even sleeping with the children. Her salary of $16 per month was collected from the parents at the end of the term according to the days of attendance and the number of children.

Life for Heinrich and Anna was one of daily toil the first year or two as they established their farm, but soon sons, Valentine, Peter and Jacob, were doing the heavy lifting in the fields while daughters, Anna Christine and Maria Eva, were managing the household indoors. Happy occasions came as their children found partners and married. First the girls married. Then on September 10, 1864 Heinrich Peter married the girl he had admired ever since he noticed her on the ocean crossing six years earlier. She had by now grown into a handsome young woman of nineteen, Elizabeth Imig.

About a year later, it became obvious to all that father Heinrich was simply unable to carry on, and to everyone's great sorrow he passed away only six years after he arrived in Illinois. Mother Anna lived another twelve years, until she was sixty-three, in the home she and Heinrich had built. It had been necessary to enlarge the house, of course, to accommodate the newly married couple and their future family. And so the Graff pioneer couple went to the grave in Gaines Cemetery near Minier having earned the satisfaction that they had brought their nine children to the new land of opportunity, established the farm, and increased their acreage to bequeath to their children and future generations.

Pioneers Heinrich Peter Graff and Elizabeth
Imig Graff – arrived 1859
—4, 5, 6,—

Although they were teen-agers when they arrived with their parents and siblings in America in 1859, Heinrich Peter Graff and his future wife, Elizabeth Imig were nevertheless of the pioneer generation. He had been born back in Louisendorf, North Rhine Westphalia, Germany, in 1838; she was born in nearby Pfalzdorf in 1845; they married in Minier September 10, 1864, after having grown up in close association with each other's family and having undergone the whole immigration experience within the larger group. Henry Peter, as he was called in Minier assumed the management of the family farm after the death of his father and after his next younger brother, Jacob, had moved on to the Seward, Nebraska, area.

As she grew to young womanhood on her parents' farm, Elizabeth Imig Graff never forgot her grandmother back in Germany who had played such an important role in her early life by sewing for her a cloth doll from nothing but scraps of fabric, black shoe buttons for eyes and the prettiest embroidered red mouth. "Oma," the German name for grandmother, had patiently taught her many hand stitches which she would need to make shirts for her brothers and dresses for herself and to knit which all the girls and women did in every spare minute. Elizabeth's sisters, Wilhelmina and Catherine, were only a year apart in age but six and seven years older than she so that they seemed to function as a team, content in their two-some, and usually too busy to include her. Oma always had time, though, and often had to protect Elizabeth from her brothers Heinrich, four years older, Carl three years younger, and Friederich six years younger. They were typical rambunctious boys who thought up the most daring games imaginable incorporating the hay loft in the barn.

By the time she was thirteen and planning the journey to America, Elizabeth no longer played with her doll, Inge, but she still loved her and laid her on her pillow each morning after she made the bed. When asked if she should take Inge with her to America, Mama replied that no, she was a German doll and wouldn't withstand the trip or adapt once they were on the frontier. Inge should go to the little neighbor girl who had no doll. Besides Mama needed Elizabeth's help on the journey with the smaller children. Elizabeth knew in her heart that this was wise advice but for a long time afterwards whenever she saw a doll she would think of Inge and hope she was loved and well taken care of! Like many girls of all times, Elizabeth had imbued her doll with something almost like a spirit.

Privacy, in a family of ten plus Oma, was a concept rather unknown to Elizabeth Imig. Everyone was crowded into just a few rooms, primarily the cooking-eating-sitting room where the large hearth served for cooking as well as warmth. A sleeping loft for the five boys, a tiny room for the three girls and Oma, and a room for mama and papa comprised the essential rooms. Leaning right up to and connected to the farm home was of course the barn where sounds of lowing, cackling, squealing, and baying were emitted and strong smells were continuously expressed. The warmth exuded by the animals completely compensated, though, for their proximity especially in the cold of winter. There were always Imig relatives wandering in and out of the house or to be seen at church or along the streets of the village of Pfalzdorf because all the farm families lived in the village and walked or rode out to their fields. Elizabeth later remembered the feeling of love and security she felt so tightly surrounded by the generations of her family and of friends. There was always someone to talk to from morning light to snuggling in bed with her sisters at night.

It seemed to Protestant Elizabeth Imig that the Catholic girls had all the fun for theirs was a religion of many feast days and festivals complete with special food, parades, music, and dancing--after church services— of course. She loved the simplicity of her faith though and could never understand how anyone could bow to the pope or tell their innermost thoughts to a priest. She would confess her sins to God himself and know in her heart that she was forgiven. It seemed to her to be simply a function of geography, however, which determined the religion one had. Whichever religion the duke chose after the Thirty Years War of 1518-- 48 was the one which everyone in his realm was forced to adopt. In the Imigs case, the Duke of Kleves chose to be Catholic so he expected all his subjects to do likewise.

Nobody asked Elizabeth her opinion on emigration. It was just assumed that as a member of the large Imig clan she would move along with them just as the current of the Rhine carried all its grains of sand along. She was definitely caught up in the excitement of the preparation for the journey, but all her life she would regale listeners with the terrors of the storm at sea: From one minute to the next the calm sea gave way to ferocious gales of wind which formed huge waves to gash against the vessel as if trying to destroy it! The ship seemed about to become air born but then descended into caverns of the deep while masses of water beat on all sides till she was sure the ship would capsize. A thunderous roar was emitted at all times from the sea and the air along with a groaning agony from the ship itself. Above deck, crew members shouted and struggled, terror on every face. Below, Elizabeth and the other passengers were on their knees praying pious vows and whimpering in desperate fear. Crowded together family members found each other's hands to fondle, children to caress, words of assurance to express. They had been ordered below deck by the captain of the "Ariel" and there to remain until he himself came to the cabin door and assured them that the danger was past.

But when the sea was calm, there was a magic in the air! How the moonbeams glistened over the water and how brightly the stars of the Milky Way flickered and twinkled above; what an enormous, brilliant blue sky enveloped their little vessel! At dusk, Elizabeth loved to lean over the stern and gaze at the trails of phosphorescence which followed their wake causing a hypnotic spell to come over her, reflecting her mood of excitement and joy. Then would gather the impromptu bands of singers, nothing highbrow but folkloric German songs everyone knew, with whom she heartily joined. Lusty and heartfelt, full of emotion and nostalgia which was sometimes pathos to Mama and Papa, the singing was at the same time a release and a passion. Suddenly the stars would be blotted out and lightning would flash. Before they could snatch up their belongings and get below, it was raining again like a waterspout!

During the day, the women and girls of the Imig and Graff clans would gather in little groups to gossip about those left behind in Pfalzdorf and Lousendorf, to express their hopes for the future, to try to unravel the mysteries of their unknown destiny in the new world, and to look around themselves for signs of potential romance among their group. The men, likewise, gathered to talk about farm techniques of the day, politics, and procedures upon arrival in the New World. Both sexes found, in their uprooted situation, warmth and companionship in these circles. At times almost a holiday spirit prevailed on board as released from normal daily cares, they relished their freedom from labors, obligations, and responsibilities. It was like being on vacation except that was a term for a pleasure unknown to our mid-19th Century folks!

Back in Pfalzdorf, both Heinrich Peter and Elizabeth had attended the village school but life on the farm was physically demanding and as they grew older their respective families needed their assistance to satisfy the demands of the never ending chores. They acquired much knowledge and a broad array of skills but book learning was not a big part of their acquisition. Instead they learned the old German fairy tales from the lips of the village story teller as well as from their parents, grandparents, aunts and uncles, for story telling has long been a centerpiece of the German home entertainment. Singing, too, was a fixture of home life where they could fill endless hours with song after song, and this tradition was one of many which they carried over to their own homestead near Minier.

Soon after the arrival of the Graffs in Illinois, the United States government, anxious to open up the land of today's Illinois, passed on January 1, 1863, the far-reaching Homestead Act. Even while conducting the Civil War it was determined that the government needed to attract settlers to western lands held in federal possession. For a ten dollar registration fee, any American could claim 80 to 160 acres of land from the U.S. government free of charge in return for five year's occupancy. Claim offices quickly rose up in hundreds of towns and crossroads from the east coast to the Mississippi River and most saw a "bang-up" business. Claims could be made on any even numbered section, except section sixteen which was reserved for school purposes and the odd number sections that were set apart as a land grant to encourage construction of a railroad. It is not known if the Graffs acquired their land in this manner but the timing of their arrival certainly would have made it possible.

As a farm wife, Elizabeth's contributions were as integral to the success of the farm as were Heinrich's and therefore she had more autonomy than her counterpart in town who was not allowed to be involved in the mechanics or business of the family livelihood. The result of her contribution to the running of the farm meant there were times when Elizabeth worried that she didn't have enough time for her children, that she was too busy to play with them or engage them individually. But that is the guilt mothers have felt from time immemorial right up to today and likely always will be a part of motherhood!

Both of the Graffs loved the rich, fertile soil which they found in central Illinois. Love of the land was in their DNA, so strong they would bend over till their backs ached while yanking fistfuls of weeds, yet find emotional rewards in the little miracle of growth they had nurtured. Agriculture is the oldest, most continuous livelihood in which humans have engaged on this planet Earth. It is the basis for man's successful dispersal from our original home in Africa to every cold, dry, high, low region on the globe. Growing food was the first activity that gave man enough wealth to stay in one place, form complex social groups, and build cities. Heinrich and Elizabeth presumably didn't know it but plant and animal domestication go back fourteen thousand years. All important crops like wheat, rice, soybeans, barley, and corn were domesticated five thousand years ago on various continents. What they did know was that they loved farming and felt irrevocably integrated into the continuity of the passing seasons.

Beside the miracles occurring out in the fields, Elizabeth and Heinrich welcomed eight little human miracles into their happy home: Charles Graff (1865—1922), Henry Graff (1867—1942), Valentine Graff (1869—1934), Elizabeth Graff (1871—1922), Anna Graff (1873—1927), William Graff (1874—1947), Emma Graff (1877—1942), and Louis Graff (1880—1944). All the babies were born at home. The Graff children attended a modicum of school as did those of other pioneer families, but it probably wasn't more than three years. They could read, write, and reckon, quote the Bible, and cure ailments with medicine made from grasses or leaves, but like Abraham Lincoln with his eighteen months of school time, they didn't count success by time spent in the classroom.

Small Emma, Louie, and William Graff around 1881

Like the other pioneer families, the Graffs all spoke German at home, at church, in the village shops, and at school when the schoolmarm grudgingly permitted it. Evenings were spent gathered by the light of the oil lamp where Mama and the older girls sewed or mended while Papa read from the Bible or told the favorite old German tales. In winter, without insulation or storm windows, it was cold so they wrapped in blankets while the wailing and sobbing of the wind, 'round the square unsheltered house out by itself in the country, enhanced the drama of the story. Sometimes, Mama and Papa would mention the name of an old friend from Pfalzdorf days, a fellow member of their church congregation or social circle, causing moistened eyes, yet no day passed when they would have returned there and forsaken this new land. Much as they sometimes wished for the society of absent friends, they could not have agreed to exchange it for the joys they had won in this new country. They were pioneers and mostly kept their gaze focused ahead.

As the years passed on his farm, Heinrich was always aware of the particular rewards of a life spent farming. He loved the outdoor work, out in the noiseless, beautiful nature where he couldn't help but take a deep breath of that clean, oxygen-rich air and know that it was good for his heart, lungs, muscles, and psyche too. He instinctively knew that it was therapeutic to walk out on his land into the yellow-green rows of corn. He even liked the smells outdoors especially after a shower when there was a freshness in the air. The beauty and aromas of reviving grass, flowers, and trees, the happy songs of birds celebrating the departure of the clouds, whether inhaled or observed, they all stirred his soul! Now and again he would persuade Elizabeth and the children to accompany him on a walk out to see the sunset over the fields, and as they walked they might flush some birds out of the undergrowth or spy a nest of baby birds in a fencepost. They were surrounded by so many living things they couldn't count them all!

Deep snow sometimes blanketed the farm, outbuildings, trees, and fields, muffling all sounds, softening sharp edges, and rounding shapes. It was beautiful to behold how the snow cover quickly built up one flake at a time, but it seemed to lengthen the distance between the Graff homestead and that of the next farm accentuating the loneliness of their outpost. Of course the snow on the roof and high up the walls offered a kind of insulation which gave warmth to the interior of the house and the barn as well. Constantly, the thin grey line of smoke rose day and night from the chimney, like Indian smoke signals, giving comfort to the neighbors that all was right at the Graff homestead.

Yes, during the winter the Graff family enjoyed a well-earned rest from their toils. Days were shorter, travel to the village more complicated, and school work occupied the children, so the family tended to cluster around the fireplace, the only heat source in the house, hands occupied by sewing, knitting, or the hand grinder to make the cornmeal for their daily use. Outdoors, though, was a special world of fun and excitement for the rambunctious Graff children. Sledding down the snow drifts, coasting down the hills, riding the sleigh Papa built pulled by their horse, building a fort from which to lob snowballs at anyone who passed was endlessly engaging to the children even though Mama's hand knitted woolen mittens soon became wet and icy-cold forcing the little soldiers to retreat to the fireplace. Snowfall began there in the 41st degree latitude around the middle of December, just deep enough at two to five inches to support a sleigh, but even a slight snow on the long grasses gave a sleigh easy flowing movement and pleasant gliding. Actually, their sleigh was just a rough box, without runners, which Heinrich and the boys set on a wagon to take produce to market or carry wood home, but in winter over frozen earth and slough, unbounded by ponds or potholes, it could take the blanket-buried riders flying under the stars, flushing out a bevy of grouse sheltering in the field, startling a deer herd in their browsing, limited only by the endurance of their steeds. Winter was also a time to set the traps for fur-bearing animals whose pelts could be sold for ready cash to the fur company agent in town.

Though winter could be harsh in central Illinois, snows were not long lasting enough to provide cover for fall crops such as winter wheat throughout the time they needed for maturity and yield. There could be intense cold but after two or three days, the mercury would rise, the sun come out, and the snows would melt. Compensation came tenfold though to the Illinois farmer with the gigantic growth of summer when conditions were about optimal for their crops.

How often Elizabeth must have paused at the end of a day to gaze up into the big night sky. Perhaps she stood with Henry in moments of serenity and peace, forgetting the noise of the children and the work of the busy day, calming her mind, opening her soul to behold the majesty of the countless stars above them. Such beauty is reserved for quiet moments; it reaches across both time and space to touch us with the radiance of creation, with God's presence, with feelings of unison with all of nature. And the magnificent sight was right outside her door each and every night, lending balance and serenity to her life.

The arrival of the merry month of March meant sugar from the Sugar Maples which grow so ubiquitously in Illinois. Folks deemed the sugar gained from the trees to far surpass the taste of West Indies sugar. It was cheaper too for the producers but a lot more work. A group of men would put a shack or camp in the midst of a grove of Maple trees, make an incision with an auger in the trees in early March, and insert a one inch diameter tube made from a sumac branch in the hole when the sap begins to rise. Frosty nights and fine days would accelerate the flow of the liquor which they caught in a bucket they hung from a nail just above the tube. Daily, Heinrich and his children had to check the buckets and if full haul them to the sugar shack where the men kept two or three five-to-ten gallon copper bowls filled with the liquor boiling over a wood fire. After the liquid boiled down, they poured it through a woolen cloth, boiled it again on a slower fire till hard and firm. That block of light tan sugar was their sweetening agent for the whole year. What they didn't need, they sold—and for a price higher than the West Indies sugar!

Even little German-born boys played cowboys and Indians in the 19th Century. Heinrich had read in the newspaper about Custer's Last Stand, the Indian massacre of Lt. Col. George Custer and the 209 men of the U.S. 7th Cavalry in Montana Territory in the summer of 1876. The story became a legend but in the Graff's day it was first page news and made a great story for Heinrich to tell his young sons. The outline of the story was plenty compelling: the vainglorious Custer was so bent on fame that he blundered into an ingenious Indian trap designed by Sitting Bull and executed to perfection by warriors who included the fabled Crazy Horse. The consequences of that triumph by the Indians was not a matter of great military significance, however, because within a year's time nearly all the Indians who took part in the battle had been rounded up and removed to reservations. Young Charles, William, Valentine, and Henry Graff re-enacted the story over and over throughout their childhood, especially elated when they let the white men win!

The Graff boys knew the names of the Indian tribes who had once roamed the land where they lived in Illinois. Ottawa, Chippewa, Pottawatomie, Winnebago, Sauk, and Fox were tribe names all boys were familiar with even though the Indians had left by the 1830s. Bones of buffalo and skulls with horns still attached were still occasionally found near watering holes while Indian spear points were more easily found when plowing a field. The boys loved to hear the stories about the Indians which then formed the basis for their play.

One day in the late 1880s, soon after the advent of a photography studio in nearby Bloomington, Illinois, Elizabeth and Heinrich decided to sit for a family portrait. All six sons and Papa dressed in suit, tie, and leather boots. Mama and the three girls appeared in gowns of voluminous fabric with a defined waist with peplum below. There were no hair products to volumize or to tame the hair in those days, but Elizabeth, Anna, and Emma knew of vinegar rinse, sheep grease and lots of brushing, so presumably that is how they achieved their shiny do's. At that time when photography was new, a toothy smile was not the fashion, so facial expressions are serious, tentative, and even fearful. Still, it was a mark of prosperity and achievement to have such a handsome photograph to display in one's home.

Standing are William, Henry, Valentine, Anna, and Emma.
Sitting are Elizabeth, Henry Peter (father), Louis,
Elizabeth (mother), and Charles.

Throughout their childhood sisters, Emma and Annie, close in age, had been practically inseparable. Their personalities meshed particularly well so that they always wanted to play together, do their chores together, simply to be together. Where one girl was, there too was the other—right up to and including their wedding day, for theirs was a double wedding! The description of their January 10, 1900, wedding in the Bloomington "Weekly Pantograph" newspaper says it all:

DOUBLE WEDDING
Interesting Nuptial Event Celebrated Wednesday Near Minier
THE MISSES GRAFF THE BRIDES

"Minier, Jan. 11—At high noon yesterday, at the home of H.P. Graff, two and a half miles from town, occurred the double wedding of their two daughters, Anna and Emma, in the presence of over one hundred relatives and friends. Miss Anna Graff with Jacob Imig and Miss Emma Graff with William Oehler, marched into the parlors to the well-known but beautiful strains of Mendelssohn's wedding-march, played by Miss Myrtle Gaines. Rev. Titke, of Danvers, pronounced the mystic word, using the double ceremony in a happy and impressive manner.

"Congratulations followed heartily, after which a bountiful wedding dinner was served to all present. Mr. H.P. Graff is one of the most prosperous and highly esteemed farmers, and while deprived of the society of his last two beautiful and accomplished daughters, he has gained two honest and upright young men, whose virtues are well known to their own communities.

"The brides wore gowns alike, made of steel gray Henrietta cloth, trimmed in chiffon and pearl. One hundred and twenty-five invitations were accepted, a large number being relatives of the contracting parties, and in accord with the German hospitality most of them were entertained until today.

"A charivari party of thirty friends and neighbors gave them the usual tin pan serenade in the evening and were entertained and treated as is the custom.

"Many costly, beautiful and useful articles were presented, nearly all in duplicate, one for each couple.

"Mr. Jacob Imig and bride will move to his farm near Seward, Neb., about February 15, where they will continue farming and cattle raising.

"Mr. William Oehler and bride are both well known in this vicinity, and will farm the coming season on the Hulvey farm near Danvers. Mr.

William Oehler, Sr., and family of Danvers, were present and also Mrs. H. Fishbeck and son of Bloomington."

Though the double wedding was perhaps the most sensational of Heinrich and Elizabeth's children's weddings they weren't the only nuptials they celebrated. Son Charles married Mary Imig, Henry married Augusta Frevort, Valentine married Alvina Wehmeir, daughter Elizabeth married John Pleines, William married Melissa Gainer, and Louis married Emma Oehler sister of his sister Emma's groom. Graffs and Imigs were still marrying each other even after the pioneer generation, seemingly to no ill effect.

Perhaps the most obvious reason for this frequent intermarriage of families was that the applicant pool was small. Travel outside the borders of their village, where young people might meet other youth of the opposite sex, was rare and led to an insular mentality. Furthermore, they were suspicious of outsiders yet could trust in their own clan. To marry a Catholic or a Jew was unthinkable. Parents just knew that when they entrusted a beloved daughter to a clansman, the whole body of the clan would be behind the couple to enforce their standards of care, protection, respect, and wealth.

Church attendance was more prevalent in those days of myriad mysteries about the physical world, about the causes and cures of diseases, and about human behavior, so families like the Graffs looked to their pastor and his Bible teachings for answers. Church teachings back then formed standards of public opinion, guided behavior, and led to teachable norms such as the concept of shame. "You should be ashamed of yourself!" was a powerful admonition uttered by a parent or person in authority to correct a person's or child's behavior.

Then, perhaps even more than now, it was recognized that a parent has the most powerful position on earth, capable of molding a relatively pliant little person into an adult with all the good and virtuous qualities to be a good citizen, loving spouse, devoted parent, and faithful Christian. Just as a parent can protect the child from all the pain in the world, she can also inflict the worst pain in the world, can spare the child from loneliness or can impose loneliness, can develop talents or can ignore them. Only from a loving home where intelligent caregiving passed from generation to generation, such as our folks knew, can the wisdom to instill the character-building virtues, on which a strong society depends, emerge. We can ask how those folks of long ago without parenting manuals nor professional advice counselors knew how to be good parents, how generation after generation they raised up sound, contributing members of society? It was with love, Biblical teachings, traditions, discipline and the insistence upon adherence to the rules.

Like every mother then and now, Elizabeth prayed that she would live to raise her children and she did. She even saw them all married, but her final days came in 1906. After forty-two years of marriage, the shared immigration experience of 1859, and the common roots in North Rhine Westphalia, Elizabeth left a sorely saddened Heinrich and went to her rest in Minier cemetery. He ended his days five years later from the home of his daughter, Elizabeth and John Pleines, with whom he dwelled.

In the Evangelical and Reformed Church of Minier, today's Church of Christ, are the beautiful stained glass windows, in the art-deco style, which will memorialize forever the names of the pioneers Heinrich Peter Graff and Elisabeth Imig Graff.

Pioneer Wilhelm Friedrich Oehler arrived 1865 and
Pioneer Marie Mueller Oehler arrived 1869
—7—

Independent, solitary immigrants did, of course, comprise perhaps the majority of those in the big wave that came across American shores in the mid-1800s. They were young men who were especially ambitious, bored with village life, disdainful of the army conscription, and above all desirous of excitement and adventure. Wilhelm Friedrich Oehler would have fit this description perfectly. Born June 28, 1848 in Weisweil, Arch-Duchy of Baden, Germany, which is in the southwest corner of the German landmass where the Rhine River first enters Germany, Wilhelm had two younger sisters, Louise and Maria, and no brothers. His father was Friedrich and his mother was Adelheid Spitznagel Oehler. Oehlers had resided in and around Weisweil for many generations farming small plots. There was a school in the village where Wilhelm learned the basics when he wasn't required in the field. The family attended the Evangelical church, where generations of Oehlers are recorded, just down the lane from their home for as all German farmers did, the Oehler home stood in the comfort of the village.

The Oehlers probably didn't realize it back in the mid-19th Century but they lived in a particularly desirable region, the state of Baden, outstanding for growing wines like the Kaiserstuhl (emperor's chair). Baden is located in the south of Germany between the Black Forest and the Rhine River and today is aligned with the state of Wuertemberg. It is a volcanic outcrop clothed since Roman days with vineyards that produce some of Baden's best reds from the Spaetburgunder grape and whites from the Gewuertstraminer grape which have an uncanny depth. The especially dry and warm microclimate has given rise to special vegetation including sequoias and a wide variety of orchids.

Fruit trees and berry bushes abound in that climate, too, the product of which folks commonly distilled into that German icon: "schnapps." It wasn't hard to do and though it wasn't exactly legal, most men of the Kaiserstuhl region took some overripe pears, apples, peaches, cherries, or plums, cooked them a bit, strained it, and ran the juice through his own private distillery and filled a jug or two with the highly potent result-- just to aid the digestion of a particularly fatty meal or to be hospitable to guests when they dropped in, of course!

Harvest festivals were particularly fun around Weisweil where the juice of the grape was center stage complete with parade, music, dancing and feasting. Wilhelm and his family spoke a dialect called "Badisch" and were proud of it even if other Germans pointed and laughed when they heard it. It sounded almost musical with a sing-song quality to it.

For royalty from all over Europe and for the very wealthy, there were famous spa resort towns like Baden Baden where from Roman times the elite came to refresh and restore themselves in the warm mineral waters which bubbled forth from deep in the earth. In Freiburg im Breisgau, stands one of the earliest universities in Germany, a Gothic cathedral which was begun in 1200, and the gateway to the Black Forest.

Baden is known too for its cuisine. Two favorites are "spaetzle" and "maultaschen," both of which are based on a noodle dough. For "spaetzle," the cook whips whole eggs and gradually beats in flour and a spoon of salt. When thick dough is formed, she places the dough ball on a wooden board, holds the board over a pot of boiling water, and with a knife slices little specks of the dough into the water. When the little dumplings rise to the surface of the water they are cooked, so with a sieve she removes them to a serving dish. Wilhelm would have eaten "spaetzle" in a soup broth, with melted cheese, or with gravy, and probably ate them most every day, because southern Germans prefer them over potatoes.

"Maultaschen" (little cheek pockets) were likely another favorite of Wilhelm. Again, noodle dough is made of eggs and flour, rolled thin, cut into circles, filled with spinach, cheese, or seasoned ground meat, and covered with another dough circle. After the edges are pressed closed they too are placed in boiling water till they float. "Maultaschen" would have been eaten in a soup broth or browned in a little butter and served on a plate.

Less than a kilometer from their home ruled a mighty presence which conferred blessings as well as demanded obeisance: the famous Rhine River on its way north to the North Sea many miles away. As a child Wilhelm and his sisters and friends waded into the cool refreshing water and even dared to "go under" on a dare. Once a small boat owner gave the boy a ride almost to the other side which was France, but they couldn't fish in the great stream because only those who had permission from the Arch Duke were allowed that privilege. Wilhelm saw the flatboats, carrying their commerce, pass by on their way to the larger world, and he was struck with the romantic dream to travel along with them out of the confines of Weisweil.

Before that could happen, though, the Rhine offered rather a lot more excitement than the boy, Wilhelm, had been desiring. All day long and all night long rain pelted the Oehler roof as it had for days until flood stage was met and surpassed. The waters of the great river suddenly and swiftly reached the foundations of their home, lifted the house up, and carried it along on its frantic power-charge ahead. The children were awoken in the middle of the night by the swaying of the house, the loud groaning and creaking as it strained to remain upright, the shouts of their father and mother beckoning them to climb the stairs to the second floor, and above all the siren sound of the water which actually rose above the thunder and lightning.

For hours the family huddled together praying and wishing for the night to end. Morning light found them still in their house but no longer moving. The house had hit a shallow spot in the river and they were stuck far from shore; as with Noah's arc they would just have to wait for the waters to recede or yell out the window in hopes someone would hear and rescue them. Eventually, a boatman came near and they climbed out the second story window to safety. The house and all their belongings were lost, though, which was quite a blow to mother and father. Now they needed Wilhelm more than ever to work and help them restore their home and possessions. Thoughts of emigration were forced aside!

But Wilhelm just couldn't forget those stories he had heard about acquaintances who had emigrated and prospered in America. Daydreams and fantasies filled his mind often as they do all teenagers then and now. Around home the conversation often seemed to veer off on feminine subjects led by his two chatty sisters. When that happened around the table or evenings before the fire, Wilhelm would get that far away look in his eye and let his mind go off to the stories of adventures in America he had read about. It was during one of these evenings when Wilhelm was seventeen years old that his grandmother noticed the dreamy look on his face and asked what he was thinking about. "America," he replied. Now she too was interested, and as they talked she impulsively offered to loan him the money for the fare across the ocean. Mother and father were aghast! Their only son was going to leave them! Like good parents, though, they wanted opportunity for their son and that certainly was not in Weisweil. Taxes had just been raised, Wilhelm was just arriving at the age for the draft, and recent harvests had been so bad it was difficult to feed the family. What could Friedrich and Adelheid Oehler do but offer their weak blessing?

Packing a few necessities and dried foods in a "rucksack" (backpack), Wilhelm walked to the nearest pier to catch a flatboat ride on the Rhine floating up to Rotterdam where he could buy a ticket on a steamship to America. It happened that the closest access to the river was actually south of Weisweil at Breisach am Rhine, so when he began his journey traveling north he went right past Weisweil. Yes, he looked but he never looked back. His passage on the Rhine was long and slow, but there was much to see from the deck. Small and large famous towns were on display: Strasbourg, Speyer with its cathedral spires, Mannheim, Worms, Mainz where the Mainz River entered the Rhine, Koblenz, Bonn, Cologne, Essen, Arnhen and Wageningen in Holland, and finally Rotterdam. This first leg of his journey could have taken weeks but what a show it was for the lad!

As soon as he could he bought passage, reduced when he hired on to tend and shovel coal into the fire to heat the boilers, on a steamer bound for New York City. The crossing was accomplished by January 14, 1866. Along the way, he enjoyed some camaraderie with other young workers on board all of whom were energized by their adventure away from the domination of parents, teachers, or overseer. It was hot and grimy in the belly of the ship where William spent most waking hours and there must have been moments when emotions swept over him. He had just left all he had ever known on earth and the folks who meant so much to him in order to venture out all alone into the wide unknown New World. It must have been the courage and daring of youth which propelled him on!

Once at the wharf in New York though he was lost in the milling, swirling mass of people from the various boats which had just come in and from the general commotion of the crowded neighborhood lining the harbor. He did hear German spoken enough to make him feel welcome, though. Immigrant Island, where the Statue of Liberty now stands, with its organized registration process did not exist until 1872 so Wilhelm simply left the ship once his duties were concluded.

His first instinct was to find a job. He wanted to send money back to repay his grandmother as soon as possible. While at a German restaurant seeking work, he learned from the owner that a dairy farmer at Patterson, New Jersey was hiring. So with the fifty cents which the kindly restaurant owner had given him for the train fare, he was on his next leg of his adventure! Such generosity was actually commonplace at that time between older established immigrants and newcomers from the old country. Perhaps the restaurateur saw himself not so many years ago in Wilhelm. For sure Wilhelm would never forget the kindness, often telling this story in later years, and seeking himself to help young men to come to America.

Fifty cents bought Wilhelm a seat on the train out of New York City, but sitting was not his main occupation while on board. Wood was burned in the steam engine to power the locomotive but often the steam was not sufficient to propel the big iron monster up the hills. Then strapping youths like Wilhelm were asked to alight and walk up the hill.

Farming was a real entry level job at that time for young men who arrived in America without specific skills or facility in the English language. Farm technology was still low, so many men were needed to labor in the fields, to care for the animals, to mend and sharpen hand tools, and of course to harvest the crops. It was still winter when Wilhelm arrived at the farm in New Jersey but he was hired to feed the cattle which he did among other chores for six months earning ten dollars a month. In this way he was able to repay the debt to his grandmother.

While at the farm in New Jersey, Wilhelm heard about one Jacob Oehler of Bloomington, Illinois, and learned through letters from Weisweil and from Bloomington, that they were cousins. Encouraged to seek his fortune in the west, he decided to join his newfound cousin. His route probably took him on the Pennsylvania Railroad through Pennsylvania, Ohio, Indiana, and finally, on the Illinois Central line, to Bloomington, Illinois. Most likely, he slept on his seat and ate at the many stops along the way for he was young and not at all spoiled. German speaking folks seemed to be everywhere so he didn't feel too lonely, though mostly he stared with wonder at towns and villages, fields and mountains, rivers and plains which passed before his eyes.

Once he had found his cousin in Bloomington and generally unwound from his trek half-way across country he quickly sought employment again. This was accomplished on the farms of Peter Springer and Nathaniel Perry just outside of town. Ten dollars a month were the wages paid for the year he spent with them. Then for several years, Wilhelm worked on farms in the vicinity of Stanford just west of Bloomington. So industriously did he apply himself and so profitably did he serve, the landowner, Mr. Perry, was willing to lease the farm to him.

Life was not all work and no play even for a poor immigrant boy of the late 1860s. Then as now, young single people found each other at country dances, church events, barn raising, weddings, July 4th celebrations, and village festivals. Wilhelm found his girl, Marie Mueller, and married her on December 2, 1872, when he was twenty four years old. They must have smiled as they felt the incongruity of their situation: two people standing face to face, inhibitions and nervousness put aside, fallen into a laughing, silly, happy hug, so glad that all the trillion chances in the universe had brought them to the same point in the whole globe at the same time from nearly the same point of origin so far away!

When Wilhelm and Marie met, she was working as a domestic servant in the home of the Thompson family in Stanford which must have been a challenge for her, because they spoke English and she spoke only German, a fine, clear, high-German. Marie's day as a servant girl began early, around six o'clock in the morning, with the dirty but unavoidable job of cleaning and lighting the kitchen stove. After breakfast had been prepared and served, the traces of the meal had to be removed from the kitchen and dining room; afterward the agenda included making beds, dusting, possibly shopping—jobs that more or less occupied the entire morning and had to be finished before it was time to prepare noon dinner. The cook performed the actual food preparation but much assistance by Marie was assumed. When the kitchen had again been cleaned, she turned to her afternoon chore of cleaning one of the rooms thoroughly. It could be 9 p.m. before the cleaning up was finished after supper and she could finally think of calling it a day.

In addition to those chores, there were once weekly ones which had to be fitted into the day such as washing, ironing, or knitting. The washing of clothes was the nightmare of the servant girl and sometimes took longer than one day. Ironing next day was only slightly less onerous. Relatively high wages compensated these girls who mid-century earned four to six dollars a month which rose to ten to fourteen by the end of the century. This was at least twice what a maid servant could earn in Germany at the time. The wages of seamstresses or female factory workers were roughly equivalent or higher, but those women had to pay for their own room and board leaving their real income less than that of a servant girl.

Marie and her sister, Caroline, had immigrated together from Altmersbaden, Prussia on May 16, 1869 when Marie was twenty years old. Her birth date was May 31, 1849. Two more of her sisters immigrated to America while the one brother and five sisters out of ten children remained in Germany. The four sisters in the Stanford area married and remained close to each other all their lives.

Wilhelm and Marie began married life as renters of a farm owned by the Warlow family south and east of Danvers, Illinois, their home for thirteen years. There they found weather patterns decidedly different from those back in Baden with its continental, mountain-influenced conditions. In central Illinois no mountain barrier blocked the warm moist winds coming from the Gulf of Mexico in the south bringing normal precipitation of at least thirty-three inches a year. Without those Gulf winds Illinois would have had a parched growing season and colder, drier winters. Tazewell County received 180 frost-free days per year, a low moisture evaporation rate, and precipitation peaks during the growing season and tapering at harvest time. Truly an ideal growing weather in addition to the previously described "gift of the glacier" soil.

A little more than a year later, on January 1, 1874, their first child was born—a New Year's baby! They took it as a good omen and named him William Frederick. How thrilled they must have been to have their own little natural born American citizen sleeping in the little wooden cradle beside their bed!

STORIES MY FOLKS TOLD ME

There must have been occasional language misunderstandings even among two Germans because Wilhelm and Marie hailed from decidedly different areas of Germany with quite different ways of speaking. Marie was from the north where the true High German is spoken while Wilhelm spoke the dialect of his home in Baden. Their children spoke their mother's German tongue, of course, and as a result could be understood by all the Germans in the Danvers area who represented a variety of the German dialects. Marie and Wilhelm spoke only German all their lives there in a completely German community.

The years from 1871 to 75 were considered favorable to Illinois farmers. Crops were good and prices were high enough to bring profitable returns; implement inventions had progressed to the point that harvesters were now standard equipment and binders which bundled the sheaves could be attached. Mowing machines cut the grass, threshing machines were improving, disk cultivators and plows all came with seats, called sulky design, but were still pulled by the energy of a mule or horse. Barbed wire fencing was available by 1874, just in time to compensate for a shortage of wood with which to build board fences caused by all the trees which had already been cut down to build fences and houses. Grasshopper infestation in 1874 caused some farmers to set straw afire in the field, cover with grass, and smoke 'em out, but central Illinois farmers were mostly spared such scourges.

In quick succession after Will, appeared Marie in 1875, Charles (Charley) William in 1878, Ida Marie in 1879, Katherine Wilhelmina in 1880, Amelia in 1882, Matilda (Tilly) Lucy in 1883, Emma Elizabeth in 1886, Lillie Susana in 1887, and Edward (Eddie) George in 1890. One baby boy died at birth, but all the others grew to healthy adulthood, most into their nineties. All stayed close to each other, none ever living more than ten miles from the place of their birth. Wilhelm could certainly consider himself a paterfamilias now, though he would have said: "Famileanvater."

This rental home had three rooms; three beds with trundle beds to pull out accommodated the growing family and a hired man. Water was drawn from a well outside in the barnyard, calls of nature were answered in a two-hole outhouse, most all edibles were grown on the farm, most clothing and bedding were hand-sewn or knitted at home. They were truly independent and self-reliant pioneers! It was a home filled with laughter as observed many years later at yearly Oehler family reunions. The girls were pretty blonds some with blue eyes and some with hazel. They knew they had to help their mother for she was always busy with a new baby in that little wooden cradle.

The winter of 1881 has become known for the many snowstorms. Roads were blocked, rails were drifted over, travel was impossible till April when the snowfall abated. Then came the year without a spring after a winter of more snowfall than all the twenty years before. Those were long winter evenings, cold, dark, and drab, when Wilhelm and Marie must have gathered their little ones around the fire where a warm, golden light from the burning logs and the natural vivacity of the children turned the otherwise gloomy environment into a merry, lively scene. When Wilhelm could finally get out to plant the corn there was still snow banked along the fences; we can only guess how late it was before the earth warmed enough for the seed to germinate!

The very next year, 1882, was known for inclement weather as well: rain, sleet, and snow with sheet metal skies. Minus zero degrees fahrenheit were the norm for the entire month of January. Baby Amelia did not let the weather deter her, though, but made her appearance in March after the sub-zero temperatures had abated a bit. Perhaps the challenges of the weather strengthened her because like most of her siblings she lived a long, healthy life into her nineties. Despite the short days and long dark nights of that winter, we can imagine that the seven rambunctious little Oehlers made bright and merry the everyday life for Wilhelm and Marie.

As soon as he was able, in about 1885, Wilhelm purchased land for his own homestead paying fifty-four dollars an acre half of which was slough or swamp and thus un-tillable in the day before tiling. It too was located south of Danvers, Illinois. There he built a home, larger than the rented one, and the requisite out-buildings. The children were growing, requiring more space for more beds, and one, the last baby, Edward, joined them there. Now that the children were of age to attend school, Wilhelm and Marie appealed to the town to build a one-room school house right across the road from their property. It was only logical then that the school mistress would board with them.

In 1855, Illinois created free, universal education with a State Superintendent of schools and a common school fund; one-room school houses, revered today as an early American icon, were found approximately every two miles in rural America. At the one room country school just across the road from their homestead, the Oehler children learned from the McGuffy readers which included wonderful stories to entertain as well as enlighten. There were examples of patriotism, civic virtue, morality, and values of steadfastness, hard work, thrift, and restraint interwoven in each story, so that generations of American children absorbed moral lessons in a painless way. Good versus evil, right versus wrong, delayed gratification, responsibility, disdain of self-centeredness, respect for authority, and 'tis better to give than receive were just a few of the virtues absorbed by the children in their tiny schoolhouse. It was almost Biblical! A Webster's speller, Kirkham's grammar, the Bible, and Pike's arithmetic were also used by their teacher. Declamation or reciting a poem or some memorized verse was a prevalent form of learning back then.

The teacher spoke to the children in English at school but at home only German was spoken, Mama's High German. For part of the school year this young recent graduate of a women's seminary actually lived in the Oehler home sharing the girls' room and a place at the table. Reading, recitation, repetition, memorizing, writing, and arithmetic were skills she attempted to imbue in the minds of her young charges.

On the new property, the Oehlers did have more space but still no indoor plumbing, no heat except the wood stove, no light except the oil burning globes or candles, and no communication except letters. Once a week, the family walked or rode horseback to Danvers to get the mail which often included letters from loved ones in Germany for there was no mail delivery not even on one day a week. It was a happy occasion too when one of Wilhelm's German newspapers arrived, for he loved to read news from home as well as the American news printed in the German language.

Although daily life was filled with farm chores, tranquility prevailed in mid-century Illinois. Lawlessness was not at all a problem, for crime and outlaw bands were a rare exception on the Illinois frontier. Horse thievery, counterfeit coins or paper money, robbery, swindling, although gossiped about, were pretty exceptional in the pastoral world the Oehlers inhabited. The 1860s period had been the twilight of the frontier in Illinois. The buffalo were gone by then as were the Native Americans.

Prairie fires, the consequence of lightning flashes, were becoming a rarity by 1880 and nothing like the earlier infernos of shimmering orange walls of fire which had awed the settlers. Wolves, though, were still a problem until well after the Civil War. In order to protect their livestock, neighbors would conduct massive day-long sweeps hunting down and killing the predators. Raccoon too aggressively ate huge amounts of corn and therefore were hunted. Long gone, though, to the westward territories were the buffalo, elk, bear, panther, wild cat, beaver and otter. Left behind to be tolerated and hunted were turkeys, partridge, quail, prairie chickens, and rabbits. The weapon used by our pioneers was the common muzzle-loading rifle, not capable of rapid shooting but due to the sheer plentiful number of game allowed easy success.

Voracious flies, too, were a torment as when a Logan City farmer needed to haul corn to distant Edwardsville for milling. To avoid flies the farmer traveled at night, but during the day he had to build a fire to keep the flies, which would attack in swarms and draw blood from the horses and animals, away from his animals. The bites could kill a horse! Prior to 1850, Malaria was the most prevalent disease in Illinois, but as the swamps and sloughs were drained the bite of the mosquito was mitigated.

Summer of 1887 was especially hot and dry, yielding a crippled corn crop and a short harvest. Translation? High prices and more income for Wilhelm and his cohort of fellow guiders of the plow! By 1891, the climate for agriculture in the U.S. was described as optimal especially compared to that of Europe where conditions were exceptionally unfavorable, causing increased foreign demand for America's commodities and rising prices. Business in the U.S. was booming generally that year which led to much industrial expansion, to the inception of the "Gay Nineties," and to an expectation of continued prosperity. But Mother Nature had other ideas sending blasts of raw, rainy, cold weather to the spring of 1892 and right on through July. Crops were planted late and in muddy soil, were cultivated in mud, and were harvested as a short crop with declining prices; it was a complete reversal of the year before. The everlasting mud arrested travel and especially the rural traffic of harvest to market and to grain storage facilities. Weather-wise, most of the years were good for Wilhelm, though, and he prospered. 1898 brought a drought in autumn followed by a deep freeze which injured or killed many of his trees or weakened them so they could not survive the heat and drought of 1901.

Wilhelm, like all folks engaged in agriculture, became a shrewd interpreter of the atmosphere around him. He spent so much of his life outdoors and his success depended almost exclusively on the weather that over time he became very prescient, able to observe and analyze the most minute or peculiar change in the sky or temperature. All his observations were shared and integrated with those of his fellow farmers so they could best chart their course of action for they were on their own without weather forecasters, the morning radio farm report, or satellite feeds!

Looking back on that era, one gets the feeling it offered more freedom for lone decision making, for individuality, more reward for the independent person who was not afraid to act, sometimes boldly, and to work hard and risk much, than in today's efficiently organized, highly mechanized, scientific discovery-driven, technology-assisted agricultural economy. Compared to later giant factory farming corporations and sprawling conglomerates, a man could be his own boss, give his all to a project which he himself designed and managed. On the other hand, that Illinois farmer, Wilhelm Oehler, who tilled his acres, walked behind his mule, not yet crowded out by the diesel-engined tractor, had to bear alone the risks of farming, whether from weather or from borrowing from the bank, and had to support his large family, feed them, sustain them through the long winter. Like his cohort farmers, Wilhelm was flush with cash after he sold the harvest, contributing to the prosperity of the village merchants and perhaps paying off debts, but always conscious that the money must last and pay for the spring seeding. Perhaps the independence Wilhelm enjoyed looks attractive only when viewed from a distance; perhaps the world we have lost might be nice to visit for a day, but we would not want to live there; perhaps the present is disturbing and the future ominous, but we don't gain anything by assigning to the past a charm for which we are not fit!

Over the years Wilhelm was constantly endeavoring to increase his acreage, eventually acquiring many acres in several pieces around Danvers. There was no absence, of course, of the usual ups and downs of farming; he experienced the trials that beset every farmer in those days, selling corn for seventeen cents a bushel and oats for twelve cents a bushel. But on the whole, he prospered. For instance, in 1935 the original Oehler farmstead sold for $135 an acre to Butch Pleines, but a member of the Oehler family farmed it until 1984.

Wilhelm put down strong roots in the Danvers area by contributing his time and effort to community interests such as the railroad which he helped to build in the early days. As an Oehler he naturally loved music and sang well, participating presumably in the men's choir club as he had with his father back in Germany. He financed a nephew of his wife who immigrated as a young man to Danvers. This Otto Fuehling (he changed the name to Fuesling) was the son of Marie's sister, Dorothea, and he remained in Danvers with a life-long bond with his aunt, uncle and cousins.

A sister of Wilhelm, Maria, two years his senior, also immigrated to Illinois shortly after him but not to Danvers. She joined the German community in Chicago where she found work and soon married Wilhelm Ehrhardt in West Chicago. They had four children: Mary, William, Lena, and Fred. She and her brother, Wilhelm, were close until her early death at the age of thirty-eight. When he received the telegram announcing her death, he left right away for Chicago but sadly arrived the day after her burial. Now, his only connection in America with his Weisweil home was severed; there was no one here who could laugh with him about the old folks and times or who could speak with him in his beloved Badisch dialect! This was yet another event which steadily turned his orientation from the old world to the new.

In a way, the German immigrants occupied two worlds: rural early America and their past years in Germany where at an early age they had learned their values of hard work, diligence, honesty, strong family ties, and a connection to the land. In Illinois, Wilhelm continued to speak only German and was allowed to continue to do so all his life because he lived in a solid German community. Living on the farm as they did, the Oehlers made their own small self-sufficient world, not much in touch with the wider world. There were occasional visits to Danvers but most experiences within the family unit took place on the farm.

Family solidarity, a quality especially visible in the pioneer generation and their children, was due in part to all they had experienced together in the immigration process. The heart-rending farewells taken back in Germany with little expectation of seeing those loved ones ever again, the rigors of the journey to America without the support and advice of their parents, the feeling of being separate in America because they spoke a different language, the isolation they experienced by living on the farm as opposed to living in the village as they would have done in Germany, and the constant adjustment to new customs and societal norms without being able to consult their parents or established community leaders led Wilhelm and Marie to develop a great strength, solidarity, and reliance on each other. Their children were affected by this reliance on each other and so felt the ties of kinship very strongly themselves.

But in addition to their strong bond, the Oehler family members were genuinely happy together and constantly sought out each others' company. Theirs was a home filled with love and laughter, in great part due to the love and respect between the parents. When, for instance, they grew up, the ten children of Wilhelm and Marie never lived more than ten miles from their homestead near Danvers. They tended to marry into other immigrant families in the area. For instance, two married Graffs and two daughters married Imig cousins. The oldest son, William, married Emma Graff; Emma Oehler married Louis Graff; Katie Oehler married Alvin Imig; and Tillie Oehler married Gus Imig. The Graffs were sister and brother and the Imigs were cousins proving the strength of kinship. Until their generation completely passed away, the siblings held an annual family reunion at the park in

Minier. Talk evoked the gaslighted evenings of their childhood where lively chatter, mending, knitting, and "Vater" reading aloud from the German newspaper competed with the joking gossip and laughter of those outside the circle of light.

In every age, in every place people have made music for their own enjoyment. The Oehler family back in Germany, and then in America, thought of themselves as musical. They agreed with Confucius who said: "Music produces a kind of pleasure which human nature cannot do without." They knew the words to the favorite old German folk songs such as: "At the fountain before the gate, there stands a Linden tree. There in its shadow, I dreamed so many beautiful dreams. I cut into its bark so many dear words, and in joy and in sorrow I feel it draw me back." Or "Must I, must I now leave my little town, and you my treasure stay behind? When I come, when I come back again, I will stay with you forever." Or "I don't know what it means that I am so sad. A tale from long ago I cannot get out of my mind. The evening is still and it is getting dark; the Rhine flows gently on. The light of the sunset just strikes the rocky peak above." Or "In a cool valley there is a mill. My sweetheart who used to stand there has disappeared." Or "I lost my heart in Heidelberg on a warm summer night. I was head over heels in love and her mouth was like a little rose when she laughed. And when we said good-bye in front of the gate, at the last kiss, I realized I lost my heart in Heidelberg – my heart lies back on Necker's shore." As in every language, the folk songs are laden with romantic, sad, longing feelings which strike a very deep chord in the listener's heart!

Today, we wonder if those German immigrants who loved music knew of their compatriots Bach, Mozart, Beethoven, Schubert, or Schumann. If not, they surely sang folksongs from the rich German repertoire accompanied perhaps by an autoharp, flute, fiddle, or recorder/flute which were common musical instruments in the German home. It was in 1876 when all our pioneer forefathers were already putting down roots in Illinois that Richard Wagner first staged his "Ring of the Niebelungen" comprising "Rheingold," "Die Walkuerie," "Siegfried," and "Die Goetterdaemerung", the ancient tales of the German folk, in Germany. One supposes they read of this musical feat in their German language newspapers.

Because Marie shared so many farm responsibilities, she actually assumed a kind of equality with her husband which she would not otherwise have attained. But of course he didn't bare the eleven babies! Much of the care and feeding of the barnyard fowl, the raising of garden plants, even field work at harvest time was Marie's responsibility, plus indoors hers was a continuous effort to produce food for the table. Canning, salting, and smoking of meat was necessary to prolong its viability. Cider, carrots, potatoes, and onions, if stored in a cool dark place, would last months. She knew from her childhood home how to pickle cabbage into sauerkraut, that timeless German favorite, to last all through the winter. Wild berries, plums, and other fruits could be canned for later meals. Wild game was plentiful and surely was a part of her offerings. Tea, coffee, spices, rice, and sugar, could be purchased in Danvers to grace the table on special occasions.

Fabrics like linsey and flannel, though purchased in Danvers, were crafted into garments in the home. Sewing machines were appearing to replace the loom and spinning wheel, so she would have had that technological assist, though dependent on her foot on the treadle for its energy. The children could happily go barefoot all summer long but by fall they each were shod in leather boots, many hand-me-downs but some of necessity bought in the village. By the 1860s chairs had replaced stools and benches for seating, and the introduction of kerosene lamps enabled Marie to sew in the evening, if she could stay awake.

Around the turn of the century the whole Oehler family donned their very best clothing, full suits and bow ties for the men and elegant taffeta dresses for the women, and drove their buggy into town to be professionally photographed. George Eastman had invented his still camera in 1875, had inspired an industry to tap into human narcissism, the desire to look at oneself captured forever on film, and had watched this popular desire spread all over the United States, even to the smallest hamlet.

As always the girls cut and coiffed each other's hair into the fashion of the day. Their blond curls were their best feature and they knew it. Every bit of jewelry they possessed was displayed for the camera as well. Feminine excitement having reached fever pitch, "Vater" (German for father) escaped into Danvers to have his mustache and full beard painstakingly groomed by a barber. Soon after, the girls began to marry and in those same dresses as white was not yet the fashion of brides. A studio portrait recorded those special occasions for each as well.

Standing are Amelia, Ida, Charles, Lillie, Matilda, Katherine, and Emma. Sitting are William, Marie (mother), Edward, Wilhelm (father), and Marie.

Nine weddings followed one another in quick succession for the Oehler children: Marie married Charles Loeffler on October 12, 1899; William Frederich married Emma Graff on January 10, 1900; Ida Marie married Henry Brenneman on September 1, 1901; Tilly married Gus Imig on June 28, 1903; Charley married Louise Burr on February 12, 1905; Emma married Louis Graff on October 20, 1905; Katie married Alvin Imig on December 19, 1905; Lillie Susana married John Buescher on September 28, 1907; and Eddie married Loretta Knapple on December 11, 1912. One year there were three weddings but Mama Marie took it all in stride. She loved happy occasions and celebrations!

Marie liked the morning light at sunrise on a cloudless horizon as it crept perceptively up spreading a warm, rosy hew over the sky auguring a happy day. Sunsets over the billowing corn fields were a special delight too which even vied with those she had seen over the ocean from the deck of her ship on her journey to America. But perhaps most magical, because it was so fleeting, was the dewy sparkle on the grasses in the field before the sun could burn it off. Those little shiny points seemed to go on into infinity but she had to be there at just the right moment in the morning to catch them!

As every mother does, and especially in those days when mothers often died young, Marie prayed she would live to raise all her children—and she did. She had had the indomitable constitution to bear eleven babies with the loss of only one. Her youngest was twenty years old when she took sick, sick enough to be taken to St. Joseph's Hospital for eight days at a cost of $46. The invoice for her hospitalization remains in family possession from which we know that board and nursing from March 30 to April 8, 1910, cost $24 at $20 per week, private nursing at $15 per week came to $17, and the operating room charge was $5. Payment was received in full according to the receipt. The diagnosis was inconclusive but she didn't last long. Just short of her sixty-first birthday, Marie passed away in the presence of her husband of thirty-seven years, their ten children, and twenty-seven grandchildren. It was a sorely sad day for all whom this cheery and pretty little lady left behind. Later they never tired of telling what a happy home she had made for them out there on the Oehler homestead.

Marie along with Wilhelm had indeed passed on good health, habits of clean living, and a strong constitution to their ten children resulting in amazingly long lives for all: William lived to age 92 and 8 months; Marie Loeffler, 94; Charley, 93; Ida Brenneman, 95; Katherine Imig, 81; Amelia Franks, 91; Tilly Imig, 87; Emma Graff, 92; Lillie Buesher, 81; and Edward, 89.

Wilhelm struggled on at the farm with the help of his son, Edward, and daughter, Amelia, who was not married. The corn harvest still came after hay-making and apple-gathering still came after the corn harvest. Nights were still frosty then, mornings and evenings were still misty while mid-day was still all sunny and bright, but the merry contentment was missing in the house; the one who gave a spark to all around her was gone!

Wilhelm decided he needed a change of environment. He actually began to make plans which other immigrants had only dreamed of—a visit back to his homeland. His parents were dead, of course, as were both of his sisters, but his nephew, Johann George Oehler, still lived in the Oehler family home and would welcome him back. Marie had been gone a year at that time and perhaps Wilhelm thought of finding a good German woman to bring back to Danvers.

That didn't happen but it was a very therapeutic sojourn for Wilhelm. He saw Weisweil and the surrounding Baden landscape with completely new eyes. Most transformative of all was the German unification which had occurred under Otto von Bismarck in 1871 making Baden one of seventeen states of the German Empire instead of one of many little duchies. 1911, at the time of Wilhelm's visit, was during a forty year relatively peaceful period in Germany which was about to end in 1914 with World War I. There had been great scientific progress from the universities and industries there. Many village folk had left farming and were working in nearby manufacturing cities. That was the time of the Industrial Revolution which saw the invention of the telegraph, camera, horseless carriage, and radio. Food was better and cheaper; dramatic advances came in hygiene and medicine. A German physician, Robert Koch, had raised bacteriology into a science and in the 1890s he identified the bacillus of typhoid, tuberculosis, cholera, lockjaw, diphtheria, bubonic plague. Surely, it was assumed, cures lay in the immediate future.

A special joy for Wilhelm was speaking his old Baden dialect, rarely encountered back in Danvers and never spoken by Marie with her "high German" with his friends and relatives back in Weisweil; in fact, this old mother-tongue dialect was the only one spoken in Weisweil by absolutely everyone he conversed with there! He was amazed how, after only a couple of days, "Badisch" easily just rolled off his tongue! On Sunday at church he stared at the men and women who wore their folkloric suits and dresses just as they had done when he was a boy. Now he saw them with new appreciation for the special stitching and the women's hats with large red yarn balls atop. Most days found him standing long at his parents' graves, his mind always flooded with memories. Assuredly, he knew the quiet hungering that comes to one who returns to the place of his origins and perhaps he even knew the ache of mis-belonging!

It was a deeply moving experience to return to his native hearth, once rejected by him but now appreciated. Memories and sensations, inspired by the sight of places he had known as a child, a rickety chair, or picture hanging on the wall, flooded his mind. He was surprised how some small passing object could set off a torrent of memories nearly fifty years old. Walking along the fields with their earthy scents brought him many hours of pleasantly nostalgic reverie. Seeing the homesteads, long in some family's possession, the thriving vineyards and orchards of Baden, the young folks now grown old, the marriages made since his departure, and the homes occupied by another generation of a family he knew, must have been a moving experience for William after the passage of so many years.

In Weisweil, the farmers still walked or rode a horse out to their fields, small plots compared to what he had back in Danvers. Though Wilhelm tried not to boast, he owned several hundred acres around Danvers in McClean County and Allin township and had stipulated in his will that each of his ten children should inherit a sizable acreage, something not possible in Germany. He noticed that the farmers in Baden still relied more on hand labor and still used barnyard manure to fertilize their crops. Conversations with them about crops, seed, methods, weather, and government policy were, like among farmers in Illinois, always very satisfying. There was an inkling of war in the air too. The farmers told how now that Prussia was the most populous and powerful state in Germany there had been a military buildup which they didn't like.

Then one day soon, it was time to catch the boat to return to America. All that Wilhelm had seen and heard back in the land of this birth had struck a very deep chord in his heart, but he was ready to leave, for he had realized that he didn't belong in Germany any more. That wasn't home anymore! Though he would always love Weisweil and wasn't sorry about that, he wasn't sorry either that he had left her. Geography had made him who he was. There was a final evening when many from the village and from church came to call, shake hands, shed a few tears, and offer a blessing, and then he was off on his second journey to America.

Wilhelm knew, deep in his heart, that he was one of the privileged few pioneers who were ever able to return to the land of their birth and then go back to his new home in the New World. His experience was truly exceptional!

Back in Danvers, Wilhelm returned to the farm life, up at dawn and toiling all day, though now unrelieved by the companionship and assistance of his beloved helpmeet, Marie. The onset of World War I, considered by the world to have been caused by Germany, brought another kind of sadness and disappointment to the aging farmer. Through his recent contact with friends and relatives in Weisweil, he knew the Germans who had already experienced enough war on their soil to last several lifetimes, knew from experience the terrible mayhem and destruction of war leading to the unification of Germany, didn't want war and certainly didn't want to fight American soldiers. He knew it to be a fact; he had just been there, talked with them, shared beers with them at the "stube," walked the lanes conversing with the farmers. Even after reading his German language newspapers, he just couldn't understand how affairs could lead to such an all-enveloping war in Europe where eventually American soldiers would be implored to come and help defeat the merciless enemy, Germany. When they did, Wilhelm joined all his German-American contingent and sided with his new homeland. Though he sympathized with his loved ones back in Germany, his ostensible allegiance now had to be with America and all the other countries so bravely trying to defeat Germany.

This was a turn of events he could never have predicted, could not have prepared for. In the confusion he felt when he read in the newspaper that even Germans in America were suspected of collaborating with the enemy or in the helplessness he felt when his pastor said the children would be not be taught, christened, or confirmed in German any longer, Wilhelm was truly disheartened. It was surely a sadness all Germans in America felt, tinged with real shame as commentators associated them with the enemy, shunned them in the marketplace, and motivated them to actions which would make clear to all their new compatriots that they were truly American, not German. Ended forever were the German singing clubs, the German language newspapers and publications, the German language spoken by school teachers, the importation of

German goods, the respect and admiration for all things German. From that point on, folks living in small German communities like Danvers turned their orientation one hundred percent to their adopted homeland, dropping any identification with the Old World, severing those ties, saving themselves from any doubt. For those like Wilhelm, it was hard, painful, and regrettable—but necessary.

Three generations of Oehlers named William Oehler
taken in 1912, the pioneer, his eldest son,
and that William's youngest son.

About the same time, 1913, a terrible fire, that bane of existence before electricity in the days of wood stoves and kerosene lamps, burned the Oehler home to the ground. No one was hurt and the structure was rebuilt, but Wilhelm took this as a sign to retire from farming and to move into the village of Danvers. Edward stayed on the farm, with his bride Loretta Knapple, to carry on the Oehler ways and traditions. Amelia moved to town with her father as housekeeper, and they settled in at 119 W. Columbia, a home which had been built in 1895 in the Queen Anne cottage style. Fancy machine-turned porch spindles, decorative gables, multi-roof lines, and a picket fence were architectural trademarks of the style. Chairs from the dining set are still in family possession. Wilhelm first brought plumbing into the house in 1917; heating was obtained first by a wood cook stove in the kitchen and a coal stove in the dining room and later with a coal burning furnace in the basement. The upstairs was not heated. A barn graced the back yard as was custom in those days, even in town, for most everyone had a horse and at least one cow plus a chicken coop. Wilhelm tore down the barn in 1916, replacing it with a garage, complete with outhouse and a coal storage room, strong indication that he was an automobile owner by then.

As was the Oehler family tradition, Christmas of 1927 found the whole family of fifty gathered together even after the children had married. None of them ever lived more than ten miles from the old homestead, but naturally it took a holiday to motivate them all to be at the same place at the same time, hectic and noisy, but surely satisfying to the paterfamilias as proof of the dynasty he had established. And how they laughed and reminisced mostly in German for the sake of the patriarch though that was growing more difficult for the grandchildren. Those same twenty seven little children remembered all their lives long, how their "Opa" (grandfather) greeted them by name and pressed a gold coin into their hand, a big surprise in his handshake which never failed to bring a smile of glee to their faces!

Life in the village offered Wilhelm enjoyable pursuits with other retired farmers and at the Evangelical Friedens Church where services were still held in the German language. He enjoyed having the time to read his newspapers and books which had always brought him pleasure. A very special occasion, a regular family reunion, was the celebration of his eightieth birthday in the home of his eldest daughter, Marie and Charles Loeffler, near Stanford. Since the average life expectancy at that time was forty-two years for a man, Wilhelm had proved to be, in yet another remarkable way, quite an exception. All of his fifty progeny were in attendance for the dinner served at noon, buffet style with the adults eating first and children afterwards, followed by the cake with eighty candles blazing from its center. Yes, June 28, 1928 was a very happy occasion!

STORIES MY FOLKS TOLD ME

That day proved to be the apex, however, from which the rest of his days were leading, as inexorably as a clock winding down, to the end. Despite his famous determination and lifelong spirit of daring, his health was failing and he just couldn't seem to rally. By the first of November he was bedfast followed quickly by the end on Tuesday morning, November 6, 1928. As reported in the Bloomington newspaper: "Funeral services were held Thursday afternoon at the Oehler home, and in order to accommodate the large number of people who wished to pay their last respects to the beloved pioneer, family received callers at 2 p.m. at the Presbyterian Church. Two pastors officiated: Rev. E.H. Rathmann of the Evangelical Friedens Church of Danvers and Rev. James Fisher of the Presbyterian Church in Danvers. A Soloist, Mrs. D.S. Ummel sang several hymns accompanied by Miss Viola Nafziger. Six grandsons, now young men in their twenties, served as pallbearers: Ivan Imig, Roy Imig, Alvin Oehler, Jesse Oehler, Lyle Brenneman, and Donald Buescher." Wilhelm is buried beside Marie in the Danvers cemetery marked by an imposing monument, easy to locate.

Wilhelm's estate, to be divided among his ten children, was valued at an astonishing $91,800, each one receiving a sizable acreage. Hard work, diligence, focus, and intelligence brought him a life of achievement by anyone's reckoning. By his own nature, he assimilated the American principle of conscious self-betterment, the ubiquitous philosophy of the time. America was a new country composed of mostly new citizens who together, without the help of any outside force, worked to develop into an enviably prosperous nation. Wilhelm and Marie, like countless others, played a significant part in that effort which incrementally contributed to the prosperity of the whole.

Pioneer Gottlieb Traugott Rost arrived 1868 and Pioneer
Anke Margarethe Wilken Rost arrived 1876
—8—

Presumably it was a particularly pious mother and father who gave the name Godlove Truegod to their newborn son on January 21, 1852 in Ruedersdorf, fifteen miles east of Berlin, state of Brandenburg, in northern Germany, and forty miles west of the Polish border on the Oder River. It is not known if Gottlieb had a nickname, but as an adult he answered to G.T. Possibly the family livelihood was the butchering of animals because that is what young Gottlieb learned.

Many of the Rost kin and neighbors, however, sought their living at the town's open-pit limestone mines formed millennia ago when the earth was covered with shallow seas and the accumulated marine life, over the eons, laid down the shells of their crustaceous inhabitants. Famous buildings and the Brandenburg Gate in nearby Berlin are constructed of Ruedersdorf limestone. By the time of Gottlieb's youth only a series of lovely lakes remained of the enormous "ancient Berlin melt water valley," and it was a very special family outing whenever the Rosts took themselves to the lake shore for a relaxing day in the sun or fishing.

Alone of his family, Gottlieb traveled with a Ruedersdorf friend to Bremen and then by ship to New York City. He was only sixteen years old when he arrived in 1868 but he had his trade and some of the necessary butchering tools. Schooling for a young man in those days was rudimentary with only reading and arithmetic inculcated, for life skills were very basic and childhood was short. Several of his few years were presumably spent in apprenticeship to a butcher in town. He liked the man and the work seemed to suit him.

The Rosts were indeed a pious family but perhaps not more than their Protestant neighbors of the day. Religious practice and knowledge of the Bible was learned in most every Protestant home of Ruedersdorf, complete with morning prayers, meal-time prayers, Bible reading in the evening, and finally night prayers. Although shelves of books did not exist in the Rost home, a well-read Bible did and was quoted and addressed for answers to daily uncertainties.

Located as they were in the heart of the state of Brandenburg, the citizens of Ruedersdorf were above all Prussians which was then a military and bureaucratic despotism in the best sense of the term. Though a population of only eleven million, its soil largely infertile, it was nevertheless a powerful well-governed state. Every department of government was commanded to function with the direst economy so that surpluses would be gained in order to afford a first-class army. Even in time of peace, Prussia remained a state disciplined for war, a militarized machine served by the best of officers. Military service was compulsory, the ranks filled by farmers, laborers, and artisans; officers came from the noble landowning families and city nobility.

When Prussia along with assistance from Austria went to war in 1864 to reclaim the states of Schleswig and Holstein from Denmark, Gottlieb was too young to march with General von Bismarck's army, but by 1866 when Prussia was no longer affiliated with Austria but actually engaged militarily in a dispute with her, the boy was seriously trying to elude the draft officer! He was interested to hear about the newly invented "needle gun" which was three times as deadly as the old muzzle-loading type but he was genuinely frightened as well. With his best buddy, he surreptitiously began to make plans to emigrate. More and more youths were taking this solution to the never ending coercion to the battle field. Germans had by then been migrating to America in vast numbers for twenty-five years; it was no longer an unusual move; young people unaccompanied by their parents were commonly setting out on their own. Gottlieb, too, was caught up in the gusher to go west!

If Gottlieb had not left when he did in 1868, he most certainly would have had to shoulder one of those new "needle guns" and muster for the Franco Prussian War which lasted till 1871 as well as for the many wars Prussia fought with German duchies to force them to join a united German Empire of the same year. His progeny can be glad that Gottlieb Traugott put his unusual name on the ship manifest out of Bremen and took it to Illinois!

He was considered a handsome blond youth with striking blue eyes, muscularly formed from his work, ambitious and eager to make his way in the new world. The two young men didn't lose time in the east but worked their way across the vast land to Petersburg, Menard County, in Illinois, where they had been advised they would find a German-speaking community and jobs. With the certificate of his apprenticeship in hand, Gottlieb was able to find employment in a butcher shop in town. First, though, he had to learn the English words for all the animals, the cuts of meat, the tools, and the English measurement of weights. His employer was German as were all with whom he associated, but his customers were not all German. In his new world, Gottlieb had to grow up fast and learn English; he had to be a man from the day he left his home in Ruedersdorf!

As Gottlieb began to catch on to the new language and as he read in the German newspapers printed right there in Petersburg, he learned about the Civil War and Abraham Lincoln who was already a legend in Illinois. Folks showed the young man the nearby hamlet of New Salem where Lincoln had lived and worked in a general store a couple of years while he studied law at night by the fire light. Petersburg residents considered Abe Lincoln their neighbor; many of them had known him personally; their own Ann Rutledge was his first love, and he would have married her had she not first taken sick and died. They showed Gottlieb her grave stone in their Rosehill Cemetery.

Residents of Petersburg also boasted to Gottlieb that their town, then populated with 3,000 residents, was actually surveyed and plotted by Abraham Lincoln himself in 1836. A year later though, Lincoln gave up his position as deputy surveyor of Sangamon County, left New Salem, and went to Springfield, Illinois, to practice law. He came back to Petersburg frequently though to try cases at the handsome county courthouse there. Though Lincoln was the town's claim to fame, most of the residents found jobs with the two railroads which stopped in town, the several grist mills, the brewery, the winery, or the small factories and shops.

Day by day, Gottlieb was leaving his Prussian self behind and becoming an American. Yet, when he decided it was time to find someone to share his new life with, he knew it would have to be a German woman. It was not only a German woman, he wanted, but a north German woman with whom he could speak "high German." For the first time in his life—and in America at that—he had learned that there were quite a few ways to speak the German language! And what ugly ways there were, too! If the truth were told, he didn't even understand some of those dialects like Swabian, Hessian, or Bavarian. Even before he met her, he heard her name, Anke, and almost fell in love because hers was definitely a beautiful north German name.

Anke Margarethe Wilken was born on December 13, 1847 in Etzel, state of Lower Saxony, Germany, in a farming community near the larger city on a North Sea bay, Wilhelmshaven. Of course, in Anke's childhood the Wilken family was under the rule of the Kingdom of Hannover. Moors, heath bogs, and even inaccessible swamps covered the area but the land, where dry, was flat and a productive combination of loam and sand yielding wheat, oats, and rye. She grew up in a large farm family where she learned to work hard and understand all the salient details of sowing, weeding, fertilizing, and harvesting as well as sewing, cooking, and caring for her younger siblings. There wasn't much time for formal schooling although Anke did attend the village school during the winters.

About 1875, Katherine Wilken, Anke's slightly older sister, began whispering to her that she was sick and tired of her life of constant toil and would emigrate to America. Though shocked at first, Anke who loved this sister best of all and couldn't imagine life without her actually began to entertain the idea of joining her. They had friends who had already made the journey to Illinois in mid-America and who wrote back letters encouraging their friends to come. It would be so easy just to take the ferry in Wilhelmshaven over to Bremerhaven where the big ships set out for New York City. Emigration from Germany had been in full force now for decades so it was no longer unusual for unescorted young women to travel. Families were large and parents could manage with a couple of fewer mouths to feed; girls could not inherit the farm yet were a responsibility and cost to the parents until they married. Mama and Papa didn't want to lose two daughters at once but were reconciled when they acknowledged that the same abandonment was being experienced by many other farm families. Young people then as now were seduced by the lure of the unknown, the excitement of travel, and enticement of independence.

Thus, Anke and Katherine Wilken fulfilled their dreams and in 1876, when Anke was nineteen, they shipped across the ocean to the United States. All the way to Petersburg, Illinois, they clung together, encouraging each other about the wisdom of their decision to emigrate, sharing their meager resources, talking each other out of homesickness, straining their minds to understand the new language engulfing them, and promising each other to stick together not only for the journey but for the rest of their lives. Central Illinois was their final destination where a family they knew from home lived in Petersburg, Menard County. Resourceful girls like the Wilkens soon found work, but not on a farm. They had had enough of that life and sought work in the town where the day did not end at sundown and chores did not begin before sunup.

Pretty Anke, with her auburn braids coiled upon her head like a crown and her warm brown eyes lighting up a room when she entered, soon had the attention of the young bachelors of the county. Whether at church, country dances, weddings, in the stores, or along the street, she was noticed as a very pretty girl, but Gottlieb Traugott Rost is the one who won her heart and on March 31, 1880, her hand in marriage. He was twenty-eight, she twenty-two. To Gottlieb's dismay, Anke stated that she would henceforth be known as Margarethe, pronounced Margaret, which sounded ever so less foreign and was more pronounceable by the Americans she was now meeting since she was learning English. It's just possible, though, that when he whispered romantically in her ear, it was "Anke" that he spoke! With her blessing, he began to be called G.T. in their circle of friends and associates.

Within a year, on February 12, 1881, they welcomed their first child whom Margarethe named Katherine Alluerdine after her beloved sister though the baby was immediately nicknamed Katie to distinguish the two. Two years later appeared John Wilken, six years after him came Pauline, and eight years after her came Theodore. Mama and Papa insisted that English be spoken in the home but the truth is that it was a struggle for the parents who often lapsed into High German, so in the end the children could speak some German as well as English. All their childhood, the Rost children grew up in close association with Aunt Katherine's family, for their mamas had long ago vowed fidelity to one another.

Especially when Margarethe with swelling heart and misty eyes was somehow in the course of a day struck by a reminder of those she had left back in Germany. Their influence, for only a few years of her life, came during the growing up years when one is most profoundly impressed. When as she said her prayers they came to mind, when a person she saw reminded her of someone back in Etzel, when it was Mama or Papa's birthday, it would warm her heart, filling her with the sensation of love, impelling her to Katherine for a good talk. Dreams too evoked the memory of those far away, gave her some pleasurable moments where she seemingly was really with her mama or papa, aunts, or friends, filling her upon awaking with sublimely warm feelings that lasted for hours, and restored her to face the challenges of her day.

Ambitious and risk-taking were traits of G.T. so it was no surprise to Margarethe when one day he announced that he would leave the butcher shop where he was employed and would open his own enterprise. He had become very skilled in this ancient trade and there was always work for a butcher here in America where folks liked to eat meat and plenty of it. From a wood frame building in the center of town, he made it known that he would buy hogs, steers, or sheep at the big door around back of the shop. If the animal had not already been slaughtered by the farmer, G.T. would take an iron bar or wooden mallet, hit the animal on the head to stun or incapacitate it. Exsanguination, the severing of the carotid or brachial artery with a sharp knife to facilitate draining of blood, followed. Usually he hung the carcass from a beam which ran the width of his shop for this purpose catching the blood, which had use in certain of the sausages he made for sale, in a pail.

Skinning, the removal of the hide or pelt with a special knife, he performed next though in the case of a pig, scalding water was used to remove the hair first. Next, evisceration involved the removal of the heart, liver, intestines, kidneys, brains and other such delicacies which sold for a premium. After splitting the carcass in half longitudinally, the butcher let it hang a few days before cutting it into smaller, more workable sizes, and then into the prescribed cuts. Careful boning and trimming work was done before finally laying the cuts in the showcase in the front of the shop.

True to his training as a butcher, G.T. did not waste one speck of the animal, not the ears nor the hooves. He was a sausage maker, as well, you see. Any self-respecting butcher to a German community must offer sausage in his showcase such as Bierwurst, Blood Sausage, Bratwurst,

Jagdwurst, Knackwurst, Thueringer, Weisswurst, Mettwurst, and Westfallen Beef Sausage among the scores of others. Developed as a way to preserve meat and enable it to be transported over distances, sausage was mentioned already in 600 BC in China, Greece, and Rome. First, G.T. would cure the piece of meat using curing salts such as saltpeter (potassium nitrate) (sodium nitrite or sodium nitrate are used today), to prevent botulism poisoning, to kill the bacteria, and to act as a preservative. It was necessary to precisely calculate the exact amount of nitrate to meat, of course, in order to preserve the meat without poisoning the one consuming it. After mincing or grinding the cured meat, seasonings like salt, sugar, herbs, spices, onion, or garlic were mixed in. Lastly, the mixture was forced into a casing or skin made from the animal's own intestines.

Sometimes, smoking of the sausage was called for as in the preparation of Braunschweiger, the trademark sausage of the area of Braunschweig from where the Buehrig family had hailed. This is sometimes called liverwurst today, made from pork liver. After the curing process and the encasing, the sausage was submerged in 160 degree Fahrenheit water for two to two and one-half hours till it reached an internal temperature of 152 degrees Fahrenheit when it was plunged into icy water before it was cold smoked at 115 to 120 degrees Fahrenheit for two to three hours.

Another favorite of G.T'.s customers was "head cheese." It was dish eaten by peasants all over Europe since the Middle Ages, and it wasn't really a cheese at all. It did come from a head though. Any animal would do, the fleshier the better, for any kind of skull contains a natural gelatin. Once he obtained a calf or pig head, the butcher removed the eyes, brain, and ears to be used in other delicacies, and boiled the skull with vinegar and water possibly adding tongue, feet and heart as well as onion, black pepper, bay leaf, allspice, and salt. Boiling for a few hours removed the meat from the skull and released the natural gelatin. Then he poured it all into a loaf pan and left it to cool, and miraculously, firm enough to allow slicing for serving at room temperature. G.T. sold it by the slice.

Margarethe was occupied with their children, the home, garden including fruit trees, cooking and sewing. Indoor plumbing was still years in the future as was electricity and the telephone, but she had her family and the company of her sister nearby, so she didn't know what she was missing! Letters from the Old Country and German newspapers informed the Rosts of the enormous changes which had transpired back in Germany: In 1871, the final consolidation of all the little duchies, principalities, and free towns made them into one country called Germany. There was now one federal government with fourteen states instead of 300, one army, one "Kaiser" (king), and one national assembly. It had taken several wars, though, to accomplish this great step forward, reconfirming once again the Rost's opinion that they were glad they were in America and not in Germany where their sons would have just been cannon fodder.

In her own home now and with her growing family, Margarethe carefully replicated the North German dishes she had brought with her to America in her head. A simple soup of broth made from bones and vegetables she had boiled began every dinner. Potatoes were a daily fare prepared in a multitude of ways from boiled to pureed to fried. A stew was made from pickled meat, red beets, sour pickles, and garnished with a fried egg. Sauerkraut, an example of food preservation by salt, was another staple at Margarethe's table. She made it herself by layering cabbage slices and salt in a tall crock which stood in a dark cool place, the basement of the house. To prepare for the table, she rinsed the kraut well, fried it in rendered fat in a pan, added slices of apple, perhaps some sugar, broth or water, covered and cooked it for hours. With mashed potatoes and any kind of meat it was pure comfort food!

Salt, so necessary to the preservation of food since ancient times, came to Margarethe from the Gallatin County saline mines near Shawneetown in the south eastern part of the Illinois. The springs there furnished over 300,000 bushels of salt annually at fifty to seventy-five cents a bushel. Later it became available from Vermilion County in east central Illinois on the border with Indiana.

Sauerkraut was but one example of food preserved to last over the winter until the next harvest. The pickling process, first mentioned in India over 4000 years ago, prolonged for months the vitality of meats, vegetables, and even fruits by the use of salt or vinegar. Before glass jars were available, women like Margarethe used tall crocks or crockery made of earthenware which she filled with cooked ready to eat hot foodstuff and then poured a brine of salt and water, or vinegar and water, to the top. She added spices and herbs before capping it tightly with a lid and then let it ferment some time till it tasted just right. Corned beef was of course a favorite in the Rost household, and it too was an example of the pickling or corning (or brining) method.

Fish dishes were far less frequent in Petersburg than in Lower Saxony near the North Sea and the little tributaries flowing into it, but now Margarethe was married to a butcher and could eat meat every day if she wished. Like all Germans they ate their main warm meal at noon. G.T. walked to and from his shop for this meal as did the children from school. Their evening meal usually consisted of leftovers fried together in a pan or bread and sausage.

Margarethe knew how, on a wood stove, to bake the famous life-sustaining German breads of hearty whole grains and the Christmas cakes and cookies like butter S and cinnamon-molasses "lebkuchen," "stollen," and cinnamon stars. She made jams and jellies from the cherry trees she had planted in their yard. As a gardner, she marveled how the rain came in Illinois at just the right intervals to nourish her plants right on through the growing season. The rains were no light, misty, drizzle that she had known coming off the North Sea but extremely dramatic storms of rain accompanied by lightning as if the sky were on fire with zig-zagging, crackling, snapping flashes of light followed by ceaseless, deep rolling waves of booming thunder that seemed to shake the earth. Finally came darkness and blessed silence, but only for a moment, then the deluge as water began from single drops, growing into bucketsful, pelting the rooftop and windows with pings of driven water. Such a power of nature, followed by a profound quiet, left the earth and its inhabitants numbed and breathless like the stories she had heard at home about fishermen caught in a storm at sea.

The state of the weather, the temperature of the air, the amount of rain which fell, made all the difference to Anke because she was a committed gardner. Sowing seeds seemed a very simple matter, but she possibly felt it was a sacred thing among the mysteries of God, that she was His handmaid given the power to summon life from the silent passive soil. In her role as partner in creation, she brought a mat from the house and knelt by the smooth bed of mellow brown earth she had earlier prepared, lay a narrow strip of board across it a few inches from one end, drew a furrow firmly and evenly in the ground along the edge of the board, repeated this until the whole bed was grooved at equal distances across its entire length. Into those straight furrows the living seeds were dropped, the earth replaced over them, and the board laid flat with gentle pressure over all the surface till it was perfectly smooth again. Then must the whole have been lightly and carefully watered.

In the days while she waited for the first blessed seedlings to erupt from the soil she was forced to watch vigilantly to protect her newly sown seeds from invasions of hungry songbirds who with their scratching, pecking, and clawing could undo a morning's work in moments. Netting pegged over the bed helped prevent their havoc but there must have been times when, infuriated, she had to repeat her entire sowing process. Later when the plants were leafy and succulent they became an irresistible lure to the three "R"s: rabbits, rodents, and raccoons, just as they are today. But oh the gratification and delight when finally all her effort found fulfillment at her table whether fresh from her garden or from the canning jars all winter long!

Through all the years of their life in Petersburg, the Rosts found fellowship with the families they knew from the German Evangelical Church. Activities besides Sunday services, picnics, potluck suppers, singing, lectures or poetry readings, took them to the meeting hall more than once a week. The services were in German and all the parishioners were German and spoke a version of that tongue so naturally a satisfying social life developed for them. Katherine and her family were sure to be included in that society as well. In that close German-speaking circle it didn't matter that Margarethe and G.T. spoke English with a strong German accent. They had a strong bond with those people and a real feeling of belonging so important to the human spirit wherever they are.

An especially happy day for the Rosts and their friends was the marriage of daughter, Katie, when she was twenty years old. They liked her groom and agreed that they made a good match. Though it always breaks the mold when the first child marries and moves out of the house, Margarethe and G.T. consoled themselves that Katie was just going a few blocks away and they would see her nearly every day. Soon, she announced she was in the "family way" for which they all rejoiced. Pauline vowed to be the best aunt ever, John though a high schooler extended his congratulations, and even little Teddy started asking what an uncle does.

Then in a matter of hours, jubilation turned to despair. Katie's labor went badly and despite prayers and doctor both mother and baby perished. There was no consoling the young father and grandparents! The light of Margarethe's life, the beautiful lively spirit in the fullness of youth and health, was suddenly gone! Grief lasted a long time, but with help and faith they kept on going.

Then one day when all was going well again in their lives, a cloud appeared on the horizon which the Rosts could not dispel. It began with a stomach ache which attacked G.T. for no obvious reason at all. Before long, it seemed that whatever he ate caused his stomach to burn and send him into paroxysms of agony. The only food he could keep down and eat without pain was soup, so that is what Margarethe prepared with the declaration that she and the children would join Papa and eat only soup as well. Oh, how boring and monotonous that was to the children! They wanted to complain but contained themselves out of fear that Papa would die and also because of the love and respect they felt for him. Later, sitting at the head of the table in his own home, John declared: "Soup will not be on the menu here! I have eaten enough soup to last a lifetime."

G.T.s doctor who came to the house regularly made quite an impression on young John, then in high school, by answering his questions, discussing scientific subjects. Observing that the lad had ambition but no specific goal yet identified, the good doctor encouraged him to study medicine. The doctor's words had a powerful effect on the young man, for that is exactly what he did. By the time G.T., only fifty-two years old, succumbed to stomach cancer on January 19, 1905, John was in medical school at the University of Illinois in Chicago.

The family always thought that G.T.s exposure to nitrates, which in high concentrations form nitrosamines and thus are carcinogens, caused his cancer. There were no CAT scans, radiation, chemotherapy, nor effective pain killers, so the family was forced to stand by helplessly as Papa suffered to the end. The sad finish did serve as a strong motivation to John to work hard in his studies as a tribute to his father and to do his part to alleviate whatever human suffering might come his way. In medical school, John was elected treasurer of his class and graduated number four out of one hundred classmates.

John Rost at graduation from
University of Illinois Medical School

On graduation day in June of 1906, the Rost family excitedly donned their finest attire and prepared to take the train up to Chicago for the graduation. Then, practically on the way out the door, Margarethe glanced at her three cherry trees and saw to her horror that the fruit was already ripe! It seemed to her that the last time she looked she had seen the glorious flowers covering the trees like a big fluff of cotton candy, and now she saw only bright red cherries hanging in luscious bunches ready to be picked by the handful. They would not last to be picked when she returned from John's graduation. What should she do? She announced that Pauline would have to stay home, pick the cherries, pit them, and can them. No amount of wailing or cajoling by Pauline would change Mama's mind, so though she was wearing the very prettiest dress she had ever owned, had never been farther from home than the state capitol in Springfield, and had looked forward to this day for months, the poor girl had to accept her fate and bid her mother and brothers good-bye.

Margarethe had always been a strict German lady and now since the death of her daughter and husband occurring so closely together and feeling the weight of her new position as head of the household, she could be rather unyielding, stern, and sober. Her braids atop her head were turning to silver now and her figure was that of a stout German woman, but she still worked tirelessly in her garden and home making all their savings last through John's medical school, Teddie's medical and dental schools, and on to her own death on May 12, 1935, at the age of seventy-seven.

When Pauline married Homer Hallstein who farmed south of Minier, Illinois, it was a happy day for Margarethe. She missed her helpmate daughter but visited her often by train especially after little Margaret and Eileen arrived. As grandmother she could be a big help to Pauline especially as the latter preferred to be outdoors in the open air, working in the fields, rather than indoors doing housework. Later when John needed her in Minier, Margarethe dropped everything and went to his aid too.

When Ted married in 1927 it was to a big city girl and a college graduate as well. Clara Tesmer was a beautiful blond blue-eyed waif of a girl from Evanston, Illinois, with a degree she had earned from Northwestern University in three years. Margarethe wondered what she would talk to her about, but that problem was solved when she learned Clara was of German descent. Anna, Clara's mother, remembered many of the old German traditions to recount with Margarethe, but she was thoroughly American and spoke with no accent. Not long after the wedding of Ted and Clara, her father Richard Tesmer was shot as he drove into his own garage in Evanston. A Chicago gangster with the Prohibition era crime

STORIES MY FOLKS TOLD ME

syndicate who killed the wrong target, the police decided, but the case was never solved. Anna went to live with Clara and Ted in Bloomington for the rest of her life, remembered for the lovely articles she knitted for friends, family, and soldiers overseas. Ted's sons, Dick and Ted, grew up in Bloomington where their dad had a dental practice and their mother was active in community affairs including the P.E.O. sisterhood. Dick practiced dentistry with his dad and Ted became a banker in St. Petersburg, Florida.

Anke Margrethe lived thirty years after Gottlieb Traugott's death, her final years in Pauline and Homer's home, but she was buried next to G.T. in Rosehill Cemetery in Petersburg where Abe Lincoln's love and all the characters in Edgar Lee Master's "Spoon River Anthology" repose. With the Rosts demise we see illustrated the way immigrants of intelligence, ambition, and tenacity transformed themselves in a mere generation. They had come to America with only a dedication to hard work and lots of hope, yet they gave their new homeland two physician sons, one of whom practiced dentistry and invented new methods for that science and one who served a small community for over thirty years as well as the United States Army in wartime.

Summary of Pioneer Generation

And so, I come to the end of the pioneer stories, each one daring, courageous, and inspiring in its own way. All of the immigrants brought pluck, intelligence, industry, perseverance, self-reliance, resourcefulness, habits of the famous German orderliness, and a strong sense of morality based on the teachings of their Christian faith. Above all, those folks had remarkable valor as expressed by the American author William Faulkner who said: "You cannot swim for new horizons until you have the courage to lose sight of the shore."

Perhaps our pioneer folks seized the opportunity of starting over in a new land as a chance to leave behind long-held fears, anxieties, embarrassments, ugliness, failure, or low self-esteem. Perhaps they saw emigration as a chance to leave their mistakes behind, to be a new kind of person, more positive, kinder, gentler, better. Perhaps the move involved redemption, a second chance. We will never know, because none left a written statement or even letters. Yet we know that their actions were universal in the history of mankind. Their migration was, like all those before and after, a response to certain economic and social ills, a very human drive to leave untenable conditions, to improve their families' lives, to turn their backs on all they knew, to leave the land where their fathers were buried, and to jump off a cliff into the unknown. They shared the bravery of giving up the known for the unknown; they shared the optimism that the future can be better than the past, that lives are what one makes of them, and that their actions controlled their destiny.

Bonds of kinship and limitations of language drew our folks to seek the society of other Germans, to gather with them into small farming communities, to join with likeminded members of the Protestant faith, and to select from that small circle a marriage partner with whom they would spend the rest of their earthly days. Amazingly, our pioneer folks were all born within a small radius of 150 miles on the European continent in today's Germany, representing several different dukedoms at that time before Germany was united as a country, and all settled in an even smaller radius of ten miles on the American continent in the Danvers - Minier area of central Illinois, near Bloomington!

The nation which received them was the epitome of a free enterprise system marked by few regulations, a small federal government, an implied understanding that free men had the right to craft their own destinies, that opportunity awaited those who would apply themselves. European contemporaries of our earliest immigrant forefathers visited America in the first half of the nineteenth century and wrote their observations about what they called the American Exceptionalism. For example, Francis Grund, the seventh son of a German baron and educated in Vienna, visited, traveled extensively, and published a two-volume appraisal, "The Americans, in Their Moral, Social, and Political Relations." Highly impressed with the core high ethical level here, he wrote that the government established in America was only possible because of the high moral level of the citizens. "The American Constitution is remarkable for its simplicity but it can only suffice a people habitually correct in their actions and would be utterly inadequate to the wants of a different nation. Change the domestic habits of the Americans with their religious devotion and their high respect for morality, and it will not be necessary to change a single letter of the Constitution in order to vary the whole form of government," wrote Grund.

Grund's observations about the U.S. would not have surprised its founders. Everyone involved in the creation of the U.S. knew that its success depended on virtue, not gentility, among its citizenry. As James Madison stated at the Virginia ratifying convention: "No theoretical checks, no form of government can render us secure. To suppose that any form of government alone will secure liberty or happiness without any virtue in the people is a chimerical idea." It was chimerical because of the nearly unbridled freedom that the American Constitution allowed the citizens of the new nation. Americans were subject to criminal law, which forbade the usual crimes against person and property, and to tort law, which regulated civil disputes, but otherwise Americans faced few legal restrictions on their freedom of action and no legal obligations to their neighbors except to refrain from harming them. The guides to their behavior at any more subtle level had to come from within.

For Benjamin Franklin, this meant that "only a virtuous people are capable of freedom. As nations become more corrupt and vicious, they have more need of masters." For Patrick Henry, it seemed self-evident that "bad men cannot make good citizens. No free government, or the blessings of liberty, can be preserved to any people but by a firm adherence to justice, moderation, temperance, frugality, and virtue." George Washington, himself, wrote: "no wall of words, no mound of parchment can be formed as to stand against the seeping torrent of boundless ambition on the one side aided by the sapping current of corrupted morals on the other." As he put it in his Farewell Address: "Virtue or morality is a necessary spring of popular government." Altogether our founders recognized that if a society is to remain free, self-government demands first of all that individual citizens govern their own behavior.

For today's readers of history, the name most known among those who made epic visits to our shores and wrote down observations about early 19th C. America was Alexis de Tocqueville of France. In his "Democracy in America," he, too, mentioned first and foremost the virtues of the citizens, that "morals are far more strict there than elsewhere." And what were those virtues so essential to the Democratic Federalism type of government established here? The founding virtues were industriousness, honesty, marriage and religiosity. Some would add frugality, self-reliance, and philanthropy because they were also traits observed in the Americans.

American industriousness fascinated the rest of the world. Besides morality, this quality was consistently mentioned as exceptional here. Francis Grund made it the subject of the opening paragraph of his book: "Active occupation is not only the principal source of the Americans" happiness and the foundation of their national greatness, but they are absolutely wretched without it. It is the very soul of an American; he pursues it, not as a means of procuring for himself and his family the necessary comforts of life, but as the fountain of all human felicity."

Henry Adams noticed that industriousness affected those on the bottom of American society perhaps even more powerfully than those on the top: "Reversing the old world system, the American stimulant increased in energy as it reached the lowest and most ignorant class, dragging and whirling them upward as in the blast of a furnace. The penniless and homeless Scotch or Irish immigrant was caught and consumed by it, for every stroke of the axe and the hoe made him a capitalist and made gentlemen of his children. The instinct of activity, once created, seemed heritable and permanent in the race."

A side effect of this passion for industriousness was embarrassment at being thought a failure. In the words again of Francis Grund: "I have never known a native American to ask for charity. No country in the world has such a small number of persons supported at the public expense. An American embarrassed by his pecuniary circumstances can hardly be prevailed upon to ask or accept the assistance of his own relations and will, in many instances, scorn to have recourse to his own parents."

Honesty was of unequivocal importance to the functioning of a limited government; an assumption that people will follow the rules

STORIES MY FOLKS TOLD ME

is indispensable for making a free market work. Founder John Adams went so far as to say that our form of republicanism could not possibly work in France or the Netherlands which at the time he considered too corrupt, meaning dishonest in their dealings and lacking in basic moral principles, adding "if the common people of America lose their integrity, they will soon set up tyrants of their own." Francis Grund again: "There exists in the U.S. a universal submission to the law and a prompt obedience to the magistrates which, except for Great Britain, is not to be found in any other country."

Marriage in the U.S. was indeed seen as a different kind of union than in Europe. Here, the concept of arranged marriages was rejected; here, men courted, women accepted or refused. Tocqueville again: "If democratic nations leave a woman at liberty to choose her husband, they take care to give her mind sufficient knowledge, and her will sufficient strength, to make so important a choice. As in America paternal discipline is very relaxed and the conjugal tie very strict, a young woman does not contract the latter without considerable circumspection and apprehension. Precocious marriages are rare. Thus American women do not marry until their understandings are exercised and ripened; whereas in other countries most women generally only begin to exercise and to ripen their understandings after marriage."

To Tocquiville, the effects on American culture were profound and had largely to do with the role that American marriage gave to their women. At the end of his famous work, he wrote: "If I am asked to what the singular property and growing strength of that people ought mainly to be attributed, I should reply—to the superiority of their women."

Francis Grund agreed: "I consider the domestic virtue of the Americans as the principal source of all their other qualities. It acts as a promoter of industry as a stimulus to enterprise, and as the most powerful restrainer of public vice. It reduces life to its simplest elements, and makes happiness less dependent on precarious circumstances; it ensures the proper education of children and acts by the force of example the morals of the rising generation; in short, it does more for the preservation of peace and good order than all the laws enacted for that purpose, and it is a better guarantee for the permanency of the

American government than any written instrument, the Constitution not excepted." The American concept of marriage, where both parties were equal contributors, demanded a lot of its adherents, but it was seen as the fundamental institution of a civil society in a free nation.

The openness of American society, the welcoming of newcomers, the mixing of classes impressed Tocquiville as well: "Local freedom perpetually brings men together and forces them to help one another, in spite of the propensities which would sever them back in Europe. The more opulent citizens take great care not to stand aloof from people. On the contrary, they constantly keep on easy terms with the lower classes; they listen to them, they speak to them every day."

Although our founders were members of the Enlightenment movement they maintained that religion was essential to the health of the new nation. To a man they held that liberty is the object of the Republic, liberty requires virtue, and virtue is impossible without religion. As John Adams said: "No government can contend with human passion unbridled by morality and religion. Avarice, ambition, revenge, or gallantry, would break the strongest cords of our Constitution. It was made only for a moral and religious people and is wholly inadequate to the government of any other." Viewed today this conviction of our founders may seem exaggerated or idealistic wishful thinking, but with the Christian Bible as one of the few, often only, books in American homes, they could be confident that its teachings of humility, self-denial, forgiveness, brotherly kindness, and the golden rule, precisely what a self-governing democracy needed, would be followed.

This relationship between religiosity and limited government was observed by many visitors to America but is perhaps best summed up by Tocquiville: "Thus, while the law permits the Americans to do what they please, religion prevents them from conceiving, and forbids them to commit, what is rash or unjust. Religion in America takes no direct part in he government of society, but it must be regarded as the first of their political institutions; for if it does not impart a taste for freedom, it facilitates the use of it. Indeed, it is in this same point of view that the inhabitants of the U.S. themselves look upon religious belief. I do not know whether all Americans have a sincere faith in their religion—for who can search the human heart?—but I am certain that they hold it to be indispensable to the maintenance of republican institutions. This opinion is not peculiar to a class of citizens or to a party, but it belongs to the whole nation and to every rank of society. The Americans combine the notions of Christianity and of liberty so intimately in their minds that it is impossible to make them conceive the one without the other."

Well into the twentieth century all four of the founding virtues of industriousness, honesty, marriage, and religiosity were seen much as they were in the first fifty years of the nation's life. They were accepted as well by our folks and their children within a few years of arriving here via the many forces which acted to inculcate new citizens with the founding virtues. Foremost was the schoolhouse! There it was the standard textbook for the socialization of nineteenth century children, the McGuffey Readers series, filled with readings that touched on the founding virtues while at the same time teaching the child to read, which dominated. This belief that school was a place to instill a particular set of virtues lasted until mid-twentieth century when it came to be assumed that the American system itself would work under any circumstances as long as we got the laws right, but then the McGuffey Readers disappeared and with them some of the idea of what it meant to be a good American.

Since the government our folks met when they arrived here was a form, called federalism, in which power is constitutionally divided between a central governing authority and the states and is based on democratic rules and institutions in which the power to govern is shared between the two, they must have felt most bound to the one closest in geographical proximity, Illinois. There they found the land office to purchase property, there they payed their taxes, there they registered their births, and so on. Additionally, the primitive state of transportation and communication kept their vision fettered to the local scene.

In strict usage of the term, according to historians Will and Ariel Durant, democracy has existed only in modern times since the American and French revolutions although then still without universal suffrage. Further they write: "Democracy is the most difficult of all forms of government, since it requires the widest spread of intelligence. It gives to thought and science and enterprise the freedom essential to their operation and growth. It breaks down the walls of privilege and class and in each generation it raises up ability from every rank and place. If equality of educational opportunity can be established, democracy will be real and justified. For this is its vital truth: though men cannot be equal, their access to education and opportunity can be made more nearly equal. The rights of man are not rights to office and power but the rights of entry into every avenue that may exist and test a man's fitness for office and power. A right is a privilege to the individual yet leads to a benefit for the group as a whole."

Our folks saw that here the "equality" referenced in the Declaration of Independence: "We hold these truths to be self evident, that men are created equal, that they are endowed by their Creator with certain unalienable rights, that among these are Life, Liberty, and the Pursuit of Happiness—that to secure these rights, governments are instituted among Men, deriving their just powers from the consent of the governed," meant equality of opportunity. In the words of economists Milton and Rose Friedman's "Free to Choose:" "A society that puts equality—in the sense of equality of outcome—ahead of freedom will end up with neither equality nor freedom. The use of force to achieve equality will destroy freedom, and force, introduced for good purposes, will end up in the hands of people who use it to promote their own interests.

"On the other hand," wrote the Friedmans, "a society that puts freedom first will, as a happy by-product end up with both greater freedom and greater equality. Though a by-product, of freedom, greater equality is not an accident. A free society releases the energies and abilities of people to pursue their own objectives. It prevents some people from arbitrarily suppressing others. It does not prevent some people from achieving positions of privilege, but so long as freedom is maintained, it prevents those positions of privilege from becoming institutionalized; they are subject to continued attack from other able, ambitious people. Freedom means diversity but also mobility. It preserves the opportunity for today's disadvantaged to become tomorrow's privileged and, in the process, enables almost everyone, from top to bottom, to enjoy a fuller and richer life."

As we see, not only was the earth ready and waiting for our folks but the system of government, equally important, was ready and waiting for them as well. Drawn into this society of exceptionalism and armed with their own many virtues, our pioneers helped to convert a wilderness into a land teeming with plenty and simultaneously achieved prosperity for themselves. Theirs is a timeless story illustrating the age-old theme of wanderers who long for a better life, seize the moment, and bring their goals to fruition. They had helped to create a nation which was the envy of others where no national church prevailed, no soldiers patrolled the streets, and no inherited leader ruled their lives. Playing their part in the great human drama, we can only hope that our forefathers had the abiding satisfaction that they had dreamed big, had dared big, and had accomplished their goal!

CHAPTER 3

Generation # 2

Mary Lizetta Henrietta Buehrig Peine
—2,3—

T HE SECOND DAUGHTER born January 8, 1863, to the
Reverend Ludwig Henry and Caroline Austmann Buehrig in Peru,
Illinois, Mary grew up in a close-knit group of four sisters made even
tighter by the frequency with which the family, due to the minister's
reassignments, pulled up stakes and moved to a new locale. Brothers did
arrive in the family but later, so Mary's orientation was within the set of
four sisters all born within six years. The four little girls, Lydia, Martha,
Mary, and Anna, liked to play with their dolls but they especially
played with the real live babies who seemed to arrive every other year,
and Mama certainly encouraged that play! The little girls learned, after
many hours of effort, to sew numerous different hand stitches in order
to make the requisite sampler of their day. Knitting, crocheting, and
cooking were presumably also their skills.

Mama had grown up in a minister's home, too, so she was accustomed
to the frequent interruptions imposed on their family life by Papa's
parishioners. Recurrently he was called from the table or from family
play to pray at a sick one's bedside or with a clutch of mourners. When
Papa was asked to officiate at a wedding in the congregation, however,
the little girls were thrilled because they, caught up in the romance of
it all, were always invited. The bride of that day did not wear white but
wore instead her best gown, perhaps sewn for her for that special day, and
carried flowers of the season. Following the ceremony which included
music from the little band of flute, fiddle, and voices, there was a big
potluck supper attended by the entire congregation. Music and dancing
succeeded, including home-brewed ale and schnapps passed among the

men, a valued custom of frivolity among the German churches but not allowed by some denominations in America.

Bible study was naturally an important occupation in the Buehrig home. From toddler age and on, the little girls were taught to recite verses not only to Papa but to friends who called. Farmer friends especially teared-up when little Mary spoke Genesis 8.22: "As long as the earth lasts, seed-time and harvest, cold and heat, summer and winter, and day and night shall not cease." Of course, the lingua franca of the home was German, and all Papa's parishioners were German speaking.

Yes, it was a pious home life, and the children had to be models of behavior for not only were Mama and Papa observing them but the whole congregation was watching what they wore, what and how they were speaking, who they were seen with, and on and on. It was tiresome to be trying so hard to be good all the time and then to hear that some gossip in the church had told Papa a total fabrication about the activities of one of his daughters. Manners, which emphasized that children were to be seen but not heard, were stressed in that day, but then as now were not easy to perform.

Because her father's occupation was minister of Evangelical Lutheran Church of the Gospel, Mary grew up in a village or town and knew farm life only when she visited her grandparents on her father's side who farmed near Ft. Madison, Iowa, or her school friends who lived out in the country. Her mother's father was also a minister, the Reverend Louis Austmann, who with his wife lived in Peru, Illinois, which too was not a farm experience.

Town life in the 1860s and 1870s, though not comprising the number of people engaged in farming, was increasing as a percentage of the United States population. As late as 1880, forty-nine percent of those gainfully employed were working in agriculture, but the second industrial revolution was in full sway and ensured employment to a growing number of workers who lived in towns. The typewriter and treadle sewing machine date from this period as do the safety pin, rayon fabric, pasteurization, the internal combustion engine, dynamite, impressionistic art, Mendel's work on genetics, and Mendeleev's periodic table of elements.

Schooling in town was lengthier and more extensive than its country counterpart. Farm children simply needed to be free to work with their parents in the fields. Town girls, like Mary and her sisters, were taught by more experienced and knowledgeable teachers, not by very young girls who were straight out of school themselves. Their teachers had precious instruments such as maps, even globes, quill pens and ink, paper, and enchantingly fascinating books. Mary loved school and was known to be an eager learner.

Women's work in the home, however, was still a daily grind of drudge chores whether she lived on a farm or in a town. Year in and year out, her toil at the washtub, the wood-burning iron cook stove, the copper water heater, the hand sewing, and the broom precluded much leisurely time for books, writing, or music. This was especially true in the large Buehrig family which eventually grew to nine children whose care and nurturing fell in large extent to the four older girls. To them this was normal, of course, and they had no idea of diversions such as telephone or television. For them, excitement came in the form of a horse and buggy which Papa kept at the town stable, but just occasionally on a pretty spring day squired Mama and a couple of the children through the streets and out to the countryside. There was not room in the vehicle for all the family!

The Reverend Buehrig's church assignments caused the family to live in an unusually great, for the times, number of towns: Okawville, Illinois, southeast of St. Louis in 1860; Sandwich, Illinois in 1861--3; Hollowayville, Illinois in 1866--9; Ft. Madison, Iowa in 1870--74; 1320 North Second Street in Minneapolis, Minnesota, in 1874--8; and Fond du Lac, Wisconsin in 1879 until his death in 1897. Presumably this peripatetic existence away from extended family, yet within the bonds of the German immigrant society, where deep roots were not permitted to form was mitigated by a feeling of tight family cohesion. Instead of long-held friendships or cousins and grandparents living nearby, Mary knew the intimate attachment to Lydia, Martha, and Anna with whom her sisterly life was intertwined always. In marriage, Lydia joined William

Bekemeier and lived in Peru, Illinois; Martha joined a pastor Simon Hoffmeister and lived in Minneapolis, Minnesota; and Anna joined a pastor Franz Beshold and lived in Belleville, Illinois. While face to face visits were seldom and the telephone not yet common, the sisters were faithful letter writers for all their lives long. For emergencies there was the telegraph invented in 1850 and a hub in every village thereafter.

Since ancient times the winds blew, unimpeded by mountains or trees, over the vast prairies of America's mid-section. Towns such as those where the Buehrigs lived had actually been laid out based on the direction of those prevailing winds. It was a crucial fact that the winds crossed Illinois from west to southwest making the upwind or western lots, located ahead of the stink of butchering or the great number of horses and mules which also inhabited the town, more desirable. The owners of the finest homes naturally wished to situate themselves on those upwind lots and usually succeeded. Dwellings in those days were constructed of wood an easy target for the devastating fires which were fanned by the wind to a downwind direction. Thus by building their homes in the upwind direction, citizens were spared the general conflagration. In the same way the winds drove the dust storms, which were frequently whipped up on the dirt streets, drove the smoke from the heating of wood and coal which blanketed the town, and drove the mosquitoes and flies which swarmed around the draft animals, downwind.

Knowledge about diseases in that day was imperfect, yet people sensed it was wise to live upwind from the garbage, offal, smoke, or stagnant water. Farmers, too, understood this principle of prevailing winds, built their house upwind from the noisy smelly barnyard, hen house, and pigpen and rarely put the barnyard north of the house. The absence of projections on the rolling prairies enabled the winds to travel long distances and gain quite a velocity before meeting the western edge of a town or the windbreak of trees which the farmer ineluctably planted on the west side of his house.

Mary was a well educated young woman for the day. After graduation from primary school in Fond du Lac, Wisconsin, where her family was then living, she had studied the classics at a Women's Seminary in Keokuk, Iowa. Though the name, seminary, implies a school for training clergy or ministers, in those days at the end of the 19th century it was a school of higher learning for women comprising high school and junior college. No doubt it was the suggestion of her grandparents who farmed just outside nearby Ft. Madison which brought the outstanding student, Mary, to further her education near them.

Mary Buehrig at the time of her graduation from the Women's Seminary of Keokuk, Iowa

Those seminaries for young ladies reflect the desire in the small towns of the Middle West to cultivate the minds and tastes of their young women. It also was an indication of the general importance at the time of self improvement efforts. Because of their much needed contributions to the immigration process, American women had long been valued and appreciated in ways not seen back in Germany. Here, they enjoyed a level of independence and elevated status because they had earned it! Far from harming the development of their best qualities, education actually contributed to their allure and formed a confidence in their own strength and maturity of intelligence, making them responsible to their own conscience, alone. They then entered marriage fortified by practical knowledge which prepared them for the realities of life. This self-confidence which education gave Mary was also projected on the subsequent generations of women in the family.

During those two years Hennig and Caroline Buehrig with their granddaughter, Mary, endeavored to catch up some of the years lost when distance had separated them. While she was then often in the company of her Buehrig grandparents, Mary continually heard the praises sung of their daughter and her aunt, Caroline, who had gone off to Minier, Illinois, with her husband Henry Peine. Oh, how they missed their baby Caroline and oh, how Mary would love her if she could only know her better. Perhaps it was Caroline, herself, who put the bug in her young brother-in-law's ear, but it wasn't long after Mary graduated that George Edward Peine of Minier paid a call on the Buehrig family and fell head over heels in love with pretty Mary. On January 3, 1883, George and Mary were married in Fond du Lac at a church wedding presided upon by the bride's father and attended by three glowing bridesmaids, Lydia, Martha, and Anna.

Wedding portrait of Mary Buehrig to George Peine

By just two years prior to that time the decision to sell out in Iowa and move to Minier had been made by the senior Buehrigs and their sons, so when the bride, Mary, moved to Minier, her heart swelled to have a ready-made extended family awaiting her. Right in the village, there were her grandparents Caroline and Hennig Buehrig plus her aunts and uncles: Caroline and Henry Peine, Caroline and Fred Buehrig, Rosina and Charles Buehrig, and Molly and William Buehrig. Of course, between them all, they had many children, now young adults like Mary, who were also living in Minier and eager to welcome her. For the first time in her life, she was surrounded by an extensive set of relatives and she just knew that she, like them, would put down deep roots in Minier. German was still the predominant language among these folks but the second generation members were, like Mary, completely bi-lingual.

Generation #2—George Edward Peine
—1—

George Edward Peine, the youngest child of Stephen and Margaret Davin Peine was born on the family farm located five and a half miles southwest of Minier on May 2, 1856. It was exactly one year before Charles Darwin published his "Origin of the Species." His parents and older brother and sister, Mary and Henry, were born back in Hofgeismar, state of Hesse-Kassel in Germany, but siblings Sophina, Hettie, and Stephen were also born in the New World. When George was only two years old, the young mother of those six small children perished, presumably in childbirth, forcing the oldest daughter, Mary, to grow up quickly and fill the shoes of her lost mother. It was all a devastating situation which happened before little George grew to consciousness, so the only mother he knew as he grew up was his older sister. All the extended family which might have been expected to assist in the motherless home were back in Hofgeismar, thousands of miles away, so Stephen and his children managed as best they could although there were no prepared meals to purchase and few ready-made clothes available.

Little George, himself, born so tiny that his head fit in a teacup, had a sickly childhood given to an allergic reaction to farmyard chaff, weeds, and dust which caused his eyes to redden, nose to run, and his whole

STORIES MY FOLKS TOLD ME

body to erupt in sneezing. He also suffered from the family choking reflex. Though never resulting in choking to death, it did scare witnesses "nearly to death!" As the baby of the family he was petted and treated very affectionately by his older siblings and spared some of the heavier chores on the farm, ministrations which must have succeeded because George lived to celebrate his eighty-fourth birthday!

Certain events stood out from the routine of his daily life, were remembered, and related by George to his own children. In 1865, his father took him on horseback to Minier, a nearby village, to view the passing of President Abraham Lincoln's funeral train. This was the famous funeral cortege which traveled from Washington D.C. to Springfield, IL, for burial there. At each stop, in its slow wandering progress, through Harrisburg, Trenton, Jersey City, Albany, Syracuse, Buffalo, Cleveland, Columbus, Indianapolis, Chicago and many lesser places, there was an astonishing turnout of mourners. People waited through the night in some places crowding along the tracks in reverent silence. It was near the end of April 1865 that the black-draped railroad car, continuing its stately pace, passed before little George's eyes. Not only was the Peine family in mourning over their mother Margaret's death, but the entire country was mourning one million fallen young soldiers of the Civil War and now their commander-in-chief as well.

All his long life George felt a kinship with Abraham Lincoln just as all Illinois folks of the day did—even the German immigrants! His presence was referred to often, his life story was invoked as a model of behavior, his virtues were proclaimed in the church and home, and he was quoted prodigiously by school children and adults alike. For instance, there was the story of young Abe, clerking in a store in New Salem, who mistakenly shortchanged an old woman two pennies, discovered the error, and walked two miles that evening to her home to return her money. A song beloved by Abe Lincoln was "Home Sweet Home," so it quickly became the favorite of all Illinois folk.

Though only Henry, oldest of the Peine brothers, served in the Civil War, all Americans were touched by the fearful possibility that the country would be torn into two entities. More than a quarter of a million men, largely unequipped and untrained, answered the call to fight for the Union led by Abe Lincoln. There were nearly thirty-five thousand casualties, two-thirds of those not from gunshot but from the deplorable standards of medicine and sanitation of the day! Many Illinois soldiers, who enlisted in numbers far exceeding the quota, fought in the first major union victory against the confederates at Belson and Fort Donelson, but they were also involved at Vicksburg, Atlanta, and the siege of Richmond.

In his youth, one of George's favorite pleasures was to walk out to watch the construction of two railroad lines into Tazewell County with stops in Minier. The Illinois Central Railroad, as it progressed from Cairo to Decatur to Bloomington to the Illinois River and the end of the Illinois-Michigan Canal and finally to Galena, included Minier on its route. Another line joined Warsaw on the Mississippi River to Peoria to Bloomington to Mackinaw with a fork to Pekin and Mackinaw. Additionally, the C and A Railroad, a branch of the Chicago, Alton, and St. Louis line stopped in Minier. These were not stray lines going to unrelated places but were well-planned and formed a true network. The building of the railroads across America was at the center of the Industrial Revolution, and at the same time it was the means whereby the people mastered a giant continent, making possible America's rise to world prominence.

Looking back to those times, it is impossible to exaggerate the impact of the locomotive on society whether on the farm or in cities and town! Rails could serve communities which were not located on waterways which were the original highways, could operate in all kinds of weather and seasons, were relatively inexpensive, comfortable, fast and safe and pretty much spelled the end of the stagecoach and wagon travel. When underway, a steam engine train could travel seventy miles an hour which was a huge advance over the horse! Soon, a trip from New York to Chicago, which in 1830 took three weeks, in 1850 took two days! Trains could speed thirty to forty miles per hour while stagecoach at best achieved six miles per hour. In George's boyhood, Illinois, though the fourth most populous state, had the second most tracks of all the states—2800 miles—and Illinois coal fired the locomotives as it superseded the wood-fired steam engines.

The ride might be slow by today's standards, bumpy, noisy, and dusty but it was about the most exciting thing there was to do in the 1860s! Just walking into the depot or station house was to enter an atmosphere charged with drama and excitement. A shrill whistle announced the approach of the locomotive; smoking, hissing, clanking accompanied its braking; an "all aboard" was called out by the conductor in a long drawn-out tone; lucky travelers scrambled up the steps to look for their seats aboard the magical conveyance; wisps of smoke and steam whipped past the window as they took the first curve. They were really on their way and the mere act of leaving was a high point of the trip! Folks wore their Sunday best to board the train, talked about it for weeks before and after the trip, and described the experience like being carried away by the wind!

To folks who had only known one horse power, it was immensely fascinating to look out the window, to see the landscape, people on the ground looking as if they weren't moving at all, houses, whole towns, and animals—all whisking past before their amazed eyes. Young George, as he stood in the field and looked, had never, ever seen anything move as fast as a train so he too looked at the passing train with amazement. Lying in bed at night out on the farm, the boy would hear the mournful whistle of the train out there, somewhere, and know that other folks were on their way, traveling to some far away destination, fulfilling the romantic notion of moving far off; just that sound carried through the air made him feel less lonely, more connected to the larger world.

In the beginning, young George heard some pretty grizzly stories of death by speeding train which happened to livestock, even children, hit while meandering along the track or by the scalding of passengers from an overheated steam engine. But perhaps the worst death came to the towns which were by-passed by the railroads. Crippled, they sent delegations to the railroad company offices to try to sway officials with bribes of free right of way and guaranteed profits if they would only include their town on the track trail.

Even the cost of postage, so important to people living isolated lives in Illinois far from their origins, was lowered by train travel. Early in the century when a laborer earned sixty to seventy-five cents a day, postage for a letter to travel four hundred miles cost twenty five cents. After the mails relied on the rails, the cost of a letter to travel three thousand miles was three cents! Minier got its first post office in 1866 actually just a room in someone's home, later in a store, and finally in 1893 in its own building. RFD, rural free delivery, didn't begin until 1900. Newspapers, too, traveled the rails resulting in increased subscriptions. Every day until he died on the job in 1954, Bully Glauser, the village mentally-challenged man, transported the mail to the train depot from the post office and vice versa in his hand cart.

As train travel grew safer and less expensive the reliance on horses, carts, and wagons for long distance treks was diminished. Fewer rural folk by the 1850s walked from farm to village or rode three or four children on one horse. The farmer still moved his cargo to town by wagon and on a Saturday evening would take the whole family to town to trade and talk. But to really transport his crops to market in central Illinois, his first choice was by rail car.

With the railroads, the use of ice to prolong the life of fresh foods was introduced. Suddenly it was possible to transport meat and other perishables over long distances to consumers far away. Chicago became the epicenter of the railroad industry in part because it could generate and keep huge quantities of ice from Lake Michigan. There it was created naturally at no cost to the producer, was clean, renewable, and infinite in supply. It had to be cut on site, lifted, and conveyed to a storehouse where covered with an insulation of hay or sawdust it lasted the year. Before ice, in hot weather, milk could be kept for only an hour or two before it began to spoil; chicken had to be eaten on the day of plucking; and fresh meat was seldom safe for more than a day.

Schooling for George consisted of the country Hicks school and later in the town of Minier at the public school there. In 1851, the first high school in the state was established at Jacksonville, cost-free, and open to women and men. By 1855, the Illinois legislature gave every child in the state the right to a publicly financed education, no more requiring parents to employ a teacher for their children. A flurry of colleges, just in time to benefit our folks, were organized as well: twenty-five during the 1850s and business colleges like Browns Business School in

Bloomington. As soon as he finished his education, though, George moved away from the farm and into town for his allergies were making his life out among so many allergens quite miserable. For three years he clerked in Champaign County at various stores like John Leise's. Then as his older brothers were doing quite well as merchants in Minier and invited him to join in the business, he happily moved back there. A quick learner and avid businessman, young George was asked the following year 1882, at the exit from the business of brother-in-law William Buehrig, to join his older brother Henry in partnership of the general store. Honored and ecstatic, young George accepted and plunged into a career which lasted fifty-nine years; and like a bird soaring aloft, he was in his element the entire time. The name of the enterprise changed from Peine and Buehrig's Store to H.A. Peine and Company.

The H.A. Peine and Company store quickly filled a need in the village and thrived until the mid twentieth century due to its reputation for quality and expert management. Henry and George established a unique reputation and made their motto, "The Old Reliable," a real and profitable asset.

Together the two brothers operated the only dry goods store in Minier, Illinois. Their business acumen, combined with an expert eye for what the public wanted in style and quality, brought them a reputation for good service, fair price, and for them, personally, prosperity. A mercantile business selling fabric, clothing and notions, carpets, even shoes but no hardware nor foodstuffs, the Peine store was a sturdy brick building in a combination of Greek revival and Italianate architecture at the corner of Central and Main Streets in downtown—or as they said in Minier, "uptown."

In those days, the store owner was most often on the floor to give his customers a kindly welcome, shaking hands with many of them, and asking them all after their families whom he well knew, before proceeding to the business of sales.

Back, past the textiles and the cigar and candy counters, was the shoe, boot, and men's suit department where one or the other of the brothers could be found presiding. When not measuring a customer's dimensions, he was generally perched on a stool behind the counter figuring discounts, correcting prices and pouring over catalogues left by the traveling salesmen from Chicago or St. Louis. It was also where folks gathered to discuss politics, weather, and the price of corn and hogs. A business office where account books were kept, a small safe, and two desks occupied a small space located up front by the door to the street and was enclosed by glass, offering a view to the sales floor to the brothers when seated. Business was strictly cash in that day before checking accounts, debit or credit cards, though the occasional barter transaction did occur.

The first counters to meet the eye of shoppers in 1883 Minier, were naturally consumed by shelves and shelves of fabric and sewing notions, quilting tools, yarns and embroidery floss, ribbons, a sampling of ready to wear women's dresses and children's clothing, a millinery department, stockings, intimates, sun bonnets, straw hats and overalls, and all things to attract the principal shopper of that day and ours—women and girls.

Household items were not the purview of the Peine brothers but were sold nearby at the version of today's hardware store. Most all household utensils of their day were made of wood. Solid hardwood was used for butter molds, butter paddles, rolling pins, kraut cutters to slice cabbage for sauerkraut, bread boards, clothespins, bowls, seats for the outhouse, and dozens of other items necessary for efficient housekeeping. But the Peines were a mercantile enterprise; they sold fabrics and ready made clothing, called dry goods.

The Union of Two Second-Generation Families Peine and Buehrig
—2—and—3—

Intermarriage between households strengthened early American society, cemented the German communities into more compact bodies, provided greater cohesion and contentment to its members, preserved and continued attitudes of religion, language, and values established in the Old Country. Such was that of the Peine and Buehrig family's conjugal union on January 3, 1883. Just one year after establishing himself in the mercantile business with his brother, George married Mary Buehrig of Fond du Lac, Wisconsin, and brought her to live in a small house at 209 N. Minier St. in Minier, Illinois.There they raised their two children, Adela, born January 14, 1884, and Paul, born August 16, 1885. Cyril Henry, born August 13, 1901, lived only three months.

Minier, in the late 1800s was a community which provided services for the primary industry of farming which surrounded it. The history of the village dates back to the 1867 founding by George W. Minier. "Father Minier," as he was affectionately known, was a prominent educator, land surveyor, farmer, ordained minister of the Christian Church, a president of the State Horticultural Society, a vice-president of the State Agricultural Society, and a president of the North American Forestry Association.

He was a friend of Abraham Lincoln and Stephen A Douglas and was nominated to the United States Congress. The land which is today the village of Minier, he received as barter payment for surveying services rendered to the Illinois Central Railroad. In 1867, George Minier founded the village and named it after himself. Shortly afterward, the sale of lots began which were purchased primarily by people from the surrounding farmsteads while newcomers from Ohio and Pennsylvania also appear on the early lot titles. Growth, though rapid, peaked at around 700 citizens, yet innovations such as its own newspaper in 1875, the telephone in 1883, and electric light in 1899, came as quickly as possible.

Competition between villages like Minier and its neighbors for designation of county seat of Tazewell County was probably robust early on, but Pekin won that rank, guaranteeing it growth and influence through the jobs of county clerk, sheriff, judge, assessor, jailer, bailiff, and county treasurer. Its court attracted lawyers, realtors, surveyors, merchants, and builder of the court house which further required a hotel, tavern, restaurants, stores, newspaper to publish government notices or official information and, of course, the best roads, bridges, and town amenities graced the county seat. All that was not to be the destiny of Minier, but it was no stagnant backwater either. Social cohesion prevailed within its borders where newcomers tended to be of German heritage, where without fanfare neighbors helped neighbors, crime stayed nonexistent, civic leaders served voluntarily, a good school was built, and village services were provided.

There, George and Mary led sound, sober lives in the community and served in leadership roles in town and church in an age when social improvements were emphasized, a variety of societies were formed, and women like Mary began to achieve purpose outside of the home. Ralph Waldo Emerson's admonition to "Hitch your wagon to a star!" really resounded with the folks of that day! Self-improvement was a new concept whose time had come to mid-America. Clubs and organizations were formed, like-minded folks gathered together in discussion groups, made their own entertainment, and followed current events. In his "Democracy in America," Tocqueville marveled at the way Americans preferred voluntary association to government regulation: "The inhabitant of the United States has only a defiant and restive regard for social authority and he appeals to it only when he cannot do without it." Unlike Frenchmen, he continued, who instinctively looked to the state to provide economic and social order, Americans relied on their own efforts. "In the United States, they associate for the goals of public security, of commerce and industry, of morality and religion. There is nothing the human will despairs of attaining by the free action of the collective power of individuals."

What especially amazed Tocqueville was the sheer range of non-governmental organizations the Americans formed: "Not only do they have commercial and industrial associations, but they also have a thousand other kinds: religious, moral, grave, futile very general and very particular, immense and very small. Americans use associations to give fetes, to found seminaries, to build inns, to raise churches, to distribute books to send missionaries to the antipodes; in this manner they create hospitals, prisons, schools."

Lecturers regaled listeners at the village "opera house" on practical, cultural, or moral topics. Though Barnum and Bailey didn't bother with villages like Minier, smaller circuses did pitch their tent in a nearby field to the immense joy of its citizens. Traveling zoos would occasionally pass their way as well charging two bits or twenty-five cents to see an elephant, two camels, a lion, and a Bengal tiger.

STORIES MY FOLKS TOLD ME

It is likely that Mary and George knew a bit of the music of their contemporaries back in Germany—Johannes Brahms, Franz Schubert and Frederick Chopin—even though they lived in the day before radio or recorded music. For sure, they knew the songs of the beloved American Stephen Foster and could sing along with their friends the words to "Oh! Susanna," "Camp Town Races," or "There's A Good Time Coming." Probably they had heard of the actress Sarah Bernhardt, the Swedish Nightingale Jenny Lind, and her contemporary the Italian soprano Adelina Patti, all of whom performed widely in the United States in their day, though it is not known for sure that they actually were able to attend a concert of that caliber.

The fiction of Sir Walter Scott, Louisa May Alcott, James Fenimore Cooper probably lined their bookshelves as did the poets Longfellow, Thoreau, and Emerson. German writers, Lessing, Schiller, and Goethe were perhaps on their bookshelf for George and Mary were fluent in German and much of their education had been in that language. It is certain, though, that the Bible was a favorite tome drawn from the shelf to entertain and enlighten the family evenings 'round the reading table!

At the Peine home, the Chicago Tribune was delivered once a week and the Daily Pantograph, in existence since 1837, each day. The Minier News, first issued in September of 1875, was delivered every Saturday to the Peine home, for curious folks of that day, before radio, relied heavily on newspapers for information. Books filled shelves, friends were invited to tea, supper parties were hosted, and good conversations were valued.

The Lyceum, lectures by local luminaries or traveling spellbinders, was the best example of that category known to the likes of the Peines. Ralph Waldo Emerson, a prominent intellectual of the day, lectured to hundreds of lyceums during his long career. Though he may not have traveled as far west or to a village as small as Minier to lecture, his ideas of self-reliance, individuality, and the possibility of humankind to achieve almost anything were surely read and incorporated into their personal philosophy. American gregariousness showed itself in a variety of social pleasures which were allowed to find expression now that every waking moment of one's day was not engaged in mind-dulling drudge labor. Parties, picnics, church festivals, holiday celebrations, as well as impromptu gatherings in the parlor or on the front porch were guiltlessly embraced by folks like Mary and George Peine.

Yes, those people took to heart the admonition of Mark Twain: "Twenty years from now you will be more disappointed by the things that you didn't do than by the ones you did do. So throw off the bowlines. Sail away from the safe harbor. Catch the trade winds in your sails. Explore. Dream. Discover!" Ever employing the metaphors he learned working on the Mississippi River, Twain captured the spirit of the Peines' day.

In her new role as wife, Mary knew well how to cook on the wood-burning stove whether baking, boiling, stewing, or roasting. An iron skillet served to fricassee a chicken and an iron pot to boil corned beef and cabbage while she, with the help of a farm girl employed by the day, canned George's vegetable harvest and fruits in the newly available glass Mason jars. Kerosene oil had replaced flickering candles by then and gave a brilliant but soft light to their evenings. Soon after their wedding she and George poured over a salesman's catalogue which he brought home from the store to choose their modern new pieces of furniture. Eastlake was the style made of beautiful Illinois Walnut, inlaid with a little Birdseye Maple, and carved to the specifications of the mode. Their bedroom set is still in the hands of descendants as are the dining room chairs though the latter are divided among many. Mary delivered her three babies in that bed.

One particular piece of furniture, part of the bedroom set, was the commode. Also of walnut, it had two drawers on one side and a door on the facing side in which the chamber pot was stored for nature's call during the night. On top of the commode sat the large bowl and pitcher of water where Mary and George washed themselves and their teeth morning and night. A pump just outside the back door of the house supplied their water needs, but of course there was a lot of conveying involved in their daily lives. Every backyard, theirs included, had an outhouse, often more that one hole with newspaper or Sears catalogue pages at hand. Sociability trumped privacy in some families especially the really big ones.

Also acquired through the Peine store was the beautiful Haviland Limoges china, the Wedding Band pattern, chosen by Mary. She purchased the dinner set and slowly but surely added more and more pieces. It was her pride and joy as it is today the pride of her descendants. Yes, Mary loved her "things!" What would Papa think? Was this a sin? Another prized possession of Mary was the black Mantilla shawl of very fine lace, brought home from the store one day to her surprise and joy, from Spain via a traveling salesman. No longer in family possession, unfortunately.

The warm meal of the day was served at noon in those days. Promptly at twelve noon, a whistle would blow from the train station so that everyone in the settlement would know mid-day had arrived; work tools were laid down, hats were donned, and the toilers would proceed to walk home where splendid aromas would greet them even before the front threshold was crossed.

Though a devoted wife and mother, Mary never felt totally confined to the domestic sphere as most women of her generation were. She was an educated woman and felt this distinction. She held strong opinions of her own, took an active philanthropic role in her community, and contributed many helpful suggestions to her merchant husband which bore fruit in his mercantile establishment. She had seen other women cowed by their fathers or husbands. Still, she would say "marriage," when asked: "What is the natural role for women?" or "What is a girl's education for?" She was probably not so much in conflict, as women were later, between female independence and womanly subservience, for although this duality is experienced by each generation of women, in her day society decreed stronger role definition. Women knew what was expected of them, and they knew exactly where the barriers were. Not of a temperament to have defied the mores of the day, Mary would have resorted to a reply: "So it is," when faced with inner conflict. All else was yet unknown.

One thing was certain in Mary's mind: she did not want to have a baby every other year as her Mama had done. Why her baby brother, Herbert Dan, was born just a half year before she and George were married! No, Mary wanted just a few children on whose education and development she could devote herself fully. Her mama had been far too busy with the new babies and helping Papa with the church to have any time for herself or time to spend focused on one child at a time. Mary took her teachers at the Seminary as a model for the modern woman of self-confidence and accomplishment which she wished to emulate.

When the German Evangelical St. John's Church of Minier (now Church of Christ) embarked on a building campaign in 1907, Mary served on the finance committee, and though it could not have beens easy to ask parishioners to contribute money to build a new church, she did it. In one instance, a farmer nearly ran her off his property when she paid him a formal appeals call in her horse and buggy. Hearing this, George was so incensed that he immediately saddled up and tore out in a fury to accost the man shouting: "Why did you treat my wife that way? She wasn't asking for the money for herself!" The beautiful red brick church with its Art Deco glass windows donated by individual members was built at a cost of $15,360 debt free, and Mary Peine's name can be seen today inscribed on the foundation stone. George, too, is inscribed on the stone as a member of the building committee.

As the wife of the chief merchant of the village, Mary was glad to drape his wares on her back as a subtle form of advertising. In 1890 the fashion was still long dresses, tailored from yards of fabric, with gigot or leg-of-mutton sleeves characterized by a very large puff on the upper arm but close-fitting on the forearm. In summer the fabric would be lightweight cotton; in winter, taffeta or broadcloth and always a hat complemented the dress. A dressmaker and a hat maker were also at her service. Men's attire also consisted of a hat but with a narrow brim; suit and tie were derigguere along with polished leather shoes or boots. One thing Victorian women didn't have were brassieres. Corsets pushed up from below, which held breasts in place, but for true comfort some women concocted slings to hold them up. As always in fashion, comfort had to withdraw to the demands of, in Mary's case, the hourglass figure.

Eventually George bought himself a "Morris" chair in the arts and crafts style of the day with its brown leather seat and back, prominently grained oak arms, a button to recline the back, and a pull out cushion to rest his feet. He was the picture of a true gentleman in his recliner, which by the way is also still in the family. Perhaps this is the proper place to mention as well that George walked up town to the barber shop each morning to be shaved and have his mustache trimmed. Like many men of his day who lived a comfortable life, George enjoyed a good cigar from time to time. He owned a humidor in the shape of an Arab sheikh with a receptacle inside for a damp sponge to maintain the correct humidity, still in family possession.

Behind the Peine home was vegetable and flower garden tended by George who had learned about growing requirements on the farm and enjoyed working in the soil. There was no stable behind the house because he preferred to rent a horse and buggy at the village stable a couple of blocks away--he and Mary just naturally walked wherever they went in Minier—but there was an outhouse in those days before indoor plumbing. Some of their neighbors did have a small barn back of the house, though, just large enough to shelter a horse or cow with room for a buggy and a tiny loft for the hay. Most of the yard was taken up by George's garden; there was grass but the idea of a lush green lawn had not yet been conceived. No one owned a lawn mower; when grass grew too high, a goat was hired to chew it down or George would take a scythe to it.

"God Almightie first planted a Garden," said Lord Bacon. "And indeed it is the Greatest Refreshment to the Spirits of Man." George agreed. Though he toiled in his garden to feed his family, he also found profound satisfaction there. The very simple, ageless tools: iron fork, shovel, spade, hoe, and rake served him well when in the spring, he first augmented the soil with the dark, velvet-smooth, scentless barn manure, then broke the clods with the hoe, worked the soil finer with the fork, combed out every stick or stone or straw or lump till the earth was as fine as meal, and finally raked all smooth and level with the rake. Only then was the soil ready for the sowing of his seeds. Clover, mallow, and innumerable weeds throve right along with his beans, peppers, tomatoes, and pumpkins so a daily pass was necessary to yank them out by hand in that time before herbicides and pesticides. George acknowledged those demands of the job and took it as a quiet time of solitude between the commotion of life at the store and the enjoyment of Mary's supper, family time, and reading before bed.

In time, the village citizens were ready to establish a bank. George was a founder, lifelong member of the board, and director of the Farmers' State Bank in Minier. Additionally in the spirit of community service, he served several terms on the Minier School Board, the village board where he served as treasurer, and a number of political and business organizations.

When Mary and George began housekeeping there were already ten street lights placed on the principle corners of the business district in Minier. They burned gasoline and later kerosene; occasionally one would explode though not very shocking to residents accustomed to frequent fires of all kinds in that day before electricity. Sidewalks were boardwalks which during the rainy season would often float on puddles of water and had to be constantly reassembled. By the late 1890s brick and stone walks were installed in the business district and finally concrete sidewalks were installed in the early 1900s.

The streets which Mary and George knew were of dirt, kept level and smooth with graders and drags pulled behind a team of horses, a quagmire of mud when it rained or when snow and ice melted, and a source of airborne dust during the hot dry summer months. Women wore paper boots and carried their good shoes when negotiating those wet or dusty streets. By 1913, the village fathers arranged to have the dirt street coated with oil each summer and did so until after 1949 when the first blacktop was laid. For the first few days the oil made the streets a slippery mess but in time it soaked into the dirt and kept the mud and dust down. Lovely shade trees of chestnut and elm, long gone now, then lined the streets of Minier increasing the pride residents felt for their village. The special Illinois soil existed in the village as well as in the surrounding fields!

A fixture of the village was the livery stable which consisted of a barn for the carriages as well as the hay and straw, a harness room, horse stables, and a Barn Man's room. Without an automobile, townspeople needed a place to board their only conveyance—their horse and buggy. The village stable was usually just a short walk from any house in Minier and, like the telegraph office or post office, became a hub where men congregated in their free time. Of course, there were no restaurants, no movie theater, no fast food shops.

Another conveyance, rather newly invented, was the bicycle. It was all the rage throughout the United States in the 1890s and had become a major pastime when the Peines were a young couple. Bicycles were everywhere—on village streets and country lanes, piloted by women in bloomers and men with droopy mustaches. They were the high tech harbinger of modernity, mobility, and sleekness! How George and Mary loved to ride with friends out to the countryside with picnic baskets tied over the handlebars. No Lycra skin-tight, moisture-wicking fabric bodysuits for those fashionable bikers, though. They wore the same suit-tie-hat combo and voluminous dresses that they wore every other day, suffering rivulets of perspiration to flow through every layer of their modish attire. Likely, a rest beside a cool flowing creek was on the itinerary. Handkerchiefs were dipped in before passing over a sweaty face and neck, and perhaps even bare toes and ankles were exposed and dipped in!

As time went by, as their children arrived and George's business took off, Mary and George began to realize that they had become pretty typical Americans. They still spoke German to their parents, in church and on many social occasions, but they felt highly patriotic as Americans; they understood and endorsed the American form of democracy which disdained class distinctions; they were materialists yet philanthropic; they were religious; they read the transcendentalist philosophers, the new poetry and novels of American authors such as Emerson, Whittier, Kipling, Longfellow, Alcott, Cooper, and Twain. Through newspapers and traveling lecturers, they felt part of the wider American society, and they just knew that it was a wonderful thing to be an American!

Adela and Paul were a constant joy to Mary and George. Both were excellent students, spoke both English and German; Paul showed signs of musical talent, was given piano lessons, and spent all his life in transport of that solitary delight. They recognized that Adela was the more out-going leader of the twosome or of any group she joined, for that matter. She had a certain self-confidence, lots of ambition, and the pluck to turn events to her liking. Besides, she was lots of fun and everyone wanted to be in her company!

George, Adela, Paul, and Mary Peine

The world of George and Mary was still very confined to the village, of course. The newspaper brought news of the outside world but there was still no radio to report minute by minute news. Horse power, their mode of transportation, did not allow for far journeys. If they did wish to travel by railroad, hotels were limited, so they stayed with Mary's parents or sisters as those visits were the only reason for them to travel. Mary corresponded with some of her girlfriends from the seminary, but essentially their lives were insular and tied to the world of Minier. Because life in a tiny cosmos could exaggerate the idiosyncrasies of its members, disagreements which in a larger sphere could find vent, sometimes found expression in family feuds. This, by following the principles of their faith, the Peines stalwartly sought to avoid.

One day George read in the newspaper that the Columbian Exhibition of 1893, commemorating the 400th anniversary of the arrival of Christopher Columbus to the New World in 1492, was finally about to open in Chicago. It had been postponed a year due to rainy weather delaying construction of the fabulous, though temporary, buildings, but now it was about ready and looked mighty appealing. Salesmen from Chicago who came to his store were excitedly describing all that was to be seen at the "White City," the enormous park-like setting beside Lake Michigan. Like a world's fair, all the new inventions pertaining to manufacturing, agriculture, the arts, or the home were to be on display. Why, there was even one of those "new fangled" automobiles! Among the multitude of attractions were pavilions to showcase the wares of forty-six countries, electric street lights and even indoor electric lighting, carnival rides with the world's first Ferris Wheel, a new-fangled moving walkway, first moving pictures, a stunning chapel which made the reputation of L.C. Tiffany, an automatic dishwasher, the first manure spreader, beautiful murals painted by known artists such as Mary Cassat, concerts by world-class composers like Anton Dvorzak, and a slide fastener which was the forerunner to the zipper.

For sure, George and Mary would attend as were some of their relatives. Alas, ten-year-old Adela begged and begged and generally promised half her life away if they would only allow her to go along, so of course since they only had a manageable clutch of two children they took Adela and Paul with them to Chicago. They traveled by train the entire way from their village which took most of one day. It was the farthest they had ever been from home, so they excitedly took a seat in the chair car, looked out the window, and exclaimed at all that passed by their eyes. Mostly they saw land under cultivation with board houses and red barns sprinkled over the vastness of the prairie and every so often some towns dotted the landscape where the train stopped to let passengers on or off. They shared a lunch from Mama's basket and wondered when the big city would appear. Farm country and widely separated houses still filled their vision when slowly and imperceptibly they saw that the farms were being replaced by the truck gardens of the city; some houses appeared straining close together along half-made streets which stretched into a vanishing distance. Then there came the new subdivisions springing up with newly built and half-finished apartment buildings and cottages, all constructed in anticipation of the World's Fair along plowed strips soon to be streets and boulevards of an ever-expanding great city. Newly planted trees were making a desperate attempt to grow. Factories, lumberyards, coal yard, grain elevators appeared; tugs, sailing vessels, steamboats on the big lake, the river, and the canal swam into view as they rattled over the switch tracks and into the increasing density of Chicago.

There they were overwhelmed by the enormity of the city. Since the Chicago fire of 1871, it had grown from thirty-five square miles to two hundred, from a population of 300 thousand to one million, half of which were German and Irish immigrants. The city which greeted the Peine family was awash with tourists from all over the United States and Europe but especially from the Middle West who had come to see the famous World's Fair. We don't know today if George had arranged for them to stay in a hotel close to the elevated tracks, newly constructed expressly for the fair, which would carry them south to the Midway Plaza where the Columbian Exhibition building stood or if they found accommodation in the many "rooming houses." Regardless, "awestruck" wasn't a strong enough word to describe the feeling the four felt when they first beheld the "Magnificent White City," as it was called in 1893. "Dumbstruck," maybe, or "thunderstruck," but for sure they felt they were in fairyland as much as any child today feels when arriving in the Magic Kingdom of Disneyland! Though well read, their experience with travel away from their village was pretty limited in that day of one-horse-power or the "iron horse," so they all thrilled at viewing the pavilions of forty-six foreign lands. It was as if they were gaining a glimpse of the entire globe!

The iconic centerpiece of the fair was a large water pool, the Grand Basin, to commemorate Columbus' arrival four hundred years before. Fourteen of the most prominent buildings were positioned around the rim of the pool: grand halls of agriculture, of women, of mines, electricity, and transportation among others and all showcasing their progress. Though built of a temporary material consisting of plaster, cement, and jute fiber, and uniformly designed in the Neoclassical style of symmetry and balance, the large buildings were a vision of splendor clad in white stucco, defining them as the "White City." The Peine family toured as many pavilions as they could and attended lectures and demonstrations on new-fangled inventions such as the telephone, the phonograph, and moving pictures. They likely felt it a privilege to witness such progress, to glimpse into the future!

Something vaguely mysterious, even frightening, to them was the new invention of electricity with all its uses. In a science pavilion, stood a fantastic tower seventy-five feet tall completely covered with electric light bulbs such as they had never seen before, turned on by the flip of a switch instead of the lamplighter with his flaming torch walking around to ignite each kerosene lamp as was done at home. Here, by the light of the electric bulbs illuminating the walkways and streets they could happily stroll about after dark or if tired of walking, they could board a moving walkway powered solely by electricity as it looped around the park. All the possible uses for electricity like the washing machine and the dishwasher simply mystified our folks as if they had stumbled onto a magician's stage. One astounding sight followed after another till Adela said she felt like Alice in wonderland. There was an enormous Venus de Milo statue made out of 1500 pounds of chocolate, a giant ferris wheel of thirty-six cars, each of which could hold sixty people, and everywhere was the sheer number of people. The impressions made even Papa's head swim. And all for the admission price of fifty cents, twenty-five cents for Adela and Paul.

It wouldn't have been a vacation without discovering new foods, and that the exhibition offered in abundance: a sweet combination of popcorn, peanuts, and molasses known as Cracker Jack; Hershey chocolates; Juicy Fruit chewing gum; Shredded Wheat cereal; Aunt Jemima Pancake Mix; and Pabst Blue Ribbon Beer—all were introduced at the fair to lasting enthusiasm.

It wouldn't have been vacation without buying a souvenir either. Papa bought Mama a ruby red claret glass inscribed: "World's Columbian Exhibition of 1893." She treasured it all her life and took such good care of it that it could be passed down to future generations of today.

Fascinating exhibits showcasing the telephone invented by Alexander Graham Bell in 1876, the electric lamp of Thomas Alva Edison in 1882, and the camera using film instead of dry plate by George Eastman in 1888 were on display. All their lives long, the Peines expressed how fortunate they felt to have had the opportunity of a travel vacation, of hotel accommodations, of restaurant food, and above all of sightseeing in that day when most folks in the middle west led prosaic lives at home.

Sadness called at the door of this seemingly ideal little family, too, of course, or it wouldn't have been the real world. Long after she had given birth to Paul, a new baby was born to the Peines, sixteen years almost to the day, in fact. While it was quite an adjustment, to face this pregnancy and start over with child-raising, by the time little Cyril was delivered they were ecstatic with joy and felt he was their little "bonus baby." This was not to be, though, for three months later the sickly baby departed from their world to lie in the family plot in Minier cemetery.

Both Adela and Paul were good students and after graduation from Minier High School enrolled at the University of Illinois in Champaign; Adela graduated from the university in 1908, Paul in 1910. Sending a daughter off to a university caused quite a sensation in the village. Colleagues of George questioned him about this and asked: "What farmer is gonna marry her if she has all that high fallutin' education? She'll just be an old maid and always yours to support!" George just smiled to himself and reflected that Adela had already announced that she didn't intend to marry a farmer and live on a farm.

A trip to the British Isles, a teaching position at Minier High School, and marriage to the new doctor in town quickly followed in the exhilarating life of their daughter, but the grim reaper soon made another appearance at the Peine home and took away forty-seven year old Mary. It had become apparent, by her breathlessness and lack of energy, that her heart had become weak in recent years. Dr. John Rost, the new doctor in town, was called to the house to examine her and he made the diagnosis of a faulty valve for which there was nothing he or medical science of the day unfortunately could do. Mary regrettably didn't last till Adela's wedding, for on February 8, 1910, she was gone and laid to rest beside her baby, Cyril.

At least, George thought, Mary didn't have to know about the Great War, World War I, for which the world blamed the German Kaiser. The four years of that horrific war changed forever the orientation of folks in the German communities like Minier. Once American soldiers went to fight against the Germans, the fidelity of folks like the Peines, Burhrigs, Imigs, Graffs, Oehlers, and Rosts was transferred completely away from their ancient homeland to their chosen one. They ceased speaking German in church, on the street, in the school, and sometimes even in homes. There would be no question about where their fidelity lay. It was a heart-wrenching time in the German settlements where slurs and prejudice were sometimes slung at the folks, and confusion and embarrassment were continuously felt by them.

The grieving George felt his loss especially when he alone had to give Adela in marriage to John Wilken Rost, the new physician in town on June 14, 1911. Also about that time, George encouraged Paul in his decision to seek employment in a shoe store in Three Forks, Montana, and so the young recent graduate of the University of Illinois headed west to seek his fortune.

One day, as George groped out of his depression, an idea seized his mind which took over his thoughts and gave him a reason to go on living: he would buy the vacant lot next door to his home and build a big modern home for Adela and John. They loved the idea and insisted that he live there with them. Within the year 1911-12, a large wooden, four square, arts and crafts style home took shape. It had a wrap-around porch at the front door, a big sleeping porch on the rear of the second floor, a kitchen in the basement which was a new location to take advantage of the cool temperature beneath ground level, a library, a living room, a dining room with dumb waiter to bring food from the kitchen to the table, and one indoor bathroom.

This domestic arrangement soon became a profoundly satisfying one for George as two little baby girls joined the family circle: Mary Adela, named for his own beloved Mary, on May 13, 1912, and Ada Margaret, given a thoroughly modern name by Adela and a middle name for John's mother, on Oct. 8, 1916. First Mary and then Ada was his constant companion walking every Sunday afternoon out to his wife's grave where they lay a bouquet of flowers from his garden. Before long George retired from the store, but not from the bank board, and was able to devote his life to the little girls who were his adoring companions every day till he went to his bedroom and they to the sleeping porch with their Mama and Papa Doc.

In his spare time George liked to putter in the new large yard where he moved some of the perennials from his former yard next door to the new garden and even installed an ornamental pool where goldfish swam to the delight of little Mary and Ada.

George bought one of the first automobiles in town but saying that he was too old to learn, never drove it. It was to be Adela's privilege to chauffeur him to his appointed rounds to check on the progress of the growing things in the countryside or to visit an ailing cousin or to his frequent get-togethers with his brothers in town. He specifically decreed that the garage built for the new contraption was to have two large garage doors, one at each end, in case Adela couldn't stop the thing and so she could start it up going forward without having to back up. No driver's license was required in those days and hence no driver's test at the secretary of state's office! Gasoline was sold at the new station in Minier.

Idyllic years passed one after another for George spent in the company of his daughter's family and his large Peine circle including his son who returned from Montana to live in Minier and work at the family store and the bank. The patriarch, George, served several terms on the school board and on the village board, once as treasurer, and continued as director of the Farmers' State Bank of Minier. The goodness of life all screeched to a halt, though, when Adela got the diagnosis in 1924! It was breast cancer for which, other than the double mastectomy she endured, there was little anyone including her physician husband and all his resources could do to save her life. Day after day, while the children were at school and John was away at his expanding practice, an anguished George sat at Adela's bedside holding her hand, reading books or the newspaper aloud to her, trying with all his heart to staunch the horrible pain she was suffering.

A private nurse, Marie Cooney, was hired from Bloomington to live in the home and care for Adela. Everything possible at the time was done for her, but inexorably the day November 21, 1926, came and as if a sharp knife had pierced his heart, George lost his beloved Adela. For George, this was the fourth woman essential to his life who was taken from him in early death. His own mother, Margaret Davin Peine, died when he was only two years old; his sister, Mary, who had been the only mother he ever knew, died when he was sixteen; his beloved wife, Mary, died when he was fifty-four; and his darling daughter, Adela, died when he was seventy years old. The broken old gentleman lived on for nearly fifteen years, but there were no more essential women to enhance his life.

The ramifications of Adela's death for her daughters, aged fourteen and ten, were insurmountable especially when eighteen months later their father married Marie Cooney and she turned out to be the proverbial wicked stepmother. Her first victim was George who, to keep peace, moved out of the home he had built and paid for and into Paul's two-unit apartment/commercial building on the business street of Minier. It wasn't ideal there with stairs to climb and no kitchen facilities, but he and Paul took their meals at the restaurant across the street, saw Mary and Ada as often as possible, and being chipper in nature generally did not complain. Besides, he did enjoy those little concerts when Paul played the piano most evenings!

Mary's graduation from the University of Illinois, followed in four years by Ada's, was a proud moment for the old gentleman as was Mary's wedding to William Peter Oehler on May 1, 1937. Rumblings of war again in Europe which might yet involve the United States were a worry and concern to his last months, but George was losing his grip on life and knew it. The loves of his life, Mary and Ada, were grown now and on their own in far away cities so he just gave up and passed away in Paul's home on January 28, 1941. His remains lie beside Mary's in the Minier cemetery. George survived his wife, Mary, by thirty-one years, and he sorely missed her every single day.

Summary of Generation #2

As we can see, daily life for these folks does not seem so very strange to us. They didn't have the electronic technology or home appliances which seem so very essential to us, yet they nevertheless filled their lives with meaningful relationships, even best bosom friends, entertainment of their own or of friend's creation, clubs, cliques, or men's and women's groups.

The automobile had not yet replaced the horse drawn carriage making travel very slow and distances limited. Although travel to distant locales or going somewhere on vacation didn't even occur to most folks, for the few who did there was the train which crisscrossed Illinois even back then. Mail delivery was very dependable, relied upon greatly in that day when a portion of every day was devoted, by many folks and to all businesses, to letter writing. News was received as well in the newspapers which came daily with the train's mail car. The absence of even radio yet made for a kind of quiet which we today can only dream of.

Members of the second generation had likely absorbed the founding concept of American exceptionalism and assumed that no other nation could do what America could do. It wasn't just their involvement of the United States in world events, but their leadership; their participation in World War I had secured the final victory which guaranteed the survival of freedom in Europe. America did not seek the position. It was her's because of her ideals and her power, and the power of her ideals. As British historian Andrew Roberts has observed, "In the debate over whether America was born great, achieved greatness or had greatness thrust upon her, the only possible conclusion must be: all three."

Temptations of the heart, food, liquor, or behavior no doubt gripped their lives as they do ours today, but there were perhaps stronger controls and restraints on misbehavior then than now. Social pressure to conform to the standards of a village, where several generations of one's family resided and cared about each other's status, where one's actions were seen and reported, where one was known by a large portion of the other residents, where one's standing in the community was zealously protected, where the reputation of the family name was of critical concern to each member, was paramount. The churches of the day, composed of small, closely-bonded congregations, provided a first-line check on misbehavior, keeping for instance a fear of out of wedlock pregnancy like a thunderbolt waiting to strike any girl affected. Knowing that her reputation and that of her whole family, even her life, would be ruined, was a strong dictator of morals. Adultery, drunkenness, laziness, shabby housekeeping, physical abuse could all be mightily diminished by the invocation of the family name, its reputation, its standing in the village of all its members. Divorce was then unheard of in villages like Minier. Perhaps as much as all the above controls was the strong sense of shame which was fundamental in society in that day, as in: "You should be ashamed of yourself!" Such a admonition hurled at a child or adult bore a very strong impetus to reform and was frequently employed.

It is true that some of the idiosyncrasies of village life, known to us in stories and novels, likely had at least a kernel of truth to them: suspicion of outsiders or newcomers, prejudice against those of a different faith or skin color, set opinions about women's role in society, and more. In that day before scientific inquiry was widespread, folks could be stubborn and unyielding in opinions, hold a grudge, feud, gossip, or insult another. Again those are all behaviors perhaps not so different from those of us today, and as we get to know our predecessors and understand the conditions of their lives we can't help but feel drawn to them with admiration and love.

Generation #3 – Adela Lydia Caroline Peine Rost
—1—and—3—

Born January 14, 1884, at home in her parents grand Eastlake bed, Adela Peine was already some distance in time away from her immigrant ancestors: thirty-nine years, in fact. She would have identified herself as American, not German; Hofgeismar and Lesse were not much referrenced in Adela's world; her roots went deep into American soil and into the glorious American culture, all its richness to be her heritage. She was named for her mother's beloved half-sister, Lydia, and her mother's mother, Caroline. Growing up in Minier, Adela knew both her namesakes even though the first lived in nearby Peru and the second in various towns not so near. A large number of Peine and Buehrig aunts, uncles, and cousins did live within walking distance of her home, however, and so formed a warm, comforting, supportive extended family for Adela which gave a decided strength and confidence to her personality. In addition she had a brother Paul, only one year younger, who was a constant companion whenever she wished. Theirs was a happy home at 209 N. Minier St., Minier, Illinois.

Paul and Adela Peine

Adela lived in the day when girls wore their hair long with the side locks pulled up and tied in a bow; her hair was blond and her eyes, hazel. Her dresses fell to below the knee where her knit stockings were visible until they disappeared into her black high-button boots. From an early age, she liked learning and had an insatiable curiosity about all sorts of subjects. Papa taught her to read before she even went to school, and together they would read the newspaper and talk about events. Like her mama before her she was expected to learn those parlor pastimes of Victorian ladies: sew a variety of hand stitches, paint china in company with her aunts and cousins, practice hair weaving, all of which she did, but most often young Adela could be found with a book in her hand.

One cherished childhood memory was of the times she was driven in the horse and buggy out to Uncle Stephen Peine's farm especially in the spring to see the newborn lambs bounding about, even allowing her to stroke their wooly flanks and soft ears. She loved to ride the pony which Uncle always kept and Papa led around like a dog on a leash. Later, when older, she appreciated the sight of the fiery sun setting over the cornfields. Living all her life land-locked in Illinois, far from ocean or lake, she had never seen the sun set over a great body of water, didn't know the flame such a sight possessed, so this was her sunset standard of comparison and a beautiful sight it still is!

When she was about eight years old the big excitement in the village was the construction of a water tower and system to replace the pump in every backyard. This advance did not replace the outhouse but it was nevertheless a great boon to the housewife and the firefighter, to name just two. It was a complicated procedure and took some weeks; Papa took Adela and Paul to see the progress often. First a six inch well had to be sunk one hundred and forty feet deep. A brick pumping house was built to house the new fourteen horse power boiler and pumping machinery. By 1897, though, a new ten horsepower gasoline engine was purchased to operate the pumps. Water mains or pipes, gradually laid to extend the village water system to all the homes, were completed by 1904. To hold a supply of water in reserve, a wooden tank was mounted on wood pilings with a stairway extending to the top. A gilt ball on a pole atop the tank towered about one hundred feet above the amazed eyes of little Adela and Paul.

A pretext for the new water system was the frequency of fires in that day before electricity. For instance, a fire which caused serious destruction to the downtown was sparked when the tailor neglected to remove hot coals from his flatiron before he closed his shop for the night. A bucket brigade could not keep up with the flames which spread in several directions, finally leveling a number of wood frame business buildings on the commercial street. That and other fires impelled the village fathers to organize a regular fire department, to dig several wells on the business street, and to purchase a fire engine they called "Little Giant." The latter was a manual cylinder pump mounted on a hand-drawn cart, and required sixteen men to properly operate. Of course, it required its own little building to house it from the elements. Volunteer firemen numbered twenty-four in those early years. By 1886, the village purchased a new hose cart and installed a fire bell on a framework built next to the fire house. When the Peine family heard that bell they were alert but at the same time they felt a new degree of safety.

Still, at one o'clock in the morning of December 24, 1888, the fire bell rang out to rouse all in earshot that a fearsome fire was raging in the business district of Minier. Ignited in a small coal house in an alley behind the most worthy structures of the main street, it was discovered by a roomer in the Union House Hotel. Fortunately, he was able to alert the sleepers who fled to safety, wrapped in blankets, without any loss of life. Rapidly the fire spread to lumber sheds one hundred forty feet in length where it naturally fed on easy fodder, and nourished, began to attack with reckless abandon all structures in its path. The existence of the wells and the volunteer fire company with their Little Giant engine were able to restrain the fire from the grain elevator and barns as well as the Peine's store and Buehrig Brothers grocery store. Those stores suffered some damage but were closed to business only briefly. The block where the fire had run rampant presented a view of utter desolation for awhile, though, a grim reminder of the destructive power of fire in that day. Soon after, a waterworks system including nine fire plugs was installed by the village.

Adela's papa, a keen observer of life and reader of a daily news paper, was a quite a story teller who delighted her of an evening with stories like the origin of a place named Starved Rock, a bluff just north of Minier on the Illinois River. It was sad and exciting at the same time for her to hear how the Illinois nation was defeated by the Pottawanamie nation not so very long before. The two tribes fought in the northern part of the state until a small band of the Illinois retreated to find refuge with their wives and children on a bluff 250 feet above the Illinois River, water on three sides, bare rock of perpendicular wall down to the river, a challenge to today's rock climbers but a formidable defense for the Indians, only accessible by a narrow passage connecting it to the mainland. There, the small group spent many days defying their besiegers, trapping and gathering for their food, lowering buckets attached to bark ropes down to get water from the river, until one day when raising the water bucket it seemed too light and sure enough, the rope had been cut. There was no water! Trying again and again without success, famishing of thirst, watching rain clouds approach but not deliver, facing a death more terrible than the tomahawk or scalping knife, miserably sitting inactive all day, the braves could stand it no longer and stole away to attack their foes. The bitter contest resulted in total annihilation of the Illinois

STORIES MY FOLKS TOLD ME

nation, their name extinct as the women and children were slain on the precipice where they had watched the fatal struggle.

Another story beloved by Adela and Paul also took place in Illinois. Indian chief Black Hawk was the tragic hero of that story. Leader of the Sauk, Fox, and Kickapoo tribes, he led a life of valor leading his braves in raiding parties against not only the incursion of white settlers but against other Indian tribes throughout middle America. Most famously, Black Hawk contested the disposition of fifty million acres of territory by the U.S. government in 1804 and the removal of all the natives to the west of the Mississippi River. In 1832 he led five hundred braves and one thousand old men, women, and children back across to his beloved Rock River area near Rock Island, Illinois, to fight for the return of their home. After many skirmishes with deaths on both sides, he fell to the superior weaponry of the whites; the Black Hawk War was over, and he had to leave the place he called "our mother." "I have looked upon the Rock River since I was a child. I love the great river!" Later, he diplomatically said, "Rock River was a beautiful country. I liked my towns, my cornfields, and the home of my people. I fought for it. It is now yours. Keep it as we did—it will produce you good crops."

When Adela was ten years old, after much pleading, she was allowed to go with Mama and Papa to the Columbian Exhibition in Chicago. They traveled by train the entire way, from their village of Minier, which took most of one day. It was the farthest she had ever been from home, so excitedly she took a seat in the chair car, looked out the window, and exclaimed at all which passed by her eyes. Mostly she saw land under cultivation with board houses and red barns sprinkled over the vastness of the prairie and every so often some towns dotted the landscape where the train stopped to let passengers on or off. She shared a lunch from Mama's basket and wondered when the big city would appear. This remarkable experience for the young girl has already been described in her parents' story, but suffice it to say, Adela never forgot her adventure, which like a travel to the future, introduced her to a world far beyond her bucolic village.

Traveling to the big city of Chicago and the fabulous world's fair had been stimulating for young Adela, but at the same time she treasured the reassuring comfort of the traditions of village life. Memorial Day was then universally known as Decoration Day because it was the day, May 31st, when families walked out to the cemetery carrying a basket of flowers from their garden to place on their fallen soldiers resting place. The day in Adela's childhood belonged to the Civil War veterans, but as the years passed it became more and more a day to put flowers on the grave of any loved one.

The Civil War veterans, wearing their blue uniforms with brass buttons and black billed caps, were the keepers of such patriotic traditions. Giving a special flavor to village life, they were the living embodiment of what most believed was their nation's greatness and high destiny. Like Adela's Uncle Henry Peine, they had years ago marched thousands of miles away to the legendary battlefields of Gettysburg, Shiloh, and Cold Harbor. They had been there. Now they stood by the Grand Army of the Republic monument in the cemetery and listened to orations and prayers and patriotic songs. To watch them was to be deeply moved!

July 4th celebrations in the village also reinforced Adela's sense of place and belonging. There at the bunting-draped bandstand, patriotism was engendered as speeches were given--often with the underlying reference to Americans as the chosen people--and all the favorite songs were sung. Titles like: "Columbia Gem of the Ocean," "When Johnny Comes Marching Home," "America the Beautiful," and always concluding with "Blest Be the Tie That Binds." It was the nation's birthday—the day to fly the flag, walk in the parade, express optimism and pride in the achievements of the United States, picnic in the park, and watch the fireworks.

That same bandstand was the gathering place all through the warm summer evenings for band concerts, theatricals, family reunions, even for fireworks. It was a small world, but ennui was not a condition of it!

Teenaged Adela and Paul

Adela's life, aided by new inventions such as the telephone, electricity, the automobile, the nineteenth amendment to the Constitution giving women the vote, and her own education at the University of Illinois allowed her to stride deeper into the larger world outside Minier. By June of 1900 The Mutual Telephone Company of Minier was organized, a phone directory with one hundred eighty-five phone listings was issued, one of which was that of George E. Peine. Sixteen year old Adela didn't immediately start phoning all her friends, though, because in those early days the telephone was not considered an instrument for entertainment but for serious, almost emergency use. An oak rectangular box hung on the wall with a black funnel shaped, metal projection into which one spoke. To hear, one lifted a black, tube-like, hand-sized, rod from which the sound of a voice emanated from one end and connected at the other end to the box by a thick cord. To make a phone call, one would turn the crank on the side of the box until a real woman's voice called out: "central!" Then, one gave the name of the home or business one wanted to call. The woman or operator, who sat in the central telephone switchboard office "uptown," would then physically join your wire to that of the person you were calling. Numbers instead of names were not used until they became necessary, for obvious reasons, in time.

This was also about the time, 1903, that Adela and nineteen of her girl friends formed a secret society, called the SOPHs. Alas, the meaning of those letters has been lost to Adela's descendants as she was the type of young woman who could keep a secret and never disclosed it. Nonmembers, even close relatives, made joking suggestions for the meaning of the letters, though, such as: "Still On Pa's Hands," "Start Out Picking Husbands," and "Some One Please Hurry." It is known, of course, that the club members were all high-minded and met to discuss books. Well, maybe the name of a masculine classmate did come up occasionally, but nobody knew for sure because it was a very secret society. What was known for certain was that their club joined likeminded young women, and the bond was life lasting. Whenever a member married, the others gave her a silver spoon with the letters of the club engraved on the handle, spoons which are still prized by her descendants.

One of Adela's household chores as a little girl on Saturdays had been to wash the lamp chimneys, fill the lamps with "coal oil" and trim the wicks. All homes, businesses, or public buildings were lighted with kerosene, gas or acetylene. Though many fires were ignited by this method, it was an improvement over whale oil or candles and extended the day from its ancient rhythms dictated by the sun.

With regularity, a big block of ice was delivered to the back door caked in sawdust, an excellent insulator, for that was the Peine's sole mode of refrigeration. An enterprising farmer or sawmill owner had cut the ice from his stream the previous winter, then buried it in sawdust, so essential to the business and very cheap, a virtual by-product or waste of the sawmill lumber industry found in every town.

Then just as Minier was adjusting to the newfangled telephone, the village fathers voted to install electric lights to the village streets. Rural electricity was still decades away but once again Minier proved to be a forward-looking village. There was no all-day electric service, only mornings part of the week, and the plant was turned off at midnight. It wasn't till January of 1920 that the current was changed to a safer 110 alternating current from 220 direct current and twenty-four hour service was provided. About that time, too, electric service was extended to rural locations around Minier.

We forget just how painfully dim the world was before electricity. A candle provided barely a hundredth of the illumination of a 100 watt light bulb. The world at night for much of history was a very dark place. Paintings of that day show family members sitting companionably at a table sewing or reading by the light of a single candle with no sense of deprivation or hardship on their faces nor sign of desperate postures trying to get a tiny bit more light to fall on a page or piece of embroidery. They simply put up with dim evenings because they knew no other kind! The kerosene lamp gave off more light than a candle but little compared to an electric bulb. Kerosene, in Adela's childhood, could be purchased at the village store, filled in a tin container, carried home, poured into a glass vessel with a wick which was lighted, and when the globe was placed around it a very magical warm yet bright light filled the room and the hearts of the family.

Such progress as electricity brought formerly impossible, in fact undreamed of, appliances for the homemaker. In 1912, a Minier resident Simon E. Schroeder received a patent on an electric washing machine he called "the two in one" which he manufactured in a wood frame building right in the village. Also with the advent of electricity came an electric pump to raise the water out of the backyard well with no effort and many other laborsaving inventions.

The role of letter writing as then practiced, before the 1895 introduction of the telephone in Minier, can scarcely be imagined today. Girls like Adela, her mother and father too, all received at least one letter in the mailbox each day often written by someone actually living in Minier; likewise, they wrote and posted several letters a day. It wasn't considered a chore but was part of the daily routine, and besides if they wrote they received!

As Adela was approaching graduation from Minier High School, discussions within the family centered on her future. Mama had gone to the women's seminary and always hoped that Adela too could further her education. Papa himself was in favor because he had learned from experience the advantage of living with an educated woman. From the way Mary could analyze information and make sound decisions, George just knew the world needed educated women as well as men. Of course, when his colleagues heard that he planned to send his daughter to the University of Illinois in Urbana, they disdained the idea asking: "How do you expect her to ever get a farmer around here to marry her after she gets a university education?" He remained mum but George knew quite well that Adela did not intend to marry a farmer!

In that day when a woman's employment options were restricted to governess, teacher, maid servant, store clerk, seamstress, cook, nurse, or telephone operator, most women felt satisfied with the role of wife and mother. A few, however, felt "buried alive," stagnating, good for nothing, bored by the life of her mother or sister. It would not be fair to say that Adela fell into that category, but her consciousness had definitely been raised by her mama who had studied at a Ladies' Seminary. She bore an inner conviction that she wanted to be all that she could in her life, and believed that that would entail continuing her education. She, like most women, limited by the convention of the day, knew, though, that to gain position in society she would need to marry. There was no alternative, yet some yearned to venture into the wider world of power and notoriety. Books by George Eliot, Elizabeth Gaskell, and Jane Austen were already being read by girls like Adela and dealt with this conundrum of the woman's role: the clash of the desire for independence and the instinct of domesticity, the quest for purpose and the need for love.

So off she went in the fall of 1902 in her wide brimmed hat, wearing the Gibson girl fashion consisting of a high necked blouse with mutton sleeves to the elbow, belted waist, long skirt slim over the hips and gathering in fullness at the ankle, a bow at her neck. Crinolines kept the skirt flaring as it progressed down to the ankle. In a special hat box from the millinery shop in Minier, Adela carried the hat she wore only for special occasions which was really huge and full of ribbon bows, fabric flowers, and a veil. A seamstress had been engaged over the summer to create Adela's new college wardrobe.

Adela the University of Illinois student

No student dormitories existed in the early 1900's, so Adela resided in a boarding house, either a private home or one run by a church, YWCA, or a sorority. Men and women housed in separate dwellings; monthly rent approximated $8.00.

At the University, Adela majored in English literature and German with the intension of teaching in a high school. Teaching was, of course, one of the few career opportunities open to women at the beginning of the Twentieth Century. Paul majored in business with the plan to follow his father at the Peine Store and as a board member of the Minier Bank though Adela was the more outgoing, daring, and ambitious of the two. Paul had a lifelong interest in music which he pursued playing both the piano and home organ. Later he liked to travel to Peoria or Chicago to attend concerts, the theater, and ball games.

Adela seemed to be in the forefront of that generation of gentle women who were finally starting to break out of their historical "place." Since time immemorial child bearing had been a woman's task, fine needlework her recreation, earning respect her obligation. Women were dependent first upon their fathers and then their husbands. The home was their only place to find fulfillment and respect. As a young woman in the vanguard, Adela was an independent thinker, could analyze abstract concepts, think critically, and arrive at a decision, confident of her own abilities. In reality she couldn't vote, she couldn't gain admission to medical school or law school, she couldn't open a bank account; she struggled with the convention of women in the home, men in the world, but the spark was ignited, her consciousness had been raised!

Though her ambitious nature drove her to fulfill her determination to earn a university degree, she still assumed she would marry and bear children. Her dreams could not include a lifetime career in that day when women were restricted to work which did not even require a university degree such as classroom teaching, nursing, seamstress, nursemaid, telephone operators, sales clerk, to say nothing of the many drudge jobs as a housemaid. Adela simply wanted to be all that her natural born talents would allow. She instinctively knew that even if she were never employed, she would acquire many advantages as an educated woman: the ability to think clearly about the answers to life's questions without reliance on superstition or myth, to better understand the issues of the day, to delight in the acquisition of knowledge for itself, and to gain the confidence which came from fulfilling all the requirements leading to a university degree. Some of her favorite textbooks still remain in family possession such as "History of German Literature."

She was one of just a handful of women studying at the U. of I. in those days; she was navigating uncharted waters, blazing the trail for women's education of future generations. When she graduated in 1907, she was the first of many of her family to graduate from the University of Illinois, the vanguard of many future descendants, but of course, she didn't know that; she only knew that she was the first in her family. Paul would follow her to the stirring strains of "Pomp and Circumstance" in two years as the second of the Peines and Buehrigs to graduate from the University of Illinois.

Another example of Adela's avant-garde style and daring ambition was her decision, and her parents' permission, to accept the invitation of her college roommate to accompany her and her parents to England during the summer of 1909. The Reverend was traveling on sabbatical and knew his own daughter's enjoyment of the trip would be enhanced by the accompaniment of her best friend, Adela. Fortunately, Mary and George saw this as a rare and unique opportunity for their daughter so they lent their financial support and encouragement for Adela's long journey far from home. In company with her dear friend and her parents, Adela thrilled at the sights along the length and breadth of the British Isles.

The four of them sailed in early July of 1909 on the "Ionian," a 9000 ton royal mail steamer of the Allan Line. In a postcard written to her parents as the ship prepared to steam from Canada to England, she wrote: "Our river pilot goes off in a few hours so I can send another card. Am well. It has been raining all day, blowing like fury and cold as Greenland. But it is getting quieter out now. They say there is lots of ice at the mouth of the river which accounts for the coldness." Alas this is the only extant mail written by Adela to her loved ones at home, for years later an attic fire destroyed a box of her letters and mementos from that wonderful summer.

Somehow a couple of ship menus escaped the fire, fortunately. On Tuesday, July 13, 1909, Adela's breakfast card offered: oatmeal porridge, boiled hominy, broiled plaice, grilled beefsteak and horseradish sauce, broiled Cambridge sausages, broiled mutton kidney on toast, boiled eggs to order, lyonnaise potatoes, cold roast beef, soda scones, plain and French rolls, dry and buttered toast, preserves, tea, coffee, and cocoa. A luncheon menu enticed with: green pea soup, broiled cod steak, hot pot, boiled corned beef and cabbage, boiled potatoes, cold roast lamb, cold veal and ham pie, pickles, sliced tomatoes, ground rice pudding, baked apples, biscuits, farls, cheese, fruit, tea, and coffee.

Sunsets over the vast Atlantic Ocean were a marvel to the girl from landlocked Illinois. Each evening found Adela gripping the railing, hair streaming, skirt billowing, eyes fixed on the wonder of the sun falling into the far edge of the ocean. For long minutes on end she thrilled as the sky then filled with the spreading, rosy afterglow. Fellow passengers seemed to know so much about the celestial sky and nightly gave little impromptu lectures about the constellations, their names, mythology concerning them, until she felt she had a whole new world opened to her. Of course, that was just the beginning of the learning which was to take place that summer. Like the curtain of a stage finally opening, she gasped and beheld wonder after wonder being presented before her eyes!

Once in London, the four took rooms in the home of a church family, settled in, and found they had time yet that first day to attend one of the many Evensongs held then as now in the Church of England churches. At St. Alban the Martyr, Holborn, Adela thrilled to hear the lovely choir voices sing the entire evening service: "Abide with me from morn till eve, For without Thee I cannot live; Abide with me when night is nigh, For without Thee I dare not die. Come near and bless us when we wake, Ere through the world our way we take, Till in the ocean of Thy love, We lose ourselves in heaven above." On, they sang for ten pages until: "Lead, kindly Light, amid th' encircling gloom, Lead Thou me on! The night is dark, and I am far from home,--Lead Thou me on! Keep Thou my feet; I do not ask to see the distant scene; one step enough for me. I was not ever thus, nor prayed that Thou shouldst lead me on; I loved to choose and see my path, but now Lead Thou me on! I loved the garish day, and 'spite of fears, pride ruled my will. Remember not past years. So long Thy power hath blest me; sure it still will lead me on! O'er moor and fen, o'er crag and torrent, till the night is gone; and with the morn those Angel faces smile which I have loved long since, and lost awhile. Amen." Adela instinctively knew those were words to guide one so far from home.

What joy for her to visit the Lake District and the birthplaces of the great English classic writers whose works she had so recently read and studied! Wordsworth, the Brontes, Gaskell, Shakespeare, Austen. Adela's entourage traveled to each of their birthplaces as would an acolyte. It was like making a pilgrimage to a shrine of her beloved poets and authors! Visits to countless churches and cathedrals were on the itinerary as well as Stonehenge, art galleries, palaces, gardens, and Poets corner at Westminster Abbey. A little bound book of Shakespeare's sonnets, which Adela bought in Stratford upon Avon, remains to remind of the grand tour.

On August 10, 1909 they visited the Old Mill at Ambleside in the Lake District with its picturesque market place, old mill, and gentle hills all around. The previous day they had sailed on Windermere Lake which was also surrounded by hills which sloped down to the water's edge. How the sun glistened on the water's surface! She was alert to the sound of ducks and waterfowl on the water, was transfixed by the shimmering of the tall trees reflected in the deep slate-green water. These were all new sensations to a girl raised so far from a large body of water. Fisher skiffs silently slipped out from shore manned by a ruddy-faced fisherman at the oars, gunnels piled high with nets, poles and line reminding her of the fishermen back home who came to the back door to sell their perch or bass.

In a horse and buggy they traveled out to view the more rugged hills of Langdale Pikes visited the rock-strewn Kirkstone Pass, and stopped by a little river where in its cool, slow-flowing waters they cooled their feet and wetted their handkerchiefs before passing them over their brows. From the hills, they looked down on the seaside village of Bowness with its long pier and fishing skiffs pulled up onto the rocky shore which they strolled along. In Granmere, another lakeside village, they also ambled admiring the ubiquitous tiny vegetable and flower gardens behind each house. For nearly an hour they sat on some rocks to rest and admire the long waterfall called Stock Ghyll Force. And then it was time to wrench herself away from this beguiling place, this idyllic summer and return to the reality of life in Minier. Wish though she might that she could stop time, like chaff before the wind, it flew on before her without pause!

Practically before she could alight from the train at the Minier station, Adela needed to report to the Minier school house where she taught high school English. Sorrow clouded Adela's days, in spite of the exhilaration she felt as she stood before her students, as it was apparent at home that her mama was ailing. Strangely, Mama was growing weak and more sickly by the day finally taking to her bed on New Year's Day, 1910. The new physician in town, John Rost, visited and examined her many times, brought surgeons from Bloomington to study her case, but surgery of a heart valve was unknown in that day. Adela, Paul, and Papa anguished for days at her bedside; the minister prayed with them; her sisters and the Peine women came to bring baskets of food for the grief-stricken family; her grandparent Buehrigs lived too far away to attend; there was nothing anyone, including Dr. Rost, could do. Quietly, sweet Mary slipped away on February 8th. aged 47.

That helpless feeling, that inability to change the march of death was expressed by John many times as the hardest duty he had to perform as a physician. Eventually, Ludwig Henry and Caroline Buehrig, Adela's grandparents, could travel to Minier to seek and give consolation to George and the family; they and the large Peine and Buehrig contingent helped them regain their equilibrium, but the home was not the same in the hands of a hired country girl nor was life ever the same for George during the thirty-one years he survived his Mary.

A sad Adela was glad to be living in her childhood home with papa and Paul. Daily life without mama was a hard adjustment, something she and papa had to do, helping each other step by step through the fog of bereavement. Adela's presence did brighten George and he was especially glad that she could remain right there in Minier, could still live at home with him, could still teach German, Latin, English, and history in the high school a short walk away.

The high school had just the year before, 1909, been reorganized under the leadership of Principal Ralston Brock to offer a four-year course in English, three years of history, two years of Latin, two years of German, and one and one-half years of Algebra, one year of plane geometry, one year of physics, and one-half year of each zoolorgy, botany, and physical geography. There were twenty scholars and two teachers, Adela and Principal Brock, who taught mathematics and science. In addition, on one day a week, vocal music was taught by Dorothea Lessing and later by Bessie Fritag.

As is always the case when one returns from travel to such far away, little heard of places like London or the Lake District in the day when most folks never traveled from Minier to Peoria a matter of thirty miles, it was hard for Adela to find anyone with whom she could rhapsodize over her summer sojourn. Friends were curious and expressed interest with a question, but when she began to answer with any length or detail their eyes glazed over and the conversation simply drifted to a stall or worse

STORIES MY FOLKS TOLD ME

to a recent banal happening in Minier. Her experience was just too far beyond the ken of her hometown friends and relatives to find mutual understanding and grasp; she yearned to meet someone who had also traveled to England with whom she could compare experiences, who could understand and identify with her experiences. But alas, except for the family she had traveled with, and they resided relatively far away from Minier rarely to be seen again, there was no one with whom to share her enthusiasm. Many quiet times of reflection were spent by Adela, though, reviewing each day's activities as written in her travel log, sadly later consumed in a house fire, and day-dreaming about where she might travel next, for she was mightily bitten by the "travel bug."

Life did not exactly stand still though, of course, for a pretty young woman of Adela's talents and energy. There were still in town nearly all of her S.O.P.H. friends to meet with, University Women's Club, leadership in the Women's Atheneum, church activities, and the Peine and Buehrig family events in that day when formal calls were paid and teas were given. But it was not long after the resumption of her life in Minier that Adela was keeping company with the new young doctor in town, John Wilken Rost. He had not in his life been farther away than Chicago, but he was not a local man either. He grew up in Petersburg, Illinois, over in McClean County, had also studied at the University of Illinois in Champaign, and had received his medical degree in at the University of Illinois Medical School in Chicago in 1908. John could make her laugh as no one else ever could and so regaled her with stories of his athletic prowess that she amazingly found herself suddenly interested in football and baseball, his specialties.

By the summer of 1911, the matter was settled between Adela and John, so that her papa sent formal invitations: "Mr. George E. Peine requests the pleasure of your company at the marriage of his daughter Adela to Dr. John Wilken Rost on the morning of Wednesday, the fourteenth of June one thousand nine hundred and eleven at half past nine o'clock, Minier, Illinois."

Wedding portraits of Adela and John.

The local newspaper printed under the headline, "A HAPPY HOME WEDDING: One of the prettiest weddings that has occurred here for a long time was that of Miss Adela L. C. Peine and Dr. John Wilken Rost, at the bride's home Wednesday morning. About fifty guests were present being received informally by the bride and groom.

"At the appointed hour Mendelssohn's wedding march was played by Paul Peine the bride's brother, and the bridal pair took their places before a bank of marguerites. Rev. P.A. Bierbaum officiated, the ring ceremony being used.

"The bride wore a gown of white marquisette, with Cluny lace, and carried bride's roses. The house was effectively decorated the color scheme being white and pink. Following the ceremony Dr. and Mrs. Rost were heartily congratulated, and all were served with a fine four course wedding breakfast, served by the Irelands. Dr. and Mrs. Rost left in an auto for Bloomington where they took the Big Four train for Colorado. A dozen or more of their friends intercepted them at Peoria with posters and rice. The cruel depot officials would not let them throw any rice; eleven little sacks might have been observed standing in a row outside the gates. But they brightened up the trunk with ribbons and flowers and hung streamers and banners on the train so people would make no mistake.

"The marriage of these young people is a pleasant thing to write up, for they are able and talented and fine people socially. Dr. Rost is popular, and is one of our most progressive citizens. His bride is a graduate of Illinois, and a leader in the social and intellectual life of the town. They have the sincere good wishes of everyone.

"The wedding occasion was enlivened by the presence of the whole S.O.P.H. Club, of which the bride was a member. Miss Alma Ewing captured the bride's bouquet. Other guests were Mrs. Rost and son Theodore, Petersburg; Miss Maude Wullenweber, Bloomington; Harry Arnold, Colfax; E.H. Peine and wife, Blackwell, Oklahoma; Paul Peine, Three Forks, Montana; Mrs. W.S. Buehrig, Presbo, S.D."

Extant photographs of Adela and John on their honeymoon show them dressed in the opposite of today's "vacation casual," he in suit and tie, she in Gibson girl style blouse and ankle-length skirt, and hat. They are sitting outside their tour car with the inscription on the photo: "waiting for the auto mechanic!"

Honeymooners John and Adela

Upon her return to Minier as a married woman, Adela was required by law to resign from her teaching position. Only unmarried women were deemed appropriate to stand at the head of the classroom in those days! She found pleasant occupation, however, in helping with the design of the new home her father was building for her and John, in assisting John with the ledgers accruing to the business side of his practice, and especially in preparing for their first baby's arrival in May. Oh how she must have missed her mother now that she was pregnant and like all new mothers had so much to learn! Grandmother Caroline was far away in St. Louis, too far distant to visit.

Happily, nature took her natural course, and baby Mary Adela arrived in fine shape on May 13, 1912, to the joy and pride of her parents and many Buehrig and Peine kin. Four years later Ada Margaret joined the family on October 8, 1916.

The Rosts were happily situated in their thoroughly modern new home, a large four-square board home with a large porch on the front and a sleeping porch on the top floor. Those were the days when on a Sunday afternoon or evening when the chores were done, folks sat on the front porch, chatted with whomever walked by always addressing each other with the Miss, Mrs. or Mr. title; perhaps they even invited them to sit with them for a glass of lemonade or tea. It was customary for friends to make Sunday afternoon calls showing up at the door unannounced but always welcome for the housewife knew to tidy up and have something baked to offer guests in just such an eventuality. In those long ago days before Sunday afternoon TV sports shows, folks made their own entertainment spinning stories with friends, telling jokes, or discussing the news of the day.

One topic of endless fascination and shock was the sinking of the luxury ocean liner Titanic which sank on April 15, just a month before Mary was born. Newspapers were full of pictures of the ill-fated ship; sensationally written articles characterizing the victims one by one appeared so often that Adela and John felt like they practically knew them!

Then came the news of the day which was the Great War or World War I. Over in Germany, after the Austrian Archduke Ferdinand was assassinated in 1914, a chain reaction followed which would be known as The Great War and was so horrific it was considered to be the war to end all wars! Old empires collapsed leaving communism, fascism, and democracy to jockey for position in the realm of political ideas. From 1914—1918, two million Germans and one million Americans lost their lives right on the soil from whence both John's and Adela's folks came. John was commissioned as a physician early on. Though most soldiers boarded ships for the European front, his charge was in New York City to restore the wounded who were transported there by ship to large hospitals turned to military use.

As the war finally ended in 1918, another thirty thousand American soldiers lives were cut short by the Spanish flu epidemic which occurred world wide in spite of the efforts of doctors like John. Adela worried that he too would succumb to it and felt compelled to see for herself that he was really all right. Resolute, she boarded a train for New York and spent some days there with him till she was convinced that he would survive and return to their haven in Minier.

That war, in which American soldiers were sent to defeat the Germans, was a pivotal point for the descendants of German immigrants in communities like Minier. Until the war, even third generation folks like Adela and Paul were fluent in German which was spoken by most citizens in communities like theirs. But at the outbreak of World War I, in 1914, their German community and all others like it completely severed its ties to the German language in order to eliminate any question of its fidelity to the United States. World reaction to German aggression was so severe that Germans in the United States, in defense, ceased speaking German or orienting themselves to the Old Country. It had been the language used in most homes, in stores, and in churches. Weddings, baptisms, confirmations, religious education, and entire church services were all conducted in the German language until World War I.

Feelings of confusion, conflicting emotions, and embarrassment regarding the war in Germany, where American soldiers fought against the German soldiers and gave their lives, ran high among German descendants in Minier. Many people still were in contact with friends and relatives there. One young woman who had come to Minier as a mail order bride had just returned to Germany to visit her ailing parents when the war broke out preventing her from returning. Her new Minier friends like Adela sent care packages of food and clothing to her family in Germany during and after the war. Though they suffered many privations especially after the war, the Germans through the goodness of friends in Minier, survived. In gratitude, after the war, the German women sent beautiful hand embroidered linens, still in family possession, to their generous friends in Minier.

1910 to1920 was not only the decade of the Great War but of the Model T automobile, the fight for Prohibition, and the long battle for women's suffrage. Adela was swept up in the enthusiasm for the amazing new technological wonder: the horseless carriage. Not everyone shared her fervor, however. One account after a first drive stated: "There is a sense of incompleteness about it. You seemed to be sitting on the end of a huge pushcart, propelled by an invisible force and guided by a hidden hand. There is also a seeming brazenness to the whole performance. I dreamed once that I walked down Main Street in my pajamas in the full tide of the afternoon promenade, and I almost died with shame before I awoke. Yesterday I had something of the same feeling as I sat there and felt myself pushed forward into the very face of a grinning, staring and sometimes jeering crowd. But it wore away after a while. Gradually I felt that I did not need the protection of a horse in front of me." Another report tells of a state which legalized the horseless carriage, but only if "so constructed and its novelties so covered and hid as not to be liable to frighten horses on the highway by its novel appearance." Needless to say, in a very few years those same horses ceased to be a major concern of the writer as they no longer were the power of their transportation at all!

John continued to make his rounds by horse and buggy for a few years, but Adela had one of the first horseless carriages in Minier. Her father bought it under the guise that he wanted to be driven out to the family farm in all kinds of weather, but since he had no intention of learning to drive it, Adela must do the driving. There was plenty of room in the rear yard to build a garage complete with two wide double doors opening opposite each other in case Adela couldn't stop the machine at just the right moment and also so she could start driving in the forward

STORIES MY FOLKS TOLD ME

position. It was a status symbol and a whole lot of excitement at the same time for the aging gentleman and his daughter.

To add even more excitement than they actually wished for, the family was driven from their warm beds and sound sleep one night by a fire in the attic. House fires were still a common occurrence in that day when wood was burned in the basement furnace. Sparks still rose up the chimney and if the wind was just right could ignite the roof which is exactly what happened. No one was hurt, thank goodness; the local volunteer fire brigade appeared with their truck full of water and a long hose. Mary and Ada huddled with Mama in their nighties till the fire was extinguished and they could go back to bed. Next morning, Mama reported that many records from Papa Docs patients were lost, but for her the greatest loss was all her letters written from England and her souvenirs.

Of course, when Adela traveled out to Three Forks, Montana, to meet Paul's intended bride she didn't attempt to drive her automobile the distance. A train with many transfers transported her. Through traveling alone so far, she once again felt herself stimulated by the various scenes continuously passing by her window, by the new impressions attaching themselves to her senses, and by the very act of going where she had never before been. Paul took her to the boarding house where he lived, showed her the shoe store where he worked, and of course introduced her to his intended and her family. Looking back, Adela always said what a happy little vacation it had been for her and how much she had liked Paul's girl. She returned to Minier convinced that she would soon return for a wedding, but alas, there never was a wedding, and Paul never explained why.

As for Prohibition, the German communities never favored that. Beer, schnapps, or wine—alcohol had always been a central part of their celebrations or special occasions. Some of the leading opponents throughout the United States were German brewers and distillers whose fortunes were at stake in the dispute and thwarted by the passage of the 18th Amendment to the Constitution in 1919. We don't know that Adela marched for the temperance movement and rather doubt that alcohol consumption was a part of life in their circle.

For all her adult life, Adela had never felt completely confined to the domestic sphere; she spoke her mind freely to men as well as women, held strong opinions of her own on subjects as the right of women to vote, behavior of children, and education. Hers was far from a sheltered life as she caught the train or drove her car to Armington or Bloomington to attend meetings of the University Women's Club. She was active on church committees, the cemetery board, and other philanthropies. This women's philanthropy work gave her and women like her valuable experience and a kind of enabling power outside of the home through which she learned how to organize, form committees, and establish networks, all new in her prevailing social structure. By far, those same women found it mandatory to marry, however, as so many professions were closed to them, talented as they were. No doubt Adela had read in the novels of Elizabeth Gaskell, Charlotte Bronte, or Jane Austen the plight of women in villages straining under the conventions of the day, helpless in the face of financial uncertainty, unable to sit in the drivers seat of their own lives.

The passage of the 19th Amendment giving women the right to vote in August of 1920 was a victory for Adela personally for she had actively campaigned for it through her University Women's Club. What finally tipped the balance for women's suffrage was the energy, resourcefulness, and reliability of women workers who had filled the places of men away at battle in the Great War. Especially in factories, where women had formerly been excluded, they proved their mettle. Both political parties had endorsed women's suffrage by 1916, except the liquor and textile trades, scared of the impact of women voters, lobbied viciously against it. President Woodrow Wilson made it official administration policy and Congress passed the legislation by June of 1919. Ratification of the 19th Amendment came in August of 1920 to the everlasting joy of American women and just in time for Adela to vote for the first time in the national election the following November. As a Republican, she had voted for the presidential winner, Warren G. Harding.

About the same time, the Rost family embarked on a travel adventure spearheaded by Adela. She questioned her friends, the few who had actually taken a vacation away from home in the day when the concept was unfamiliar to most folks, thought about her desire to go away from the heat and humidity of Illinois summers, and decided to travel north to the Great Lakes. Her memories of travel in the Lake District of England still captivated her thoughts suggesting that perhaps she could give those same positive impressions to John and little Mary and Ada. Through the railroad company she was able to book passage on a Lake Michigan steamer out of Chicago. They traveled by train from Minier to the big lake harbor in Chicago where they boarded the steamer. Slowly, they steamed northward with the temperatures noticeably cooling by the hour, refreshment and relaxation working a continuous balm to their spirits. Though travel away for even a night would have been impossible to their farmer friends back home, John was able to engage the help of a fellow Minier doctor to care for his patients. It was easier to find a substitute for sick humans than for the farm animals!

Dr. Rost, Ada, Mary, and Adela

Accommodations were far from that of today's cruise ships but they had a stateroom, personal servants, and fine food featuring lake trout freshly caught each day by local fishermen who rowed up to sell their catch to the chef. Mary and Ada had never seen such a big body of water nor a sunset over the water and so were entertained just walking the decks, playing croquet, and generally accepting the admiration of fellow travelers. No stops were made until the ship arrived at the Harbor on Mackinack Island which is at the juncture of Lakes Michigan and Huron hundreds of miles north of their port of embarkation. There they left the ship for the first time to walk on land, ride by horse drawn coach to the Grand Hotel for tea, and walk the gardens and back down to the harbor to board their waiting steamer. The railroad company owned the Grand Hotel so a stop at the hotel was mandatory for all their customers thus providing a lifetime memory for the two little girls.

As she had in England, Adela delighted to see the shimmering, rippling village as it was reflected in the water upon their arrival in Mackinack. When the little girls begged to take off their shoes, walk on the sand, and finally ankle-deep in the cool water, she naturally acquiesced. They were on vacation after all! The pine trees were again being re-established on the island as on the mainland now that the clear-cutting of all the Michigan virgin forests was finished. Trees were about man-tall at the time, a far less glorious sight than they had been just twenty-five years prior, but the rough-necked loggers and their equipment were gone, elegant summer homes were being constructed, the banks of lavender lilacs were blooming below the old fort, and elegant visitors from all over the Midwest were coming to vacation at the Grand Hotel.

Back in Minier, Adela was busy with her civic duties on the cemetery board, at church, S.O.P.H., and University Women's Club of women from the entire Tazewell County including Bloomington, and of course overseeing her daughters' school work. She still loved to read and by example instilled a lifelong love of reading in her daughters. She employed the help of a farm girl, for even in 1920 the housewife had to chop wood for the stove, clean the lanterns, and carry water from the pump. The whole family, except for Grandpa, slept summer and winter in a big sleeping porch, windowed on three sides, on the top floor of the house. They had one of the first telephones in the village because John had to be available at any hour to his patients. Life was good!

And then she received the diagnosis. Only forty years old, always hearty and hale, to the point of becoming a bit stout, in fact, she felt the lump in her breast. John confirmed there was a lump which had to be removed right away. He didn't have surgical privileges at the hospital in

Bloomington but engaged the best of his colleagues who did to perform the mastectomy operation. Afterwards, Adela recovered and all seemed just a bad dream as she tried to get on with her active life. The idyllic life of the Rosts never quite resumed, however, because new aches and tender spots appeared. In the early 1920's before cat scans or even x-ray machines, all a physician could do was to cut open the patient's vital parts and have a look. This the surgeon did and immediately closed Adela's incision for the cancer had spread far from the breast. There was nothing even her dear husband John could do. No radiation or chemotherapy treatments existed at that time, no reliable pain medicine was available either, only crying and moans of agony were there for her to draw upon. A private nurse, Marie Cooney of Bloomington, was engaged to her care, but Adela suffered unspeakably and so did her husband, father, and daughters. For two years the torment they all felt never let up until November 21, 1926, when Adela succumbed to the cancer at home, in her own bed at the age of forty-two. It was over for Adela but for her daughters, her death was a permanent wound which would affect them all their long lives.

A last picture of Adela Peine Rost

As was customary in that day and particularly cruel for the little daughters, the body was dressed to be displayed right in the living room of the Rost home, visitors came to gaze and whisper laud, and a black taffeta wreath was hung on the front door seemingly to torture Mary and Ada for the requisite one year of mourning.

As a memorial the family had stone gates erected at the entrance to the Minier cemetery with the inscription: "In Memory of Adela L.C. Rost, November 1926." Her remains were interred just ahead along the drive with her Peine and Buehrig family members.

Generation # 2 – John Frederick Wilken Rost
—8—

John Rost was born December 1, 1882, in the small German community of Petersburg, Illinois, in Menard County just a bit west and south of Minier. Both of his parents had been born in Germany and met each other after settling in the Petersburg area. Village life for the Rosts at the end of the 19th Century was similar to that of the Peines when considering the state of technology, participation in one's chosen church, or their commitment to a social circle. However, there were differences stemming from the Rosts' lack of formal education; their status as immigrants; their lack of connection to the community leaders; in short, their lower social standing in the community.

To a growing boy like John, however, those differences were inconsequential. He was endowed with an optimistic, outgoing, fun-loving character which drew a plethora of companions to him. Those qualities combined with keen intelligence, drive, and athletic ability, made the butcher's son a standout in the small town, the equal of any boy at whistling, walking on stilts, climbing a tree, catching beetles, kindling a fire without a match, walking on his hands, using a jackknife, fighting with his bare hands, swimming in the Spoon River, or leg racing. All-American sports like baseball and football were burgeoning across the land in those days, claiming young John for an adherent, captivating his imagination and day-dreams in which he would one day play on a big league team!

John's extant Confirmation memories and autograph book, with prayers in the German language, from the day of his formal admission into the

Evangelical Church is revealing because each of the attendees signed their name and the place of their birth, including his parents, pastor, and friends.

John Rost at his Confirmation celebration

John did make the Petersburg High School teams for baseball and football. His time free from home chores and studies, in those days without the distractions of TV, internet, telephone, or family vacations, was spent perfecting his hitting, running, catching, and kicking. He made sure he had time for sports, disorganized as they were back then. The only incident which slowed his ambition and actually side-lined him was a serious tackle on the football field. Rudimentary medical care gave him a slight limp for the rest of his life, but his love of baseball and football never faltered.

As crushing a blow as it was to give up active sports participation, that was really a small problem compared to his dad's cancer diagnosis. No amount of wishing or praying it away helped. Dad just got weaker and weaker. The doctor who came to the house impressed young John with his knowledge and skill, and he took time to explain and console. In time the kindly doctor had become a role model, saw the intelligence of the young man, and helped John to discover his life trajectory. John, full of ambition, strove to qualify for medical school after undergraduate studies at the University of Illinois in Champaign.

The University of Illinois had only recently in 1867 been founded. Abraham Lincoln signed into law the Morrill Act of 1862 which established land grant colleges and universities all across America, making an affordable college education broadly available to the average citizen. Passed during the Civil War it was an act of faith in the nation's future. Illinois was one of sixty-nine colleges funded by those land grants.

Graduation from a university at the turn of the twentieth century was more than unusual. It represented an extraordinary less than 10% of all the college age population of the United States. In the entire country university student graduates then represented only 28,762 men and 8,437 women. In that very elite milieu, John graduated from the University of Illinois in Champaign and was accepted to the University of Illinois Medical Department College of Physicians and Surgeons in Chicago. From there he graduated fourth in his medical school class of one hundred men in 1906 while also elected by his classmates as treasurer of his class.

Yet in spite of his intelligence and conscientiousness, one of John's most endearing qualities was his playfulness. He had a merry way and hazel eyes that crinkled often as he played tricks with his folks and friends. Later as one of the village doctors in Minier he would try to put a little child at ease by asking her to say "Popocatepetl" and then laughing with the child when her tongue twisted while trying to pronounce the word. We are mystified that John knew of that active volcano, located 31 miles east of Mexico City at an altitude of 17,782 feet, named "smoking mountain" by the Aztecs! As a father, he loved to play April Fool jokes like making waffles with a cotton ball mixed into the batter and baked, or in order to get his daughters to eat more, he would cut up their food into tiny squares which he called pills and said "the doctor says to take all the pills!" Margaret Pleines Tanner, classmate friend of Mary, still recalled in her 90s his humor, his playfulness, his sunny outgoing personality, his fun-loving spirit which she had experienced in sleepovers in his home. In short, John Rost was high-spirited, fun-loving, very popular person whose optimism and joy d'vivre would serve him well in the coming ups and downs of his life.

In 1906, typhoid fever was the leading cause of death while tuberculosis, diphtheria, cholera, smallpox influenza, scarlet fever, and dysentery were close seconds; by 1917 the leading cause of death in the United States was tuberculosis. The role of bacteria in disease transmission was still a new discovery so that quarantine with the dreaded yellow sign posted on the front door was part of the treatment method. Amazing as it is to us today, the discovery that microorganisms cause disease has only been accepted for about the same time that the telephone or electric lights have existed! Calomel, a mercury containing purgative now known as a dangerous neurotoxin, was the remedy of choice for many illness in Dr. Rost's day. Caster oil, mainly used today in brake fluid, paint, and other industrial products, was also on the doctor's shelf then.

There were just an awful lot of ways to die at the turn of the century. Whooping cough killed about ten thousand children every year from 1840 to 1910. Measles killed even more. For awhile it was thought that diseases such as cholera struck only the poor, but then it began to strike down people in well-to-do neighborhoods as well, and very quickly the terror became general. People had never been so unnerved before by a disease. But even worse fears gripped folks in 1918, when the flu epidemic grew to world wide proportions, affecting even the war in Europe. Cleanliness was then as now a bulwark against disease and always the doctor's first line of defense in an epidemic. Papa Doc, as the little Rost girls called their father, insisted on frequent hand washing at home and forbade going barefoot as: "germs could enter the foot as well as the mouth!"

Dr. Rost had enlisted in World War I and as a first lieutenant served as a physician to injured and sick American soldiers brought back to the States on battleships. He spent his entire time stationed at hospitals near the port of New York City tending to sick and dying who surely were so glad to be on home ground, buoyed by the cheerful competence of the young Dr. Rost. From August to November of 1918 he was assigned to Camp Upton Base Hospital in Brooklyn, N.Y.; from November to May 1919 he was at Post Hospital Army Supply Base; and from May to July 1919 he was at Camp Merritt N.J. Base Hospital. His discharge was from Hoboken N.J. in July of 1919. To the doctor's delight, his dear wife, bitten by the "travel bug" so long ago, traveled by train to visit him, tour the city, and especially to lighten his days.

John Rost served in World Was I

As late even as the early days of the twentieth century, a country doctor like John would accept payment for services in barter form. It was not uncommon at all for the chicken which graced the Rost Sunday dinner, the jellies which lined the pantry shelf, the ironing placed crisply in the basket, or the steaming pie scenting the whole house to have been payment for services rendered. He wasn't at all the kind of man to carry a grudge, but John could be forgiven if later a glance at a baby now grown up could still elicit the image of a freshly baked ham!

The 1920s saw great advances in medicine; treatments were learned for diphtheria, whooping cough, measles, and influenza. Life expectancy was creeping up. At the office John kept an incredibly heavy iron safe with a combination lock entry known only to him and Adela in which

STORIES MY FOLKS TOLD ME

he secured the drugs he dispensed. He was his own pharmacist, first grinding the blocks of drugs by the piece, which he bought from a traveling pharmaceutical salesman, in a mortar and pestle, then carefully measuring on his medical scale, and finally tapping into small paper wrappers the individual dose. The resulting powder was, when prescribed, mixed with water to be swallowed. That very same safe, still operational but with changed combination, is even now in family possession.

Curing illnesses or treating maladies took much of John's time, but delivering babies was a very big and just possibly his favorite part of his job. Women, in the early 1900s bore four to eight babies, perhaps more, in the course of their lives; especially fruitful were the country women who formed the bulk of his patients. John was not immune to the gravity of his position in the village as illustrated by his comment in June of 1942 when he attended Emma Graff Oehler (mother of Bill whom he had delivered and was now a classmate of Mary), who had been felled by a stroke: "I see it all. It's so happy when they come and so sad when they go!"

It was indeed an emotionally weighty job John had dealing with suffering and death on a daily basis, but there was compensation to spare in the recovery of a patient to health, in the safe delivery of literally hundreds of babies he delivered far out in the country under less than ideal conditions, and especially in the love he found with Adela in their home. He never left the house to make his rounds without first going to her with a kiss on his lips. He would have agreed with Sophocles who said over 400 years before Christ: "One word frees us of all the weight and pain of life. That word is love."

Together they lived the good life in early 20th Century Minier. They lived in a large prestigious home, drove a car, traveled, dressed themselves and their two daughters well, had friends in Bloomington with whom they exchanged dinner parties, and entertained at boisterously merry card parties. They asked each other: "Could life be any better?" Why, they had actually had a "honeymoon trip," practically unheard of in Minier! All the way to Colorado to see what mountains looked like! They took their little daughters on a Lake Michigan steamship cruise just to get away from the heat and humidity of Minier one summer.

Oh, there were times when the insular environment of a small town could approach the suffocating level as when patients would tempt John to deny his vow to doctor-patient secrecy by asking pesky, intrusive questions about another patient or when gossips circulated untrue or exaggerated statements about a church friend or when jealous claimants spoke mean, half-truths about a more successful friend. But for the most part Adela and John were comfortable with their lives in the village where like all others of the day public opinion was the powerful regulator of behavior. In Europe, standards had been set by the monarchy, aristocrats, the institutional churches, and other ancient institutions but in small town America one's behavior was guided by family pride, the concept of shame, and the churches.

Aware of his position in the community yet forced often to walk along dusty, muddy lanes to visit a patient and genuinely enthusiastic about his sartorial self, John was fastidious about his appearance. Near the door where he exited the house each morning, stood a hand crafted box eighteen inches square and no matter how hurried he was he bent to open the lid, stepped one shoe onto the three inch high mold of a shoe sole, grabbed the nearby paste polish and a brush from the box and shined his shoe. The act was then repeated on the other shoe. John's son-in-law Bill Oehler later in the 1950s, so enamored of the box which came to him at Dr. Rost's death, turned out in his basement woodworking shop nearly a dozen oak replicas of the shoe box to give as Christmas presents. Several exist today in family possession.

One of John's favorite stress relievers was to amble over to the village ball field and watch the young men hit a few, maybe call out a suggestion or two to the batter, and generally kibitz with the players on the bench or his friends in the stands. He still knew a thing about the game and delighted to just talk the talk though relegated by his injury to the sidelines.

Watching Adela steadily decline after her breast cancer diagnosis and mastectomy in 1924 was the hardest thing John had ever been subjected to. There he was, a doctor, claiming all the knowledge to heal and cure; yet, he could not stop for more than a few months the inexorable progression of her disease. He was in agony! She was in agony! Her father was in agony! The little girls were frightened to death, acting one minute like the carefree eight and twelve year olds that they were and the next minute like traumatized little old ladies. Those two years were a kind of hell for them all. Life seemed to contract and stop with nothing making sense outside of Adela's four bedroom walls. There they clustered, pleading with all the forces they could muster for a pivot of the inevitable. George, especially, never left the bedside reading to her, talking, just holding her hand till John got home.

When the end came on November 21, 1926, they were all exhausted and beset by profound grief. John's mother came from Petersburg to keep house for the bereft family. The funeral filled the church and the cortege to the cemetery was endless. Mary, now fourteen, refused to get out of the car and stand at the grave-site, but John had not the energy to command her. "Let them talk," he said to himself, "We each just have to get through this in our own way, somehow."

They were groping their way now, Ada the next Mother's Day refusing to take part in the school program for the mothers (and hating that day for the rest of her life), John looking at Mary at an eighth grade event, seeing how sad she looked standing there and how her dress was of the wrong cut, not at all the latest style it would have been had Adela been there to choose it.

By July the concrete gates erected at the entrance to the cemetery, as a memorial to Adela by John and George were ready for the dedication ceremony, another pronouncement that Mama was gone never to return, painful for Mary and Ada despite the laudatory words, the chorus performance, and the five hundred people in attendance. Adela had been a charter member of the cemetery board, served as its secretary, thus it seemed a fitting memorial to her.

John was still miserable too, distracted yes by his work, thankful for his mother's help, but at the same time felt surprisingly lonely and disoriented as if an earthquake had gone off beneath his feet and sent him flying to a distant land where he saw nothing familiar and didn't understand the language.

Mysteriously, he kept running into Marie Cooney, the mid thirty year old nurse who had come to the house to care for Adela during her illness. Whenever John was making rounds visiting his patients in the hospital in Bloomington, it seemed she was always crossing his path with her pretty smile, light blue eyes, and head of golden, auburn hair. He was lonely, flattered to have the attention of an attractive young woman, and at the same time he felt guilty for wanting to keep company of someone of the opposite sex. Still in his early forties, he couldn't help feeling he was missing out on life; it was a quandary that he felt himself drawn more and more to be with her.

Marie's Roman Catholic religion was a definite obstacle to John when he thought of marriage. Her desire for children, contrary to his own plan for the future, was also a barrier. Still, she was fun, could talk football with the best and shared with him an interest in the medical field. Before he knew it, he was bringing her to the house to join in activities with Mary and Ada. He noticed the sour looks on the girls' faces but was sure he could change their minds in time and just hoped for the best. John, himself, was so happy now that if Pauline, Teddy, Paul, George, or even his own mother tried to talk him out of the marriage they didn't get through to him, and the simple wedding at the Justice of the Peace office in Bloomington took place before the year was out.

The newlyweds were barely back from their honeymoon trip when the stress began. First Margarethe was sent packing, for a kitchen is rarely big enough for two women. Marie was actually a good cook but the entrées were unfamiliar to the little girls; Mama had cooked German style while Marie was of Irish descent. A great admirer of hand stitching, Marie determined that Mary and Ada should learn cross stitch and took them to classes where they turned out a couple of pretty hand towels still in family possession. Through her priest brother's connection at Notre Dame University in South Bend, Indiana, she procured tickets to football games there, delighting the Rost family no end.

But Marie could somehow never win over the little girls, still miserable over the loss of their mother, not understanding how their Papa Doc could actually marry any woman, resenting that another woman would move into their home, use Mama's Haviland dishes, her place at the table, her bed. Of the opinion that the girls were spoiled, Marie began to demand that they assume cleaning chores in the house even though there was a county girl who did that; Mama had felt they should spend their time on book learning instead of women's work, should read the good books she lined the shelves with, should read the newspaper and learn to discuss the current events. Marie would pick at them and nag all day long until Papa Doc came home when she became sweet as syrup. Her first real victim, however, was George Peine, the venerable builder of the house she lived in, the still grieving father of Adela, the non-adversarial gentlemen of the village whom she literally drove out of the house to live with his son, Paul, back from Montana and living for good in Minier because of Adela's death.

Something like a complete personality change or perhaps mental illness came over Marie for she was making life miserable for each member of the family even John, intentionally neglecting to tell him when sick patients had phoned for him, whose very career as a doctor and his standing in the community depended on a quick response to their cries for help. For a doctor, constantly at the beck and call of his patients such obstinate behavior was unforgivable forcing him to ask the central operator at the telephone exchange to collect the calls for him instead of putting them through directly to his home. He was working himself to the edge now not wishing to be at home where cutting slurs about his sinful Protestant beliefs were hurled at John daily, where food sloppily prepared was slung to his place at table when he arrived far later than the usual dinner hour, where lies about Mary's status at the University of Iowa were contrived. Divorce which had never occurred in his family, had never occurred in the village as best he knew, crossed his mind, even discussed with his daughters, but social convention held him back.

Behind closed doors unknown to neighbors or fellow Minier citizens, perhaps even to relatives including the larger circle of Buehrigs and Peines, the ongoing ordeal experienced by John, Mary, and Ada was discussed only within their intimate circle, only at the doctor's office after visiting hours when the grown daughters were in Minier. Visits to their paternal home where they had grown up could not be offered by John to his own daughters, their husbands, and three small granddaughters because Marie forbade them; though she tried to sever completely the ties between father and daughters, she was unsuccessful. Meetings, clandestine, hurried, and devoid of the comfort of home were held at least monthly when Mary stayed with her husband's Oehler family in Minier and Ada stayed with Willis and Della Peine of Minier.

Sadness, a part of every human life, was then as now the special purview of the country doctor, privy to the most secret, most embarrassing, most intimate of human interactions, and for all his open gregarious personality, John was a discrete man, able to keep the many secrets illumined to him in his role as physician. When Pauline called John out to the farm to have a look at her teen-age daughter, he had to confirm the suspicion that the girl was indeed pregnant by her teen farm boyfriend. What stunned him though was the announcement by mother and daughter that the baby would be kept a secret, be delivered by him and then be given up for adoption, a decision which ironically and unknown to them at the time meant that Pauline, whose daughters would both marry but too late to be mothers, would never know the joys of being a grandmother!

As was appropriate to all men above the manual worker station, John wore a fedora, a low soft felt hat with a brim, gently curled and lengthwise creased, so popular from the late 19th century and into the early 1950s when casual attire ascended to fashion in society. Its two pinches at the top of the crown, one on each side, were perfect for the owner to grab the hat to don (put on), doff (take off), or tip (a non-verbal greeting to an acquaintance, a woman, or a person of a higher position in society when encountered while walking on the street). Etiquette decreed that a man never wore his hat indoors. At the same time a man like John never exited his home unless dressed in a two-piece suit, necktie, starched white shirt, and perhaps a vest whether he was going to work, church, the home of a friend, meeting hall, or even to a picnic, a walk along country paths, or to the ball field. He owned no bluejeans but he did remove the jacket and tie to mow his lawn!

Work alone filled John's days then with very little joy, interspersed by the weddings of his daughters, Mary to William Peter Oehler on May 1, 1937 and Ada to Charles Franklin Seales, Junior, on May 1, 1943. Their visits to Minier, eventually with granddaughters Susanne and

Kathleen Oehler and Linda Seales, brought welcome family warmth to the man, remorseful that he could not invite his progeny to sleep in his home or share a meal there, much less share a mundane activity as listening together to a ball game on the radio or playing a game of dominos he was so fond of. Despite hateful tirades and threats of suicide hurled by Marie, John did occasionally and briefly escape to Moline and Lakewood, Ohio, where his daughters lived.

By the time John reached his sixties, the stress of life with a hysterical, perhaps mad, woman had taken its toll on his health, sending him to the Mennonite Hospital in Bloomington in early 1949 with heart disease symptoms. Home again, he resumed his schedule of seeing patients in his office situated on the commercial street of Minier and driving out to the farms to deliver babies or tend to the sick or injured. But on a Sunday, February night he was stricken with a major heart attack and within hours his bittersweet sojourn on this earth ended. According to his obituary in the Minier News: "Dr. Rost's sudden death is keenly felt by everyone and he will be missed in the community.... The many floral offerings evidenced the esteem in which Dr. Rost was held by everyone....Sixteen doctors from Bloomington and surrounding vicinities, with whom he had associated during his many years of practice, served as honorary pallbearers....He served during World War I in eastern camps and held the rank of lieutenant. During World War II he again served but this time at home in a wide vicinity, calling night and day on the sick, in communities who were without doctors due to the war....He was a member of the American Legion.... His faithfulness and patience will long be remembered. A poignant scene Wednesday morning was when the school children called with their teachers at the funeral home to pay their respects to the "Doctor," many of whom he brought into the world." The good doctor held membership in the American Medical Association, the Illinois State Medical Society, and the Tazewell County Medical Society.

In that day before health insurance, when there was no recourse to the country doctor if his bill went unpaid, when payment might be a couple of chickens, glasses of jam, or part of a newly butchered hog instead of currency, John nevertheless made an ample living, able to leave a generous estate for his daughters. Savings account, bonds, life insurance policies, and the house in Minier were divided evenly between his daughters enabling Mary and Bill to build their dream home in Moline, Ada and Chuck to do likewise in Arlington Heights, Illinois. For Marie there was a modest life insurance policy to get her resettled in Bloomington and back to work as a nurse.

Yes, Adela's death was a permanent wound for the family she left behind. John, her passing left vulnerable, weakened to make one fatal decision which cost him his happy lot in life, his sunny disposition, his happy home, even his health. As a successful country doctor he was accustomed to fixing people's broken parts, to restoring their health, to returning their happiness, but he never could find a way to solve his own twenty-year-long problem.

Of course, John recognized that no life is truly full and deeply lived when there is no sorrow. It molds and teaches us that there is a far deeper significance to life than might be supposed if one passed through this world forever happy and carefree. True as that may be when one has come through the sorrow and is looking back at it, but for John it never ended, could not be seen as character strengthening or instructive but only as a bitter pill which he had to take each and every day until he died.

John Rost's remains lie beside those of Adela in Minier cemetery—at peace from his ordeal at last.

John Rost near the end of his life

STORIES MY FOLKS TOLD ME

Generation #2 — Emma Elizabeth Graff Oehler
—4—and—5—and—6—

Arriving seventh of eight children of Peter and Elizabeth Graff on May 6, 1878, Emma Elizabeth grew up in a household she relished for the rollicking good fun of five boisterous brothers and two adored older sisters. German was the language of the home and church; customs though were a mixture of those from the old country and those of America learned primarily at the country school she attended for approximately four years, lastingly impressed by the young American woman who taught her there. Because Emma, like her siblings, learned English before they were thirteen years old they spoke both languages without a foreign accent.

Though she might have preferred to attend school more years, Emma like all farm children of her day was needed in the field, from the earliest moment possible a unit of production, participating in a type of work far more desirable than factory work or mining. Knowing that farm children would not be allowed to attend school in fine weather, the mistress of the school house only presided during the winter months, taught all ages of children bearing a slate and chalk instead of paper and pencil, and won their respect by the wonderful stories she told and books she read to them.

As a little farm girl, Emma was completely embedded in the bucolic life: the joy of spring, the labors of summer, the relief and appreciation at the bounty of fall, the quiet and rest of winter, the need for rain, the surfeit of rain, the weather and the commodity price worries which were the burning concerns of each day. Too much rain in the Spring meant Papa and her brothers couldn't get into the flooded fields to plant at the appropriate time. Too much rain in the Fall meant the corn would be too wet to harvest, in that day before artificial dryers; there wouldn't be enough time for it to dry in the field before the killing frost. It was no wonder Emma developed a reputation as a little "worry wort!" Like all country girls, Emma knew those thunderstorms so awaited by Papa could be terrifying to her, as they approached from afar with rolling, growing, growling, and finally roaring, cracking, pealing thunder. Lightning, which cleft the sky, came moments later, illumined the objects in her dark bedroom, metamorphosed them into ghastly, scary, frightfully magnified forms, and could last half the night, causing her to cling terrified to her bedmate, Annie, also lying in wait as if for her doom.

Emma's day began at daylight when came the little homely everyday duties connected with feeding not only the family but their domesticated animals so dependent on them. She loved it when it was her turn to go out in the gloaming to call the cows home to be milked, and she happily sauntered back to the barn behind the patient slow-gaited creatures. Emma loved the homely murmurs of the farm: the feel of the warm breath of a cow on her hand, the smell of the rich warm dung in the shed, the cluck of the hens, the screech of the cock, the clank of pails at the well. She belonged to the soil and was rooted to the earth as generations of her forefathers had been. Evening darkness in her country home gathered all the family members together in one room, forced them to settle to some sedentary employment like knitting, story telling, or Bible reading, around a candle or gas light till sleep came and ended the day. It was as if the warm glow of love, not only the lamplight, enveloped them in their circle!

When in the course of the growing season rain was desperately needed, the whole family joined Papa out in the field searching the sky, stress lining his face, waiting, yearning, willing the clouds to open and the big Illinois raindrops to fall. He had wagered everything he had on this crop! Then just in time, true to Tazewell County history of temperate climate, exhaustless soil, and exactly the desired amount of precipitation to offer abundant return for their labor, the rain arrived accompanied by deafening crashes of thunder and blazing streaks of lightning. Not only the corn drank in the gushing bounty, but the jubilant children ran amidst the drops, faces uplifted, mouths open, to taste the cooling, life-giving sweetness.

Emma quickly mastered the seamstress skills from her mother and older sisters, sewing first the chambray shirts for her brothers and later for her husband and four sons, her own girlish calico dresses and those of her doll. Likely, she first perfected the necessary hand stitches on a "sampler" as was customary in her childhood. Clothing she fashioned on the family Singer treadle sewing machine, but the many quilts Emma made throughout her lifetime were sewn by hand in a crazy quilt or even a formal pattern from fabric scraps taken from garment remnants. When a piece of cloth was unsuitable for the quilt it was relegated to the "rag bin" still usable for many functions before paper towels, kleenex, or plastic bags were invented. "Waste not, want not" was a dictum of the new country as well as the old.

As she grew to womanhood, Emma acquired laudable cooking skills though performed without the use of measuring spoons, cups, or a scale, with recipes wonderfully imprecise calling merely for "some flour" or "enough milk." Her recipe for lemon chiffon pie for example: Bring to a boil one cup water, butter the size of a walnut, and one scant cup of sugar. Add two tablespoons corn starch dissolved in a little water. Cook until clear. Remove from the stove and add yolks of two eggs and the grated rind and juice of two lemons. Beat two egg whites sweetened with two tablespoons of powdered sugar. Fold into the lemon mixture. Pour into a baked pie shell. Put in oven till meringue is set.

In the kitchen, a black wood-burning stove provided warmth as well as the means for cooking and together with the black cast iron stove in the main room, vent pipe rising and letting smoke exit the house through one of the walls, it heated the house. If wood was scarce on the farm, corn cobs were burned, until eventually coal was the fuel of choice for the increased amount of heat if offered over wood.

A typical young woman of the turn of the century, Emma mastered the home canning process known as the "open kettle method" to preserve the fruits and vegetable harvested by the family for winter consumption. It was another arduous job which took place in the hot kitchen of late summer: glass jars filled with beans or berries, sweet syrup or boiling hot brine poured to the tip top, tightly closed with screw lids, and cooked for the requisite time in huge pots of boiling water. Emma knew the consequences of a bit of air at the top of the jar or not heating the contents enough to be sterile. A lid not entirely sterile could be infected with bacteria which would grow over the months and cause sickness to the person who ate of that jar! Therefore, following all the hard work she inspected the jars looking for bubbles, promptly though reluctantly, discarding those which bore the tale tell signs of spoilage.

Laundry duty was another chore which fell to young Emma, and chore it was in those days near the end of the century. Before detergents, laundry had to be soaked in soapy water with lye for hours, then pounded and scrubbed on a washboard, boiled if necessary, rinsed repeatedly, wrung through a roller-wringer to remove excess water, and finally hung on the line outdoors if weather permitted or draped around the stove indoors. Needless to say, folks were encouraged to wear their clothes as long as possible before throwing them in the laundry. Difficult or delicate fabrics, velvet or lace had to be treated with the greatest of care, often taken apart, parts washed separately, and then sewed back together. Because most dies were unstable, it was necessary to add precise doses of chemical compounds to the water of every load—Alum and vinegar for greens, baking soda for purples, oil of vitriol for reds—either to preserve the color or to restore it. There were recipes which mother passed down to daughter for removing various kinds of stains.

Incredibly those were also the days when men and women wore starched collars and cuffs, waistbands, and blouses. Starching was such a big job that it was left to a following day, a process which began by first making their own starch: mix a large spoon of cornstarch with a mason jar of water, stir till cloudy, dip the garment part in or pour the solution over the cloth, let almost dry, and press with the iron, hot from the stove but not so hot as to scorch!

Ironing was another massive and daunting job. Several irons were employed with one wooden handle to which an iron once heated on the wood stove was clasped by a metal hook. Generally, there would be one on the go and two heating on the fire grate. The irons, heavy in themselves, had to be pressed down on the fabric with great force to get the desired results. But because there were no controls, they had to be wielded with delicacy and care so as not to scorch the fabric. Heating irons over a fire made them sooty, too, so they had to be constantly inspected and wiped down. If starch was involved, it stuck to the bottom of the iron and could only be laboriously removed with sandpaper or an emery board. If anything drove the Graff family members to bed early it was not the dim lighting but exhaustion! Whether on the farm or in the factory, the day of labor was long and arduous!

Still, the Graffs would be the first to remind us of the good times, spent all ten of them together, in the midst of their daily lives. The five boys were terrible teasers, big and brash, loud and funny, given to boxing and wrestling, driven by Mama to "Go to the barn! You can't act like that in here!" Told by Pa to meet him behind the proverbial wood shed, they knew what that meant too. They were the ones though to saddle up the horse and wagon, drive the family to Danvers for the church ice cream social, for the July 4th parade and speeches, or for political gatherings before an election. Much of the fun of those events was in the preparation, itself. Japanese lanterns were strung from trees and posts, tables were improvised with rough boards, tickets were printed by hand. And then there was the ice cream! Made from good fresh country cream, turned by hand in the bucket set in ice cut the previous winter from the pond, covered with sawdust a natural insulator, and stored in the ice house, the ice cream was a worthy treat, served sometimes with cake and strawberries like having a little heaven on earth!

Today one must plan ahead, make arrangements in order to immerse oneself in nature while Emma had only to walk outdoors to be reminded that nature has a plan and she was a part of it. She didn't know it but even Aristotle knew this and said for all eternity: "Nature does nothing uselessly." Emma probably observed that nature reminds us that rootless things die, that there is an order to beauty, that there is a reason for everything, that nature does not waste time. Nature teaches patience which is the companion of wisdom, anything valuable is going to take time; we must wait for the seedlings, for the rain, for the harvest. Waiting gives us something to look forward to! She never asked herself where she would like to go on vacation, in which restaurant she would choose to eat, which cereal she should buy, or which TV show she'd like to watch yet, if asked, she would probably have described her life as rich and full.

True to the custom of the day, Emma's family were church-going religious. Thievery, bullying, disrespect, public insult were rare in those pastoral communities of long ago where a spirit of truth and goodness pervaded lives. Folks, indeed, knew right from wrong, recognized truth from sham, and behaved in a manner to acknowledge so. Those same folks could be seen today, though, as stubborn, suspicious of outsiders especially Catholics and Jews, unfamiliar with the concepts of multiculturalism or equality of outcome, yet they brought to their society just the right qualities to ensure its health, happiness, strength, and success.

Still it must be acknowledged that even during ostensibly happy times and at an early age Emma occasionally suffered from a kind of melancholy, seized by tears she couldn't stop, for reasons she knew not, a silent misery she had to endure yet subjected on others as well for they naturally thought they had done something wrong, said something to offend her when of course it was no one's fault, just brain chemicals not synapsing in the normal sequence. Today she would have popped a pill, but back then she just had to get beyond the mysterious "dark times." Perhaps it was a result of so many Imigs marrying Graffs.

Of consoling importance to Emma was her special relationship with her sister Annie, but also her love of the outdoors of farm life. The barnyard sounds of cattle lowing, the cackle and clatter of chickens, the dawn beginning with a line of yellow in the sky, spreading horizontally, taking in more and more tints of gold and wine, the orange sunsets over the luscious green fields, the spectacular starry nights above, the special light yellow green of new leaves in Spring, the wonder of the apple tree in blossom, the fragrance of mown hay or the warm fermenting smell of the hay drying in huge stacks, fields long—all struck a very deep chord in the heart of the tender girl.

Every day of her life Emma spent with her big sister Annie and every night she lay next to her in the big bed talking over the events of the day: Mama "picked" on them because they didn't haul water for the dishwashing fast enough, teacher read them such a wonderful story, friend Maude was sure proud of her new shoes, they would never brag like that. Soon enough their whispered moonlight conversations tended to boys. Who was cute or who was funny? Just as girls the world over have always done, amid giggles and shrieks of glee followed by Papa's

STORIES MY FOLKS TOLD ME

shout to "pipe down!" the two expressed the many universal phases of girlhood.

By the time Emma was twenty-one and Annie was twenty-four they had promised themselves to William Oehler and Jacob Imig, respectively. The double wedding, already described as printed in the "Daily Pantograph," followed on January 10, 1900, with Papa and Mama pulling out all the stops to fete their girls. Months long preparations of sewing, baking, and cleaning had led to the the big day as if life were wholly suspended in one big logistical project. After all, one hundred friends and relatives were expected at the ceremony to be held indoors in their own home in the dead of winter! They all had to be fed! There had to be room for the organ and organist, coats and boots, extra chairs, borrowed dishes and tableware. The Graffs had a large home occupied by eleven people, but this double wedding surely strained all bounds!

Wedding portrait of Emma and Will Oehler

The big double wedding day brought the culmination of Emma and Annie's togetherness, their identical grey dresses trimmed in pearl lace, their shared happiness, the final expression of their common childhood. Now they were fully women and wives, oriented to their husbands instead of each other, looking to a future from their own homes—Emma and William on a farm near Danvers, Illinois, Annie and Jacob on a farm near Seward, Nebraska.

Social life for Emma and Will, even after marriage, continued with the younger set of both their large assembly of siblings. Birthdays, holidays, festivals in neighboring villages, bonfires, hayrack rides, church carnivals, barn raising were all occasions to mingle; the marriage of Emma's younger brother Louie Graff to Will's sister Emma Oehler was surely a romance fostered by Emma and Will.

Out on the farm with William, Emma knew how to perform her daily chores of cooking and cleaning, bread baking, sewing, tending the vegetable garden, canning and preserving, tending to the chickens, and carrying the "slop" or garbage out to the pigsty. Likely to her amazement the distaff work of the household filled every moment of her day without Annie to help her ease her burden. With William and the hired men out in the field all day, except when they came to her kitchen for the noon dinner, she couldn't help feeling lonely though at the same time she was far too busy to indulge in self-pity. All those waves of loneliness were dispelled some months later when on August 5 she gave birth to little Alvin William. He was coloring-wise a little replica of her with his blue eyes and wavy, auburn hair, a pride and joy to his young parents. Only eighteen months later, March 2, 1902, Delmar Henry arrived also with hazel eyes and sandy red hair, followed in another three years, March 30, 1905, by Jesse Dean with brown eyes like his papa and blond hair. It's fair to say that now Emma was one busy lady—and she loved it! But scarcely before she could recover from the birth, just nineteen months later on October 29, 1906, Lyla Elizabeth, blue-eyed and blond, arrived. At last a girl! A break of nearly six years then ensued during which they had moved to town before William Peter, brown eyed and blond, joined the Oehler family on June 16, 1912.

Lyla, Jess, Delmar, and Alvin Oehler

Annie, out on the farm in Nebraska, turned out to be a prolific young woman like Emma but spectacularly so when she produced twins, Edwin and Erwin, before 1900 was out. Vera followed in 1902 and Jacob in 1907. Over the years, the two sisters maintained their close bond by writing letters and even traveling by automobile with children in tow, to each other's homes. It was a long drive of many days along winding, two-lane roads through villages and towns like Peoria and Galesburg on their trajectory traveling northward to the bridge at Rock Island over the Mississippi River, and then straight west through all of southern Iowa to cross the Missouri River at Counsel Bluffs into Nebraska and finally to Annie and Jacob's farm near Seward. Although Emma's children all vied to go along, hotels were scarce and expensive, motels were non-existent, houses along their route with "rooms for rent" signs in the window didn't always appear at the right intervals to be of use to them, and sleeping space in the car was limited to two children maximum in addition to Emma and Will, so one year she took the two oldest boys, another Lyla and baby William, and another Jesse and Billie.

Rural life was granted to Emma and Will from the first days of their marriage, but though both had grown up on farms and knew the methods and techniques required for successful farming, it didn't suit

Will's temperament. Will had an ambition to build a business in the village; Emma longed to leave the isolation and drudgery of the farm. So it was that a severe drop in commodity prices in 1910 was the last straw for them and they left the farm to become entrepreneurs. Taking their possessions, they moved to a rental house on Eastern Avenue in Minier, and Emma found herself the wife of a manufacturer as Will partnered with Henry Valentine Schroeder in the manufacture of grain elevators.

Soon after Billie was born Will and Emma, flush with success of their business, built a home of their own at 205 Main St. in Minier, a "four-square" design with four bedrooms and a bathroom on the second floor, large foyer, living room (then called parlor), dining room and kitchen on the first. Many decorative "craftsman" features of cross-sawn oak embellished the rooms from built-in cabinets to newel posts which divided the living room from the foyer on one side and from the dining room on the other. A staircase led from both the foyer and the kitchen to a common landing, with a large window to the north yard and garden, and then on up to the second floor. The bathroom there was large and dominated by the grand, claw-foot bathtub, hot and cold running water piped to it. A "privy" or outhouse with two seats still stood in the back yard just out of custom, one bathroom in the house adequate for even a large family in those days. The chicken coop, a little two-story structure with a sloping entry board which could be raised up and closed to protect the resident rooster, several hens and chicks from town dogs or even foxes at night, supplied the family's eggs and fryer for Sunday dinner and consumed another portion of the yard. Emma's vegetable garden and strawberry patch lay on the north side of the house with all day sun as it rose in the east till it set in the west.

This home was truly spacious for the day. Four bedrooms, lavish for a family of seven, were apportioned to Will and Emma, the four boys together, Lyla alone, and a guest room for visiting relatives like Annie from Nebraska or grandparents making the rounds of their children's homes.

A large garage with space not only for the automobile but a tool shed and a workshop where all the boys learned woodworking skills was built after the house by a couple of years and stood separate from the main structure. It was a good thing too because when the big fire started, consuming the entire garage, Will was lucky to get the car out safely without having to worry about the house and contents. No one today remembers the source of the fire, but they sure remember the excitement and shock it caused! Saving that automobile was crucial to Will though he rarely drove his precious possession the few blocks to the center of town to his office and manufacturing plant. No, he walked "up-town" and home twice a day as was the custom back then. Then, as now, a man's automobile was somewhat of a status symbol in addition to a mode of transportation!

Coming six years after her last baby, after she had a studio portrait photographed of her "complete" family of four children, after she had given away all the infant clothes, Billy was truly a bonus baby, an unexpected surprise for Emma who rather doted on him. She entered him in the Beautiful Baby contest at the Tazewell County Fair and to her delight he won the blue ribbon. Billy sat on her lap till his feet reached the floor, he got more trips to visit the Nebraska relatives than anyone else, and though his big brothers didn't hesitate to discipline him Emma just couldn't.

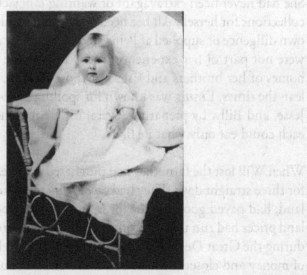

Emma's baby, Billy, won most beautiful baby award at the county fair.

The war years when the United States military fought the German people back in the place where her parents had been born and raised, about which only reverential descriptions had ever been imparted to her were very conflicting, embarrassing, and disappointing for Emma. She continued to speak German to her parents and Will's dad but no longer was that language spoken at church, school, or social events in the village in order to prevent suspicion of loyalty to the national enemy that was Germany. To her own children, Emma did not speak German so although they heard that language spoken by grandparents, other relatives, and their minister among others, they grew up fluent only in English.

Almost like a country dialect, however, the English spoken by Emma and her generation, raised in households dominated by the German language, taught English in school for only four or five years of their childhood, uninfluenced by modern communications such as the radio since it didn't even exist, tended to be spotted with what we would today call grammatical errors such as: "we was," "ain't," "they was," "you was," "we done," and "they seen."

The years of the Great Depression, 1927—32 were tough for Emma. She had never been extravagant or wanting fancy clothes, furniture, or collections for herself. All her needs were pretty much met through her own diligence or supplied at Peine's store; vacations or restaurant dining were not part of her experience; social life for the Oehlers was in the homes of her brothers and sisters or those of Will, but no matter how lean the times, Emma was known for spoiling her boys, Alvin, Delmar, Jesse, and Billy, by preparing several different dishes at a meal so that each could eat only what he liked.

When Will lost the farm they had purchased over near Decatur she cried for three straight days. They had saved long to make that investment in land, had payed good money for it, perhaps too good in the day when land prices had run up with corresponding interest to pay. Then one day during the Great Depression the value of the land fell, the banks ran out of money and closed their doors. Will's business suffered near collapse from lack of customers and Will could not meet the interest payments on the farm. But it actually got worse! Probably the lowest point came when Emma had to take in borders, to cook, clean, and serve for them. It didn't last long but she felt it was degrading after she had earned some status in the village as the wife of a small manufacturer to be placed in such a subservient role. Times were hard for everyone, though, in those days when employment was rare and cash was non-existent. To make matters even more dire, Will was left in the grain elevator manufacturing company with large debts. Compelled by integrity, Will worked for many years after the depression to pay back what he owed to suppliers and the bank.

As always a kind of consolation came to Emma when she immersed herself in her garden: tender spring, glowing summer, ripening autumn, stern winter; she found beauty and majesty in each season. She needed to be there hours at a time, of course, to plant, feed, weed, water, and pick the vegetables and strawberries she grew there for canning and for the yearlong sustenance of her large family. But it was also there that she surely found comfort and refreshment. Gardens have had a powerful hold over folks from time immemorial, always a source of healing, a magical place of beauty and wonderment which comforted when low feelings arose. The very act of planting a seed in the earth has had in it something very beautiful to men and women since the dawn of time. Emma probably did it with a joy that was mixed with awe, thinking how one of God's exquisite miracles was going on beneath the dark earth out of sight, turning the speck of a seed into a nourishing vegetable or exquisitely beautiful flower. Cut off from the presence of God within the walls of the church when she spurned the pastor, it was most likely in her garden that Emma was able to maintain her connection to the spiritual realm, led by the little everyday miracles there even to prayer.

Working with the hand of Nature as she did season after season, year after year surely returned her equilibrium to a state of happiness, refreshment, and joy many times. Flowers, too, she grew for the special gladness they gave her and gave to the recipients of her generosity. Such a sensitivity as Emma possessed must surely have recognized the supreme dignity of each flower with its reminder that life is fragile, life is transient, life is amazing. It was there, coincidentally, in her beloved garden in June of 1942 that Emma passed the last conscious moment of her life.

To the delight of Emma, right next door lived her oldest brother, Valentine or "Val," pronounced Vaul. He and his wife, "Vinie", pronounced with a long i, and short for Alvina, and their only child, Leah born in 1900 and who lived to the age of 100, could be counted on to provide many good lighthearted times. Emma's sons and daughter were pretty frequent visitors to Uncle Val and Aunt Vinie's back door where the word from inside was always a hearty: "Come on in!" Val had retired early from farming so could be counted on as a fun companion of the boys at cards and games when Vinie wasn't dishing up some special treat for the growing and always hungry boys.

Especially during the winter when outdoor chores had abated, Emma found employment and even great pleasure in the social activity known as quilting. Remnants left over from sewing for her daughter and sons, cloth from old clothes which was too good for the rag bin, and also newly purchased fabric would find their way into her "crazy" quilts or patchworks. In the afternoon after dishes from the noon-time dinner were washed and put away and the kitchen floor was mopped, Emma would set up the wooden framework in the living room for the arrival of her quilting friends. Then the fun and laughter would commence as conversation turned to gossip, to the exchange of recipes, or to announcements perhaps of a pregnancy. Though the purpose of the gathering of those half-dozen women was to create and assemble a warm bed covering, possibly the greater good came from the release from their household duties for a few hours and from the sense of joy at creating a thing of beauty together. All the women had by then mastered the many hand stitches required for quilting; indeed they had learned by stitching a child's "sampler."

All the dozens of chambray shirts Emma, with Lyla's assistance, made for her husband and four sons attested, too, to her sewing skills as well as her devotion to duty. She kept the treadle humming for hours on end, a comforting familiar sound to her children, recalled in their own later years. Emma may only have attended the country school three or four years, book reading was not a frequent occupation of hers, but based on the accomplishments of her children she was an intelligent women of many skills and talents with lots of loving ways to shower on her children and grandchildren.

Emma Graff Oehler

She could also shower her friends with loving attention and sometimes that took the form of cooking. Emma loved to entertain with all the organization, planning, issuing the invitations, securing the ingredients, setting the table in a pretty manner, and finally getting to work in the kitchen to make the event a success. When a woman, friend to Emma and to many in Minier, was about to move away from the community Emma prepared a famously spectacular luncheon in her honor filling the dining room to brimful with girlfriends. Then she repeated the exact same thing the following day so that the woman could say "good-bye" to all her friends, no one would be left out! But what a duplication of effort for Emma! What a loving heart and caring soul she had!

She could, however surprisingly, be offended, become angry, take the extreme measure of severing ties, and muster a stubborn streak to sustain the break. It is no longer remembered why, but in 1918 or so Emma became so outraged by a disagreement with the minister of the German Evangelical Church just down the street from her home that she declared that she was never going back, and she never did. Nor did her husband and children which resulted in a break, at a young age, in their religious training with long-lasting ramifications: her children never knew the special loving warmth that would have been bestowed on them had they shared a pew with parents, aunts, uncles, or cousins; they knew not the blessed spirit of God that comes to each member when a family prays together; they were denied the heightened degree of happiness which statistically accrues to church-going people; Billy"s marriage to Mary Rost had to be held in a hotel in Bloomington instead of Mary's church, the one Emma had broken from; Bill never attended church anywhere until his late 50s; Alvin never attended church again ever; and Lyla, Delmar, and Jess were adults before they returned to church-going. Yes, Emma's was an act of uprooting just as surely as when she tore a weed from her garden bed. As for herself, Emma likely felt that she entered the presence of God whenever she stepped into her garden!

An adamantly strong feeling against alcohol was also somehow embedded in Emma's character. We will never know for sure, but it is easy to think that perhaps someone she had grown up close to drank to excess and while under the influence had affected her life negatively or undoubtedly she was influenced by the temperance movement in America gaining prominence at the turn of the 20th Century until it became law by amendment to the Constitution in 1920. Alcohol abuse, with annual per capita consumption of 2.6 gallons, was considered then to be quite a serious problem, a public health issue contributing to domestic abuse and poverty whether in rural areas, villages or cities. Lectures against the evil to her sons were commonplace, no bottles were allowed in her house, no tale-tell licker breath was permitted over her threshold, until later in their own homes the boys had to hide it under the kitchen sink with the cleaning liquids when she visited.

Gifts, in the day when the farmer's wealth was in the form of land not convertible cash to make a purchase and especially during the Great Depression, were often sewed by Emma, generous hearted and thoughtful, fashioning a very special object with her own hands. When the two year old daughter of a neighbor in Minier died, Emma, alone and unbidden, selected a lovely fabric at the Peine dry goods store and overnight sewed a pretty dress for the toddler to be buried in. Sympathetic and tender-hearted, Emma was a caring, loving kind of woman.

As her own daughter, Lyla, wrote on a 10 degree January day in 1982 from Bloomington, Illinois, to a questioning niece, Kathleen Oehler: "As to my mother if you and I had a few days together I could tell you more. She was a homemaker all the way. For one thing she baked all her bread, coffee cake or doughnuts for a family of seven. She had a tiny bread pan and a little round pan about four inches diameter and every time baked a little loaf of bread and coffee cake for my tea parties. Your Daddy and a friend had a tea party one day when I was in school (he was about four) and he broke a cup and another time a saucer from my dishes. Each time I think of it I remember crying tears over that.

"Also I remember she baked sugar cookies—big round ones—and kept them in a stone lard jar with a round board lid, and we always hit the cookie jar right after school. She also did all the sewing. Made my clothes and all the four boys' shirts, blue chambray for school and light stripe or check for Sunday. She had me at the sewing machine sewing on aprons, etc. by the time I was ten. Your Dad even sewed plain seams for her. He loved the sewing machine. Also she always knotted a new comforter and pieced and quilted a quilt every winter. She used to sit at the machine and would treadle with her feet and use her hands and always sang church hymns as she sewed.

"Also I remember that when she died she had eighty-five floral pieces. Many came from kids she had fed cookies to, girls she had made a new dress for that couldn't get one, and people she had helped and kept in our home. She was a plain woman, never asked for much but gave the only thing she could and that was food and kindness."

Nicknames, though the "cat's pajamas" as they said in the twenties, were not to Emma's liking especially when they pertained to her boys! Because he liked to eat potatoes so much, Alvin was nicknamed "Spud" from high school to his dying day; because he liked to fish the local ponds for perch, Delmar was forever known as "Perch;" Jesse Dean became simply "Jess;" the younger two children were content with Lyla, and Bill. Emma and Will continued to refer to their older sons, though, by their given names no matter what the craze!

Emma, always ambitious for her children took great pride in the advanced education her sons aspired to. Her firstborn, Alvin, went all the way to the University of Wisconsin in Madison because he wanted to go to college but the University of Illinois did not at that time recognize his high school degree from the unaccredited Minier High School. There Alvin studied business administration, pledged Phi Gamma Delta fraternity, and finished the one year there required for admission to Illinois in Champaign, IL, where he subsequently transferred. The Oehler's finances were flush in that year around 1920 so they could afford the fancy clothes and out of state tuition, the fraternity membership desired by Alvin. But the reversal gradually came as the general economic depression gathered steam all across the nation. Delmar attended Illinois State University in Bloomington, Jesse Dean attended Brown's Business School in Peoria, Bill attended Augustana College in Rock Island, IL, while living with Alvin and his wife Katharine in Moline for a year and then two and a half years at the University of Illinois in Champaign.

1927 was a particularly sorrowful year for Emma. She had already lost her mother in 1906 and her father in 1911 plus sister Lizzy and brother Charles, but she was completely unprepared that her beloved Annie would go at age of fifty-four, final good-byes never uttered because of the many miles between them! Emma resolved amid her tears that the strong connection between her family in Minier and Annie's in Nebraska would never fray and indeed they extended for another two generations as Lyla and Bill took their children to Seward to visit Annie's daughter, Vera and her daughter Marguerite Ann and son T.R.

Yes, the long trek to the Nebraska relatives continued as long as Vera, Annie's daughter, lived. Bill and Mary with their daughters visited in the 1940s, Bill and Lila sent their daughters to visit her in 1955, and then the meetings transferred to central Florida when in the 1980s and 90s Bill and Mary lived in Inverness and Marguerite Ann (now Marg), Vera's daughter, lived in nearby Leesburg as did Annie's granddaughter by son, Edwin Imig, Barbara Jean Pfeiffer, and Annie's grandson by

Edwin, Donald Imig. With Annie's son and twin of Edwin, Erwin, the Illinois cousins remained associated as well. Annie's grandson in Lincoln, Nebraska, Jacob Imig, rose there to executive office of Deloitte Haskins and Sells. Those bonds would have warmed the sisters' hearts! Yet another generation of connection followed with the close association in Florida of Bill's daughter Kathleen and Marg until her death of lupus complications in 2010.

All Emma's children, too, went on to lead successful lives and she lived long enough to see that it was so, having raised them like all good mothers in a sort of crucible for making good character called family life. All those motherly warm smiles, caressing touches, hugs, and constant chatter between mother and child which children crave and which bring out the best in both mother and child, all the rough and tumble, chaotic banter between siblings, all the discipline from mother and father day after day, year after year is like a vessel where tin and copper are heated in a big metal bowl till they become bronze, a substance stronger than the sum of its parts.

The bonds of kinship established in the village of Minier were very important to society as a whole, established and strengthened by frequent celebrations in the park, complete with music from the bandstand and speakers from the podium, some still proclaimed in the German language. Games and races involved the children; 125 gallons of ice cream were sold. Emma proudly watched Alvin take first place in the fifty-yard dash, Jesse take first in the under twelve year old boys race. In the 100 yard even race, under sixteen, Alvin took second place, Jesse took second in the under twelve age group. She was likely glad to see all that energy, so troublesome and unmanageable at home, could be focused to a positive end in front of all her friends and relatives!

When on May Day of 1937, Billy married Mary Rost, the daughter of the family doctor who had delivered Billy, Emma and Will saw all their children married. But they still were not grandparents! That was out of their control, Will assured her.

Happily on December 2, 1939, Lyla was delivered of Rita Jeanne who brought almost as much joy to her grandmother Emma as to her mother and daddy, Delmar Johnson. Proximity of the Johnson farm just south of Minier made it possible for Emma to enjoy almost daily interaction with the new baby girl. Many happy hours were spent helping Lyla and acting as baby sitter, but Emma considered the pleasure all hers as she truly bonded with Rita Jeanne and relished her new role as loving grandma. As soon as Rita could stand beside her in the kitchen or perch on a counter, Emma bought a child-sized bread pan and a similarly scaled cookie sheet so together she and Rita would bake miniature treats to take home to mother. Another tradition involved a small, china, button-top shoe in which they placed little flowers they had picked from Emma's garden to take home and replenish at each visit. The little boot has continued to grace Rita's home always!

Then in March of 1941, Bill and Mary adopted Susanne who was already fifteen months old, in other words only one month younger than Rita Jeanne. Susie was brought to visit her grandmother once a month from Moline, the grandparents visited Moline, and so warm relations were forming between Emma and her granddaughters. Like her daddy, in Emma's eyes Susie could do no wrong. Once while sitting in the high chair with a bowl of cereal before her, Susie decided to pick up the bowl, turn it upside down and and squeal with delight when the contents fell off the tray onto the floor. Her mother Mary was shocked and sternly told her not to do that again, filled the bowl, and watched aghast as Susie repeated the previous fun exercise. When she began to lift Susie out of the chair to paddle her backside, Grandma Emma pleaded not to spank the child and so the toddler was spared and handed over to the loving grandmother for more tender pets.

Scarcely a year later on January 19, 1942, Mary was delivered of Kathleen Adela in Moline. Grandpa Doctor Rost was in attendance but Dr. John Gustafson was the presiding physician. Then the asphalt between Minier and Moline really began to heat up! Emma got Billy's old brown wicker baby buggy down from the attic for the new infant but truthfully, she could hardly lay the baby down in it for the joy she felt holding the little bundle close to her heart. Those happy months were limited though for Emma's high blood pressure was causing her to feel exhausted, a condition for which there was, unfortunately in 1942, nothing in Dr. Rost's bag to help her.

The end came on June 6, 1942. Two weeks earlier as Mary descended the stairs after nap-time with Kathleen in her arms and Susie at her hem, she stood at the landing between the kitchen and foyer looking out the window at the sunny day, when she spied Emma lying prostrate on the ground, the newly picked strawberries scattered. The scream "Bill" that Mary yelled stayed with little Susie all her life never to be forgotten! Bill and his dad carried Emma into the house, Dr. Rost was called and came right away, but Emma had suffered a stroke and never regained consciousness. During the ensuing two weeks while she lay lifeless in bed, Mary, Lyla, and Katharine supplied for her care. Spud and Bill came on week-ends after work hoping in vain to find an improvement in their mother's condition. As soon as Susie spotted her daddy's car in the driveway she somehow ran out of the house, clambered into it, and refused to leave, because in her toddler's mind that way she wasn't going to be separated from him again.

The end for Emma was quiet and almost imperceptible, her loved ones sitting helplessly at her bedside, sensing that an unseen hand was irretrievably upon her which neither skill nor prayer could remove. Bye and bye she would be taken away, no more with them, the agony that never finds solace, as she slipped seamlessly from this world to the next, too young at sixty-four but the way of many in those days before drugs were discovered to lower high blood pressure. And just as she was embarking on her joy-filled new role as loving grandmother! Those grandchildren, never to know the loving ministrations which only a grandmother can contribute to their well-being, suffered the loss as well. Dr. Rost's words said it best: "I see it all. It's so happy when they come and so sad when they go."

Emma was buried in the Minier cemetery in a very large plot presciently chosen by Will with his five children and spouses in mind.

Generation # 2 — William Frederich Oehler
—7—

The young immigrant couple, Wilhelm and Marie Oehler, could rightly deem it a good omen that their first little American baby was born on the very first day of the year 1874. As little William Frederick would perhaps later learn, some rather well known people would also first see the light of day in that year, but none on the very first day of the year: statesman Winston Churchill, poet Robert Frost, magician Harry Houdini, radio inventor Marconi, author W. Somerset Maugham, and President Herbert Hoover. Having arrived in Danvers, Illinois, without parents or supporting clan the young father and mother were by this baby's birth founding their own dynasty, a lineage which would see the Oehler name endure and prosper in their chosen land.

Wilhelm and Marie took their first baby on the 17th of August to the German Evangelical Lutheran of the Peace Church in Bloomington for baptism by Pastor Alex Arronet. Witnesses were Wilhelm Berner, Lizbeth Nakdasser, and Emma Finger. These details are known because the baptismal certificate still exists in family possession.

This, their first baby arriving two years after their wedding of December 2, 1872 and eighteen months before their next child, Marie, allowed them the time and space to shower him with the special love so often reserved for the first-born. The twenty-five year old new mother, far away from her own mother, grandmother, and aunts likely filled their absence with murmured sweet words of love and cooing sounds such as are always part of the intimate exchange, though unwitnessed, between young mother and infant. She spoke to him in the clear High German of her Prussian home, so that is what he spoke all his life though he understood completely the Badisch dialect of his father.

From his father Will learned daily the lessons of farm husbandry. From feeding the chickens he graduated to the more responsible chores of herding the cows from pasture to barn to eventually learning to drive a team of horses, to repairing or crafting anew the simple tools of their trade. Working in the fields, where a problem might occur and he had to figure out a solution on the spot and move on, just naturally taught him to be a resourceful, independent thinker. It was a classroom about life, as any farm boy can attest, teaching besides a sense of independence, an empathy for animals, a love of the outdoors, and a strong work ethic which stayed with him his whole long life through.

Early farmers had to be mechanically talented, able to repair their tools or even craft new ones themselves. No dull rustics, those men like Will Oehler, but the precursors to later engineers, architects, environmentalists, professors. Books though were hard to come by and not everyone was a reader. Will's dad picked up the German language newspaper when he was in Danvers, and the family had a German Bible, translated by Martin Luther into their tongue three hundred years before. Those Bible stories of David and Bathsheba, Judith, Esther, Solomon, the Queen of Sheba, Job, and of course Jesus Christ surely became common knowledge during the childhood of Will and his siblings. For more than two centuries children in Germany and America had learned to read by way of the Bible, so it is not likely that our folks were any different.

Story telling in the evening gloaming around the fireplace was another likely tradition in the Oehler home. Surely the parents knew by heart the old German fairy tales told for eons back home around family hearths, committed to memory and passed along generation to generation. "Cinderella," "Red Riding Hood," "Hansel and Gretl," "Rapunzel," and "The Wolf and the Seven Little Kids" were likely favorites of Will and his siblings. Singing too was a probable activity after chores were done and the family gathered together before bed. As later relatives in Germany told their American Oehler visitors: "Oehlers are musical!"

Humor undoubtedly found expression in those long-ago bucolic evenings as well, for a sense of humor contributes to the enjoyment of life and helps in the endurance of life itself. Humor gives aid as well as comfort, buffers against the assault of injury, and provides a weapon against insult. The taste in that day ran to satire and burlesque with pomposity a favorite target and came in the form of little story, tall tale, or joke. Even years later at Oehler family reunions, the bubbly, girlish laugher of the seven sisters could still be heard as they appreciated some comical remark.

Living on the farm, immersed in nature every waking moment, shaped his thinking, attuned him to the subtleties of weather and the seasonal changes, stirred him deeply by the vastness of the sky and countryside that went on forever for as far as the eye could see, by the wind whistling in the trees, the bird songs, the enormous flocks of migrating birds darkening the sky, and the smell of freshly cut pasture grass. All spring, summer, and fall he was outdoors, a regular little shadow to his "Papi" as he called his father by the German word for daddy, planting the seeds, tending the animals, weeding the endless rows, fighting the pesky flies around the animals, manure pile, and ponds; harvesting, taking the bounty to market, and putting away for their own winter consumption completed the cycle. This bucolic picture was truly a small world where his horizons were confined to the farm and Danvers village, yet glimpses of the wider world must have appeared when his parents talked of their homes and folks far away across the wide ocean back in Prussia and Baden. Many evenings must have been passed in descriptions of those distant places and times and of the folks back there inhabiting them.

As with all farm houses, Will entered his through the rear door, stepping into an entry space where boots and coats were kept, a pitcher of water with a bowl and bar of soap to "wash up" with stood on a table; the toilet was not far off but outside the house. Just beyond this little entry was the kitchen with its wood-burning stove for cooking as well as general warmth, sink with hand-pump for water, and as the family grew from just Will to nine more children, the continually enlarged table with chairs. This room was the heart of the home, of course, because that's where "Mutti" as they called their mother always was except when she was tending her vegetable garden or hanging out the laundry. Marie was a small but mighty woman capable of bringing eleven babies into the world in sixteen years, all survivors except one infant boy, of nurturing them to adulthood, of strong enough stuff to enable them to live till their eighties and six into their nineties, always living within ten miles of their birthplace.

The barn was a special place to the growing boy where because of the animals it was always warm even in the winter, and the smells were strong but familiar and intrinsically, inherently odoriferous; a simple rope and ball there could provide hours of fun with his brothers and sisters. Siblings did arrive in pretty rapid succession. When Will was eighteen months old his sister Marie arrived in the family followed two years later by a brother, Charles William; thirteen months later brought Ida Marie; a year later on Christmas day came Katherine Wilhelmina;

two years later, Amelia Augusta; one year later, Matilda Lucy; three years later, Emma Elizabeth; one year later, Lillie Susana; and lastly after three years, Edward George.

It was in the barn, too, that "Papi" had his workbench and his basic tools, hammer, chisel, hand-drill, clamp, and saw, to craft and repair household items and farm implements alike. At his side, Will learned the rudiments, increased his skills, and acquired a love of putting his ideas down on draft paper, drawing to scale, sawing the wood, till he assembled the pieces into a real object. When he was around twelve, Will and "Papi" built a "junior" chair, slightly smaller than a full-sized chair, which is still treasured in family possession, his initials carved under the seat.

Privacy and a space of one's own were not concepts familiar to the Oehler children nor to their parents, thankfully, because the house only had two bedrooms plus a loft for the three boys. The seven girls were so close in age that they likely shared a room and wardrobe of dresses though the studio photograph we have of them shows each fashionably dressed in yards of taffeta and silk trimmed with lace. To further confound present-day ideas of space allocation, the schoolmarm even boarded in the Oehler home for some months of the year! Of course, school was only held in the winter months when the children were not needed to perform the role of farmhands. Will and his brothers probably attended school for five years at most, less for his sisters.

In spite of farm duties and long hours of work, there was still a desire for social life away from the family hearth. At the core was the custom of neighborly visitation with Sunday dinner, as an important feature. Children were included but custom relegated them to the second or third seating after the adults had vacated the table-side chairs. Likely they were having too much fun playing outdoors on the expansive lawn or in the barnyard getting all mucked up to eat anyway. With the elders, talk drifted along the usual channels: the condition of the crops, the price of hogs, the local gossip, and politics including news from the Old County gleaned from the German language newspaper. The women discussed children and recipes, the newest dress patterns, quilts, and of course gossip which of course can be expressed in every language, their's being German.

Friend, be it man or woman, greeted friend in those days with a hearty hand shake just as they had back in Germany. No embrace, air kiss, or buss on the cheek would have occurred to those folks nor would it have been deemed appropriate to show such emotion or affection except between mother and child. Father and son bid each other good night with a hand shake as did sister to sister, and it had nothing to do with a German alleged proclivity for sternness, severity, or strictness but was a universal behavior among all civilized folks in America as well until much later generations.

The youth Will Oehler as he departed for Iowa

About the the time he reached the age of eighteen it was determined that Will should get some experience on a farm other than his dad's, so rather like an apprentice he was shipped off with his brass-trimmed, black trunk (still in family possession) to Iowa for a year. One of Will's first purchases from his salary in Iowa was a baby goat which he sent as a present to his little toddler brother, Eddie, back home. Eddie was, indeed, thrilled with the present especially when "Papi" hitched it up to a little cart for him to ride in 'round and 'round the barnyard. As the goat grew bigger and friskier, though, he became a problem by butting his horns at the pigs, eating the clothes hanging to dry on the clothes line, stomping too close to the chickens, and such. One day, the decision came down from the "pater familius" that the pet goat had to go. Little Eddie was so sad but the others agreed that that was one mighty fine tasting meat!

Employment in the Danvers area for young girls like Will's sisters in the late 1800s, unlike in cities where there were factory jobs, centered on farm or domestic work. Though a few women were to be found in other occupations such as those who could attend special schools to become teachers or nurses, the vast majority were either "hired girls" working as servants or cooks in a family home or seamstresses. Factory work in large cities was the best paid and most widely heralded. A girl could earn $3 a week in a New England cotton mill but only half that as a domestic. In the case of the Oehler girls it appears that they were needed on their parents' farm and so remained there until they married when in their early twenties. Their father relied on the labor of all his children to make ends meet. While "Papi," Will, and Charley, until Eddie was old enough to help, worked in the fields, "Mutti" and her daughters ran the household and kept the kitchen garden. In addition to preparing all the meals, drawing water, tending the stove fire, cleaning the house, feeding chickens, washing the clothes, the women sewed and mended clothes, knitted hats, gloves and socks, churned butter, possibly made soap, and trimmed the oil lamps that illuminated their home in that age before electricity.

After a year or so away in Iowa, Will returned to the homestead where he, as one of only three sons, was needed. The farm was a co-operative family effort and besides, his parents were buying more and more farmland which all had to be worked by the three men assisted presumably by "hired hands." Even in the late 1800s the typical family size in America was declining so that the Oehler family of twelve was quite a bit larger than the new average nuclear family of five or six members. But it is distinctly possible that Wilhelm and Marie, so far from their roots, were subconsciously attempting to establish their own dynasty, with its inherent attributes of property and blood lineage, in their chosen land. Still, it was expected that the children would in due time marry and leave the farm which is just what Will did when he married Emma Graff on January 10, 1900. Their noteworthy double wedding with Emma's sister, Annie and Jacob Imig, has already been described.

Will and Emma began married life working a farm owned by the Hulvey family near Danvers, Illinois, continuing what they had always done, what they had learned day in and day out to do growing up on their respective farm homes. But this time it was different: they were working for themselves or rather for the entity which they had become as a result of their marriage. As a tenant farmer, Will provided his own tools, seed, draft animals, kept two-thirds of the harvest proceeds, and remitted one-third to the Hulveys. In due time, of course, the babies began to come, for in those days "that's what happened you got married," it was observed. Alvin William, Delmar Henry, Jesse Dean, Lyla Elizabeth, and William Peter arrived in the next twelve years.

Gradually over years of good crop prices and bad, Will saved up enough money to begin buying land of his own, and of course both Will and Emma inherited acres from their parent. The acquisitions were exciting to Will, perhaps intensified by the risk involved in borrowing money from the bank to buy the parcels, and he did it as often as possible for he was an ambitious young man. Those were the days before there were today's variety of equity or bond investments, vehicles in which to invest one's money for gain, such as mutual funds stocks, EFTs, and hedge funds. Land was a farmer's method to put his money to work. Bonds existed but had become an aversion to the whole Oehler family when Will's sister, Amelia, lost her entire patrimonial inheritance when she sold her inherited land and used the proceeds to buy bonds from an unscrupulous bond broker from Chicago, bonds which immediately lost their value.

There were stresses in the life of a farmer, no doubt about it: weather, weeds, insects, commodity prices, the need to borrow money from the bank just to operate the farm and support the family until the crops were sold and income was derived, and the sheer hard physical labor. Compensations abounded, though, in the minds of Will and Emma:

their pride in ownership, their independence, their being outdoors in nature, witness to daily sunrises and gorgeous red sunsets over the fields of grain. The sky itself was like a giant canvas on which nature displayed a continuous variety of colors and shapes during the day and at night a glorious starlight display like no city dweller ever saw.

Yet sometime between Lyla's birth in 1906 and Billy's birth in 1912, Will and Emma left the farming for good and moved into Minier so he could become an entremaneur, a partner with William Schroeder in the manufacture of grain elevators known as the Schroeder Elevator Company located at the north side of Central Ave between Maple and Minier streets. Schroeder had invented, in 1895, the portable grain elevator, a horse-powered device to lift corncobs into the corn crib or oats into the barn, a thoroughly labor saving device. His machine shop measured 23,500 square feet, employed a score of men, and was located at the north end of the commercial street next to the railroad tracks. Amazingly, Will's scant years of schooling, his lack of training in business skills or engineering did not hinder him from success. He somehow could lay out his designs on drafting paper, translate that to sheet metal cuts, and weld the pieces together. Business acumen, too, had to be pieced together to keep accounts straight, apply for bank loans to acquire working capital, promote his elevators, and close the deal through salesmanship. Despite the steep learning curve, traditional values of hard work, tenacity, honesty, and pride were enough in the first decades of the 20th century to achieve success.

Although ninety percent of Americans were still engaged in agriculture at the time, the nation was resolutely moving toward industrialization. Through innovations in management, technology, production, and distribution, business leaders were building the United States into an industrial power. Opportunity was there and Will seized it. Important to his business was the railroad which supplied his raw materials and then after manufacture transported his grain elevators to market. By 1900, 193,000 miles of railroad track crisscrossed the nation— more than in all Europe, including Russia—and the tracks passed, fortuitously, right beside his factory.

Of course, it was quite a change for the life-long farm boy to move to village life: the noises, the frequent encountering of those not family members, the need to be sociable, the little unwritten rules of etiquette unknown back on the farm, the sartorial requirements, the way the sun seemed to set faster and cast more shadows behind the houses instead of lingering long over the flat pastures and open fields, the need to take care in one's dress, the knowledge that his behavior and that of his children was being observed and even judged. It all took some adjustment, but he and Emma seem never to have regretted the move.

By around the year 1912, in the flush of his newfound prosperity, Will had a large family home built at 416 N. Maple St. as described earlier. Those were generally good, optimistic times in America, before the first World War and the Depression, when one out of three families owned an automobile. "Hard roads" were constructed to enable mobility even among farmers; the radio had been invented enabling folks to be in touch with national as well as local news. Will built a large garage for the new house and attached to it was Will's woodworking shop where he crafted or repaired many household articles and taught his four sons his love of woodworking, working with their hands to fashion useful articles and in some cases works of art. The toddler sized rocking chair he made for the last addition to the family, Billy, has been lovingly used, passed down three generations, and is still in family possession.

This was also the peak time, 1880 to 1920, of local passenger rail trains. Even in a village like Minier several rail lines passed through and some stopped at various times of the day. Rail service was a small town institution as much as the public square or Main Street, the day's events were tuned to "train time," the train whistle announced the hour of the day which formerly church bells had tolled, and a form of entertainment was to walk to the depot to see the trains come in. Buggies, surrey, and carriages filled the street near the depot making it a gala event especially on Sundays when leisure hours prevailed. Though a vast network of branches criss-crossed Illinois, it was the Illinois Central Railroad with its steam locomotive, or engine, to drive and pull all the following cars: tender to hold the coal fuel, mail car, baggage car, "smoker" car, ladies' car, and passenger cars which served Minier. Always a large employer, the railroads required a minimum crew of engineer, fireman, mail clerk, baggage master, conductor, and brakeman.

Still in Will's day, a generation after the assassination, the identification with fellow Illinoisan and hugely famous former president Abraham Lincoln was keenly felt. Many there were, perhaps Will among them, who had learned in the country school house to "speak" the words of poet, William Cullen Bryant, on the death of Lincoln:

> Pure was thy life; its bloody close
> Hath placed thee with the sons of light,
> Among the noble host of those
> Who perished in the cause of Right.

Stories about him were quoted and passed on in every home, every pulpit, and every school room. He earned the moniker, Honest Abe, for instance while working as a sales clerk in a general store in New Salem near Springfield, Illinois. When reconciling the cash box and records at the end of the work day, Abe discovered he had mistakenly shortchanged a woman customer two cents, so after store hours he rushed on foot to her door, several miles distant, to repay her and apologize. Later, when living in Springfield, serving in the Illinois State Legislature, and hurrying to an important meeting at the capitol he encountered a girl struggling with a overladen basket and insisted on carrying her burden to her destination thus cementing his reputation for compassion for the weak, for essential goodness of heart, for willingness to bear the burdens of others, and for indifference to his own appearance of dignity.

Abe Lincoln was even featured in one of Will's favorite jokes told over and over by him through the years: A city slicker stopped his big sedan to ask a farmer walking his field near the side of the road to ask: "Can you direct me to Oak Ridge Cemetery? We want to visit Lincoln's tomb." The farmer replied: "Sure! At the next crossroads, turn left, go about five miles, turn right, then the next right too … wait a minute, that's not right!" "Go about five miles straight from here, then turn right at a big brick house, make a couple of lefts … wait, that's not right either!" After more head scratching and pointing, the farmer announced: "You can't get there from here!" Will always gave out a hearty laugh right along with his listeners at this point!

During the early years of Will's manufacturing business, especially during World War I from 1914 to 1918, when farm prices soared because European farm production was disrupted, U.S. agricultural prices more than doubled and farmers' income rose significantly. Of course, when farmers had cash they spent it on Will's grain elevators. This boom proved to be a mixed blessing, though, because with their new wealth farmers took on debt to expand production, then felt hard-pressed when commodity prices fell after the war. Yes the Oehler family knew some very prosperous years, but the roll of the good times eventually lost momentum.

No one in America, not even Will with his family harmony and manufacturing prosperity was unaffected when the stock market crashed in the autumn of 1929. The farm communities felt the pinch long before the crash itself, as their depression began as early as 1920 with bank foreclosures and crop failures; but those, of course, had always been a part of the farmer's reality. For all Americans, the 1920s had been a decade of uncertainty, disappointment, unemployment for one-third of the workforce, and stress for all as bank after bank closed their doors unable to meet cash withdrawals. On inauguration day 1933, all the banks in Illinois were temporarily closed by the governor in order to prevent more "run on the banks" or demand by depositors to withdraw their savings deposits beyond what the banks actually held. The Chicago Board of Trade closed on the same day. To aid farmers, Governor Horner suspended the collection of the property tax, but still Will personally knew farmers who lost their land to the banks when land and crop values plummeted, yet debts continued at their original interest rate and could not be payed. The repeal of Prohibition in December of 1933 brought liquor tax revenue into the state coffers as did the introduction of a sales tax around the same time, yet together those measures were insufficient to dispel the national economic depression.

Unemployment and unrest continued unabated nationally though hardship was perhaps less severe in Will's village where life was led closer to the soil and less dependent on city folks' factory jobs which closed. Even if he couldn't realize a profit from his crops, the farmer could still feed his family same as he ever did. Still, five per-cent of farms in Illinois fell to forced sales because of tax delinquency and mortgage default. Desperate efforts by stressed farmers led in 1931 to their withholding grain and livestock from market in a failed attempt to increase prices.

All through the 1920s farm prices were in decline; from 1929 to 1932 they fell by sixty per-cent. The European economies collapsed in 1931, two years after America's fall, making it a world-wide depression. Some folks blamed speculators in the market buying stock on credit, some blamed the Federal Reserve Board for failing to assure an adequate money supply. Whatever the causes, and they are still being argued today, 5500 banks closed by 1933, unemployment cost thirteen million workers or 25% of the workforce their jobs. The lucky ones, like Alvin Oehler at Deere & Company in Moline took pay cuts and knew not to complain, for they saw the hopelessness on the faces of men in the bread lines or on the faces of the hobos passing through on trains bound, they hoped, for better times.

Hope for an end of the Depression in Illinois finally appeared only when the prospect of war in Europe increased. Around 1938 a demand for war material began to mount, farm products were in high demand to feed a hungry world, scientific advances in fertilizers and insecticides were made, and after the attack by the Japanese on Pearl Harbor in 1942, the defense effort demanded rapid industrial expansion. The war truly pulled Illinois out of the Depression: in 1939 one million workers were unemployed and on "relief," whereas by 1945 only 214,712 were left stricken.

We will never know for sure but it is easy to imagine that Will suffered terribly when his business met a financial crisis caused first and foremost by the Great Depression but also by an advance in technology that reduced the demand for his type of grain elevators. New harvesting machines removed the kernels from the corncob. Farmers stored their corn less and less in cribs, sent the grain to large silos for storage or sale. By the 1940s business had deteriorated but debt continued. Abandoned by his associates, Will worked long and hard to pay the company debts.

Throughout his career, he had known success, pride of ownership, and after returning the business to solvency, he also knew redemption, his alone. Perhaps Will expected that at least one of his four sons would show interest in working for him in his manufacturing plant but except for summer breaks from school they never did. They set their sights on brighter lights, fancier offices, bigger towns; they seemed to want to leave behind the "close to the land" life of their childhood. Why, some of them never even had a garden!

Will was content with his life in Minier, walked "uptown" twice a day to his factory office, located conveniently beside the railroad tracks of the Chicago, Alton, and St. Louis Railroad as it ran from Bloomington through Minier to Jacksonville, brought him the steel and wire he needed in his business and then took his finished product to far away markets. In the office his only staff was secretary, Miss Leah, at her typewriter and filing cabinet. At the sound of the noon siren, he walked home for dinner, returning back "uptown" again for the afternoon. In the shop though were several employees to assemble the grain elevators he sold. To a degree now hard to imagine, Will's achievements accrued despite lack of a high school degree to say nothing of a college education, no formal technical training, no friends in high places, no financial backers, no government subsidies!

Will remembered well the day when the C. and A. ran morning, noon, and evening passenger trains each way, north toward Chicago and south toward Alton, but gradually as roads improved folks began to drive their own cars to their destination. Throughout his boyhood the railroad station had been the busiest place in town when a train pulled into the village. In those days all the merchandise coming into or leaving town, all the passengers, and all the mail were carried by rail if the distance was beyond the range of horse and wagon. When the local freight train pulled into the station, stacks of merchandise of all kinds were unloaded onto the depot platform to be picked up by the local drayman and hauled by horse and wagon to the merchants who had purchased it. Considerable time was spent switching— to spot or park carloads of lumber, coal, sand, gravel, cement, flour, potatoes, or other merchandise in the proper place for unloading. Carloads of grain were picked up at the tall village elevators and empty cars were left there to be filled and picked up another day. Yes he remembered well when it was a form of entertainment to walk to the depot to watch the train come in and thrill to the ensuing excitement of puffing engine, clanging bell, and shrilling whistle, the sight of disembarking strangers suggesting far away places, the arrival of large bundles and boxes of mysterious-looking goods destined for Peine's store, or the look on the faces of those lucky folks who boarded the train headed for the lure of the unknown.

By 1940 normalcy had crept into his life, the children were all grown and married, the house was empty except for week-end visits. Lyla bore Rita Jeanne, Will and Emma's first grandchild at long last, at the end of 1939. Eighteen months later Bill and Mary brought their adopted daughter, Susanne, for Minier family inspection. She and Rita were baptized together in the St. John's Evangelical and Reformed Church there surrounded by the full extended family, including Emma. The offending minister was long gone!

Will did suffer a moment of agony over little Susie, however, when one of his sisters, at a sibling dinner soon after Bill's announcement that Mary was pregnant, declared: "Now Bill and Mary will have to send that precious little girl back!" Will had to leave the table; he was so upset he couldn't eat and had to rush off to phone Bill who naturally assured him that that wasn't the way adoption worked. Susie was legally theirs no matter what happened. Bill and Mary's daughter, Kathleen, born in 1942, and Lyla and Delm's son, John, born in 1943 completed the set of four grandchildren.

Then in June of 1942 the big blow came: Emma was felled by a stroke, without warming, completely unexpected, life-ending for her, life-changing for him. Now instead of walking home for noon dinner, he drove his car out to Lyla and Delms' farm south of Minier each day where many of the dishes were familiar to him as every daughter learns from her mother. Little Rita Jeanne was a special joy to Will, her every childish antic drawing him slowly but surely out of his deep grief.

Although Will kept a much smaller garden than Emma had, he still kept the chicken coop in the back yard to supply eggs and Sunday dinner. He was a master at catching a chicken, grabbing it by the neck, swinging it around till the job was done, plucking, and cleaning it for cooking. That had always been his job so there was no change "on that score," as he liked to say. Those ancestors of today's chickens were half the size of ours, only laid ten to fifteen eggs per year and never during the winter compared to ten times that today where they are bred for egg production and live in a stiflingly confined space. Will's well-tended chickens lived for years whereas today's are slaughtered at seven weeks. The two-seater outhouse still stood in the back yard till well after World War II although he was the only one who used it anymore.

The demise of the family garden was rather exemplified by Will. He simply found it more convenient to choose canned goods from the village grocery store or fresh produce at farm stands when harvested during the summer months than to suffer the exigency of growing his own produce in a backyard plot and canning it for out-of-season consumption. After World War II, metal cans full of all kinds of vegetable, fruits, meats, and every conceivable edible began to appear on grocery store shelves at reasonable price so that fewer and fewer housewives felt the need to garden and can for their own families. This trend only continued, magnified by the appearance of frozen foods during the 1970s. It was then though that in response to media reports of food poisoning that ascorbic acid was deemed by the federal government a necessary additive to canned foods. Years later this acid is recognized as a cause of the ubiquitous acid reflex disease.

In 1949 Jess and Nelle returned to live with and care for him in Minier, to help dissolve the elevator company, and especially with Spud's cash investment to establish a John Deere dealership selling a good line of implements. The daily drive out to Lyla's table was no longer necessary with the addition of a woman in the home, but Nelle was a career woman as well who kept books for doctors in Bloomington.

Because of his interest in the dealership and the business there, Spud was a frequent visitor, often twice a month to the paternal home. Bill and Mary with Susie and Kathleen were also frequently at Will's home as were Lyla, Delm, Rita, and John. Without Emma it was a big help to have the "boys" eraser clean the living room wall paper or help clear out the clutter in the attic and basement, but basically Will was able to keep up the maintenance necessary for the big house and yard. Years passed, he continued his walk "up town" to look in on Jess at the dealership; the Moline family visited monthly; he saw his siblings, all of whom lived not more than ten miles from their Danvers homestead birthplace, frequently; he attended the Oehler Family Reunions annually to keep up with extended families of his siblings; he frequented the Minier Homecoming festivities each summer; he attended young John's basketball games and Rita's dance recitals; he enjoyed good health; he visited Bill and Alvin in Moline; his interest in farming offered seasonal changes and nostalgic experiences like walking the paths that wound among the corn, passing beneath the apple trees along the hedges, listening to the crickets chirping in the stubble, eyeing the cows peacefully ruminating in the shade, or spying the quail fluttering in the newly reaped field. In the custom of the day, Will dressed in suit and tie, wore a straw hat in summer, a felt hat in winter. He was always a quiet man but had a hearty, ready laugh!

One day in the mid-1950s Jess and Nelle announced that they wished to build a home of their own on a property adjoining the north of Will's. Coincidentally, one of the very first senior retirement centers in the entire country had just opened its doors in nearby Hopedale under the direction of Dr. Lawrence J.Rossi,Sr. Soon, Will announced to his flabbergasted children his plan to move there to be among the first residents along with his close friend Charley Tanner. The modern, one-floor "home" was staffed by local Mennonite women who were excellent cooks, bakers, and care givers. The little town of Hopedale, only twelve miles from Minier and not exactly foreign territory to him, was fine for walking; he still had his car; and he could still smoke his cigars and enjoy his Jack Daniels before supper. In short time, daughter-in-law, Dorene, joined the staff of Hopedale House as Activities Director which made life for him and Charley even more meaningful and interesting. Yes, the years rolled gently on.

In June of 1961, Will proudly attended Susie's graduation from the University of Illinois in Champaign, Illinois, in company with Bill and Mary, Kathleen, Alvin and Katharine, Ada Rost Seales and her daughter, Linda. Then just a couple of years later, Susie brought her fiancé, Hans-Peter Keller, to Will to be introduced. To everyone's amazement, Will conversed with the young German man in flawless high German, his mother tongue, which though little used anymore was nevertheless still available to him. Along with a full contingency of relatives from Minier, Will attended Susie and Peter's wedding in Moline the following August of 1963.

Will could not have missed the irony when Bill revealed to him in 1964 that Deere and Company was sending him and Mary to work and live in Heidelberg, Germany, just a few miles from where his father, Wilhelm, had emigrated exactly ninety-nine years before! Did he consider traveling back with Bill to his ancestral home, meeting the relatives who Bill discovered there, seeing for himself the places his father had surely described to him? Yes, he did consider it long, but his age of ninety rather precluded any action. Jess visited them in Germany as did Alvin and Katharine, Susie and Peter with baby Christopher, and Kathleen with little Kammy and Paul, but Will was content to stay behind at Hopedale House.

No matter how often he saw Bill and Alvin, he still hand-wrote letters, short with some misspellings and full of observations about field conditions, weather, and family, to them most weeks. "Minier is two weeks ahead of Moline weather-wise," though separated by only 125 vertical miles, he advised his city living sons. That meant all the farm activities happened earlier around Minier than in Moline. Will was a keen observer of all things in the agricultural world sometimes to the point of reporting farmer complaints to his farm implement designer sons who would then give assurance they would attempt to remedy the problem in the next design.

Will's last letter to Bill was addressed to Heidelberg, Germany, home to his youngest son and Mary, and was written just three weeks before he went to sleep, at home in his own bed, and never awoke: "Thursday, July 21, 1966. Dear William and Mary, Well I have been getting several letters from you, so I am writing one today. And the weather has been quite warm. But is cooler today and the temperature is around 80 today. Was over 100 last week. But farmers are all caught up with their work. Well tomorrow Home Coming starts at Minier but don't think I will go over. Well it sure will be quite a thrill for Kathleen with the kids.

Well I am feeling quite well again so am quite thankful for all that and will be glad to see you when you come to the States. By the way has Mr. Edgar Smithhalls ever called at your house? Will write more next time. Respectfully, Dad" He was 92 years and eight months.

His remains lie next to Emma's in Minier cemetery, joined later by two sons and their wives: Delmer and Dorene, Jess and Nelle.

CHAPTER 4

Generation # 3

NOW I COME to the generation many of us knew personally. No longer will phrases need to be prefaced with "perhaps," "likely," "probably," "presumably," and so forth. The following folks were known to us on a personal, daily, years-long basis. We know their personal attributes, their personalities, their desires, and accomplishments; we can describe their physical appearance because we saw them face to face; we can even define their idiosyncrasies, foibles, faults, and mistakes because we knew them so well. The shadowy veil placed by time to cover the previous folks does not yet obscure the lives of the following men and women. Still, because they are no longer with us and because we loved them so deeply and miss them still, we may ask to be excused if we look at their lives through particularly rosy lenses.

Alvin William Oehler and Katharine Elizabeth Miller Oehler
—4,—5,—6,—and—7—

Firstborn of Emma and Will Oehler, Alvin saw the light of day on August 5, 1900, giving him bragging rights for appearing in the first year of the new century, the Twentieth Century! A farm boy born and raised, yet a man of city and industry, showing ambition and cunning from an early age when he won first place in the fifty-yard dash at a county fair or second place in the 100 yard even race for boys under sixteen. Most days, though, were spent in helping with farm chores, learning the ropes from his dad, and assuming the leadership skills which naturally come to the oldest brother. School was walking distance at the country schoolhouse but high school in Minier required transportation of wagon, buggy, or pony, we know not which.

Alvin, went all the way to the University of Wisconsin in Madison because he wanted to go to college but the University of Illinois did not at that time recognize his high school degree from the yet unaccredited Minier High School. There Alvin studied business administration, pledged Phi Gamma Delta fraternity, and finished the one year there required for admission to Illinois in Champaign, IL, where he subsequently transferred. The Oehler's finances were flush in that year around 1920 so they could afford the fancy clothes, the out of state tuition, and the fraternity membership Alvin desired. But the reversal gradually came as the general economic depression gathered steam all across the nation.

Alvin graduated from the U. of Illinois with a degree in Business Administration, launched himself on a course to a position at John Deere Company in Moline, IL, in the engineering department of the Harvester Works despite his lack of an engineering degree, eventually achieving the position of chief engineer for the second largest manufacturing plant of the entire company. For many years of his career, Alvin was occupied with the design and construction of "the combine," a factory on wheels which picked the corn, soybean, wheat, barley, sunflowers, or oats, separated the grain from the chaff, propelled the edible grain through a spout to a truck moving along side the combine like a barnacle on a whale. it was a state of the art technological achievement for which Alvin was responsible—and more than a bit proud too.

By the fall of 1931, Alvin had waited long enough for his sweetheart to grow up. Pretty blue-eyed, light brown haired, Katharine Elizabeth Miller daughter of a prosperous Bloomington lumber yard owner, Roy Glenmore Miller, was born on October 21, 1908, and at twenty-three years old was ready for marriage. Preparation for the meeting of their parents at a dinner cooked by Emma in her home became an anxiety-ridden project for Alvin who in order to impress the Millers presented his mother with an exquisite set of Hutschenreuter porcelain china on which to serve the meal to his prospective parents-in-law. As newlyweds "Spud," as he was now addressed by everyone except his mother, and Katharine set up housekeeping at the Wellington Apartments at 1215 Fifteenth St. in Moline, IL, where they met other young couples: Mabel "Bil" and Swisher Wilson, Ruth and Ed James, Margaret "Muggs" and

Fred Hansen, Martha and Hjoesta Hellberg and formed lifetime bonds. Spud was employed at the John Deere Harvester Works where lay-offs due to the Great Depression occurred among factory workers, and for those spared unemployment, salaries were reduced two or three times during those difficult years. Katharine was a good manager; they, like everyone they knew, adjusted and were glad for Spud's job. In keeping with his feeling that he had married "up," Spud continued to find funds for Katharine's cleaning women, weekly manicures, hairdresser, and penchant for elegant, silky lingerie.

Loving gestures begun early on in their nuptials became habits which continued on through the years of their fifty-eight year marriage and warmed the hearts of any so lucky as to witness them: Before leaving for work in the morning, the two kissed with not one peck, not two, but three! During the course of each evening, no matter the spat of the day, Katharine stole into their bedroom to turn down the bedcover from off Spud's pillow. Little loving gestures for sure!

Moonshine and bathtub gin enlivened the parties at the Wellington, and the brides tried out new recipes. Jello and packaged puddings were new to the market, glamorized by advertisements, and frequently found their way to Katharine's table. Her mother was from Virginia, a southern lady who cooked "southern." As Katharine said: "Mama cooked string beans for hours and boiled her meat forever!"

Such references to her Mama came out frequently in her conversation even though Gertrude Stephens Miller had died suddenly and mysteriously when Katharine was only fifteen years old. Thereafter, the girl was sent to a Virginia girls' school where she finished her high school years and formed life-long friendships. In Bloomington, her best friend was Mildred Mecherle, daughter of a founder of State Farm Insurance Company. Together they were a couple of mischievous little girls but nevertheless unsurprisingly found employment at the big insurance company. Katharine attended the University of Illinois a couple of years, even pledged Alpha Chi Omega there.

Spud always felt he had plucked a highly positioned plum in his conquest of Katharine, for among other reasons she brought three very prestigious objects into the marriage: a dazzling pear-shaped opal ring, her birthstone, having been born on October 21, 1908; a large oil portrait of Thomas Jefferson's mother, Jane Randolf Jefferson, her ancestor, painted by Thomas Sully; and a chair from that family's home. "When I die, this painting has to go to the Smithsonian Institution!" she liked to say. But after hanging in a place of honor in her home for over sixty years it went to her brother's daughter, Mary Katharine Miller Campbell in Kalamazoo, Michigan.

Space in the apartment at the Wellington tightened quite a bit when in the fall of 1932, Spud's brother, Bill, and Katharine's brother, Roy Glenmore "Jack" Miller, moved in to begin their freshman year at Augustana College. It was not exactly what the honeymooners had signed up for, but times were tough and families had to help each other. Katharine tried to be a serious disciplinarian, strained to accommodate the insatiable appetites of the teen-age boys, prodded them to study and complete assignments, but generally was rewarded with disrespect, back-talk and impudence. That arrangement lasted but one year. Bill transferred to the University of Illinois in Champaign. When he was shy just one semester for graduation from the business school there, his brother Spud and he coincidentally met one week-end at the family home in Minier 'round Emma's dinner table. "The economy is gradually improving," Spud said, and "Deere is hiring again. If you want a job, you better go up to Moline with me now!" That was all Bill needed to hear and though a college degree was honored, no one around the table after those long years of economic malaise could disagree that a good job with a good company like John Deere was like winning the lottery. Bill left college, was hired by the engineering department of John Deere Planter Works, and thus began, after scarcely knowing each other due to their twelve years age difference, decades of close brotherly relations.

Both Spud and Bill saw numerous of their inventions for farm equipment registered at the United States Patent Office in Washington D.C. The registrations were, of course, not in their names but in that of Deere & Company, only a footnote mentioning the actual designer, all proceeds accruing to the firm.

By the early 1940s the young couple, Spud and Katharine Oehler, had saved enough money to buy a lot at 2404 Twenty-third Ave. B in Moline and build a white frame house. Of course, the Miller Lumber Store in Bloomington provided the choicest board feet and finest millwork to ship to Moline; both sets of parents drove to Moline to check out the progress, admired the finished product of two bedrooms and a bath with blue china fixtures, living and dining room filled with beautiful chippendale-style furnishings, and large kitchen with a booth for eating which looked out a large window onto the passing scene of the neighborhood street. There the young couple blended quickly into the horseshoe shaped cul-de-sac of young families whose many children paraded on decorated trikes and bikes on the 4th of July, and a cute baby always served as king or queen of the parade. Again lifelong friendships with Betty and Ray Shetter, Louise and Clarence Bendle, and Elizabeth and Jerry Bloom were formed.

To their presumed but never uttered disappointment, no babies were born to them. Katharine volunteered generously to the YWCA; served as a Grey Lady at Moline Public Hospital; joined a King's Daughters circle and a Masonic Lodge circle; knitted army-green hats, gloves, and sweaters for the soldiers at war; knitted skirts and sweaters for Rita, Susie, Kathleen, and Mary Kay; doted on their collie "Laddie;" spoiled Bill and Mary's daughters, Susie and Kathleen, Lyla's children, Rita Jeanne and Johnny; and her brother's children, Jack and Mary Kay; and later worked in the office at Hellberg Paint Store; but a hysterectomy around the age of forty revealed she was beset with fibroids. In the hospital, Spud told her if she got well he would buy her a Cadillac, so she did—and he did!

He himself drove Ford Motor Company products. A series of Thunderbirds, known as personal luxury cars, small but not a sports car, were his pride and joy in the late 1950s and into the 1960s. Thereafter he graduated to the Lincoln brand, one after another, though Deere disdained cars made by its arch rival Ford, and with unspoken word discouraged employees from driving them. Spud did not sit on the board of directors, had an independent spirit so ignored the taboo!

During all the years of Spud's forty-one years of employment at Deere & Company, his work field-testing harvesters and later combines took him out of the office and onto Deere's experimental fields near East Moline, IL, and in the winter to Texas and Mexico. The work was dirty and grimy, days were long, frustrations with the failure of field-testing to measure up to his calculations at his desk were high, exhaustion was expected—but he loved it! He loved being outdoors under the blistering hot sun, he loved the tinkering and the technical problem solving, he loved the mechanics of seeing how a little twist here or a little tap there could make a huge difference and improve the entire implement. The smell and touch of the damp earth spoke to him. It was in his genes. Generations of toilers of the soil had lived before him and formed his DNA, all the way back into the misty shrouded lives of his ancestors in Germany.

It was on the farm where he spent his boyhood that Spud learned independence, honesty, and integrity. Patience too was learned where one had to wait for the seeds to sprout, the rain to come, the ripening to emerge. When the farmer encountered problems in the field, he had to figure out himself what to do next. He had to create a "fix" with materials at hand, using his own ingenuity. That was a great classroom for the boy Spud, as any farmer can tell you, and the sense of independent thinking stayed with him a lifetime. He went on to become established in a main stream industrial career where those early lessons were a boon to his inventiveness. Even in retirement, which he took from Deere at the age of seventy, Spud liked to stay close to the soil. He golfed some but usually spent hours toiling in his yard planting trees, seeding worn patches of grass, bore-feeding his trees, and trimming them with the help of Frank Wiese, Chuck Fulton, Christopher Keller, and Stephan Keller. Like a miniature barn, an upscale looking tool shed always graced his back yard, hiding from sight the lowly tools of his passion: rakes, hoe, shovels, scythe, sickle, pruning hook, splitting hammer, chain-saw, and power mower. His attire for the yard work was pretty scruffy for his address at 3505—26th Ave., Moline, but the yard was a real traffic stopper. Likewise, at his home in Sarasota, Florida, he loved getting close to the soil.

He wasn't a talker or a boaster, but if he did speak others stopped and listened. Taciturn by nature, yet capable of deep friendship was Spud. When his friend Swisher Wilson fell victim to a serious car crash on his return from a northern fishing trip, Spud visited him every single night at the hospital, during his months-long recovery, to bolster his friend's spirits.

Many of those same years Spud was running his John Deere dealerships in his spare time selling tractors, implements, and service to farmers of that superior soil, the gift of the glacier referenced earlier. Most week-ends or a good long day thereof he drove alone to Paxton, Colfax, or Minier, all in central Illinois. He left day to day operations to a resident manager but drove to the sites to oversee performance and check the record books himself on week-ends. Those managers included both Katharine's brother, Jack Miller, in Paxton and his own brother, Jess Oehler, in Minier. It was a situation which at times strained taut but never severed family relations.

Each of those week-end drives occasioned a visit to his Dad and sister Lyla in Minier. Later after Will's death Spud continued his close attachment to his sister right up to the end of his life. Who knows what their conversations covered but we can surmise they hinged on mutual memories of their parents, old times in Minier, their siblings, and Lyla's children, Rita Jeanne and John, and husband, Delmar Johnson. Likely Spud even felt he was nearer his mother during those intimate meetings where he needed no pretense and could just be himself. In Moline he often appeared unannounced at Bill and Mary's door, then proceeded to spend an hour huddled in confidential exchange with his brother.

In his youth, Spud had been honored to be asked to join the Scottish Rite Lodge in Bloomington and became a 32-degree Mason of the Peoria Shrine Temple. He never transferred his membership to Moline but attended events and especially contributed to the Shriners' Crippled Children's Hospital through the years. Moline Elks Club also was a favorite haunt of Spud over the years not so much for the meetings but for the camaraderie he and Katharine found at the clubhouse where the bar was always open and the food was always "tops," in his words. In retirement Spud took up golf so a membership at Short Hills Country Club in East Moline was required. Katharine and Spud enjoyed the camaraderie there at the bar and the dining room where everyone knew their name.

Another favorite activity for Spud was to follow the stock market. He was a serious, savvy investor in the day before the ticker tape ran on TV for 24 hours, CNBC talking heads filled the line-up, and economic reporters informed. Only Louis Rukeyser's "Wall Street Week" on Friday evenings fed his hunger for knowledge of the markets. In those days, men like Spud with money to invest could not work independently through Charles Schwab or Fidelity but had to go through a broker and pay 1% to 1 1/2% commission. Spud bought only individual stocks, especially Schlumberger which he owned a lot of, because mutual funds were in their infancy while ETFs and Index Funds were nonexistent. As a result many mornings Spud could be found downtown Moline at Stiffel Nicholas' Fifth Avenue office to watch the ticker tape, buy through a broker there, and generally kibitz with other investors in the lobby. Since First Midwest Bank, also on Fifth Avenue, had a brokerage service he dealt there as well. Disputes and distrust were always a part of the relationship with brokers, but that's a fact of life, and Spud was clearly knowledgeable but dependent on them for the transaction. For sure, he was one gleeful man when the Dow Jones average hit 1000 in 1972 although it slid 40% just six months later. By his death in 1989, the average was 2168, so no wonder he found it a pretty compelling game!

Spud was seventy years old before he could bring himself to retire from Deere and Company. For some there is just no fun like work! His last few years of employment involved several overseas trips to destinations like Argentina where near the end of the 1960s his combine expertise was essential and to Germany where coincidentally Bill and Mary were stationed by Deere. Katharine joined him on those trips making them more like extended vacations. During those 1960s years they also traveled to the island of Roatan which lies off the coast of Honduras for deep-sea fishing. Also coincidentally, niece, Susie, and family were then living in Honduras sparking a visit to them.

Several fly-in fishing trips to the boundary waters of northern Minnesota were a highlight of Spud's retirement bestowing camaraderie with fellow fishermen like Bjorn Lenox, Clarence Bendle and John Lingris, beach campfire lunches prepared by their Native American guides, and quiet nights under the stars. Walleye was Spud's favorite eating fish from those northern trips while Grouper was his preference when wintering in Florida.

Late in life, Spud began to see that he was not going to need all his millions and so began methodically searching for worthy recipients. His first deserving beneficiary was the United Church of Christ in Minier, the very same one his mother had severed with so long ago. Learning that the minister there needed office space, Spud met with an architect who with lots of input from the donor designed an addition to the church which looks like it had always been there employing the same stone and roofing materials. A carved stone sign over the office door reads: "Oehler Addition." Inside, a plaque dedicates the addition to his mother and father, William F. and Emma Graff Oehler. He and Katharine also bequeathed sizable amounts to his three nieces and nephew and to her niece and nephew upon their deaths.

For decades Spud and Katharine went to Rochester, Minnesota, to the Mayo Clinic for their physical exams making a little vacation of their stay at the adjoining Kahler Inn Hotel. He was so impressed with the facility, the doctors, the research, the accomplishment that he decided to will one million dollars to the institution upon his death! His name is inscribed there in stone to this day as a generous benefactor. Spud's prostate cancer had been found there and removed without the necessity of chemotherapy so he blithely went on with life until years later the verdict came that the cancer returned. Despite his eighty-nine year age, belied by his lean, fit corpus, his doctor recommended surgery from which Spud never awoke, and he was moved in a coma to Moline Public Hospital to die on October 18, 1989. Ironically, he died at the hands of those he had most trusted with his money!

Katherine survived her husband seven years dividing her time between their homes in Moline and Sarasota, but it was in Moline where she slept away in her own bed on May 17, 1994. Spud and Katharine's remains lie in City of Moline Cemeteries at 5001 Thirty-fourth Ave., Moline.

Generation # 3—Delmar Henry Oehler and Dorene Tanner Oehler
—4, 5, 6, 7—

Emma and Will's second son Delmar, called Perch after the fish, was the tallest of the boys with light auburn hair, hazel eyes, athletic physique, and he was a dedicated fisherman. Born March 2, 1902, like all Emma's and Will's sons Delmar helped out on the farm, later at Will's shop, and carried his weight in chores at home. A degree from Illinois State College in Normal where he pitched on the baseball team for two years, led paradoxically to a teaching position in the Minier School and a return to Emma's home and table. But that domestic arrangement lasted only until he and Dorene Tanner, daughter of their friends and fellow Minier folks, Charley and Leta Tanner, married in the Minier Christian Church on August 11, 1927. They had known each other their entire lives but when both were teachers at the Minier school, where he taught high school manual arts and she the lower grades, their paths crossed often and love was ignited. A pretty blue-eyed blond with porcelain skin, Dorene, born February 4, 1901, was an accomplished pianist and singer, poised, and confident despite the embarrassment she felt about her hands. Just like her father, Dorene, an only child, inherited the condition where one of the joints in each finger was missing, shortening the length, but not the use and ability, of each hand.

Delmar became principal of the school in time, but when Dorene was married even though they had no children, she was not allowed to teach school. She could finish out the school year, however, and in her classroom was Ada Rost sister of Dorene's future sister-in-law, Mary Rost. Two cute family stories stem from that year: Ada was charged by her classmates to ask the newly married teacher if the students should call her "Miss Tanner" or "Mrs. Oehler?" "Mrs. Oehler" was Dorene's smiling response. Another incident happened on desk inspection day. When Mrs. Oehler asked Ada to open her desk, her shocked exclamation was: "Why, Ada, your desk looks like a pig sty!"

Sometime afterward during World War II and after serving twenty-eight years in the Minier schools, Perch accepted a job in Wilmington, IL, north and east of Minier on the way to Chicago, in the business office of a strip coal mine firm, Northern Illinois Coal Corporation. He participated in community philanthropies there and served as president of the school board. There Dorene was active in their church, home tutored students, gave speech correction help to children, and wrote poetry and children's stories for publication, principally in the children's magazine of the Modern Woodmen Insurance Company. But still no babies appeared in their home. Perhaps Delmar's chronic kidney disease was the cause, family surmised. The disease cut short Delmar's life when he was only fifty-four years old.

Perch's nephew John Johnson remembers: "In the spring of 1956 I was in the 7th grade. I came home from school one day and Uncle Perch and Aunt Dodo were there. That was unusual because we normally saw them on weekends for family dinners; not during the week. Uncle Perch had come to Minier to tell Mother that he had an incurable disease. And that he wanted me to come to Wilmington after school was out to fish with him. He took me outside and gave me my first lesson on how to cast with a fly rod. And then he told me to practice every day. It takes skill to cast a fish line with a fly rod from a boat! After school was out, I took the bus by myself from Bloomington to Wilmington. I was there for about 10 days. We fished every day – on weekends and after work on weekdays. Sometimes we went out with his fishing companion "Monty" Montgomery. We caught lots of fish. Uncle Perch knew how to fish. It is one of my fondest childhood memories. About 6 weeks later, he died. When I was fishing with him in Wilmington I had no idea that he was sick with a terminal illness. Today one with nephritis could get a kidney transplant."

John: "During one visit to the farm, Uncle Perch taught me how to throw a slider. He was also a baseball player like my dad. According to Uncle Jess, he was a very good pitcher."

After Delmar's July 19, 1956, death, Dorene, alone, moved back to Minier where her parents, Charley and Leta Tanner, and her mother's identical twin sister, Fleta Afflis, were ensconced just north and across the street from the Oehler home. Dorene's own home was almost directly across the street from the Oehler's. About that same 1958 time, Dr. Lawrence J. Rossi, Sr. established the first Nursing Home in the state of Illinois, the first assisted-living home in Illinois, the first alcoholic rehabilitation centers for the elderly in Illinois, and the first residence for senior citizens in the United States, called Hopedale House Retirement Home in nearby Hopedale, IL. Folks were living longer, didn't want to be a burden and live with their children, had funds from savings and social security, so the concept of senior living came into being.

Dorene was curious, interviewed with Dr. Rossi, and together they concluded she would be a perfect activities director, one of the first in the nation to hold that designation. For the next twenty years, with both her widowed father, Charley Tanner, and father-in-law, Will Oehler, in residence some of that time, Dorene explored and created all the possibilities of fun activities for the elderly: arts and crafts, singing and music, games, shows, performances by local school children, lectures by local college professors, and reading aloud to name a few. Her work, and that of Dr. Rossi, was considered ground-breaking in the 1950s so Hopedale House was frequently visited by social scientists, medical professionals, and others who wished to consult with them before opening like establishments of their own all over the United States. Many awards and much recognition justifiably were given Dorene especially for her her innovative work as an activites director at Hopedale House. The very concept of a retirement home and activities director were completely new in the 1950s when she wrote the lesson plans for the many activities she invented. She defined the job of activities director for herself and for those who followed in the days when there were no reference books for such, nor anyone from whom to seek advice.

Dorene survived Perch by nearly thirty years, lived a full and active life of contribution to her Christian Church, Hopedale House, her many friends and family in both Hopedale and Minier. She ended her days in an apartment on the grounds of the retirement community she had helped put on the map, leaving an estate at her death on February 5, 1981, the day after her eightieth birthday, with bequests to her three nieces and one nephew and many, many other recipients close to her over the years who needed some financial help. Dorene wrote her own funeral service, her last impressive act here in this world. She and Delmar are buried in the Oehler plot in Minier cemetery; her parents lie just steps away.

Generation #3—Jesse Dean Oehler and Nelle Forsythe Oehler
—4, 5, 6, 7—

Emma's and Will's third son Jesse Dean, began life on the family farm, on March 30, 1905, mimicking his older brothers, participating in the rough and tumble boys-only escapades and wrestling play of three toddler boys. Like his brothers before him, Jesse channeled that energy into running races, winning first place in the under twelve year old boys fifty yard dash and second place in the boys under age twelve one hundred yard dash! Before he was grown, though, the family moved into the village, Minier, where from an early age his artistic ability was apparent especially in Dad's woodworking shop in the garage. Creating beautiful objects out of wood became his lifelong passion and pastime!

Jesse Dean, married Nellie Forsythe, of Paris, Illinois, in the early 1930s; he served in WWII stationed at Fort Leonard Wood. An artist at woodworking and generous with his creations so that examples exist today in loving family possession, Jess surely found diversion from his black moods when absorbed in the creative process. Carefully wrought tables, hanging wall cabinets, chairs, bowls, and goblets saw their birth at Jess' hands, astounding to all who observed.

For a few years after his discharge from the army, Jess spent at a job in Portland, Oregon. But when his dad announced he would close the elevator company and retire in 1949; when his brother, Spud, expressed his wish to open a John Deere dealership in the factory premises and asked Jess to join him as partner, Jess seemed to recognize it as the natural progression of events. He and Nelle moved back to Minier and into the Oehler family home where they could keep an eye on Will and make it their home as well. Buoyed by the responsibility of the position as John Deere dealer for the farm community, stimulated by the demands of the opportunity, feeling welcomed by the village business people, and deriving the satisfaction of recognition from his fellow residents of his hometown, Jess settled in and throve.

Once his dad announced his plans to move to the newly opened Hopedale House, Jess and Nelle seized the opportunity to design and build their very own home on the vacant lot to the north of the Oehler home. Mose (Maurice) and Jean Peine, their close friends (and member of our folks Peine family), bought the big Oehler home and modernized its appearance by removing the front porch outside and some of the arts and crafts details inside (since laboriously restored by subsequent owners).

A faithful member of the Shrine Lodge of Peoria and of the VFW (Veterans of Foreign Wars) association in Minier and, Jess spearheaded its many philanthropic projects around Minier. Attendance at Johnny Johnson's basketball games took precedence over any social gathering and the watchful caring of his dad was a constant priority for Jess. From his reserved seat down front near the basket, Jess was a constant though muted cheerleader. If Johnny scored, a soft "Way to go, Buster!" was elicited. If Johnny failed to score, came a hushed "You can't make 'em all, Buster!" Both Jess and Nelle attended basketball games just to witness Rita in the cheerleading squad.

To a lifelong smoker of cigarettes like Jess, it was perhaps not a complete surprise when he got the diagnosis of bladder cancer in his early sixties. "Coffin nails," the doctor called them! Jess took the news with stoicism, acknowledged the role of the cigarettes, but knew deep down they had also served to medicate him away from the dark moods. Even at the Mayo Clinic in Rochester, MN, the doctors could only confirm the diagnosis and attempt to make him more comfortable. Family and friends trooped to his bedside at the hospital in Bloomington, sad that the gentle man had to suffer such agony, both physical and mental. The end came there on November 29, 1968.

A dusky beauty, reflecting her Native American forbear, Nelle followed the fashion which her slim figure showed off to perfection. Nature had intended her warm instincts to find expression in a mother's duties, her heart yearned for children, and her longing often vented in tears. But that was not to be. Instead, her nurturing ways were expended on her widowed father-in-law as she kept house and cooked for him, on Rita and John Johnson, and later at the Bloomington office of orthopedic surgeon, Dr. John Wright, whose books she kept and later served as his personal secretary. Diabetes, diagnosed in mid-life restricted her activities, but her disciplined nature guaranteed that she followed the diet and wordlessly injected herself. In widowhood and retirement, Nelle felt the solitude in their home oppressive so moved to the new condo building on the commercial street of Minier, the former village opera house. She was expecting to enjoy the easy socialization with other owners in the building, was disappointed when none of the other five units sold, and she found herself perhaps even lonelier there. When the December 19, 1981, end came, a complication of her diabetes as she lay in bed one night in her seventy-second year, there was no one to hear her calls, so she simply slept away to be found later.

Jess and Nelle are buried on the Oehler family plot in Minier cemetery.

Generation # 3—Lyla Elizabeth Oehler Johnson and Delmar Johnson —4, 5, 6, 7—

Arriving in the wake of three mischievous boys, the oldest just six, a baby girl must have been a great relief and joy for Emma and Will Oehler! Lyla Elizabeth appeared on October 12, 1906, out on the family farm but just as the family was making the transition from rural to village living. Once she outgrew the cradle beside her parents bed, she was given her own bedroom, a luxury, but possible in the large new four-square family home in Minier. Though she might have wished for a sister, it was another boy who joined the family when she was six years old. That meant Lyla's assistance was expected from that early age to shoulder much of the daily chores in the home. She was naturally a sympathetic and quick learning little girl who sensed her mama's needs almost before they were expressed.

It may appear that Lyla was the lucky girl of the family who didn't have to share a room or bed with anyone, but that was not exactly the case. To her discomfort, though she was but four or five years old, her privacy was somewhat pierced when her widowed grandpa, Heinrich Peter Graff, stayed with Emma's family as he rotated himself among his grown children living a few months at a time with each until he died in 1911.

Sewing came easily to Lyla at the foot-treadle machine; hours were passed from a young age of nine or so in sewing most of the clothes her

STORIES MY FOLKS TOLD ME

brothers wore; blue chambray fabric was stacked high at her side where almost like a factory girl she turned out their everyday shirts. The work load didn't subside when her brothers went off to college or business school, though! The boys came home most week-ends bringing their dirty laundry to be washed and ironed by their sister—before Sunday night!

Did resentment creep across Lyla's psyche? Of course! But at the same time, she loved her brothers, accepted her role in life, saw that her mother truly needed her help, and later was rewarded with their undying devotion. As her brothers left and she remained in Minier, Lyla was gratified that they returned often to her home for long confidential talk whether or not a meal was involved. Usually, though, a meal was involved. Lyla always made a special occasion out of a meal, setting her table with care, preparing many dishes, including those time-consuming offerings like deviled eggs or home-made noodles. You could say she went all out! She seemed to know that a meal prepared by someone you love—especially for you—is a gift, an expression of love. Spud gave her a fine ring with a turquoise-colored stone in appreciation for all she had done for him over the years of their lives and left a generous bequest to her children at his death.

By high school age, Lyla was drawn to the drama team, acting in school plays and later in adult productions at the Opera House "uptown." Garrulous and quick thinking, Lyla loved to talk with her friends and family. She loved her cousin, Vera, getting to know her Nebraska relative when their mothers, Annie and Emma, made the big trek back and forth between Seward and Minier. Soon after high school, Lyla began a real job which payed her real money, encouraged her imagination and flair for drama, and became "the job I loved!" in her words—a sales clerk in the clothing department at Peine's store "uptown." In time, the Peines promoted Lyla to buyer whose main supplier was the wholesale arm of the Marshall Field Company in Chicago. Heady with success, Lyla organized fashion shows at the Minier store as well as a quilt show there. Shopping ladies surely flocked to her shows and subsequently to her cash register!

Lyla had known Delmar Johnson forever since he was her brother Spud's classmate and best friend. That made Delm six years older than she so likely he didn't actually notice her until she was a high school graduate and successful "uptown" merchant. But with her merry blue eyes, sandy curls, and cute figure, she did catch his eye! When they married in Bloomington on Augurst 28, 1933, they traveled by train to Chicago and stayed at a loop hotel—provided by her business connection at Marshall Field's! Card playing friends, Margaret and Lyle Brenneman, tagged along, though assuredly not as guests of Marshall Field! Lyle Brenneman's mother was Lyla's Aunt Ida Marie Oehler Brenneman, sister of Will, her dad, and thus her cousin. Margaret Buehrig Brenneman was the granddaughter of Charles Buehrig, son of the immigrant Buehrigs, and Rosa Weber Buehrig and she was the daughter of Charles Buehrig and Pearl Livesay Buehrig; thus she was the cousin of Lyla's future sister-in-law, Mary Rost Oehler. The web of relationships in Minier was extensive and ubiquitous!

At the Chicago World' Fair of 1933, the honeymooners were mightily entertained at the House of Tomorrow where new building materials like gypsum and drywall panels to replace plaster walls were introduced, futuristic architecture amazed, and the exhibit of "dream cars": Lincoln, Nash, Packard so sleek and fast impressed. But of special interest to lifelong baseball fan, Delmar, was the first-ever Major League Baseball All-Star Game held at the state of the art Comiskey Park. We doubt he actually saw that game on July 6, featuring players Babe Ruth and Lou Gehrig, but we can imagine that he and Lyle did attend a game at the grand park. Folks at the time said those events, like a beam of sunshine during the rainy season, were a bit of a reprieve from the Great Depression!

Marriage to a farmer meant Lyla moved to the farm right after she married. Her father-in-law, John Johnson, was still living there, but he was building a house in Minier and moved there soonafter. For her husband, Delmar, there was no move necessary for he had lived in the farmhouse his entire life except for a few years when he was five years old; that was when his mother died and he lived with his grandparents Beal in Minier a few years. "I don't think she particularly liked farm life. But she accepted her role. She was the quintessential housewife

– cooking, canning, washing clothes, and raising children was her occupation. She did the inside work, our Dad did the outside work. She almost never left the fence outside the house," John again.

Thrasher dinners, with as many as eight or ten farm workers gathered round the kitchen table, allowed Lyla to display her extensive culinary gifts with several meats, huge bowls of mashed potatoes, green beans from her garden, her special deviled eggs, and pies and cakes galore. No sooner did the last boot leave her kitchen than the big wash up began. First the mounds of dishes and pots had to be washed and dried by hand by her alone; then she was down on the floor scrubbing it till you could practically eat off it. Only afterward could Lyla be found stretched out on the living room sofa enjoying one long cigarette break!

Their big vegetable and flower garden took input from both Lyla and Delm, but was primarily the handiwork of the distaff member. Rita remembers: Believe it or not, there was no hose connection at the house to bring water out to the garden twenty feet away! But it didn't matter! The soil was so fabulous that Mother's vegetables and flowers flourished to prize-winning size on their own. Oh, in a drought we would haul water from the pump on the other side of the house and give each plant a tin can-sized splash of water, but otherwise they were on their own!"

Motherhood brought a special happiness to Lyla and Delm, perhaps especially because they had waited a time for it to happen. They went to all of their children's school activities–Rita's dance recitals, school plays, band concerts, boy scouts, girl scouts which she helped organize in Minier, Johnny's baseball and basketball games. They didn't miss a one! Chauffeuring Rita to weekly dance classes in Bloomington or sewing each of her many dance costumes perhaps fulfilled an unrealized childhood dream of Lyla's, yet cost her dearly in time and energy as a mother.

In her leisure time, Lyla found enjoyment in her vegetable and flower garden, crafts, needle work, rugs, quilting (examples are still lovingly held by her children), and especially in talking to her friends. She served on the Minier cemetery board. Delm enjoyed fishing, pool, cards, gardening, ball games. He had played on the high school baseball team and later on the Minier adult team. He served on the grade school board, brought Little League baseball to Minier, Armington, Hopedale, and Stanford, and anonymously payed for boys' uniforms when their families could not afford them.

John remembers: "Daddy listened to all the St Louis Cardinals games on the radio. Every night! Or the Chicago Cubs if the Cardinals weren't playing. Everyone in Minier was either a Cardinals fan or a Cubs fan. He was a Brooklyn Dodgers fan. I think Duke Snyder was his favorite player. He played on the baseball team in high school. He hit a lot of balls to me after supper. I didn't know it at the time, but he helped start a little league in Minier and the surrounding towns – Armington, Hopedale, Stanford, Danvers. This was while I was in Grade School. He was one of the organizers. I remember there was a meeting of coaches from all the towns on our screened-in front porch at the farm house."

White faces on a brown coat, or white-faced cattle, were what Delm bred and raised over the many years. He raised his own feed to supply their needs and daily, even when there was a ballgame on the radio he listened to WGN out of Chicago to keep up with the morning, noon, and evening reports of prices being payed at the stockyards in Chicago so he would know when to rent a truck and drive his stock to market. There, in a dorm-like accommodation near the stockyards he spent the night before driving back to the farm. Rita remembers: "Once he noticed that the man in the next bed had a distinctly shifty look about him. But what the heck! It's only for one night! But sure enough, the next morning he discovered that his pants were missing! And his wallet (not yet filled with the proceeds of his sale)! And his shoes! A quick trip to a resale shop made him respectable for the drive home, but their ill-fit meant lots of laughs and a good story around Minier!"

John: "Farming was hard work compared to today. But I think he was in pretty good condition. Not overweight and generally healthy. I think the harvests were the hardest. Long days. You had a short window to get the crop in or you could lose it. The depression was hard. But at least they had food. I think they grew or raised most of the food they ate. Later, most of the crop was fed to farm animals. Hay for cattle and

STORIES MY FOLKS TOLD ME

sheep. Corn and oats were ground up for hogs and cattle. Excess was sold to the coop elevator in Minier.

"One summer Susie and Kathleen were staying with us on the farm for a few days. It was oat harvest time. Daddy came in from the field late, maybe around 7:30pm. He was tired from a long day. He took a shower in the basement. (That's where the shower was. We didn't have a shower in the bathroom.) We were all at the kitchen table having supper. After his shower, Daddy came up the basement stairs with a towel. Mother said, "Close your eyes while Uncle Del runs through the kitchen to go up stairs." He said, "No he's not. I'm too tired to run!"

"I never heard him say he liked farming. But I never heard him complain either. For him I don't think there was a choice or alternative. His father expected him to work on the farm after high school. So he accepted it. He could be his own boss. It was better than working at Caterpillar. He was friends with the other farmers. They shared work—baling hay for example with the Darnell's and Lovins's. My favorite farm experience was when I was old enough to go to Darnell's and Lovin's to help."

Lyla and Delm moved to town, Minier, in 1960, retiring from farming completely in 1965 when Delm was sixty-five. Their address at 602 N. Main was as always a gathering place for friends and family, though letters addressed to them from fellow Minier residents would give only "city" under their name since the postmaster knew where everyone in the village lived. As Illinois farmers customarily did, they wintered in Florida beginning in 1964. They drove around the state, stayed a few days in several different places, and finally settled on Daytona Beach. They went back to Daytona Beach every winter thereafter, last in 1981. In September 1981, they moved into Westminister Village, a senior residence in Bloomington. Delm didn't last long there, succumbing on November 11, 1982, to complications from diabetes.

Lyla persevered another nine years, continuing in her favorite role as grandmother to Mary Ann and John Witzgall and Elizabeth and Timothy Johnson, establishing for herself a reputation at the residence as an indispensably helpful woman, comfortable around people who were sick or disabled, and would help them. She took her evening meal in the dining room, for instance, with a woman who was blind, would take her to the dining room and read the menu to her, talk to her and generally lighten her burden.

All her life, Lyla was always helping other Minier people in need. Not with money particularly, but by doing something for them like cooking a meal, washing their clothes, or paying them for housework. When she was in high school, she made a funeral dress for a young girl in town who died. The family was poor. John: "When I was growing up, Hobos would walk along the railroad tracks across the road from the farm house. Often they would come to the house for something to eat. She never turned them away and always made them a sandwich and some coffee. And then she would sit on the front steps and talk to them. I think Hobos had a network and knew where they could get something to eat."

I would describe Mother as 'unremarkably remarkable.' She did not go to college. She only had one job for a few years, other than housekeeping. She didn't read much and did not seem to be that interested in current events–national or world. Her life was her family (which was large) and her friends. She loved her family and friends and was very loyal to them. After Grandma Oehler died, she had Grandpa Oehler out to the farm for Sunday dinner almost every Sunday until Uncle Jess and Aunt Nelle moved back to Minier. After Grandma Johnson died, Grandpa Johnson came to the farm almost every Sunday for dinner. All the family holiday meals were at our house. Growing up, I don't recall being anyplace but home for Thanksgiving, Christmas, or Easter dinner. She sent lots of postcards to Elizabeth and Tim when they were young. When I told Tim (he was 4) that Grandma Johnson had died, he said, 'But who will send us cards?'"

Rita and John agree, their mother's legacy should be: "She helped other people!"

Lyla and Delmar Johnson lie together in the Minier Cemetery since her death on January 5, 1990.

William Peter Oehler — Generation #3
—4, 5, 6, 7—

"It's a boy! "Well, I have a girl for your boy!" Dr. Rost presciently proclaimed when he saw the baby he had just delivered to Emma Oehler. That was on June 16, 1912; a quarter century later those two babies, all grown up, did claim each other in marriage!

Emma and Will Oehler named their little "bonus" baby who came six years after their last child and twelve years after their first, William Peter, after Will and his dad and Emma's father, Peter Graff, but from the beginning everyone called him Billy. Born in the new Oehler home in Minier, this child had different experiences than his three older brothers from the onset: less running barefoot through the fields—more well-shod adventures throughout the village where everyone knew his name; less rough and tumble antics of three little boys born very close in age—more experiences in grown-up company; less thrown into the same kettle with each other to do the same thing at the same time as the others—more individual activities.

With his blond curls and hazel eyes, the new clothes he wore (all the hand-me-downs from his brothers having long been given away), displayed proudly through town in the new brown wicker pram, Billy was a "show-stopper" as babies of proud mamas often are. Lyla and the boys petted and pampered him; his many aunts, uncles, and grandparents indulged him. Why, he was so cute he won first prize for the cutest baby at the Tazewell County Fair! Emma continued to spoil her little "cutie," establishing a very close bond with her last child. Billy sat on her lap till his feet touched the floor according to his older siblings.

Reports of Billy were not always flattering of course. When invited to the Rost's big house to Mary's fourth birthday party, he drank too much lemonade, got too excited over the newness of a party with fun and games, and consequently, humiliatingly, wet his pants! Another time just a few years later he suffered a whipping from his furious big brother, Perch. It was a Saturday night when folks got "cleaned up" and strolled "uptown" to see and be seen. Before Perch drew his weekly bath in the big claw foot tub, he carefully laid out his attire for the evening, including a new pair of brown socks, on his bed. Those new socks cast a spell over the passing Billy who, overcome with daring and mischief, slipped them on and ambled up into the gathering crowd "uptown." The thrill was of short duration though, because it didn't take Perch long to put two and two together, race "uptown," collar Billy, and wrestle him to the ground to remove the prized socks from his stinking feet!

Billy must have been a real thorn in the side of Perch in those days. One year he was actually the student, Perch the teacher—in the same classroom! Mouthy and disrespectful, bored and fidgety, Billy challenged his brother every single day until many a one he spent sitting in his desk isolated out in the hall. But at home, around the common family dining table, never a word of rebuke or complaint was issued. Not once! Every Saturday, up in the boys' shared bedroom, on Billy's corner of the dresser a shiny quarter or fifty cent coin magically appeared, "spending money" so hard for a village boy to acquire.

It was about that same time in the early 1920s when Billy sat down at his small boy-sized roll top desk to write the most important letter he had ever composed in his life. He had spent quite a while thinking about what he would say and how he would say it, and because the actual act of writing was so challenging to him, he had procrastinated until the deadline for the postmark was nearly at hand. But finally it was now or never so he sat down at his desk to write the requisite whole paragraph telling why he should be the one to win the pony. Every day he asked Dad if a letter had come for him, every night in bed he fantasized the fun he was going to have with that pony until slowly he guessed someone else must have won the pony and the whole dream sort of faded away as childhood preoccupations do. In fact, Billy might never have thought again about that letter if years later, when refinishing the desk for his own daughters, he had not found it amber-edged and faded stuck up in the roller mechanism!

Billy's cousin Glenn Imig, younger son of his Aunt Tillie and Uncle Gus, was just a few years older than him, lived on the farm, and knew a lot about the world and—GUNS. Yes, Glenn kept a rifle under his bed in case he needed to scare off chicken thieves from the barnyard chicken pen. He showed a bug-eyed Billy all its details: how to load it, cock it, handle it, stopping just short of shooting it. Then all night long, at the slightest sound from without their bedroom window, Glenn would poke Billy and tell him to go to the window to look out for chicken thieves. It made for an exciting but sleepless night for the little town boy!

On a balmy summer Saturday evening in the late 1920s well into the big band era when every good-sized town had a dance hall or outdoor pavilion, Spud was squiring a dreamy-eyed Katharine around the Bloomington version of that milieu when he glanced at the knicker-garbed boys straddling the banister at the rim of the floor. Why? Was it? Could it be? "Billy! What are you doing here? How did you get here?" Simply put, someone let him and Smitty, his constant companion, tag along for the show that evening. Later when a bit older Billy was captivated by the big bands of the day himself and the ubiquitous dance halls. He and his buddies drove all the way to Chicago to the brand new Edgewater Beach Hotel then famous for it's enormous and grand ballroom. Presumably that time it wasn't to watch the dancers but to join them on the dance floor!

Other days after school and into the evening, Billy and his friends and brothers attempted to assemble a radio kit. It was a struggle with lots of trial and error in the early days of radio, before ready made versions were available in the stores. Frustrating was not the word! When a workable result finally resulted, maybe months later, they were jubilant, but reception was usually so scratchy they could hardly hear the score of the baseball game coming out of Chicago or St. Louis or understand President Franklin Delano Roosevelt's Fireside Chats. Still, radio in the 1930s had an impact comparable to the internet today. For the first time in history, world leaders could project a voice thousands of miles into the living rooms of strangers creating boundless opportunity to inform of current and world events or even persuade. A new style of family entertainment, serial stories or "soap operas," appeared or weekly programs like "Fibber McGee and Molly," "Amos 'n' Andy," "Philip Morris Playhouse," and "The Jack Benny Show." By then the radio was a piece of furniture, a cabinet of fine wood standing several feet tall, full of tubes, with a grill-faced silk cloth through which the sound emanated, and several tuning knobs protruding, in living rooms all over America. Information and news coming over the radio was instantaneous, more up to date than the only other news purveyors: newspapers, magazines, and movie theaters. Suddenly evenings were livelier as folks looked forward to their favorite radio programs!

It can perhaps be said that Billy's favorite hours were spent in his Dad's workshop out at one end of the garage. From his Dad and then from his brother Jess, Billy learned to use the simple, non-electrified, hand tools. From first hammering nails, turning screws, drilling holes in anything and everything, sawing little boards, always using cast-off scrap wood, Billy progressed to actually assembling an object from a carefully drawn pattern. Candlesticks for Mom, small wooden cars, a little wooden stool, or a wooden tray were some of his early projects. How he liked to lie in bed and think about what he might make, get up and draw the parts on paper, write down the measurements of each piece, day-dream about how he could overcome the inevitable obstacles or correct the mistakes he had made. Whenever he looked at a piece of furniture and later at a whole house, he liked to mentally figure out how it was put together. Or, even better, he thought about how an object could be made better, be improved, be customized. That's what he was surely doing when folks, like his parents and teachers, said he wasn't paying attention or listening!

If Billy got in trouble at home, he could always slip out the back door and rap on the door just across the yard at Uncle Val Graff's (brother of his mother) and Aunt Vinie's big house. They were always overjoyed at his visits, showered him with their completely non-judgmental love, and were never too busy to play cards with him or just joke around. He knew Uncle Val always had a piece of his favorite horehound candy in his pocket. Retired young from farming, they had moved to town for their only child, Leah, a victim of a mild case of polio excluding any paralysis. She never married, was somehow delicate, and required care but nevertheless lived to the age of 100, later after her parents passing in the care of Frank and Clara Thomas, and after their passing, in a Bloomington care center.

Billy's high school graduation portrait.

It was when Billy was in his teens on a visit to the Seward relatives, perhaps for Vera's marriage to Ted Hughes, that he first witnessed the extraordinary gift that musical talent, the playing of an instrument, could play in a person's life. Ted Hughes was a masterful player of the piano of popular songs or classical pieces. He drew folks to the piano, played with their emotions up and down as he spoke the language of music and cast a passionate spell over his listeners. When Bill, as he liked to be called now, asked Ted how he learned to play the piano he got this little story: "I was the youngest in the family. My mama had tried to get every one of my brothers and sisters before me to stick with the piano lessons she insisted on, but she met with failure every time. When I came along, she knew it was her last chance so everyday when I practiced she stood by me with a man's belt over her shoulder. If I tried to procrastinate going to the piano or cut short the practice period, she would haul out that belt and even whipped me a few times. As a result I took those lessons and practiced those pieces till I was all grown up. One day recently she and I were up in the attic looking for something when she spotted that belt and began to cry for remorse, but I just hugged her and thanked her for giving me my gift." Bill was in awe, the idea was planted in his head that one day he would take music lessons, and that's exactly what he did some years later.

When still in his early forties, soon after he and Mary built the new house in Crestwood Hills, Bill bought himself a home organ and continued the music lessons he had been taking with Eddie Simon at his downtown Moline store and studio. The lessons had begun earlier on the piano but in spite of practice Bill didn't make the progress he desired so they switched to the "chord" method and soon he was able to conjure up a pretty good rendition of popular songs like: "Ragtime Cowboy Joe," "Among My Souvenirs," "Arrivederci, Roma," "Glow Worm," "Silver Bells," "I Left My Heart in San Francisco," "Whatever Will Be, Will Be," "Indian Love Call," "Embraceable You," "St. Louis Blues," "Tea For Two," "When Day Is Done," "April Showers," "Missouri Waltz," "Let Me Call You Sweetheart," "Shine On Harvest Moon," "Alice Blue Gown," "The World is Waiting for the Sunrise," and countless more from his stack of sheet music still extant.

However much he would have liked to replicate his idol, Buddy Carl, at the piano he knew he was "pretty middling," but nevertheless derived immeasurable pleasure at the keyboard. How Bill's heart swelled, how his attitude improved, how his everyday worries subsided when the emotions intrinsic in the music caused him to pour out his feelings from the depths of his soul. It was a bit disconcerting, even hurtful, though when Mary grabbed her book and huffed off down the hall to her bedroom, closing the door in a manner he could hear even over the volume of the organ; never a word of acclaim, only toleration, of what for him was a transporting experience. A little complement from her would have gone a long way but alas never came. Once in awhile a dinner guest would request a song, though, a compliment to make him glow!

Family members still remember how Bill sang in the car along with the radio. "Show me the way to go home. I'm tired and I want to go to bed. I had a little drink about an hour ago and it went right to my hear. Show me the way to go home..." Or: "Five foot two, eyes of blue. Oh, what those five feet can do! Has any body seen my gal?" He knew the words to many popular songs of his day, felt the buoyant lift that music gives to the soul, was gladdened by the mysterious mix of tone, time and tune.

Even Confucius spoke of this feeling: "Music produces a kind of pleasure which human nature cannot do without." Famous pianist Byron Janis spoke of its healing power: "What an extraordinary gift music has given us besides its beauty. It has a scientifically proven ability to help heal both physical and psychological problems. Listening to your favorite music does help but playing an instrument has a greater success. Playing well or badly doesn't matter, just using one finger to plunk out a tune is sufficient—you can come away with a feeling of well-being. It is music's unstoppable ability to uplift and inspire that makes playing so rewarding." Years later in the mid 1960s when Bill found his Oehler relatives in Weisweil, Germany, there was a piano in the home and to his swelling heart he was told: "Oehlers are musical!"

Yes, Bill loved making music and just knew someday his daughters would be grateful to him for paying for their lessons and making them practice. "As long as you girls sleep under my roof, you are going to take piano lessons!" he barked more than once. And so they did, with only two weeks break in the summer, right up till graduation from high school. Perhaps he was thinking that the only thing he knew about Susie's birth father was that he was "musical," but for sure it was his own love of hearing them play which made him so resolute in the matter. In 1968 when Susie and her husband lived in Costa Rica for John Deere, Bill even shamed his son-in-law into going halves with him to buy Susie a Yamaha upright piano. "Susie has always had a piano to play. I think she has waited long enough since marrying you! We better get her one right now!" Financially, the moment didn't seem apt to Peter, but Susie was ecstatic to resume her daily hour at the piano.

In a way perhaps not remembered today, the 1920s saw a profound social and cultural change in America. For the first time urban population outnumbered the rural. Leisure time was for the first time attained by the working class which of course counted most everyone. A radio bringing network news and entertainment was in many homes, movies were shown at a theater nearby for twenty-five cents, mass magazines like "The Saturday Evening Post" were available, new household appliances made women's work lighter, store-bought clothes appeared, super markets with canned foods began to replace home canning, commercially baked bread was cheap (but not as good), and Mickey Mouse debuted in 1928.

But surely above all the inventions to improve the lives of ordinary people like our folks it was the automobile. In 1910, the auto was still a plaything of the rich, whereas by 1920 there were eight million on American roads, even on country roads where they reduced the isolation of farm families tremendously. Ribbons of asphalt rather quickly began to be woven through the land; gas stations, billboards, restaurants, and tourist cabins followed. By 1922 there were 10,000 miles of paved roads in America whereas 1941 saw 600,000 paved roads. 1926 saw the advent of road maps and a numbering system for the roads: odd numbers for north-south roads, even numbers for east-west roads.

Bill, like all American boys loved cars, bought his first around the time of his 1937 marriage, and drove countless cars over the years of his lifetime as he traded up about every three years. For some years he drove Chryslers but Nash Rambler, Buick, Pontiac, De Soto, and Studebaker among others got parked in his garage too. All his cars, except when he lived in Germany, were American brands. Japanese cars didn't arrive to compete with Detroit until way after the war, and European brands were excessively expensive. Besides, to drive foreign cars, even high-performance German vehicles Bill considered unpatriotic. One particularly memorable car was a red Buick convertible with Robin's egg blue leather seats he bought for Mary in the late 1950s. He even let his daughters take it to the university to park in front of the sorority house during "rush" to impress all who walked past to enter their house. All along, though, his goal was to own a Cadillac. That day eventually came, a day when he really felt he had "arrived," for an automobile is much more than transportation. It states the rank of the owner, the degree of boldness, the personality, the power!

Just sitting behind the wheel out on the highway sent him into a kind of nirvana where all was right with the world, where the sense of power and independence intensified, where for the moment he was king of the road. At times like that he actually sang for joy the popular songs of the day like "That Old Black Magic," "I'll Be Seeing You," "Don't Fence Me In," and "Sentimental Journey" as they streamed from the radio. Like most men in those days he washed his car with a hose once a week and carefully dusted it off before driving to dinner at friends home or sending Mary and the girls to church. "When in Rome, do as the Romans do," he said to Mary as he drove up Wielandstrasse in Heidelberg, Germany in his black Mercedes Benz sedan, and he enjoyed every minute he drove that car! But he didn't take it to Moline when he moved back there. Instead, he had invested in a 1936 Rolls Royce to drive around Moline in nice weather before he sold it to a collector as an investment.

Automobiles were magical to those like Bill who got in on the ground floor of their advent. He still remembered when his own dad got his early cars; his own mother never drove a car; he never was given his own car as an entitlement when he turned sixteen. He had to dream long and hard before his ownership of a vehicle was a reality. For him, a car meant individual freedom; in a car he could go wherever he wanted, whenever he wanted, subject only to his ability to put gas in the tank. Scoping the dealership when new models came out, talking "cars" with friends, buying a VW Bug for Kathleen when she married Paul Beich in Germany, buying a Plymouth for Susie's wedding gift, sustaining friendship with Arnold Huikeshoven at the Chrysler dealership in Moline, and rejoicing with Woody Curtis, president of Deere & Company, who stopped by the house on 29th Ave. Ct. to show him his new car were all part of his love affair with the automobile. But only American cars! When he asked his son-in-law, Peter, how much he paid for his new BMW and heard the amount he exclaimed: "My God! You could have had a Cadillac!"

Likewise, Bill followed with interest the progress of the gasoline engine tractor which introduced in 1915 transformed farm life, though it wasn't until 1945 that they overtook horses on American farms. The number of dray horses peaked at 25 million around 1920; it took four of them to pull a plow. The life of a farm horse was short, though, only about three years. They required frequent rest stops, they couldn't till as deeply, and they were a genuine cost factor requiring much of the yield for their fodder. One man with four horses could only manage to cultivate forty acres, or a square one-fourth mile on a side, so that was the typical size of an American farm. Each tractor did the work of two or three horses but at the price of $750, a fortune in those days; the horse, mule, and ox continued as the mainstays of the farmer right up to the '30s.

But back to the carefree village life of our boy in the 1920s, whose days were spent tossing a ball with pals in imitation of their hero Babe Ruth or in evading his school assignments. There crept into his carefree, halcyon life a cloud called The Great Depression. It wasn't called by that name in those days, of course; in fact folks didn't really understand what was happening; they just knew they were feeling mighty poor. After World War I, in 1920 the federal government no longer needed to buy huge volumes of wheat and corn from the farmers to sustain the Army. European agriculture was reviving, the US had tariffs to protect its farmers, but that only depressed exports further. Between 1919 and 1921 farm income fell 60%. Farmers who had borrowed to buy land and equipment then found it difficult to pay on the loans. The American Farm Bureau appealed to Washington for help, but two different price-support bills were defeated, and one was vetoed by President Calvin Coolidge causing farmers to abandon their traditional Republican ties in the 1928 election to vote Democrat. At the Oehler house in Minier, boarders, probably evicted farmers, were needed to make ends meet. Only Lyla and Bill were still at home so space was available, but Emma suffered the humiliation and burden of the extra work.

Unemployment was actually worse in the cities. An average salary was $40 a month, eggs cost eight cents per dozen, bread was ten cents a loaf, milk was twelve cents a quart, and coffee was thirteen cents a pound. Yet money for those things was hard to come by! Breadlines, mortgage foreclosures, evictions, homelessness, lost opportunity, and despair after the stock market crash of 1929 was more the picture of urban America. Cook County was the hardest hit in Illinois with 700,000 unemployed. Although the unfortunate people were not ignored by charitable organizations, government agencies, family, friends, and even strangers, in the end all philanthropies were overwhelmed. Dozens of important measures were enacted by Congress in the early 1930s under the umbrella of the New Deal work programs. A quarter of a million able-bodied unemployed men and women were given work to build recreation areas and national parks, forestry improvements, lay sidewalks, dig drainage ditches, paint murals in post office lobbies, and plant trees among hundreds of projects. Wages, at $30 per month, were less than the prevailing local standard but it was dignified labor, sustained them, and taught them valuable skills. The alternative might have been violence or destruction if so many young men and women had nothing to do. In fact, Illinois workers depended on the projects until the summer of 1941 when the same workers were needed to prepare for war, and the draft call took them to another form of service.

Country people could take care of their own, could raise food to feed themselves. Non-farm unemployment had been at 20% in 1930, but as the economy worsened, it rose to 50% in the winter of 1932—33. On the farm, low market prices led to the dreaded mortgage foreclosure. Most folks didn't have impressive statistics or fancy names for what was happening to them. They knew it simply as "hard times." Hopelessness and the loneliness of isolation on the farm and village of the 1930s was at least sometimes lessened by the advent of radio, static-laden as it was. Farmers and villagers received daily reports on weather and livestock and grain markets. In rural areas like Minier with often nearly impassable roads, radio provided a new connection between their community and the world. Gabriel Heatter, Walter Winchell, and H.V. Kaltenborn became familiar and friendly voices to distant listeners. The desperation and tension, brought on by unemployment and unpaid bills were assuaged to a degree by President Roosevelt's "Fireside Chats" on the radio, offering hope and encouragement.

All that time whether in the country or city, the fear of job loss was intense; the experience of The Great Depression left a deep psychological scar on most Americans. Bill's brother, Spud, already employed at the John Deere Harvester Works in Moline experienced multiple wage reductions yet kept his position in the engineering department and felt very fortunate. Deere was good to its employees and in the exchange won the career-long fidelity of its workers. Prohibition, making liquor illegal, occurred at the same time as the depression but young folks like the Oehler brothers still obtained "moonshine" or made their own "bathtub gin" and later looked back nostalgically on "some pretty darn good times."

Despite her own meager education of perhaps three years at the country school, Emma Oehler was ambitious for her children. By the time Bill graduated from high school in 1929, the Great Depression had just begun, banks were closing, cash lost all value, suddenly everyone was poor. There seemed one way though for him to attend college: live with his brother, Spud, and his wife, Katharine, in their apartment in Moline and attend nearby Augustana College. Katharine's brother, Jack Miller, was invited to do the same becoming Bill's instant roommate and companion in high jinx. Katharine, only four years older than her charges, seemed always to be nagging them to study and thereby gaining only their ridicule. The boys constantly tried to wheedle the use of Spud's car; then when he did agree, with restrictions, they abused the privilege or caused him no end of worry and loss of sleep when the curfew hour was ignored. The arrangement lasted just one year, but Bill's college education continued in Champaign, Illinois, at the University.

When he was shy just one semester for graduation from the business school there, his brother Spud and he coincidentally met one weekend at the family home in Minier 'round Emma's dinner table. "The economy is gradually improving," Spud said, and "Deere is hiring again. If you want a job, you better go up to Moline with me right now!" That was all Bill needed to hear and though a college degree was honored, no one around the table after those long years of economic malaise could disagree that a good job with a good company like John Deere might be a once in a lifetime opportunity. Bill left college, was hired by the engineering department of John Deere Planter Works, and thus began, after scarcely knowing each other due to their twelve years age difference, decades of close brotherly relations.

Those were the days before a degree in engineering was required to actually work as an engineer. Many men in management didn't have a college education themselves so they couldn't very well test for aptitude or skills. Bill was capable of astonishing mathematical computations in his head, comfortable with a slide rule, and accomplished with the drafting board, squared-off paper, and a sharp pencil from his dad's workshop days. He took his place in the row of standing draftsmen and proceeded to diligently add modifications to John Deere's 1936 line of planters.

No more invitations from Spud and Katharine to bunk with them; this time Bill lived at the YMCA on Moline's Sixth Avenue. 1936 still today holds the record as the hottest summer in Illinois history. Bill often recounted the misery he and his fellow residents met trying to sleep at night: "We went stark naked to the shower, stood under the cold water as long as we could, then lay wet and naked on a cot in a tiny nearly windowless room with the door open to catch any passing breeze, hoping for a few hours of sleep." No air-conditioners, no fans, just water and evaporation existed to soothe the sweltering bodies. At least at the office, windows offered cross ventilation and fans blew from above!

Bill got along exceedingly well with his boss, the general manager of the Planter Works, Charles Harold White (C.H.), who soon became his mentor. Together they traveled by car to Arkansas where field testing of their new planters was done on the Sam and Betty Howe family plantation near Helena, Arkansas, or by train to McAllen, Texas or northern Mexico, always during the winter months when it was not possible to till in the frozen experimental farms near East Moline. Needless to say, those trips in the company of an older man experienced in the ways of the wider world, a great story teller and raconteur, those meals taken in elegant restaurants, those accommodations in hotels which he was experiencing for the first time in his life were an education in themselves. And Bill was a quick learner. He liked the life modeled for him by Harold White, was ambitious, strove to earn such a high position for himself, and emulate the life. In short order, Bill became the youngest-ever chief engineer of a John Deere factory.

When Bill married Mary Rost the next year, Mr. White increased his salary sonorously intoning, "because two cannot live as cheaply as one and besides you earned it." The newlyweds rented in the eponymous White Apartments at 2720 - 11th Ave. where Bill took on some of the management, physical plant and yard work to garner a lower rent. When in 1940 the Oehlers built their Cape Cod on 27th Street, Bill served as real estate broker for Mr. White, selling lots he owned, and pocketing the commission to pay off his mortgage on Mary's loan from her grandfather, George Peine. Bill didn't like to be a debtor; he paid cash for cars and paid off a mortgage in record time.

The affection between mentor and protege extended as well to the social sphere with Bill and Mary, and eventually their daughters, invited to dinner in the White home, at 2706 Sixteenth Ave., a testimony to the egalitarianism, the lowered class barriers in America vise a vie the class system back in the Germany of their ancestors. Cocktails were mixed and served by Mr. White; dinner was prepared and served by Mrs. White, her only employees a weekly cleaning woman and a gardner. When greeting little Susie and Kathleen, whether in his home or theirs, Mr. White never failed to pass them each a shiny fifty-cent piece in his handshake. Here was the man who held the highest position at John Deere Planter Works, with perhaps 200 employees including the foundry, socializing with an engineer on a level playing field. Bill likely could have felt inferior based on the job rank and age difference, but he still felt free to express his opinion, even to counter those of his superior, indeed was encouraged to do so. The older gentleman instinctively knew this kind of exchange was desirable in American industry as a way to arrive at the truth, at the best, the most efficient, the most cost effective design. Freedom to express one's opinion, even when proved wrong, was essential to the achievement of high quality. This was a wholly American concept unknown in other countries; it was a new kind of freedom which contributed mightily to American business excellence and success.

That is not to say that Bill never encountered "office politics," efforts to impress the boss, in his years at Deere & Co. Obsequious bowing and scraping or "brown nosing" as he called it was an anathema to him, but he recognized it as unfortunately a part of human behavior. Like his first boss before him, as related to me by Chuck Stralow, Bill believed in allowing his engineers the freedom to fail, to freely express their opinions right or wrong, even to make mistakes, for he too believed that was the straightest route to the truth. "An engineer who is afraid of the consequences of making a mistake, is afraid to take a risk, will never come up with a brilliant design," Bill said. "Often the best design is the result of many failures, many wrong turns, many evolutions!"

Air flight had come to Moline by the mid 1930s, and Bill was an avid participant. He belonged to a flight club whose members, together, owned a small single-engine propeller plane. How he loved to go out to the airfield, at the south edge of town where the runways ran east-west to catch the all important prevailing winds used in take off and landing, on week-ends or as soon as possible after he left work at the 4:30 p.m. closing bell. Barnstormers, like his friend Rusty Campbell, impressed him with their daring aerial acrobatics; Bill stood at the edge of the tarmac to see those solo fliers come close and low, "buzz" the viewers, and take off again; he never tired of the show. This was the time of the advent of hero worship in America, and Charles Lindbergh was the epitome of this after his 1927 record breaking flight across the Atlantic Ocean. Flying in those days required the pilot to have mechanical skills as well as courage and nerve. He had to be able to register a flight plan full of mathematical calculations, and he had to be familiar with engines for the pre-flight check routine. Of course, all that carefree fun ended the day he became a father; he was too responsible a man, and flying was still too risky a pastime to press his luck in the boundless blue skies, much as he enjoyed it.

Of course, he didn't have to wait too long before he could actually board a twin engine airliner at the new Moline Air Terminal as a thrilled passenger. Business trips sometimes even required it. But just for the fun of it, during the 1940s, he would sometimes take his little family out to the airport to watch the planes take off and land, then top off the event with dinner at the terminal restaurant. In about 1957, Bill decided it was time his two daughters go aloft for the first time. Susie was considering the glamorous-sounding career of airline stewardess so Bill seized that as his rationale, phoning first the Chicago headquarters of United Airlines to request an interview with a personnel employee. On a sunny summer day, clad in their navy blue pencil skirts, white sleeveless blouses, and red Capizio brand ballerina flats, the girls followed their dad up the boarding ramp, and took their seats by the window; no suitcases were required because they would return later the same day! It was truly a thrill of a lifetime, never to be forgotten, but all too short a flight. In thirty minutes they were on the ground again. At the job interview which her dad and sister also attended, a crestfallen Susie learned at the very beginning of the interview that she would not qualify for stewardess—because she wore glasses! Twenty-twenty vision was required in those days. Bill cheered the girls with a coke in the cafeteria, followed by a spellbinding tour of the huge O'Hare Terminal with all the people scurrying around them, and then it was time to board their second-ever flight back to Moline.

Long throughout Bill's life he loved any excuse to climb the gangway steps into the fuselage passenger compartment with a glance into the cockpit and words with the pilot when possible, take his seat by the window, wait for takeoff, watch with the eyes of a skilled mechanic the wing with flaps and slats in action, listen for the engine to roar and the wheels to retract, lean back and marvel at the reality of it all. Surely the pinnacle came the day he and Mary flew from Europe on the supersonic Concorde!

Perhaps the nadir came in 1969 while researching rice cultivation in Central America as Deere's director of worldwide rice mechanization and not so coincidentally visiting Susie in San Jose, Costa Rica. Son-in-law Peter Keller, assigned to Central American sales by Deere, had arranged for the two of them to visit a rice "finca" via a flight to the interior of the country. A phone call came while the men, Mary, Susie, Christopher, and baby Cynthia were at the breakfast table asking how much each of the men weighed. They naturally fudged the numbers quite a bit higher than the truth for just that one time!

Man's narcissistic tendencies were rewarded in the late 1930s with the mass marketing of the home movie camera, and once again Bill was in the vanguard with his Bell and Howell 16 millimeter camera. Movies, still in family possession, star a newly married Mary serving their young couple guests a slice of pie; another stars Bill testing his implement designs in a windy, dusty field in Texas; but most star his growing daughters and their antics. A picture truly is worth a thousand words! When he lived in Germany in the 1960s, Bill bought a German "Minolta" camera, famous as a spy camera brand as it was so small it fit in the palm of his hand yet took such good pictures; he used it exclusively for years. That camera is still in family possession.

For some it is a walk on the beach, reading a book, playing the piano, bowling, knitting, sewing, or sailing. For Bill that special joy of being completely absorbed in a task, losing all sense of time, forgetting his worries, feeling completely transported came when he entered the world of his "workshop." In his spare time in Moline, Heidelberg, Kimberling City, Gainesville, or Inverness, Bill always found great satisfaction in woodworking. His "shop," usually in the basement of his home was a marvel of an impressive amount of tools, the small ones: chisels, screwdrivers, hammers, clamps, drills, and calipers hung according to size on a peg board above the workbench. Standing on the floor, so clean you could eat off it, were band saw, table saw, drill press, circular saw, and bench grinder. All nails, screws, bolts, and washers were carefully organized, sorted, and stored as only a perfectionist would have it. To the side stood the old sawhorses, spattered with paint, that his dad had made and used so he couldn't part with them, nor could the present generation, for it was leaning over them in his boyhood that Bill had learned important life's lessons like: "measure twice, saw once."

The paint cans were lined up according to shade, lids firmly on, marking tape labels attached to describe bath, living room, kitchen, or exterior (always barn red). On the pegboard were carpenter's tools, each hanging according to size: hammers, everything from tack to six and eight pound sledges, single and double-batted, a hand brace and a staggering number of bits, screwdrivers and chisels in ascending size, hacksaws, keyhole saws, pulp saws, rip and crosscut saws wearing a blueish film of oil. In a beautiful cabinet of his crafting, measuring approximately three by four feet, of maybe forty drawers, each differing from the others by different exotic inlayed wood mosaic labels, held: nails, graded by size and type; wood screws likewise; stove bolts, rivets, brads, tacks, and staples. Under the workbench were boxes labeled: switches, plugs, outlets, electrical cord, and a variety of string excepting only that too short to save.

Ever respectful of the power of electricity and the potential for ruin of water, Bill hired those tasks to professionals: Herman Gephardt, grandson of Katherine Wilken, sister of Mary's grandmother, Anke Margaretha Wilken Rost, lived in East Moline and was an electrician at a Deere factory. He was only too happy to "moonlight" and reminisce with Mary and Bill the family stories. For the plumbing details, Bill relied on pals from the Planter Works like Bob Reeder. While his second home in Moline was under construction in Crestwood Hills, Bill went every evening after work, slide rule, tape measure, and architectural plans in hand, to check on the day's work, later phoning the contractor when for instance the fireplace was rendered wrong.

Quitting time at Deere was 4:30 in the afternoon, his commute was never longer than ten minutes, a change into his old clothes was quick, supper was at 5:30 to the radio news report of Fulton Lewis Junior, and then he slipped down to tackle his project "du jour." Without fail as he set about his hobby, the cares of the day vanished from his mind, feelings of tiredness abated, and his mind and spirit were engaged in a pleasurable, often challenging pursuit. Just a few of a lifetime of projects were: knotty pine recreation room at the home on 27th Street; bedroom, bathroom, and playroom for his daughters in that home; a separate barroom, paneled in pecky cypress complete with swinging doors off the recreation room at the Crestwood Hills home; recreation rooms at the homes of Spud and friends, Herman Linde, Hjosta Hellberg, and Roy Christiansen; Christmas gifts of shoeshine stands modeled from that of Doctor Rost, spice cabinets modeled after an antique of Mary's, and handy foldable luggage racks for gifts; conversion of Ada's porch into a den/TV room; finished empty space over the garage at the Inverness house into a guest bedroom and bath including reversing the direction of the access stairs; finished an empty room in Susie's home into a guest bedroom so he and Mary would have their room when they visited; and work as a carpenter on the construction of his retirement home in Kimberling City, losing thirty pounds in the process and loving every minute.

All along whenever an object broke or began to look worn, Mary, Susie, or Kathleen would put it on his workbench and the next day it was all fixed, good as new. Who could say, whatever the size of the project, how much pleasure he derived when he planed a board after cutting a shape, joined the part to others to make a whole, sanded, and smoothed to a certain feel on his hand, then stained, and coated a finish to the article? He instinctively knew that woodworking made him happier, that caring deeply about the details magnified the pleasurable experience, that anything he did with care became a pleasurable path to happiness at the moment. Meticulous about everything, Bill never failed to sweep all surfaces clean as a whistle before pulling the string to extinguish the overhead fluorescent lights and heading up to bed.

Thankfully, Bill perpetuated the family hobby of woodworking by teaching the skill to his grandsons, Paul and Jamie Beich and Christopher Keller. Together in Bill's shop they labored over the wiring of electric lamps; the construction of toy cars, airplanes, carts, trucks, boats; the construction, staining and painting of gifts for their mothers; and the boys found the fun of making something from pieces of wood they found in their grandpa's "scrap box." Those lessons began early in the little boys' lives for he brought them each a child-sized carpenter's workbench, filled with small hand drills, hammer, screwdrivers, planer, and to their mothers' horror, a saw—all from Germany in 1968.

When war with Germany came again in 1941, there was no divided loyalty, no dichotomy of feelings, no suspicion of people with German names like Oehler, no anxious moments, no fears of the enemy within. Bill and his family were wholly American with absolutely no connection to family in Germany. They didn't identify themselves as German; they were American! Bill served as block warden to aid his neighbors in case of attack by Germany, but it was just a precaution, never necessary to realize though well practiced. Likewise, Bill had the only vegetable garden of his life, a "victory garden" as requested by President Roosevelt. Like every good citizen he bought war bonds, knowing full well his small acts of patriotism was nothing compared to the 300,000 Americans who gave their lives! At the Planter Works, agricultural implements were side-lined to make parts for the war effort. His brother Jess served in the army, though, at Fort Leonard Wood, and his cousin Roy Imig served the army in Belgium. Both happily came home at war's end!

The end of World War II brought dramatic changes in American culture. It ended the Great Depression once and for all; it stimulated an unprecedented economic boom which enabled millions of Americans to become middle class citizens. Sixteen million Americans had gone to war in 1941. The return of the fortunate ones was dramatic! They had seen the world and returning home was not always easy. But this time, postwar years did not bring economic slowdown. In fact boom times burst forth with jobs available in nascent industries. In just a few short years following 1945, television arrived and quickly entered homes, the pent up demand for consumer goods caused an upsurge in productivity, the federal government began the construction of interstate highways and airports, industrial production took off, home construction soared. Soon the "affluent society" was born.

Bill liked Ike, President Dwight David Eisenhower, that is, who was elected in 1953. He liked his politics of moderation, his incremental expansion of New Deal programs like social security, his building of the interstate highway system crisscrossing the whole country, his reduction of taxes, his lessening of government interference in private enterprise, his halting of atmospheric testing of nuclear weapons, and his appeal to those seeking security and the good life. Yes, Bill was a conservative. "I can't understand how anyone can be a Democrat!" he could be heard to bellow throughout the years.

Yes, Bill was a Republican, and a free market capitalist to the core. Blasting the "God-damned government" frequently, he believed that limited government, the sanctity of private property, and prices set by the marketplace are what lead, when based on personal responsibility and voluntary cooperation, to peaceful and prosperous lives for all. He believed that the productive resources of land, labor and capital are guided to their best use when left alone without government interference in the marketplace, that the constant feedback provided by the profit-and-loss statement, the supply and demand of the marketplace, and the lack of discrimination when government's hands are off ultimately provided the most prosperity for the most people.

In Bill's day, the social order rewarded hard work and drive. Equal opportunity was the core of America's promise. With talent and drive anyone, regardless of background, had the chance to succeed; luck and pluck might play a part but there were no systemic barriers to success. He was convinced that capitalism succeeds in practice, even though it appears to be based on greed or self-interest, because the freedom to trade and do business with others is in harmony with our God-given nature. He knew that from the dawn of history until the

18th century, every society in the world was impoverished, with only the thinnest venire of wealth on top. Then came capitalism and the Industrial Revolution. Everywhere that capitalism took hold, national wealth increased. Where it didn't, people remained impoverished, and that dichotomy only continued. Capitalism lifted the world out of poverty because it gave people a chance to get rich by creating value and reaping the rewards.

Free trade as a component of capitalism was also endorsed by Bill. Whether between people at the community level, across nations, or between nations, free and open trade leads to division of labor. People can specialize in what they do best and trade with others for what the others do best making everyone more productive and more prosperous. In contrast, self-sufficiency at the individual or national level may be a romantic ideal, but it also means subsistence living. Likewise, after property rights and trade, Bill recognized that market prices are established most equitably when suppliers and consumers interact in the marketplace based on the information and resources each possesses and without regulatory intervention by government.

Still he was aware that there were counter arguments to his opinion: that our economic system should not be based on selfishness but on caring, that international trade leads to the exporting of jobs to low-wage countries, that the best and brightest should be assembled to plan the economy because the plans of ordinary people reflected in market prices are not informed, and that discrimination and unfair treatment are everywhere if employers are free to hire, fire, pay, and promote without oversight. Bill thought those arguments may sound nice by appealing to the emotions, but he still felt deep in his heart that for peaceful and prosperous lives, based on personal responsibility and voluntary cooperation, capitalism was the way. Especially in the latter years of his life, Bill saw millions of people worldwide escaping poverty as their countries moved away from command and control economies, toward capitalism and freedom.

Also in his latter years he began to observe in his own country a kind of corruption of capitalism which led his fellow Americans to accept the mind set, contrary to his own, that when someone got rich, it is because he made someone else poorer. The mood of the country was indeed changing dramatically from the historic celebration of economic success Bill had grown up with. There had appeared a kind of collusive capitalism or crony capitalism whereby the people on top take care of each other at shareholder expense. But beyond that and on an even bigger scale was the collusion engendered in government. Every business operation and bottom line were beginning to be affected by laws set by legislators and bureaucrat regulators with the result of corruption on a massive scale. Concurrently ran the separation of capitalism from virtue which had been the cornerstone of American society. No longer did folks accept the judgmental stand that required them to believe that some ways of behaving are right and others are wrong always and everywhere. No longer was found the sense of stewardship that once was so widespread among most successful Americans nor the sense of seemliness that led successful capitalists to be obedient to standards of propriety. Yes, capitalism and conservatism were incrementally headed for disrepute only to end in the economic collapse of 2008, long after Bill's day. But he saw it coming. He didn't live to see the labyrinth of regulations, the irrational liability law, nor the bizarre tax code which resulted from the collusion, but he would have instinctively known that the solution required a return to the vocabulary of virtue when talking about capitalism, a return to a sense of seemliness and concern for those who depend on one, a return to principled stewardship which can nurture and restore one's heritage of liberty. "Capitalism is not a perfect economic system," Bill acknowledged, "but its the best mankind has come up with yet to spread the wealth!"

Bill was dismayed at the media's views on corporate America and business in general. He did not consider American businesses to be immoral. He would say that businesses create jobs, prosperity, investment and tax revenue; they are the essence and the requirements of a democracy. Far from an immoral system, Bill believed, U.S. capitalism is the wonder and envy of the world.

Soon after World War II or at least by the early 1950s Americans, like Bill, were introduced to the "cocktail hour," the double-edged sword. There had always been bars, beer, and boot leg spirits, but the concept of serving special alcoholic concoctions of bourbon, scotch, gin, rum or vodka in drinks like "Slow Gin Fizz," "Highball," "Manhattan," "Old Fashion," Whiskey Sour," "Martini," or "Daiquiri" in one's own middle class home was new. And it caught on like wildfire! Known as "the cocktail hour," in the time before the advent of wine, the spirits were high octane and to be sipped slowly each in its own special glass in the company of fancy bites called horsdouvres served with their own special plates and utensils. This was attitude readjustment between the office hassles and family time at its finest! Perhaps Bill and Mary began observing this new custom only on week-ends but soon, due to its effectiveness, it became a daily ritual not to be missed. Bill had found his medicine against his black moods at least temporarily!

In every home thereafter, Bill built a kind of shrine to his pleasure: a small bar, in which he displayed bottles of every "spirit" known to man, decorative glasses and horsdouvres plates, coasters, napkins, hand-carved wooden bottle stoppers, and of course a recipe book for every obscure cocktail to come along. In his second Moline home, there was even a small bar room, paneled in pecky cypress, and three barstools. His guests were always entertained at the display; he went to so much effort, who wouldn't be complimented? But woe to the guest who was late or didn't show up for the sacrosanct hour! That was an affront and not sanguinely suffered. Mostly, all went well as Bill presided over the pleasure of his guests. A great raconteur, Bill never relied on the sit-coms of the previous evening's TV for subject matter but could analyze the current events of the day, could decipher the meaning of the newest twist or turn in the economy, could explain an analytical puzzle for all to understand. He could also tell great stories and loved to exchange jokes with his guests; in short, Bill was a great host. But he did tend to dominate the conversation as the alcohol loosened his tongue.

Alcohol turns to sugar water in our bodies so it probably caused Bill's type 2 diabetes, his heart fibrillations, and the life ending kidney failure on the day before his eighty-third birthday. His family in later years, especially Mary, struggled against his sometimes cantankerous comments, wished he would not drink so much, avoided him when belligerent. But he was not alcoholic; he did not miss a day of work; he did not touch a drop before the 5 o'clock start of the cocktail hour; he did not wish to quit drinking; he still felt he was just having "a darn good time."

Also just after World War II, backyard grill constructions began to appear. Those were not a portable Weber grill but a stone and masonry stationary structure of supports for the wood and fire, later charcoal, the metal grill shelf, and the chimney up which the smoke billowed. The same kind of meats were grilled back then as are today, but Bill and Mary particularly liked steaks, the bigger and juicier the better. Lea & Perrins Worcestershire Sauce for him, A1 Sauce for her. Their dinner parties often featured prime aged beef steaks served on special platter-like crockery plates and steak knives from VL and A on Wabash in Chicago. Over time, Bill perfected other methods of cooking steak such as smoking, requiring hickory and mesquite wood blocks. The Oehlers ate steak as often as they wanted, often stocked the freezer with pounds of it bought on sale.

In many ways, American life was becoming materialistic after World War II. Shopping became a form of entertainment in the new era of leisure time and discretionary money. In Bill's case shopping was also therapeutic, a mood enhancer, diverting his thoughts to the pleasure of the hunt, filling his psyche with positive vibes as the clerk complimented him on his appearance, or feeling important at paying for a big ticket item. In his case, as a consequence of shopping, Bill was known as a great dresser. With a full head of wavy brown hair, a trim five-foot, nine-inch figure, he wore the clothes well, was a good looking man. The hat shelf in the coat closet held a long row of fedoras, his tie rack contents, including bow-ties, were frequently updated, and he wasn't opposed to wearing a handkerchief in his breast pocket or two-tone leather shoes on his size nine feet. His Burberry coats, purchased in England knew long lives when given to son-in-law, Peter, when Bill moved to warmer weather, and finally worn by a granddaughter, Ingrid Keller Conroy, in her teeny-bopper phase. Bill instinctively knew that dressing well made him feel good and besides everyone knew "clothes make the man!"

The incipient affluence of the 1950s also drew men like Bill, whose previous vehicle for putting their money to work had only been government bonds with maturity of ten to twenty years, into the stock market. In the year1960, the Dow Jones average was 742; with encouragement from Spud and assistance of Cal Ainsworth in 1950, Bill boldly went in.

Leisure time was a part of the post-war world of Americans, too, and so had to be filled. The Oehlers, like their fellows, were enjoying TV programming by the 1960s which far exceeded the offerings at the time of their first set; there were three national networks: CBS, ABC, and NBC. Now the feature of their den was a cabinet model TV of beautiful wood and design—a real piece of furniture! They followed weekly appearing programs like "Beverly Hillbillies," "Flintstones," Donna Reed Show," "Perry Como Show," "Perry Mason," and "My Three Sons." Bill had outgrown his previous attraction to movies in a theater, but he sure watched westerns on TV! As well, he was drawn to the exotic and new Chinese restaurants such as the Polynesian room at the Plantation in Moline or the little hole in the wall King Hong in downtown Rock Island. Pizza arrived on the Moline scene then, too, and to his amazement could be ordered over the telephone and picked up at the storefront downtown, later even delivered to his door. That was the extent of Bill's knowledge of Italian cuisine; they had always eaten spaghetti and considered it American!

Movies had to pass the Production Code of the Motion Picture Association of America in those days which decreed no profanity, no ridicule of religion, obscenity, nakedness, abortion, sexy dancing, or sex outside marriage. Homosexuality was never mentioned. Still folks thought nothing could beat the top movies of 1963: "Cleopatra," "Bye Bye Birdie," "The Great Escape," and "Charade!"

Still a kind of cloud lurked over the lives of Americans like the Oehlers during the 1950s and beyond: Communism. After World War II, two superpowers emerged—the United States and the Soviet Union—with profound economic and political differences. They faced each other in a state of heightened political and military tension, resorted to outlandish propaganda, espionage, rivalry at sporting events, and technical competition such as the "space race," so that citizens of both nations feared all out nuclear war. Those years were called the Cold War because though threats were made by the member states of the Soviet Union on one side and reciprocated by the Americans and their European allies on the other side, though both sides massively increased their stockpile of armaments, though the media fanned the flame until the man in the street quaked in his boots with fear of a Soviet atomic bomb attack, no bombs fell on either side. There was no large scale fighting directly between the two sides, yet both heavily armed themselves for a possible attack by the other. In fact, the nuclear capability that each side had became recognized by the other as a deterrent to attack. An attack by one would thus result in complete destruction of the attacker or "mutually assured destruction." Each American town, no matter how small, had an early warning system complete with an air raid siren set to test each Tuesday morning at 10a.m. School children were taught to respond to the test blow by diving under their classroom desk.

Crime was low in the 1950s; Moliners often left their doors unlocked; muggings occurred only in big cities like Chicago. Illegal drug use wasn't an issue for another ten years, but people drank like fish and smoked like chimneys! Race relations were a problem in the American south where the races were still thoroughly segregated. In the north, laws of segregation were long gone, but the neighborhoods of Moline tended to be all white except for the few shanties clustered by the Rock and Mississippi rivers close to the factories.

The famous cultural landscape of the 1960s was taking shape everywhere in America, though, as the Civil Rights issue was becoming the dominant U.S. domestic issue. As revealed on TV and in newspapers the shocking disparity of income, education, and occupation was starting to raise consciousness in folks across America while in Moline due to the scarcity of Negroes it was a quiet scene. In Washington DC, however, in August of 1963 a quarter of a million people famously marched, filled the Mall, and concluded with Martin Luther King's "I have a Dream Speech." The momentum for legislative change was suddenly unstoppable.

Baby boomers, a fundamental part of the cultural landscape, were teenagers that year and presented themselves as an abnormally large group of the population, contributing to the pace of change. They

STORIES MY FOLKS TOLD ME

swooned to Elvis Presley and spent their affection on the Beatles who played for the queen in 1963. Bob Dylan's "Don't Think Twice, It's all Right" was their theme song throughout the '60s.

A Gallop pole in 1960 revealed that church attendance was high whether rich or poor, white or black; half of Americans said they had attended church or synagogue in the last seven days. Eighty percent of moms stayed home and out of the workforce, while ninety-eight percent of men aged thirty to fifty were in it. The issue of the status of women had not yet led to a movement in that day when they were expected to get married, keep house, cook meals, raise children, and cater to husbands. Women who didn't were considered oddballs. Teaching and nursing were nearly the only occupations open to them. But that changed when in 1963, Betty Frieden published her famous "The Feminine Mystique," ushering in a sweeping impact on society.

Of course, the introduction of the birth control pill to the market in 1960 and the rapid spread of its use made possible all kinds of change in women's lives. Sexual mores had remained established and static for millennia when for the first time in human history the pill gave women a convenient and reliable way to prevent pregnancy and still have sex. Even on the spur of the moment and without the cooperation from the man! The little pill gave independence to women which is hard to exaggerate today. Freed from a continuous mom job, women could get a paying job which could lead to more education which could lead to job advancement, more income for the family, and a better quality of life.

Michael Harrington's "The Other America," published in 1962 proclaimed that forty to fifty million Americans lived in poverty. Taken up by the liberal wing of the Democratic party, it became a part of the policy debate, and with the elevation of Lyndon Johnson to the presidency after the November 1963 assassination of John F. Kennedy, led to sweeping changes in legislation. Bill didn't agree with the statistics nor Johnson's Great Society solutions especially when fathers had to leave the home in order for women to become dependent on federal assistance. But the train had left the station, and his view was in the minority. Rachel Carson's "Silent Spring," appearing in 1962, became a New York Times bestseller and set off the environmental movement.

Ralph Nader's "Unsafe at Any Speed" established the consumer advocate movement. Yes, the cultural landscape of the 1960s was achangin'!

But back to Bill: A rather big door, big as a barn door, of opportunity presented itself to him in 1964 when he was fifty-two years old: he was asked by Deere & Company to transfer to their newly acquired Mannheim, Germany, manufacturing plant and executive offices as Technical Director for Europe. He consulted Mary but there was no contest there; she was as excited about the prospect as a puppy let off of the leash! Hurriedly before he left Moline, Bill arranged a job interview for his new son-in-law, Peter Keller, with senior executives of Deere & Company: Comart Peterson, Harry Pence, Neil Christenson, and Bob Deffenbaugh, on a Saturday in the Peterson home which coincidentally Peter and Susie bought for their own just six years later. Peter's fluency in four languages naturally directed him to the international John Deere Intercontinental branch of the company where he subsequently worked for the next twenty-five years.

The Oehlers had toured Europe just four years before which paved the way for their ready acceptance of the opportunity to live there. They chose to house hunt in beautiful Heidelberg on the Neckar River, the medieval town famous for its university and for the ancient castle towering above the cobbled lanes, stuccoed buildings, and orange terra-cotta roofs. There in a newly constructed three-flat they rented two floors or two apartments to accommodate their $11,000 air shipment of furniture from Moline. Katie and Chuck Frazee, also a Deere executive, rented the ground floor unit. In the basement, Bill set up a small workshop, outfitted with newly purchased 220 volt German tools, to make the customizing modifications he always deemed necessary wherever he lived.

Bill's position required him to travel to the Deere factories of Arc-les-Gray in France, Getafe in Spain, Zweibruecken and Mannheim in Germany where he was charged with the task of adapting the latest specifications of Deere's U.S. implements to those of the European plows, planters, disc harrows, bailers, and rakes. His responsibility was for the implements; engines, tractors, and combines were another's purview. Bill strove valiantly to master the German language by studying with a tutor, but more and more it became apparent that the French, Spanish, and German technicians he dealt with spoke better English than he was capable in German. Of course, the few German phrases he heard as a child: "rous mitcha!" ("raus mit dir") or "get out of here!" didn't do him any good either. Oh yes, there were a few funny times of language confusion. Once at a bar, Bill ordered a dry Martini only to be served by a stone-faced bartender a tray of three Martinis, for "drei" in German means three!

Fond and lasting friendships were struck in Bill's Mannheim days when he was a foreigner living in a new country, in a new culture far from his family and friends in Illinois, sensitive to the kindness and warmth shown him by others. Herr Georg Hauser was his driver, spoke English, and thus frequent companion, with whom Bill kept a lasting connection till his dying day, always exchanging gifts for Christmas and letters between time. Bill loved to regale his guests with the story of how Georg had married his own mother! That is, when Georg's father died, Georg married the widow, Anneliese, only slightly older than he! "How simple could it be?" Bill would ask. "There was no change of name nor change of address involved." Among those gifts exchanged over the years were two framed needle-point tapestries, one of a Rothenburg on the Tauber scene and the other of a renaissance boy, both still in family possession. Herr Hauser's last gift arrived at the news of Bill's death: money to plant a tree in his memory. That too still thrives on family property.

Nina and Dolf Colot of Arc-les-Gray also became lifelong friends who later visited the Oehlers in the States and sent their daughter, Ann Catherine, to visit them as well. The owner of the farm outside Mannheim, used by Deere as an experimental farm, Herman Bachmeier, also became a good friend. It was he who introduced Bill to a favorite fall event, the "Schlachtfest" or butchery and gorging on the many kinds of "wurst" made from the slaughter of the steer and pig. The Bachmeiers and their adult children also visited the Oehlers after they returned to the States.

But it was a total stranger who came to Mary and Bill's table at a Heidelberg restaurant on November 22, 1963 to offer condolences. "For what?" Bill asked. "You don't even know me." "For your president John

F. Kennedy. He was shot today and just died," the man answered. That is the way the Oehlers got the news!

Many people say they are going to search their roots and find their distant relatives in distant lands, but Bill really did it! He knew the fabled story of his grandfather Oehler's trek down the Rhine, steam across the Atlantic Ocean, and venture halfway across America to Danvers, Illinois, so he knew his ancestor was from Weisweil, just south on the Rhine from his new home in Heidelberg. Therefore, one day he engaged his driver, Herr Hauser, to drive him down to Weisweil and especially to act as interpreter at the village church where in their records he planned to begin his search for relatives. With no trouble at all he saw the name of his grandfather registered at birth. Then, to Bill's astonishment, the minister asked if he would like to meet his cousin! A short walk of a block or two brought him to the door of Liesl Oehler Ehret who answered with dour reserve, later explained as fear that Bill was coming to claim some long-settled inheritance of Oehler property. That issue settled, the two with Hauser's assistance became fast friends, continuing the relationship with a visit of the Ehrets to the Oehlers in Missouri and the continued contact of Susie and Peter Keller with Liesl on their visits to Germany in the 1990s.

Both Susie and Kathleen with their small children, Kammy, Paul, and Christopher visited the Wielandstrasse home as did Bill's brothers Jess and Spud with Katharine. Bill encouraged his dad, Will, to travel to see the land his father and mother had left, but nearing the age of ninety he didn't see the worth. Indeed, Will departed this great green earth while Bill was still living in Germany.

Back in Moline in 1968, Bill was assigned the position of Worldwide Director of Rice Mechanization with an office in the new Eero Saarinen designed John Deere Administrative Center located not along the Mississippi River with the factories but out on an Oak filled bluff overlooking the Rock River on its way to join the Father of Waters. The job offered much travel opportunity because of course most rice fields are located in Asia, Indonesia, India, and Latin America. Bill, along with Mary in many instances, visited them all and in the process added many pegs to the world map in their home displayed to show all the places they had been over the years.

It was while working in Ceylon, today Sri Lanka, that Bill met Ray Widgewaredene, son of an English mother and Ceylonese father, an engineer trained in England and large rice cultivator in his homeland. Ray and his wife, Nina, became life-long friends of Bill and Mary visiting each other in their homes several times. Life on the Widgewaredene plantation near Colombo 7 was a new experience for the Oehlers. Despite the steam heat of the island so close to the equator, a high-level formal etiquette was strictly followed including "dressing" for dinner, attending cricket games, and strict observance of Ray's Buddhist faith— all with only ceiling fans to assuage the heat. One night in one of Ray's guest cottages, Bill was awakened by the sound of rustling on the wall. He turned on the light to see to his and Mary's horror, scores of lizards, salamanders, and chameleons scurrying up and down and all around the four walls. Naturally he thought it his obligation at breakfast the next morning to advise his host of this infestation. "No, no!" said Ray. "Those animals are our friends! They control the bugs and mosquitos for us. Without them life here would be intolerable!" On a visit to the Oehlers in Inverness, Florida, while in the U.S. for a meeting at the United Nations, Ray amazed his friends by traveling so far and so long with only a case slightly larger than an attache case. When he appeared dressed to attend church services with his host, "There he stood wearing a sport jacket, tie, and silk handkerchief in his coat pocket! We never figured out how he got so much in that little bag!" was Bill's comment.

The Oehlers never learned how to travel light, but they always admired those who did. On a cruise ship vacation years later, they noticed that a woman, assigned with her husband to their dinner table each evening, wore the same beige knit dress to each meal. She highly decorated her simple dress with a beautiful silk scarf, a different one for each dinner, "and after all the scarf was what we saw while sitting," Mary described. "Then we saw them at disembarkation at the end of the cruise, and wouldn't you know? They both carried the tiniest suitcases we had ever seen!"

Near the end of Bill's long career with Deere & Company and after spending over fifty years of his life in agriculture, he could look back with pride at his accomplishments and those of his fellow innovators in the field. Not only had his field of agriculture lifted billions of people world-wide out of starvation, but a centuries long trend was about to reverse: the use of land for farming. Although they didn't know it yet, Bill and his compatriots in agriculture stood at the pinnacle of cropland use: in the future, less land would be given to the tiller and more would be spared for Nature. Globally, the production of a given quantity of crop required 65% less land than it did in 1961, thanks to fertilizers, tractors, mechanized farm implements, pesticides, better varieties, and other factors. Even corrected for different kinds of crops, the acreage required to feed the world was falling at 2% a year. Though corn production almost quintupled in the U.S., the acreage devoted to growing corn actually fell. Similar divergences appeared in other countries such as India where wheat production increased five-fold while acreage crept up less than 1.5 times. Similarly, Chinese corn production rose sevenfold while land use merely doubled.

Even with increasing world population and growing affluence which drives demand for meat, farming efficiencies have been able to counteract the pressure on land use. It takes two to ten calories of corn or wheat to produce a calorie of meat, depending on the animal, so carnivorous eating demands more cropland. But as a country gets richer, total calorie intake soon levels off; even as wealth continues to rise, the change in meat consumption actually decelerates.

Like his brother, Spud, and probably under his influence, Bill was a confirmed investor in the stock market. He initially was guided by Calvin Ainsworth, a young broker in downtown Moline with a reputation for trust and dividends. With Cal's advice he purchased shares in one of the first mutual funds available to investors: American Funds, still prospering today. Bill thought so much of Cal that he even drew Ada from a Chicago suburb to his services. In time though, Bill graduated to the brokerage department at the First Midwest Bank of Moline. Also like Spud, and a good deal of investors, contention and distrust with his brokers ran high. By the end of his life, Bill severed ties completely with "those blankity, blank brokers," bought only individual shares, demanded the certificates of ownership, and kept them in his basement safe. They were only blue chips like Proctor and Gamble, Exxon-Mobil, GM, and of course Deere. By the time of his death in 1995, the Dow Jones average stood at 4000, so he too profited from his investments in the market. "A million dollars isn't what it used to be," he would grouse, but others countered that it's actually more because of all the vehicles available to put one's money to work for him.

When Bill was fifty-eight years old in 1970 he had the good fortune to be offered a retirement contract from Deere & Company which he could not refuse. His pension combined with investment income, savings, and social security looked to provide a comfortable lifestyle for him and Mary, so he very happily accepted. Their research on retirement locations, for they did not go blindly into uncharted waters, led the couple to Kimberling City in the Ozark Mountains of Missouri. Armed with the vigor of a younger man, Bill worked each day with the carpenters building their retirement home, losing thirty pounds, growing a mustache, and purchasing a motorcycle to travel from the motel where he lodged, up the mountain to the construction site in the process.

Bill piloting his houseboat on Table Rock Lake

Once the house was completely customized to his specifications, once he had dabbled in golf, had made new friends like Mary and Mac MacCall and Leanna and Marsh Edinger, had explored nearly every cove of Table Rock Lake in his thirty-five foot houseboat, had begun to attend weekly church services and a men's prayer group, Bill grew restless. His solution was to sign on as a volunteer of the International Executive Service Corps to advise fledgling manufacturers in developing countries. The first assignment was to Ibague, Colombia, where his assigned entrepreneur desired Bill's help to design and build self-propelled combines. Together they labored over the design drawings, consulted the cost charts, approached banks for an operating loan, and generally faced-off each other in disagreement. Trying to summarize the point of contention, a frustrated Bill finally blurted out to his colleague: "If we succeed in building the combine you want, there's no way we can get it out the door! What you want is way too big for this factory!" The chastened man settled for a more modest, but reasonable project, and accomplished it with Bill's help.

A second assignment found Bill and Mary in Mersin, Turkey, a location on the Mediterranean coast near ancient Christian sites like Ephesus, Smyrna, Pergamum, Sardis, Tarsus, Konya, and the antiquity sites where they followed in the footsteps not only of St. Paul but also Alexander the Great and King Croesus. Museums or ruins, the Oehlers toured all they could while stationed in that fabled part of the world so far from Illinois. From both foreign assignments, the couple brought home many purchases from the exotic bazaars they loved to wander, most memorably a silken Turkish prayer rug still in family possession.

Of course, when Bill returned back to his home in Missouri, back down to earth from those highly diverting travels, he had to confront the elephant in the room: his estrangement from his brother, Spud. On display was yet another facet of the complex man, a repeat of his mother's fury and depth of rage, one of the seven deadly sins we call wrath, a state of Biblical proportions. And it was all a result of a falling out over a disagreement which can transpire very easily in family life; similar cases could undoubtedly be found in my previous stories but because of the shroud of time covering those folks, I couldn't delineate them.

Bill had severed the close tie with his older brother on the day after Kathleen, Kammy, Paul, and Jim Ashby fled, in fear, his accusatory threats in a vain attempt to stop their marriage plans. The young group drove the short distance to the home of Spud and Katharine where they sought refuge until the next day. But before dawn, they stole away without a word and without revealing their plans nor destination. An anxious Spud phoned Bill that morning to report the exit of the group. When he arrived minutes later, Bill shouted: "Why didn't you phone me to say they were here?" "I was going to call you in the morning. I had no idea they would take off in the middle of the night!" was Spud's helpless retort. "You should have called me! Now, I don't know where they are!" seethed Bill. Yes, he grabbed this rationale to blame someone else instead of himself like a drowning man catches a life-saving ring and clings to it with all his strength. To blame himself for the scene of the previous evening which sent his daughter to flight would have been untenable for the pitiable man. Instead, he blamed his brother for the split in his family; psychologists call such an unconscious redirection of feelings from one person to another "transference." The cleavage with his brother he kept alive like a red hot tong at the blacksmith's forge, never allowing himself to doubt his own actions, but transferring all his anger to his brother, just to keep his own equilibrium.

Hand wringing by Mary, an attempted but aborted consultation with Kathleen's Episcopal priest, and heartfelt ministrations by Ada and Lyla, did nothing to bring their daughter and grandchildren back, so the quagmire continued for nearly five years. But even after his reunion with his daughter and meeting little Jamie who would become in the ensuing years his cherished grandson, he couldn't bring himself to reconcile with Spud. Like his own mother, Bill could get mad and stay mad—year after year. In fact, it was only about one year before Spud's death in October of 1989 that the two brothers reconciled.

What caused Bill to end his vendetta with his very own brother, Spud? Perhaps those discussions at the men's Bible study group prompted his change of heart. Certainly there he was for the first time exposed to fundamental tenants of Christianity, which his mother's actions so long ago had denied him. Like forgiveness. Perhaps the age old lessons which he should have learned as a boy in Sunday School like the words of St.

Francis finally reached him: "Make me an instrument of your peace. Where there is hatred let me sow love, where there is injury let me sow pardon.…for it is in pardoning that we are pardoned." Or perhaps he read for the first time the Lord's words in Colossians 3, 12—14: "Put on then, as God's chosen ones, holy and beloved, heartfelt compassion, kindness, humility, gentleness, and patience, bearing with one another and forgiving one another, if one has a grievance against another; as the Lord has forgiven you, so must you also do." Perhaps he finally saw how miserable his wife, sister, daughters, and grandchildren, who were naturally drawn in, felt. Perhaps time doused the fire!

Long before that day of reconciliation with his brother, however, he thankfully knew rapprochement with Kathleen. It's not possible to find the words to describe the joy Bill found in the reestablishment of his grandfatherly role with Kammy, Paul, and Jamie. They lived also in Kimberling City with their mother for several years, so he could watch and nurture them on an almost daily basis, could plan activities with them, could teach the boys together with their visiting cousin, Christopher Keller, how to use the tools in his workshop, how to rewire an electric lamp, how to build wooden toys, how to operate an old fashioned sling-shot. Even on the hottest summer days he drove his six grandchildren (Kammy, Paul, and Jamie Beich; Chris, Cynthia, and Ingrid Keller) to Silver Dollar City theme park, to the many nearby water slide parks, and to the far off the Dogpatch park across the border in Arkansas. Bill was known to have a soft spot for children!

When he told Christopher's mother that he planned to give the boy a wristwatch for his sixth birthday, she demurred: "But he doesn't even know how to tell time yet!" "How can you expect him to if he doesn't have a watch?" was Bill's response. When the same boy tried to get a piece of candy by opening his mother's new china cabinet causing a whole glass shelf to fall breaking many of her treasured glass objects, she passionately berated him verbally. Bill who happened to overhear the crash and altercation, calmly investigated the new piece of furniture, and announced: "It wasn't the boy's fault. The bracket for the shelf is way too short so that any slight movement could have dislodged the shelf and cause it to fall. Yes, Bill had a soft spot for children! When the toddler, Susie, crawled out of her crib that first morning and came to his bedside, he lifted the covers to let her in whispering as he did so that she was his little adopted sweetheart. He called Kathleen "Babesie," a shortened version of "Babesie Dumpling" until she married!

Rita Johnson Witzgall, Lyla's daughter remembered her Uncle Bill: "I had ridden back to Moline after Christmas with you. Uncle Bill took me to Davenport across this big bridge to an ice skating revue the next night after he had taken you. For a ten year old from Minier, it was like he had shown me New York and Hollywood. He felt bad that he didn't have a ticket for me the night he took his family, so just Uncle Bill and I went the next night." Yes, Bill had a soft spot for children!

Toward the end of the seventies, Bill was again looking for greener pastures and warmer winters, so the couple put up a house-for-sale sign and followed Kathleen to Florida. Gainesville was their first landing spot in a golf community with a grandiose club house where they expected to meet new friends. Activities surrounding the university were part of the attraction to that city, too, but they soon found that Gainesville was part of the Old South, that they were deemed "Yankees" and different, that that city was not a good fit after all, and so they moved on farther south to Inverness. Their home there was also in a golf community and on a lake complete with boat house and dock, with plenty of opportunities for Bill's inclination to customize with his woodworking, paper-hanging, and painting skills.

Throughout his years, Bill had always followed the political scene and discussed it openly and opinionatedly with anyone who would listen. He didn't approve of Lyndon Johnson's Great Society. "Too many government give aways! Who's going to pay for it?" he asked meaning the war on poverty, housing aid, and extension of welfare. He believed in the Civil Rights Act to end Jim Crow, but he was never a marcher. Bill voted for Richard Nixon, identified with him since they were of the same age and times, watched every session of the Watergate hearings on TV in 1977. He didn't like the inflation Nixon's policies caused, was shocked at the revelations of wire tapping, perjury, tampering with evidence, and general dirty tricks, but impeachment was too excessive, too cruel in his opinion.

But Bill loved Ronald Reagan. He supported his presidency and treasured Nancy and Ron's greeting card he received on his and Mary's 50th wedding anniversary. In Reagan, Bill saw all his valued conservative policies exemplified: taxes lowered, interest rates dropped, regulations reduced, inflation tamed, unemployment dropped, Cold War ended, Berlin's wall torn down. When GNP rose ten percent, when the Bull market of 1982 saw the Dow Jones hit 777 he was ecstatic. Between 1983 and 1989 the economy roared 4.4% per yearly average, one year saw 7.3% growth. Under Reagan's leadership the economy grew by one-third, disposable income increased twenty percent, and eighteen million new jobs were created. Despite lowered taxes, government revenue increased twenty-seven percent!

For a person so analytical, so mathematical, so logical, an engineer for heaven's sake, one wouldn't necessarily expect to find creativity, but nonetheless Bill was a very creative, inventive man. Down in his workshop he found boundless expression for it. For instance, while motor boating on the endless system of rivers and lakes from his Florida home boat dock he discovered that low bridges prevented many boats from fitting under them, denying them entry to the waters beyond. His solution was to design a boat with a fold down cabin! He drew the specifications, made a toy-sized model, and even planned to apply for a patent, never realized, before his health began to fail and his interest to wane.

In 1984 when Lee Iacocca led the draft to restore the Statue of Liberty and Ellis Island where the ancestors of so many Americans first registered to enter the United States, Bill enthusiastically supported the effort with contributions enabling him to place the names of both his and Mary's ancestors on a plaque despite their having entered between 1845 and 1865 at the predecessor immigration center at Castle Gardens. Emma Lazarus' sonnet inscribed on the base of the Statue of Liberty, "Give me your tired, your poor, your huddled masses burning to breathe free!" resonated deeply with the patriotic, sentimental Bill Oehler.

Though a lifetime reader of "The Reader's Digest" and "The Wall Street Journal," Bill was not an avid reader of books, with the exception of "Letters from the New World," a collection of letters written by immigrants in America back to family and friends in Germany during the 1800s. The writings plus analysis and interpretation helped answer his age old question: "How could they have left family and home and all that was familiar to travel, often alone, so far into the unknown?" Bill was too grounded in his familiar Illinois surroundings, too bound to his siblings and many cousins both Graff, Imig, and Oehler to imagine such a wrenching act. Representative of the time when love was not expressed verbally nor with an embrace at greeting, he yet showed his caring feelings by preparing an elaborate meal, giving a gift created in his workshop, or just by sharing a good story or joke.

Times spent together with Lyla or Ada or Spud or cousin Marguerite Ann Hughes Sukoff over the years of Bill's life touched a deep chord within him. Conversation with those most near and dear, who had also known folks dearest to him from his childhood, who had also known the place Minier and the times, could easily invoke within him his mother or his dad. They knew her sweetness, her affectionate ways. When they spoke he could suddenly see through swelling eyes and hear his mom again, as if she was standing or sitting there with them. That was the real power of relatives from the past. They had special gifts. They could bring his loved ones back. A certain spell was cast transporting them as if they were in a bubble, floating back in time to Minier, the place where their loved ones had been. Time stopped, feelings intensified, and loving emotions surged. Chuckles too. It worked right up to Bill's last days when he lived in Inverness and Marg was just over in Leesburg.

Known for his insights and frank retorts, Bill is remembered for some of his particularly knife sharp observations: "The last thing a restaurant does before it goes out of business is raise prices!" "Your home is worth exactly what someone will pay you for it and not a dollar more!" "Don't you believe in safety?" when his son-in-law proudly showed him his new car which didn't have seat belts in the days before those now ubiquitous straps were standard equipment.

Like most sojourners here on this great green planet, like the others depicted on these pages, Bill was not perfect. Yet he was undisputedly a well-meaning man, a person who wanted to be loved, who positively influenced the next generation, who had a positive life on balance, who was simple and complex at the same time, and who found love and redemption in his marriage and family. Bill went to his Maker on the day before his 83rd birthday in the Inverness Hospital, suffering from kidney and heart failure. His cremated remains lie beside Mary's in Minier Cemetery, just steps from those of his parents, siblings, aunts and uncles, and cousins.

STORIES MY FOLKS TOLD ME

CHAPTER 5

Generation # 4

Mary Adela Rost Oehler
—1, 2, 3,8—

B ORN ON MONDAY May 12, 1913, in Minier, just three weeks
after the sinking of the famous Titanic ocean liner, Mary was
delivered at home by her own father, Dr. John Wilken Rost, into an
environment of loving protection and plenty. Both her parents were
University of Illinios graduates, imaginative, and self-confident from
their own accomplishments. The home which the new family inhabited
was newly built, was payed for by Mary's grandpa who lived there also,
was outfitted with the latest inventions of electricity and telephone,
included a garage for the automobile they owned, had a large grassy yard
and wrap around porch, and boasted indoor plumbing and running
water. Missing from the list of accouterments to the house, though, were
any locks; no double-bolt, deadbolt locks on the doors were desired or
needed back then in Minier. Ensconced in such an imposing home,
conscious that she was the daughter of the village physician, sensing
from a young age her prestigious position, though later learning that
her position was that of a large duck in a small pond, Mary always bore
a strong sense of pride, even hubris.

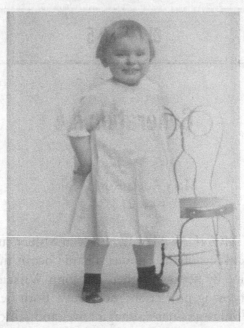

An early look at Mary Rost

Although her Minier grandmother, Mary Buehrig Peine, had already died, Mary did have a grandmother, Anke Margaretha Wilken Rost, just a county away in Petersburg, Illinois, who, newly widowed, visited often, bringing sonTeddy, still in high school, with her. Mary's Aunt Pauline, married to Homer Hallstein, lived on their farm just south of Minier and soon provided Margaret and Eileen as cousin playmates. Lots of aunts, uncles, and cousins on her mother's side also extended Mary's family circle and enriched her life there in the village. Her sparkling dark hazel eyes and dark brown hair reminded folks of her "Grandpa" on her mother's side, George Peine, coloring from his French grandmother, Mary always said. Her quick intelligence, temperamental nature, feisty spirit, and quick tongue guaranteed Mary a lively long life.

Girls of Mary's day wore dresses, falling to mid leg, no matter what the occasion, only the color and fabric changing with the season. She wore high button shoes before the "mary jane" style came to replace them, and her legs were covered by stockings for half the year, a problem in that day before the invention of nylon or any fiber with elasticity to keep the stockings from stretching, sagging, and bagging. It seemed to Mary that Mama was constantly admonishing her to "pull up your stockings!"

Mary Rost with a favorite doll.

From pictures we see that Mary wore her hair in a short bob, bangs pulled to one side and off the forehead, a bow for decoration, and that was pretty much the way she always wore her hair throughout her long life, minus the bow of course. Very long hair or the pony tail style did not ever suit her. "I've got that fine, straight German hair and this is the way I've got to wear it," she would often say.

For as long as Mary could remember, her most constant companion was her "Grandpa," George Peine, her mother's father. He lived with her family, was retired from the Peine store, and was never too busy to spend time with her; he read the newspaper aloud to her carefully choosing the humorous articles so they could laugh together; he even taught her how to read from the newspaper before she ever went to school. Every Sunday Mary would accompany him on the walk out to the cemetery to lay fresh flowers on his wife Mary's grave, though it seemed so far to little Mary it was like she was walking to perdition. Grandpa could never say "No" to Mary, spoiling her a bit, but why would he do otherwise, he asked himself, when she so obviously loved him so tenderly back? When Papa Doc and Mama went out visiting for the evening, Mary was allowed to sleep with Grandpa in his big feather duster lined Eastlake bed, made of mahogany with cherry inserts, high carved headboard, still in family possession. Unlike the rest of the family who slept together in the big sleeping porch, winter and summer, without heat or lights, Grandpa slept in his own room, smelling faintly of cigar smoke, where he could read in bed, get up any time he wished, turn on the light at any hour, and even finish a cigar there undisturbed.

Especially when Papa Doc went off to be a soldier or more specifically a physician in World War I and when Mama went to New York City to visit him during a brief furlough of R and R, Mary clung to her Grandpa like a little tick. The country woman who came to keep house, launder, and cook was rather surprised when she was not called upon to be a baby sitter too. The old gentleman was certainly an amazing creature!

As it turned out, that R and R period had contributed mightily to Rost family life, for soon after Mama returned home she carried a secret under her heart. By her fourth birthday Mary learned that her days as an only child were about over, and sure enough on the next October 8, 1916, exactly nine months after Mama's visit to Papa Doc in New York City, she got a little sister, Ada Margaret. Mostly Mary was glad but there were times when she thought Mama was spending a bit too much time with the new baby, times when friends and family gushed a bit too much over little Ada's cute figure and precious personality, times when her friends begged to include Ada in the play though she certainly didn't want to, times when even Grandpa wouldn't stop coddling and petting her. It was all enough to make Mary stamp her foot and show her temper!

Once when Ada was sick in bed, Mary was so miserable with worry that she gave her sister her own favorite doll. That really did seem to help Ada and soon she was well and out of bed. Ada still had the doll

STORIES MY FOLKS TOLD ME

and loved her immensely, carried her with pride, and ignored her own dolls until Mary announced that she wanted her doll back. Poor Ada had to give her up, but with her sunny disposition, inherited everyone said from Papa Doc, she never held a grudge. Over the years growing up together, facing trials and tribulations, joys and triumphs together, the sisters forged a bond noticed by all, envied by some, and amazing to most.

Mary and Ada with their Buehrig cousins
Grace, Margaret, and Mary Buehrig

Mary was one of those few lucky little girls who was given birthday parties in her childhood. One of the first was when she was turning four years old and so invited some of her first playmates, some with whom she was in contact her entire long life of ninety-two years. One in particular even became her lifelong partner, William Peter Oehler, but of course cupid didn't shoot his arrow at that early date!

Through her school days in Minier, Mary was a diligent, top student, always knowing that she would follow her parents to the University of Illinois over in Champaign-Urbana. Girlfriends like Mauna Hainline, cousin Mary Buehrig, and Margaret Pleines (later Tanner) were her companions now, relegating Grandpa to less time but no less loving affection. Like girls of their day, they played with their dolls, skipped rope, jumped the hop scotch diagram chalked on the sidewalk, tossed jacks, collected rocks, pulled taffy, popped corn, told ghost stories, had sleep-overs, and generally had a grand, carefree time in their little world of Minier. Papa Doc's profession ordained that she could not make or receive telephone calls, though, for she was taught that she must keep the line open for sick folks, but telephone use as a form of entertainment was not actually recognized yet anyway.

John, Ada, Mary, and Adela Rost on their front porch swing.

Once when Mary went to Ada's classroom to pick her up for the walk home, she found little Ada sitting on the teacher's lap and together they were deciphering the mystery of the alphabet letters. One of Ada's first teachers at Minier Elementary School was Miss Dorene Tanner. Neither of them knew it then but one day Miss Tanner would be Mary's sister-in-law when Dorene married Delmar Oehler and Mary married his little brother Billy. But I am getting ahead of my story. As teachers now do too, Miss Tanner announced one day that she was going to inspect the inside of desks that day. When Ada opened hers, Miss Tanner could only gasp and exclaim: "Why, Ada, that looks like a pig sty!" Later that school year, Miss Tanner announced that she was to be married to Mr. Delmar Oehler. It was Ada who was charged by her classmates to ask Miss Tanner how she should be addressed, Miss Tanner or Mrs. Oehler. Very seriously, but with a merry twinkle in her pretty blue eyes, the teacher replied: "Mrs. Oehler."

Menu items in the Rost family reflected the German heritage of Adela and John as well as the tastes and availability of foodstuffs in the early 20th Century. During the growing season a continuous parade of country women would appear at the back door offering beautiful vegetables for sale. Cabbage and root vegetables were still a mainstay of the diet, but tomatoes, eggplant, peppers, broccoli were special treats when in season. When she planned to put up vegetables in Mason jars, Adela would contract with the green grocer in Minier for the amount of product she needed, hire a country girl to help her, and together would spend several days in the steamy basement kitchen washing, chopping, blanching, and processing the vegetables into jars to feed them all through the coming year till next harvest. Adela may have been a rather fancy lady with a university degree but homemaker was her first title and that meant putting a meal on the table three times a day for five people.

Occasionally just for the fun of it and to satisfy a sweet tooth which they all had, Mama would get out the big block of marble and they would make taffy, pulling and stretching the mass of sugar till it was cooled and ready to eat. Fudge, popcorn, carmel corn, and peanut brittle were more of the home-made treats of the day.

The Rosts ate their main meal of the day at noon, consisting of potatoes or noodles, rice not yet introduced to the American palate, chicken, pork chops, or a beef roast, usually baked, vegetables, and stewed fruit for dessert which Adela had canned herself or on special occasions a pie which she excelled at baking. Supper was made of leftovers from noon, usually fried up together in a skillet, with home-baked bread. The German taste for pickled foods endured in the Rost home, for example in a summer salad much requested by all: in a shallow bowl arrange fresh tomato slices and large white onion slices, sprinkle or pour plain white vinegar over, top with a few ice cubes which when somewhat melted diluted the vinegar dressing. "Tart and refreshing!" they all agreed, just the way they liked a summer salad!

Mary and Ada liked to watch the preparations preliminary to a visit of Mama's University Club members for all the hubbub of special house cleaning, baking, and import of fancy cakes and teas. Mama's S.O.P.H. club meetings would also regularly meet in their home. They were mama's oldest friends and Mary had known those women all her life, but she never did find out the meaning of those letters in spite of all the attempts she made to guess and for all the whoops of laughter her guesses elicited from Mama and the members.

On one important day in Mary's childhood Uncle Ted brought his fiancé, Clara Tesmer, to dinner. Mary and Ada were allowed to sit quietly at the table with the grown-ups and stared completely awed at Miss Tesmer's beauty and charm. Though they didn't say much, the girls made a very exciting, even shocking, observation: the young affianced couple were holding hands under the table! Douglas Fairbanks and Mary Pickford could not have appeared more romantic to the two little girls!

The concept of travel on a summer vacation was indeed novel in America in the 1920s, but Mama having been to England and she and Papa Doc having been to Colorado on their honeymoon, to New York City in 1916, and having both been bitten by the travel bug were ready to pack their travel bags at the slightest provocation. In 1920, therefore, the four Rosts, gear packed in big steamer trunks, train tickets purchased to Chicago, household management turned over to Grandpa, and doctor's office responsibilities assigned to fellow physicians, set out on a steamer tour of Lake Michigan. Not to be confused with today's cruise ship vacations, their ship was a long, narrow lake transport steamer carrying loads of ore, coal, steel, or freshly milled wood for manufacturing in Chicago where the ship was the reloaded with finished goods and shipped out to other ports of call along the route or finally out the St. Lawrence River to foreign lands. A few staterooms were rented out for vacationers who could enjoy restful days reclining on deck chairs, breathe in the fresh, crisp air, eat the hearty fare prepared in the galley, fraternize with the other paying guests, and generally indulge their lazy streak which folks back then had as well as they do today. One stop Mary remembered all her life was when the ship docked on Mackinack Island and they all got off to board a horse drawn carriage for dinner at the Grand Hotel. A special white dress of dimity fabric, full of flounces and tucks, had been packed in the trunk for her to don on that special occasion.

Yes, life was good at 211 North Minier Street in Minier, Illinois. Oh, there were times when Mary sassed her Mama and got slapped across the face for it or she "picked on" Ada and everyone including Grandpa took Ada's side or she didn't pick up her toys to satisfaction and was then denied a privilege, but essentially her world was worry-free, comfortable, and stable. Her parents instinctively knew, because they had learned it in their own homes, how to cultivate a sense of motivation and self-discipline in their children, how to defer gratification through a structured learning environment, how to use a network of relatives and friends to help them through harried times, how to plan ahead, how to form strong, lasting relationships, and essentially how to assure that their daughters would become self-reliant, capable adults. Social scientists tell us that self-discipline, delayed gratification, and restraint are essential traits in a person to find success in a market-based economy such as that of the United States where business enterprises demand hard work and sobriety from their employees.

That day when Mary was a child was before those same business enterprises who demanded hard work from their employees began to also advertise their goods and services to stimulate a desire for a world of pleasure and play. That abundance fostered by a market-driven economic growth lent itself to prodigality rather than prudence, to a gap between those people who can, due to education, finances or ability, and those who cannot keep up, and to the need for more government, as opposed to kinship-based help. Dependence on governmental support often leads then to indolence and indifference to work; governmental policies may actually discourage the presence of a father in the home, leading to poverty and instability, just what the welfare state public aid was designed to correct in the first place! But that vicious circle is topic for another book.

Before long, Mary had grown to love reading just like her Mama. She could spend hours lying on her bed with a book taken from the shelves of the library room on the first floor of the house, the collection at school, or purchased. Sometimes when Mama called her to come down to the kitchen to help with some chore, Mary even feigned deafness in order to avoid interrupting her book. Mama and Papa Doc had invested in a twelve volume set of children's books published by Harper and Brace Company out of New York which Mary read every page from. Once, when impressed by all her mother knew and showed it, her mother replied: "Oh, Mary, I've already forgotten more than you know!" Mama further revealed that she hoped Mary and Ada would go far away to college because then she would have an excuse to travel there to visit them. Mary, a bit struck by fear and curiosity about leaving home, liked to day dream about what that might be like, assuming that it might really happen if Mama said so.

Mary around the age of twelve.

Though twelve years old, Mary still liked to snuggle, cuddle, and tickle with Mama, sometimes even when someone else was looking. Like all children she needed it in fact; it was a kind of nourishment that her soul craved. But it ended from one day to the next and she never got it back causing Mary to search for that intimacy all her life yet never let anyone get that close again, for destiny played her a cruel scenario. When Mary was twelve years old in 1924, she began to notice the conversation between Mama and Papa Doc abruptly halt when she entered the room, the frown lines across Mama's forehead grew more pronounced, the household had to be quiet because Mama was resting. She and Ada guessed that Mama was somehow sick but surely Papa Doc would fix her up like he did everyone else. It was a huge surprise then one day when Papa Doc announced that Mama had to go to the hospital in Bloomington where a surgeon friend of his would perform an operation on her. "She has breast cancer," he said solemnly, "but after the operation she will be fine."

When Mama returned home, a nurse from Bloomington, Miss Marie Cooney, was engaged to care for her in her convalescence, and for some months Mama did improve, got up from bed, resumed her routine, and believed she had dodged the bullet. But that was in the day before chemotherapy, radiation, or knowledge of the restorative benefit of a plant-based diet. The cancer returned with a vengeance sending Mama back to bed and Miss Cooney rehired. Mary and Ada were terribly frightened; yet they had never known anyone who had cancer and they certainly didn't know anyone whose Mama had died, so that couldn't happen to them! Yet sometimes when Mary passed by Mama's room, Grandpa would be sitting by her bed, holding her hand, talking to her in a soft, serious, heartfelt way. Sometimes at night, lying in her bed, she could hear someone crying, down in another room. It was hard now to let loose and just be joyful, silly, crazy like a girl!

The end came on November 21, 1926; Mama was 42 years old, Mary was 14, and Ada was 10; all were too young to suffer such a fate; the little girls were not ready to suffer a massive, tragic, and permanent wound with lifelong repercussions. Grandma Rost came from Petersburg to transition the family, someone hung a black crepe wreath on the front door, immediately establishing Mary's lifelong aversion to door wreaths whatever the season or reason, Mama's friends came bearing strange, ill-tasting foods when no one in the family felt at all like eating, huge bouquets of flowers stood in vases all over the house till they turned putrid and gave a sickening smell mimicking the foul, sick feeling in the core of Mary's stomach. At the cemetery, dressed in her obligatory black dress hastily stitched by their dressmaker, Mary, anguished at heart and dismayed in spirit, could cope no more and causing quite a stir refused to get out of the undertakers's car. She refused to watch them lower Mama's box into the big hole and cover it with black clods of earth. She had cried so much and so long that she couldn't produce any more tears just then, but she couldn't go out and face the huge congregation of mourners either because if she did she'd have to admit that Mama was really dead. Upon reentering the house at the 211 Minier St. the terrible void really hit them all, as if the life light of the home had been extinguished.

The following days, weeks, and months reinforced that fact. Some nights in a dream, Mary could see Mama, be with her, talk to her. Oh, she never wanted to wake up from those dreams! Papa Doc seemed to throw himself into his work, staying long hours at the office he kept "up town." Grandpa was there for the girls but he too was despondent and less playful. After the following Mother's Day celebration and recitation at school, Papa Doc came home, asked Mary why she wore that ugly, ill-fitting dress, and was guilt ridden when she said that was all she had. They all knew the reason: a woman's touch, a mother's hand was sorely missing from their midst! The catastrophe had broken the crucible in which every family, then as now, is fired, molded, cured, and strengthened. Mama would have known that the style for girls in 1927 was a skirt to the knee worn with a sailor-suit collared blouse and a scarf. On the first Christmas after Mama died, to her profound chagrin and disappointment, Mary received from ever practical Grandma Rost a very utilitarian gift of an appliance for the kitchen, revealing Grandma's opinion that Mary was spoiled, when what the girl really needed was loving touches and affectionate words.

Perhaps that was the reason Dr. Rost began keeping company with Miss Cooney, their mother's former nurse; perhaps at the age of forty four he sought the company of a pretty young woman; perhaps he could see he needed the help of a feminine hand with his daughters; perhaps Miss Cooney, not yet married past the age of thirty, desirous of a comfortable home like she saw when working for the Rosts, or exhausted from the grueling yet tedious work of a nurse of that day, selected and made herself available to him. We will never know for sure, but to most observers of the day of the marriage, May 8, 1928, it all seemed a natural progression of the course of events.

From the very beginning it seemed to Marie that Mary and Ada had been far too indulged, had not enough chores around the house except for making their beds and drying dishes, so right away she revved up the participation of the girls around the house "just for their own good." No longer could they dawdle walking home from school with their friends or participate in after school enrichment activities; they had to hurry home to assist Marie in some "make work" schemes of housekeeping, cleaning and polishing, to learn to make perfect square corners of the sheets on a bed, or to learn cross stitching of tea towels (an example of Mary's is still in family possession). All this was happening while Mary was building a temple in her mind to Mama who could do no wrong, was the most perfect, smartest, best, and most accomplished person who had ever graced God's green Earth. She tried to complain to Papa Doc but he only half believed her and as Mary said: "he was always an appeaser!"

Somehow, through native diligence and habit, Mary was able to continue to excel in her schoolwork. In her sophomore year, Mary won Honorable Mention for her essay, "A Good Citizen."

How Mary and Ada would huddle together and laugh at Marie's attempts to portray herself as the fancy lady. When she would put the catsup bottle on the table instead of putting the contents in a little bowl with a spoon as Mama would have done, insisted on using Mama's Limoges Haviland china inappropriately, or shopped for clothes in a store which Mama had disdained, the girls held their tongues until they were alone and then let the guffaws and hilarious imitations loose. They actually liked Marie's fun loving Irish relatives who came to visit from Bloomington. They were all Catholics, of course, but never tried to make them feel less Christian or insulted them over being Protestant as Marie constantly did. One of her brothers was a priest at Notre Dame University and occasionally got them tickets for football games there to the Rosts delight. But to the girls, especially when Papa Doc was out of the house, she was critical to the point of abusive, mean and vindictive, untrustworthy, and especially seen in their extreme need for affectionate gestures, unloving. Mary and Ada lived in constant suspense, stood in dread day and night, never were sure when Marie would lash out at them with humiliating criticism, hysterical ranting, or screaming fits of dish-breaking fury. But as Mary so often said in later years: "If Marie had just tried with us, we would have responded, Papa Doc would have noticed, and she could have had the world!"

The little girls were not the only target of Marie's bad temper, of course. Equally made to suffer was dear old Grandpa. He tried so hard with his personal charm to find her good side and get on it but never succeeded. He finally had to move out of his own home to bunk with his son in a second floor apartment Paul owned "uptown," just to keep the peace.

May of 1930 brought Mary's graduation from Minier Community High School; the class of eight consisted of: Mary Rost, Mauna Hainline, Anna Gottschalk, Margaret Pleines, Walter Schmidgall, Clifford Schmidgall, William Oehler, and William Kuhfuss. The tendency of all of them to remain in Illinois, their close bond built over twelve years of classes together, and reunions of all Minier graduates held at regular intervals over the ensuing years meant that ties were maintained and treasured over their lifetimes.

Unlike for Ada, escape came for Mary when she was eighteen, graduated from high school, and was accepted at the University of Iowa in Iowa City. She had intended to go to the University of Illinois where Mama, Papa Doc, and Uncle Paul had studied but over the summer prior to classes in the Fall she was diagnosed with a thyroid ailment which required surgery, kept her home sick under Papa Doc's care well into the first semester of classes, and required her to take a tablet of Synthroid every day of her life thereafter. By the time, the correct medicine was identified and she was strong enough to leave home, it was too late to start classes in Champaign. With some investigation, however, Papa Doc learned she could still slip into classes in Iowa City, which Mary desperate to get away seized with all her heart and gifts of persuasion. When a family from nearby Armington, friends of Mama and Papa Doc, asked if she planned go through sorority rushing, and if so they would like to offer the required recommendation to pledge their daughter's sorority, Gamma Phi Beta, Mary, flattered, impulsively replied yes. All her life long, Mary thanked her lucky stars she had agreed because she treasured many bonds then as an active member and later as a member of various alumnae chapters. For a girl without a mother, the sorority surely served as a home away from home right down to the "house mother" who lovingly cared enough to help develop and bring out the best in each and every girl.

The United States was still recovering from the Great Depression and very few from her high school graduating class had funds to further their education, so Mary knew she was indeed very fortunate. In the 1930s, hundreds of thousands of unemployed men, from farm and city both, took to the road, hitchhiked by rail or car looking for work to escape the poverty at home, subsisted on food and humanitarian treatment provided them in the towns they passed through, some dying while jumping the trains or falling sick to disease, appeared at back doors requesting food, nearly always given, slept in jails and out the next morning, but they were definitely not tramps or bums. Mary was aware of this situation, but it was not her reality.

After two years at Iowa, Papa Doc suggested she come back closer to home for financial reasons, specifically to transfer to the U. of I, where she now had the credentials for admission, and that Mary dutifully did. It helped that there was a Gamma Phi Beta chapter there where she would automatically be accepted as a sister; though never living in the sorority house, she lived nearby in a dormitory on West Nevada Street, and could attend all chapter meetings and social events. To Mary's horror, Marie, ever the proverbial evil step-mother, spread it around Minier that Mary was leaving the university because she had been suspended from the University of Iowa for stealing, which patently was a lie. Papa Doc accosted Mary with the charge, she tearfully tried to defend herself, but it wasn't resolved until the doctor telephoned the Iowa administration to be told that Mary's record there was pristine; there was absolutely no truth to the story!

Building step by step, events such as just described culminated in so much acrimony that one day Marie hurled a charge at Mary forbidding her from entering her own home again. Mary could never go home! The proverbial ultimate damnation had been uttered! She could never again sleep in her old childhood bed surrounded by her beloved mementos, under her favorite quilt, in the safety she had always known under her father's roof; she could never again, while sitting in a favorite chair reading, listen to the idiosyncratic moaning and rattlings of the house responding to Papa Doc's footfall or the wind; she could never again sit on the top stair surreptitiously listening to the music emanating from the living room, letting herself be transported by the melody; she could never again enter the back door and be carried away by the smell of dinner steaming in the oven; on and on the finality of the situation became manifest. And it was bleaker because Papa Doc appeared helpless to alter the fact.

At the U. of I., Mary majored in history and minored in English which combined both her lifelong love of reading and curiosity for other times and other places. Occasionally she would bump into others from Minier who were also on campus, like Bill Oehler, studying Business Administration, working as a waiter in another sorority house, sharing a small apartment on campus with some pals. They partied a few times together but nothing serious came of it.

Mary's University of Illinois graduation
picture showing her sorority pin

Graduation brought Mary the favor and pride of her father and they both wished Adela could have witnessed the grand occasion too. After the ceremony and festivities, though, she had to face the Great Depression's bleak employment picture. She was prepared to teach high school English or History but no schools were hiring. She couldn't go home where Marie tyrannized! Papa Doc to the rescue again: he found her a job in the Bloomington Brokaw Hospital laboratory testing blood samples. Though not her major, science had been an interest of hers and with a bit of training by the department head, Miss Elaine Strayer, she performed admirably and liked the work. Miss Strayer only a few years older than Mary became her mentor and friend, helping her navigate the protocol of the hospital and introducing her to other young people, becoming the first older woman in Mary's lifelong search for a mother figure. By this time in Mary's life when she could not go home, for Marie had so declared, a friend like Elaine was truly a lifesaver and sanity provider, the first of Mary's many mother substitutes. Ada was safely at the University of Illinois, living in the Gamma Phi Beta sorority house, and in her own words: "having the best years of my life!"

Photos of Mary taken around the time of her graduation from university reveal she had inherited the square jaw of her father and his sister, Pauline, and surely therefore from her grandparents either Anke Margarethe or G.T., we know not which since photographs do not exist. Her figure was hourglass with an especially ample bosom, a lifelong challenge to conceal. Always modest, a "lady," Mary never once appeared in décolleté though she had the figure for it, never adopted the tight sweater look of the 1950s, never was described as anything but modest. She and Ada were justifiably proud of their legs, however, even trimming their hemlines happily with the fashion when they retreated above the knee as in the 1960s.

When Bill Oehler came back into Mary's life in 1936, she was ready. She had had very few dates in her life, was actually shy around men, though very attractive, diminutive, classy-looking, with an hourglass figure. Because of the Depression and scarcity of jobs, Bill had left the university, even though he had only one semester to complete his business degree, to take a job with Deere & Company in Moline, Illinois. On his way from Moline to visit his parents in Minier or vice versa, he began stopping in Bloomington to see her. One week-end he drove her with him to Moline to see the big town where he lived and worked, the famed Mississippi River, the John Deere factories, and to stay with his brother and wife, Spud and Katharine. Mary was impressed; in fact, she was sold! This was a life she could be happy living! This was a perfect escape from her life in Bloomington and her homeless condition in Minier! Suddenly the relationship between Bill and Mary rocketed to super charged level; they set the date for the next May Day, the first of May 1937, a Saturday. Bridal showers were given for Mary in Minier, gifts were received by the score.

Mary would have preferred that the wedding ceremony take place in her lifelong family church in Minier, the German Evangelical Church, the one where her grandparents' names, Mary and George Peine, were inscribed on the foundation stone, but Bill's mother was still seething about a row she had had there years earlier and refused to consider that location. Instead, they chose the Mandarin Room of the Illinois Hotel in Bloomington presided over at 10 a.m. by the Reverend W. A.Mueller from Mary's church in Minier, attended, of course, by the sole bridesmaid, Ada, in Delft blue silk, and given away by Papa Doc. The motherless girl chose her wedding gown on a shopping trip with a substitute mother and next door neighbor in Minier, Vivian Theis. A Redding Coat of intricate lace extending to a small train over a satin slipper dress, tiny buttons of lace marching down the center front, it was subsequently worn by two of her granddaughters, Kathryn Mary (Kammy) Beich Young and Cynthia Keller Patti. At the time of her wedding, Mary stood five foot two and weighed just slightly over one hundred pounds, Ada a bit shorter, even less. For the ceremony Mary and Bill stood on a small Oriental carpet, a wedding gift from Papa Doc, and still in family possession. In addition to Bill's parents, all his siblings and their spouses attended.

Mary Rost marries Bill Oehler. Ada is bridesmaid.

Like her mother before her, Mary had been bitten by the travel bug and quickly infected Bill without resistance. For their honeymoon they drove, after the first night at the Illinois Hotel, to Gatlinburg, Tennessee, in the Great Smoky Mountain National Park, overnighting along the way in those days of winding, hilly, two-lane roads, full of blind spots, slow trucks, and "Sunday drivers." But what did they care? Each day was a new adventure, new sights, new marital experience, new future lying before them, and they excitedly talked it all over there in the close confines of their small Chevrolet on the drive to Gatlinburg. Though known in 1937 as a nature lover's paradise and the first national park, the Smokies did not yet attract hikers, an activity still unknown to most folks like Mary and Bill at that time. Hundreds of miles of trails and the 2000 mile Appalachian Trail still were in the future, but roads for driving along fast flowing streams, vistas from high peaks overlooking valleys of flowering dogwood, idyllic picnic locations, Indians as if on location from a movie, hamlets of log cabins, an altitude of cool temperatures and relief from summer's intense heat in Illinois, and a comfortable hotel for them abounded. The final destination of the honeymoon trip was to attend the Kentucky Derby.

Their return route, of course, did not take them to Minier but to Moline where the Mississippi River flows east to west, not north to south, where together with Rock Island, Illinois, and Davenport, Iowa, across the river, it was called the Tri-Cities. It was to a studio apartment complete with a "Murphy bed" that folded up into a closet when not in use, the Windsor Apartments, owned by Bill's boss, Harold White, at 2720 Eleventh Avenue, that Bill brought Mary to begin their married life. For acting as building resident manager of the six unit brick property, Bill got a substantial discount on the rent. Several other young couples occupied the structure and became their first guests, for entertaining in their home became a favorite activity of theirs lasting throughout their long married life wherever they lived. An early photograph shows Mary proudly entering the scene bearing one of her famous fruit pies.

Mary and Bill had early in their courtship discussed the pros and cons, the advantages and disadvantages of life in small American villages like Minier, ten blocks long north to south and seven blocks wide east to west, where they had both grown up. They acknowledged the comfort one feels in a close-knit community of kindred spirits where everyone knows your name, the small daily pleasures of friendly interchange with neighbors and storekeepers, and the satisfaction one feels from the support and encouragement of those also occupying that small circle. But decidedly both Mary and Bill had long desired to leave that comfort zone behind them. Together they defined the disadvantages of life where folks not only know your name, but they know just about everything you do—what your parents, grandparents, cousins do too! They agreed that anonymity was impossible, that the pressure to conform could be oppressive. Yes, it was an easy decision—and a mutual one—to depart the safe haven which all their forefathers had claimed when they immigrated from Germany.

Furnishings for the honeymooners in a world still reeling from the Great Depression consisted of a lot of early attic and late cellar; translation: their parents told them to go upstairs or go downstairs in their homes and help themselves to whatever wasn't nailed down. From the Rost attic they acquired the Eastlake bedroom set of Mary's grandparents, still treasured and used by descendants. Other pieces of furniture for the living and dining rooms, such as the camel back sofa still in family possession, they ordered at Peine's store in Minier where Grandpa guaranteed the price would be very favorable. Also at Peine's, Mary chose her sterling silver flatware, International's Riviera pattern, which she increased over the years from a service of eight to sixteen and later gave to her granddaughters Cynthia and Ingrid Keller, and her Noritake porcelain. Mary also acquired her mother's Haviland, in the wedding band pattern, which later over the years she increased to two dozen place settings to be dispersed and used by later generations of the family.

Katharine and Spud, established at the Wellington Apartments at 1215 Fifteenth Street in Moline, immediately introduced them to their circle of friends, Margaret and Fred Hansen, Mabel and Swisher Wilson, Alice and Herman Linde, Martha and Hjoesta Hellberg, Lydia and Bruce Connell, and Ruth and Ed James to name just a few, who readily admitted them to their rounds of supper parties. Mary had another special source of social contacts, the alumnae chapter of her Gamma Phi Beta sorority which had just been formed in the Tri-Cities, bringing her lifelong friends: Gladys Lasser, Gladys McKahin, Phyllis Johnson, and Peg Smithers. Like her sister-in-law Katharine, Mary volunteered as a "Grey Lady" at the Moline Public Hospital, wearing a uniform, assisting in various capacities, generally spreading cheer, and answering questions about services, in the day when married women no matter how extensive their education did not entertain any notion of a career. It was presumed however that they would keep a tidy home, prepare mouth-watering meals, and after a year or so produce an offspring. Soon Mary was asked to join the Emma Kough Circle of King's Daughters and there made another lifelong friend, Helen Curtis, whose husband later became president of Deere and Company. Though it was later in the mid-1950s, Mary was invited to join the P.E.O. sisterhood, an honor and privilege she valued all her life, even to engraving the letters on her tombstone. Membership at the First Congregational Church in Moline meant a lot to Mary for she had a spiritual life and though not accompanied by Bill, rarely missed a Sunday in attendance, joined the Mary Martha Guild, a philanthropic women's group at church, and worked hard at its causes and social events.

About twice a month Mary and Bill, until wartime rationing of gasoline prevented that frequency, drove to Minier to see their parents, overnighting at the Oehler home, visiting Papa Doc, now called Dad, at his office "uptown," and often stopping at Mary's request either coming or going in Bloomington to visit her dear friend, Elaine Strayer. After a couple of years though, Mom Oehler signaled that Miss Strayer had too great an influence on Mary, an influence which should be the preserve of her husband only, and the relationship was harshly cut off, Miss Strayer never mentioned again by Mary, though her wedding gift of a fold top Duncan Pfeiff side table was always prominently displayed in her home and continues today in family possession.

Perhaps Mary and Ada, who after all they had been through together were still extremely close, cooked up the idea based on reports heard all their childhood from Mama and Papa Doc, but Mary had already learned that with Bill she had to "plant the seed" of an idea, wait for him to "mull it over," and then one day announce a plan as if he had thought it all up himself: a vacation in the Rocky Mountains. Sure enough, the seed had been planted, encouraged, and bore fruit. The three drove to Colorado the next summer, relished in the refreshing cool air of the mountains, looked thunderstruck at the magnificence of the landscape so different from the flat cornfields of their native Illinois, overnighted in tourist cabins which by then lined the highway along their route through Iowa, Nebraska, and Colorado, and stayed at a rustic lodge in the National Park. No car troubles with the radiator spewing forth boiling hot water as Mary's parents had experienced on their honeymoon in the Rockies was reported, only that a wonderful time was had by all.

About the same time, Bill and Mary were wondering why no little Oehlers had yet come to their home despite the fact that they were following all the time honored procedures. When the course of adoption came to mind, suggested by Bill's boss and wife, Edna and Harold White themselves parents of an adopted daughter, Polly Ann, Mary went straight to her Gamma Phi alum friend, social worker Margaret Decker, for advice. Margaret, in that day before aid to dependent mothers allowed unwed mothers the ability to afford to raise their children, before the shame of illegitimacy had melted away, and long before the invention of the birth control pill, was only too happy to help place an infant in such a home as the young Oehler couple. In fact, there was no shortage of children available for adoption, especially baby girls, which the Oehlers requested, for when the baby was a boy the father usually married the mother. Another prerequisite of Mary and Bill was to obtain a girl who would be a candidate for university level education, and that, Margaret advised, meant a child who was old enough to be tested, thus eliminating a new born infant.

To Chicago and the Illinois Children's Home and Aid Society at 206 W. Washington drove Mary and Bill several times for interviews, questionnaires, including a visit from a social worker to inspect them in their home. When they had passed all the necessary requirements with flying colors it was time to visit the Home and see the children. Excitedly they went to meet fifteen month old Susan Johnson in her foster home, observed that she had exactly their coloring, had big shy eyes, seemed chubbily healthy and bright, but they were completely won over when they learned that her birthday was January 1, the same day as Bill's dad, a sign they took that they should choose Susie! A week of thought and prayer was required by the agency so they returned alone to Moline, but the following trip to Chicago was their last childless one, for Susie, now officially named Susanne, the German version of Susan, came home with them to their new home at 1177-27th St. in Moline, Illinois.

Three new little dresses hung there in her closet waiting for her and a toy box full of the latest, most desired children's playthings and stuffed animals stood nearby but at first Susie clung to a little stuffed puppy which she brought with her from her Chicago world, a world which after a few days seemed to slip imperceptibly and inevitably from her memory. Mary delighted in her new "mother" role, carried Susie in her arms, read to her, played endlessly with her on the floor, and then just before Bill was to come home from the Planter Works she washed Susie, put a freshly ironed dress on her, and combed her hair, for the evening belonged to Daddy.

How happy Mary felt now that all the frustrating years of trying to conceive, the meeting with failure, the dreaming of establishing anew the kind of family that she had lost so many years ago, were over. How relaxed she felt now, how calmed, how she and Bill seemed to increase in compatibility now that this little unifying force joined their disparate wills into a common goal of Susie's welfare and happiness, how purposeful, how fulfilled her life now seemed to her. Is it any wonder that scarcely three months after Susie's arrival, Mary was told by Dr. John Gustafson that she was pregnant?

Mary wrote on June 5, 1941 to her sister at the Saranac Apartment Hotel, 5541 Everett Ave., Chicago, IL,:

My dear Ada,

Your letter arrived and I'm sorry that I haven't written to you sooner.

Dr. Gustafson tells us we are to have a new addition to our family about Jan. 11. I have been feeling pretty awful but everyone says I'll feel better soon. I am trying to get some part time help doing the washing and cleaning etc. but I haven't as yet been able to get any. Don't say anything about it. The doctor said not for us to make too many plans for I might miscarry and that's why I'm trying to be careful.

We are planning on going home the fourteenth.

Gladys and Blake were just here. Gee, Blake is a cute little boy.

Well lets hear from you.

Love in Pi K E (the Gamma Phi salutation)

Mary

Susie is fine.

Dr. Gustafson did advise, though, that although the pregnancy appeared normal Mary should engage a woman to assist with household duties and the care of Susie who was now in a particularly active stage.

Through one of Bill's friends from his rooming at the Moline YMCA days, Glen Engberg, they learned of a fellow Swedish friend of his family living just two blocks away on 26th Street, so one afternoon Mary and Susie walked up the hill to meet the woman, Hildegard Linnea Carlson, Mrs. Algot Carlson. In front of the house, bouncing a ball, and looking very shy was her twelve year old, blond and lanky son, Bill, who in his taciturn manner informed them his mother wouldn't be home for an hour or more. A second walk up the hill was more productive for the three soon bonded and Mrs. Carlson agreed to walk down the hill every Wednesday and Friday morning to help Mary. Thus began a long, almost familial relationship, between Corsie, as Susie struggling to pronounce Mrs. Carlson named her, and the four members of the Oehler family.

Born Hildegard Linnea Person, on June 4, 1904, the thirteenth of eighteen children, in Saxon Barmland, Varmland, Sweden, Linnea scrubbed the pinewood floors of her family farmhouse and milked the cows when she was only eight years old, cooked and baked before she was much older, and helped her mother bake the bread to dry and hang in a shed to last many weeks which we call wasa bread, but she dreamed of becoming a nurse. She did not want to be a prolific mother like her own "mor;" that she made very clear on many occasions. By the time Linnea was seventeen and long finished with school with no prospects for nurses training in sight, she followed three older brothers who had already emigrated to Illinois hoping to further her education there. While still in New York City and just off the boat, she ate a banana, the first she had ever seen in her life. It tasted so good she ate another, then another and yet another until she was doubled over in extreme gastric pain. She wouldn't do that again but it did make a good story to laugh over later!

The enticement written by her brother to pay for her education if she would immigrate to America was immediately thwarted by his wife, so Linnea went to work in that brother's boarding house where she was also living. The warm embrace of the large Swedish community in Moline eased her adaptation to life in America but she slowly but surely knew she had to learn English so that is what she studied at night. It wasn't long before a handsome blond, blue-eyed, patrician-looking Swede, Algot Carlson, who took his meals at the boarding house began courting Linnea. On September 18, 1923, they married and he, too, moved into the house. A fine wood-working craftsman trained back in Sweden, Algot soon built them a two-story wooden home at 1171 Twenty Sixth St. With a porch on the street side, carefully crafted newel posts for the staircase leading to the second floor, a hedge of lilac bushes, like both knew in Sweden, planted in the back yard, and a garage for Algot's car, the Carlsons were ready on Christmas Eve of 1926 to welcome baby William Algot into their home.

Blessed with a sunny, optimistic, fun-loving personality and a quick mind, full of vitality, dedicated to hard work, pretty in a brown-eyed, brown-haired, non-Nordic way, Linnea was a known fixture in the Swedish community as she co-hosted a Saturday morning radio show in her native language, served as officer in the VASA club, and created beautiful linens decorated with her embroidery artistry. She never drove a car but that didn't stop her from taking the only employment open to countless unskilled, plucky immigrants: house cleaner. Linnea wanted her only child to have a college education and was willing to work to accomplish that goal, so she toiled many years at Youngberg Antique Shop in the large, historical home of its proprietor, Anna Arnell Youngberg, near Augustana College in Rock Island. Two days a week she worked in the Oehler home where she slipped ever so easily into the hearts and lives of each member.

Son, Bill, did go Augustana College and there was influenced by its outstanding geology department head, Dr. Conrad Bergendorf, to major in that field. A teaching fellowship at the University of Kansas in Lawrence led to his Masters Degree in Geology and a very proud Linnea. Even with the goal of educating her son accomplished, Linnea continued to help her friends with their housekeeping chores. It helped her afford the generous gifts she liked to give and kept her close to those she had truly grown to love. It became a tradition in the Oehler home to eat her "potato baloney" at Christmas Eve dinner and for Mary and Corsie to bake Swedish spritz cookies (one pound butter, one cup sugar, two eggs, four cups flour, and 1 1/2 teaspoon almond extract beaten together and put through a cookie press with the star disk); "peppakakor" spice cookies, and sugar Christmas cookies together in Mary's kitchen.

STORIES MY FOLKS TOLD ME

Of especially long lasting favor was Corsie's "Swedish pancakes." Those she made in a special "platt" cast iron pan from a batter of one and one-half cups flour, three tablespoons sugar, half a teaspoon of salt, three eggs, two cups milk, and two tablespoons melted butter. The pan's seven round recessions produced seven unique little pancakes that charmed every diner whatever the age.

One Christmas, Algot crafted cradles and Corsie fashioned the linens for Kathleen's and Susie's "sparkle plenty" dolls; another year, he made bunk beds and she the linens for their "sweetie pie" dolls complete with a doll-sized chest of drawers for the doll clothes; when the girls moved upstairs to their new quarters, Algot made a grown-up sized dressing table and stool which Corsie covered with a gay chintz fabric. Each item is still in Oehler family possession, treasured by two additional generations.

Once the housekeeping chores were done for the day, Mary and Corsie would sit at the kitchen table over a cup of coffee commiserating the news of the day, dreams for the future, or a personal affront ascribed to one of the husbands just as women have exchanged with a confidante since time immemorial. When Kathleen and Susie arrived home from school the conversation changed to answer the girls' plea, "Tell us about when we were little!" And so they did. And what good stories the two women could weave about the funny antics the girls had performed in their earlier years. And how they laughed. And how they gained knowledge about themselves to face one of the mightiest questions any human being contends with in those difficult pre-teen years: "Who am I?"

Corsie continued her "grandmotherly" ministrations in the lives of Susie and Kathleen after Algot died in 1968, teaching them in their Moline homes to work with yeast, bake rye bread, cinnamon rolls, and Christmas cookies, and help care for their children until she moved to be near Bill and Christine in the Denver, Colorado, area. Four trips back to Sweden to introduce her son and grandchildren to her family there highlighted her widowhood years. She never let the lameness in her right arm, a result of a minor car accident in 1959 which sent a blood clot to her brain, restrict her life but instead taught herself to write with her left hand so she could continue her extensive letter-writing circle of friends. Corsie was truly an amazing, inspiring woman, affecting those around her with her love and merry ways till the day she died at the age of ninety-four.

Kathleen: "In remembering Corsie, I find my senses bombarded with those blurred images of childhood: the scent of lilacs that she would bring to us in June, the color of the petunias I would pick along the side of her house until nary a one was left on the plants, the taste of the Christmas cookies, rye bread, potato sausage, and coffee breads she artfully prepared and shared with my family; going to her house on Christmas Eve and discovering the cradles one year and the bunk beds the next, so precisely smoothed and crafted by Algot's hands with the beautifully handmade linens Corsie had created (how elegantly our dolls "slept" in such surroundings!}; and turning on the radio and listening to her lilting voice speaking in Swedish on Saturday mornings when I couldn't understand a word of what she was saying but listening with rapt attention anyway because it was her voice.

"For fifty-six years I have had the comfort of knowing she loved me, just the way I am, not for what I might become."

Once summer of 1941 came bringing the high temperatures and humidity to Moline, Mary and Bill felt the lure to the cooling waters of Minnesota. There in a rustic cabin, Mary by then ballooning into her pregnancy figure and Susie in the throes of potty training, the little family enjoyed fishing expeditions, motor boat rides with the resort owner and his little daughter along with all the restorative virtues which come from a change of place and pace.

Like most women who feel that her home is practically an extension of herself, Mary was enthralled with the little red Cape Cod style home she and Bill had built at 1177 Twenty Seventh Street in 1939. She and Bill had poured their heart and soul into it's design and execution, giving the project all their concentration of time and thought. Their love of home was truly a uniting element in their marriage. They both responded to the sight of, almost the caress of familiar objects in a room, the arrangement of their possessions, the provenance of them, the special meaning of each item which no one else could see or know quite the same way as they did.

Standing on the little footstool, forged in Bill's planter works foundry and needlepointed by Mary, beside the window looking out at 27th Street, one of the main arteries of Moline, Susie pointed and said "bus." "Oh, Bill," Mary exclaimed, "Susie just said her first word!" Absent a television, the view from a window out to the passing scene was the closest they came in the early forties to a moving picture show. Traffic over the brick two lane street, canopied with American Elms now long gone, was actually very light back when the economic constraints of war prevented much driving, so a lumbering bus moseying along was sure to catch the attention of the toddler.

Twenty-seventh street was then a major artery of Moline. It followed the dry bed of a former tributary which had flowed sloping to the north into the Mississippi River. In fact, many streets and avenues in that town, situated between the Mississippi and Rock rivers, claimed thoroughfares from former creeks, rivulets, and streams of the major drainage system of the Mississippi Valley. The resulting ravines with verdant hillsides descending from flat plateaus actually offered interesting and unique home building sites.

Inside their barn-red Cape Cod, in a neighborhood of bungalows, four squares, and tudor cottages, were two bedrooms, a bathroom with a deep tub, a kitchen with a back door to the alley, a dining room, and a living room. A thoroughly modern touch was a clothes chute in the bedroom to drop soiled linens and clothes from the main floor directly down to the basement where the washing machine stood with its electric agitator but hand-cranked wringer. The most astounding attribute of the house, however, was the central air-conditioning, a rarity of the day and one which took all of Bill's engineering skill to operate. Small as the house was, they somehow found room in the living room for a baby grand piano, always a bit of a space issue but worth it, which Dr. Adeline and John Petrie, older friends from their White Apartment days, had given them when they retired to California. A wood burning fireplace, a sofa wrapped at one end with a small table and lamp for reading, a cabinet radio, and two comfortable chairs also filled that space. Built-in shelves there held Mary's books while corner cabinet shelves in the dining room held her glass and china treasures. An Eastlake bedroom set, garnered from her parents' attic by the Depression Era newlyweds, was in their bedroom while bunk beds, built by Bill, soon served the little girls in their room. Many finishing, customizing touches were provided by him in his basement wood-working shop.

The construction of the home, at a cost of $4750 including an extra $300 for the fireplace, was payed for by a loan of $3000 from Mary's Grandpa, George Peine, and repaid in monthly IOUs accelerated by Bill selling lots for property owned by his boss, Harold White. A small niche, open to the kitchen and to a hall near the two bedrooms, conveniently held the shiny little black telephone firmly anchored by its very short cord. A milk cupboard with two doors, one to the kitchen and one to the alley so the Sturdevant's Dairy milkman could put the bottles into their designated place, and Mary never had to step outdoors to get the milk. A swing set filled the side yard where it and the clotheslines competed for space; a screened porch projected from the sunny south-east side of the house, the perfect playroom for several months of the year and always a place where Mary could snuggle close to her girls on the porch swing as she read them a story.

Yes, Mary's lifelong love for books found a new expression when she gathered her daughters, one on each side, to read them a story. Like so many mothers before her, she instinctively knew that to curl up with her children and a good book was one of the great civilizing practices of domestic life, an almost magical means of cultivating warm fellow feeling and a common cultural understanding. "Long ago there lived a widower who had one daughter," Mary read. "For his second wife, he chose a widow who had two daughters. All three had very jealous natures…" And she was off, taking her little girls by the sound of her never-to-be-forgotten voice, transporting them to the magical world of fairy tales, pulling them emotionally and physically into their own private, joyful world.

A one-car attached garage was approached from the gravel-surfaced alley which left 27th Street at the south border of the property and curved behind the house to exit onto 11th Avenue B after serving four homes. Just before the alley curved, the driveway to the garage made a sharp right-angle turn and descended to the basement level under the dining room giving access into the house via the garage. Stacked flagstones formed a wall on both sides of the decline so that erosion would not send muddy water into the garage. Also on the basement level was the laundry, a rough bathroom with shower for Bill's own use, a pine paneled party room which Bill had finished off, and most importantly his workshop of woodworking tools.

In time, Bill finished off part of the attic so the girls, as they were called, had their shared bedroom, bathroom and playroom up there. New slipper chairs purchased with money from Grandpa Doc and a dressing table crafted by Algot and covered in chintz by Corsie signified that soon to be young women occupied the space. Twin beds, replacing the bunks, were where Mary placed a new garment she occasionally purchased for one or both while they were at school, and her words: "Have you checked your bed yet?" sent them, heart pounding, racing upstairs. The playroom was alternately an office, a hospital, a school, or a restaurant always with their dolls playing essential roles. It was up there also that Mary would steal silently to a daughter's bedside, kneel down, reach out her arm to touch her, and in a penitent tone ask forgiveness for an angry outburst of temper she had exhibited that day. A sleepy "yes" was all that was necessary to make both their worlds whole again, atonement complete, injury forgotten.

But of course all those amenities did not make the house a home. It was what happened inside, day by day, step by step, which like a crucible of character took parental love, mixed it with discipline and positive example, blended in story books which exemplified solid morals, weekly church school, and the regimen of piano lessons and daily practice that taken together over the years forged the characters of Susie and Kathleen. It was perhaps not a conscious effort on the parents' part but instead a kind of replicating of the traditional home life they, themselves, had known growing up or in some cases an intentional repairing of instances of fault they had experienced. The lessons of self-discipline, delayed gratification, and restraint learned in the home have always been requisite to building self-reliant, capable adults, for the family is the first school of human values. The traditional family is a good which society cannot do without!

Here this writer would like to insert a personal note as I describe those years: I see now that my whole outlook on life, my vision of the world, was shaped way back in that little house on 27th Street in the daily lessons quietly conveyed and infused with love. I know too how fortunate I was that my happiness and stability were never clouded by illness or accident, job loss or divorce, destructive behavior or selfish ruin. It is not a particularly dramatic story but, thankfully for me and for all of society as it played out in countless Cape Cods in America, it contributed to a healthy and strong nation. As I often like to say: "Happiness is still homemade—and so is goodness!"

It was to this home that Mary and Bill brought their second daughter Kathleen after the requisite two week hospital stay from her birth on January 19, 1942. Oh, how Mary relished her role as mother to two little girls, a role she had perhaps unconsciously absorbed from her own mother while growing up in a family of two girls. Whenever possible, Mary dressed her daughters alike in "sister dresses," fashioned their hair in the same style often wrapping their long tresses in narrow bands of dampened fabric called "rags" to set curls overnight, took them to a photography studio since she never owned a camera, or took them to Mrs. Gosline's home in Rock Island to choose a new outfit, clothes that were a notch above those available in department stores.

Kathleen's arrival allowed Mary to experience motherhood from her baby's first breath. Her dad was in attendance but Dr. Gustafson was the delivering physician for the "normal" delivery. Cute and precocious, Kathleen talked before she walked. Mary liked to tell that when carrying her baby in her arms, if her attention was diverted and she would remove her glance from the baby's face, Kathleen would grab her face in her pudgy little hands and turn Mommy's face to look at her saying: "I talka you!"

Wartime rationing put only a small crimp in the Oehler's life. Butter was unattainable at Mr. Stormont's nearby corner grocery store where Mary walked to do her shopping, so margarine was invented; no one seemed to know what was in the clear, one pound-sized, plastic bag with a bright red button-sized circle in the middle, but if Mary kneaded the contents of the bag long enough the mass turned to the color of butter and could be eaten on bread, baked in recipes, or fried, all in place of butter. Leather too was rationed but friends could be counted on to share and pool their ration stamps if new shoes were really necessary, especially for growing children. Whatever the deprivation in the wider economy, the little Oehler girls were nevertheless afforded the Kenwood wool coats and leggings to ward off the winter blasts. Only the gasoline for the car which drove them to Minier every couple of weeks was a conundrum, causing the little family to miss an occasional trip or two to the grandparents, John, Emma and Will, in Minier.

One trip to Minier they did not miss was in 1943 for the May Day wedding of Ada to Charles Franklin Seales of Springfield, Illinois. The two had met as students at the University of Illinois, not dating however, because was Chuck was a waiter in her Gamma Phi Beta sorority house, and it was against house rules for a Gamma Phi to date a waiter. A friendship ensued nevertheless and continued after graduation when Chuck pursued a law degree at U of I, and Ada went to Lincoln, Nebraska, to found with Phillis Armstrong, a new Gamma Phi chapter and earn her Master Degree in Psychology. Standing erect in his brown army dress suit, Chuck was glad for his leave, narrowly won in time of war, from active duty to marry his Ada. Mary was, of course, her matron of honor. Just before leaving Lyla and Delm's home in her long flowing gown, she went into Rita's bedroom to kiss little Susie good-bye. Susie sat straight up from her nap-time bed and exclaimed: "Oh, Mommy, can I put on my nightgown and go with you?"

Mary and Bill saw to it that no hardships of war ever penetrated the world of little Susie and Kathleen. Bill's assignments at the John Deere Planter Works pivoted from planters to panzers, he was the designated warden of their block in case of an unlikely invasion, and he planted a "victory garden" on a nearby vacant lot as requested by President Roosevelt in a radio address. That was the Oehler's one and only vegetable garden! All their lives though the girls remembered standing out on the sidewalk in the early June evening of 1945 hearing the sirens and honking horns, the shouting and general frivolity as the end of the war was announced. Two of their older friends, the Quilty girls, ran to them jubilant that they had been excused from washing the supper dishes that night in celebration of the war's end!

Mary and Bill with Kathleen and Susie in 1944.

Then just about the time tomatoes were ripening in home gardens of middle America, preparations went into high gear for Kathleen and Susie to make their first sojourn without their Mommy and Daddy. First had arrived the letter from the childless Aunt Dorene and Uncle Perch, Bill's older brother, inviting them to visit them for a week in Wilmington, Illinois. Then came the days-long discussions regarding their readiness to travel alone and to actually function without Mommy there to coordinate their every move and tuck them in every night. As the oldest Susie was full of bravura and confidence, at least in the safe confines of her home, but Kathleen, two years younger, required some convincing.

In the course of the next few days though, Kathleen was completely won over when Mommy showed them the traveling outfits she had bought them: "sister outfits" of blue plaid skirts with matching solid blue blouse tops over white cotton slips, black patent Mary Jane shoes, lace-trimmed

STORIES MY FOLKS TOLD ME

white anklets, straw bonnets, and of course the requisite white gloves. As if that wasn't enough finery, Mary drew out of her shopping bag something brand new to the market, two small boxes labeled: "Toni Home Permanent." It didn't seem to matter that Susie had naturally curly hair because when you have two little girls so close in age you toss them both into the same time frame, treat them practically as twins and what one gets, so does the other!

It was a bit mystifying that Mary, who went weekly to Mrs. Berndt's beauty shop in the basement of her nearby home to have her own hair washed and rolled onto curlers and got a permanent wave every three months of her entire adult life, would suddenly decide that she had the ability to give her daughters a home permanent, but that must be a testimony to the "Which Twin has the Toni?" advertising campaign. Kathleen looked really cute after the perm but Susie looked like someone had stuck her finger in an electric socket. Her hair "took" the perm and was tightly curled but no amount of brushing would make it lie on her head. Of course the straw hat which tied under her chin happily served the purpose of corralling her hairdo at least for the journey.

Dressed in their new clothes, the sisters followed the porter to their seats on the Rock Island Zephyr heading east. No sooner was the train out of the station than they ripped open the brown bag lunches Mommy had given them just to see what they contained, exclaiming at the extra treats and a note professing her love. To their consternation, some ladies who got on at the next stop actually pointed at them, whispered, and laughed. "What is so odd about us? Is it my hair? Why are those people laughing at us?" they asked each other. Puzzled, they tried not to let the mockery dampen their spirits even when a second and third group also pointed and chuckled. Both girls were grandmothers themselves before they figured out that those folks were probably saying to each other: "Look at those little girls! Aren't they cute?!"

What a wonderful time Susie and Kathleen had at Aunt Dorene's and Uncle Perch's! Days were spent playing with an endless supply of paper dolls, sewing aprons to take home to Mommy, and going to lunch at Aunty's friends. But as soon as Uncle Perch came home from work at the strip mine office, they changed into bathing suits, loaded up the picnic supper, drove out to the flooded mine pit for an evening of jumping off the diving board, screaming like banshees, and splashing into the refreshing pool. As they drove home by moonlight, Aunt Dorene's sweet voice serenaded them with "By the Light of the Silvery Moon," "Chattanooga Choo Choo," "Don't Fence Me In," and "I'll Be Seeing you in All the Old Familiar Places." The girls can hear and see her still!

The week sped so quickly by that Kathleen and Susie really didn't have a chance to get homesick, but the last minutes in the kitchen before going to the train station were full of commotion and exasperation as they looked and looked for Kathleen's train ticket. It had just been sitting there on the counter as they waited for Uncle Perch to come in from picking some tomatoes for them to take home to their parents—and then it was gone! Uncle Perch suddenly announced that there wasn't time to look any more if they wanted to catch the train. He would just buy another ticket at the station. Oh no, the girls thought: the ticket would cost $3. But that's what he did!

Back home, the little girls were glad to be in Mary's embrace when the phone rang. It was Aunt Dorene calling to say they had found the train ticket! Tissue paper thin, it had blown off the counter and stuck to the wet sole of Uncle's garden shoe where it stayed till it was dry and flaked off!

Still, not all was always blissful and tranquil in the home of Mary and Bill. Like the monster Medusa, dissension would raise its ugly head from time to time, causing spoken words of hurt and consequent tears, causing flashes of Mary's hot temper or in the case of Bill, given to swings of mood, periods of a moody silent treatment lasting days, his face glowering or filled with hurt, stubbornly refusing to talk. Mary called it "the silent treatment" which he could keep going for days. Would his spell have been broken if Mary had given him a big sloppy kiss on the mouth and said "I love you?" Perhaps she did, but we'll never know. Confused and helpless, Mary confided in her dad in one of their many huddles in his doctor's office after all the patients had gone home. It was in the day before psychology was included in the training of physicians so all he could offer was the time-honored words of consolation and council: "You can't be right or get your way 100%

STORIES MY FOLKS TOLD ME

of the time, it may look like you don't even get it 50% of the time, and may seem like you get it only 25% of the time, but silently over time a kind of balance emerges and you will see that you do get your way half of the time. No one can be completely happy if his partner is miserable and so to establish their own equilibrium they will eventually do whatever is necessary to raise the spirits of the other." Just talking her problem over with her dad, Corsie, and later with Ada always helped, but it didn't cure Bill's moods!

For all her days on this earth, Mary hung a framed sampler-like picture in her home, a present from Bill upon his return home from a business trip in the early days of their marriage. Testifying that at one time he was full of love for her and could show it, it read:

> Wherever I roam,
> Whatever realms
> To see. My heart,
> Untraveled, fondly
> Turns to thee.

Bill had trouble expressing his affection, and when love was not nourished, not expressed, even the feelings fell into disuse. "My dad never left the house without kissing my mom good-bye," Mary would sigh. Bill called her "Mom," not Mary which perhaps indicates conflicted feelings as well. Yet at the very end of his life, he avowed his love for Mary, told her he appreciated her, apologized for his mean spirit, and asked for forgiveness. It meant everything to her, late though it was!

Whatever their interpersonal problems, though, Mary and Bill were united in their love of their daughters, the enjoyment and fulfillment they derived from the activities involved in their development, the challenges and pleasures of acting as a family. When early January birthdays prevented the girls from starting kindergarten after the December 31 deadline, Mary enrolled them in the Villa de Chantal, a private Catholic girls' school in the convent of the Sisters of The Visitation in Rock Island, which had no age restrictions. The school was a 1901 Gothic Revival-style edifice of towers, belfry, rose window, pointed-arch chapel windows, ornate and prestigious, for boarding and day girl students. A green school bus driven by Mr. Edwards drove Susie and later also Kathleen to and from school; the kindergarten teacher, Sister Angela, captured their hearts especially Susie's whom she paraded from room to room introducing as her "little Hummel" because of her big brown eyes, cropped brown hair, and chubby cheeks. A highlight of the school year was "May Day," when the entire beautiful campus was decorated with the flowering shrubs and trees, senior girls wove ribbons and danced with them around the May pole as countless generations of girls had, parents and alumnae were in attendance, games were set up, thespian and singing acts were performed, a parade bearing a statue of Mary progressed through the grounds, and chances were sold to win a little doll dressed in the habit of the teaching nuns. Kathleen had her sights set on that doll and was inconsolable when she did not win it, so on the following day Mary phoned the school to ask if she could buy such a doll. She could and did buy the "Sister Doll," to Kathleen's supreme joy, still in family possession!

With a twinge of surprise and alarm, Mary observed her daughters unfathomable love of the nuns. The little girls spoke of the mysterious looking habits which the nuns always wore. Did they have hair like Mommy behind the white wimple and under the black veil? They exuded a certain smell, not disagreeable, from the long black tunic secured by a woolen belt which held the dangling, constantly clacking rosary beads. The cross on a long chain around her neck often caught in a girl's hair as the nun leaned over her desk to help with a troublesome lesson; a silver ring was the nun's only jewelry and worn just like Mommy's wedding ring. Sweetness and goodness personified, yet stern, were Sister Angela, Sister Rita, and Sister Mary Rose, and the others; benevolent and other-worldly, yet strict, were those fascinating creatures! They quite captured the hearts of Susie and Kathleen until Mary, a true WASP in America finding Catholic teachings and beliefs completely incomprehensible, grew fearful. Flashbacks to Marie's bigoted behavior completed the nightmare scenario that the girls might ask to convert to Catholicism. Since that must be avoided at all cost, Mary withdrew the saddened girls at the end of the school term, Susie's third grade and Kathleen's first grade.

As the world economy began to recover following World War II, the Oehlers began to think bigger travel thoughts. Gasoline was again available for the American family cars, the Petries were writing from their home in Banning, California, that they missed them and they really must visit—the sooner the better! Mary busied herself with maps at the table while Bill spent evenings in his workshop building a platform for the backseat of the car to be used as a bed/playroom for the little girls during the long drive across country. Seat belts had not been thought of yet nor deemed necessary. Then almost at the last minute they decided to travel by train. All slept together in a "compartment," but during the day a steward folded the beds away and the little room became their private sitting and play area. They ate in the dining car, walked the aisles to stave off ennui, marveled at the tumbling tumbleweed, the mountains, the changing landscape, and the sunsets they saw from their window. Clever Mary entertained the little girls too with a story book and the magic she conjured from her handkerchief. Yes, from the simple "hankie" she drew from her pocket Mary could make two mice in a blanket or with two separate handkerchiefs she could make a doll for each of the girls to play with. Unfortunately that "old timey" skill was not passed on to the next generation though it had come to Mary from her forbears.

The ubiquitous paper tissue or "kleenex" of today was still awaiting its discovery in that day hard upon World War II. The white handkerchief or "hankie" was then always in the possession of the well dressed man or woman, still seen waving from the window of a disappearing train or automobile, still dropped in the hope of being picked up and retrieved by a handsome man, still the source of games and crafts of the good grandmother, still carefully washed and ironed by the dozens each week, and still considered the appropriate gift to a friend, teacher, or hostess. The paper towel, so indispensable today, also awaited invention in those days. "Go get me a rag!" Mary ordered her daughter who would then hurry to a tall wicker, lidded basket, called the "rag bin," in the bedroom to retrieve one from a large assortment of various sizes and fabrics of worn out linens or garments, used over and over, washed, dried, folded, and returned to the basket. A similar rag basket held prominence in Bill's basement workshop as well.

Of course, it was a loving welcome they received at the Petrie's little desert house where the sun shone every day and Adeline's trilling voice recounted story after story of their experiences since becoming Californians. Their introduction of that happy conception, "the cocktail hour," became a ritual in the Oehler home before long as well. Moving northward by train, the little family arrived in Whittier where former Moliners Bob and Jane Gamble with Martha at Susie's age and Wicker at Kathleen's age took them "trick or treating," to visit Knott's Berry Farm, a forerunner of Disney World, and many other fun vacation experiences. Lastly, the train took them to Portland, Oregon, where Bill's brother Jess and wife, Nelle, lived. With them they drove up the nearby Mt. Hood mountain to play in the snow.

Those were indeed the days when travel for folks from the middle class in Middle America, if they were so fortunate as to have the money to travel at all, usually meant staying in the homes of friends and relatives. Grand hotels were few and only in major cities. "Tourist Courts," consisting of tiny one-room cabins often lined the road in six or eights, but the Oehlers never overnighted in them. It was also in the 1940s after the war that they traveled by car to visit the Nebraska relatives. The contact between Bill's mother's family and that of her sister, Annie, though both were gone by then, was still strong, so early one summer morning Mary and Bill, Susie and Kathleen, set out by car to log the 500 mile trek to Seward on two-lane highways in one day. Knowing that it would be a tedious time for the little girls, Mary devised an ingenious game for them: if they were good and played nicely for one hour, they each could reach a hand into Mary's big paper bag and pull our a little gift-wrapped prize in the form of a garment for a doll, paper dolls, a coloring book, or comic book. Needless to say, it worked!

At the palatial residence of Vera, Annie's daughter, and Ted Hughes awaited Marguerite Ann and T.R. and their many fascinating toys including a real carousel horse to ride on in the backyard. Kathleen and Susie were in heaven even if Bill did tie a string around the latter's loose tooth, connect it to the proverbial door handle, and slam the door shut all before little Susie knew what was going on. Kathleen experienced her share of drama too when the inner tube she was clinging to in the country club swimming pool capsized and she was held head down, feet up until her daddy noticed, jumped into the kiddie pool with all his clothes and shoes on, and rescued her. Not too many years later the Oehler girls traveled with their cousin, Rita Jeanne, Lila's daughter, back to visit Aunt Vera, further cementing the relationship between the Illinois and Nebraska branches of the family.

Other travels instigated by Mary included a drive to visit her Iowa Peine relatives who farmed near Pella. Two sisters, Edna and Ethel, and a brother, Charles Liese, rather like Marilla and Matthew Cuthbert in "Anne of Green Gables," which Susie had just read, never married but carried on the farm as they had known it growing up. Like all farmers, Charles queried Bill about Deere products and offered suggestions and complaints while his sisters impressed with their bountiful meals and stitching artistry. A tour of the barnyard to see the baby lambs, chicks, pigs, and gave Kathleen and Susie lasting memories.

But the most memorable event of that trip was when Kathleen fell out of the car as it fortuitously slowed to forty miles per hour to take a curve in the road. Chewing gum had recently appeared on the market and become a favorite of Mary and the girls. They were allowed to chew in the car but to freshen the flavor needed a new portion of a stick with some regularity. Kathleen had just received a new piece from Mommy, intended to roll down the window to throw away the wrapper, instead grabbed the door handle, and out she flew! Fearing that her mommy and daddy wouldn't notice and drive on without her, she was actually able to get to her feet and run after, tears of pain and anxiety streaming down her face. Of course, Bill pulled over immediately, jumped out of the car, and carried her to it. A visit to a doctor in the very next village revealed that nothing was broken but seemingly hundreds of tiny abrasions from the cinders of the road shoulder marked her entire little frame and forceps were required to remove those still embedded in her skin. She looked like a walking mummy for a few days and had trouble bending one stiff knee causing her the next morning to knock a cleaning woman's pail of water down the grand staircase of their hotel eliciting yet more exclamations and embarrassment but profound relief that nothing more serious had befallen the little girl!

Several themes converged to prompt a 1949 train trip to Chicago: Susie had been introduced to ice skating at Riverside Pond and even fancied herself becoming a famous ice skater when she grew up; Corsie mentioned that her compatriot Sonja Henie, the renowned Swedish (actually Norwegian) figure skater, was appearing in Chicago; and a Christmas present idea for Corsie was sought. Bill and Algot were in agreement that the two women and two girls should travel to Chicago for the performance and stay overnight at the Palmer House. Even Mary, who had never been on ice skates in her life was enthralled as Miss Henie pirouetted, spun, performed figure eights, assumed camel position, jumped, and lunged; costumes, lights, and music were amazing! Long after the super charged performance, the little girls wore the white plastic pin of figure skates which Corsie had bought them from a stadium hawker.

Though travel was always a bond between Mary and her husband, a strong nesting instinct or love of their home was another shared quality which unified Mary and her Bill. There they created an environment where they surrounded themselves and their daughters with old family pieces of furniture mixed with new ones of their own choice, photographs and paintings, collections of porcelain figures and of boxes, books, and antiques, treasured objects all which spoke louder than worlds about who they were and what they valued and held dear. Truly their refuge and retreat, their home, actually numbering eight in all over the years, sustained them, united them, and gave meaning to their lives. "No matter how modest your home is, never feel ashamed of it! It's who you are at a point in time," was Mary's retort when later a daughter lamented the small size of her home. She knew that "home" connotes more than its size or even the sum total of its elements, evokes very special feelings and makes a deep imprint on our hearts. That a house becomes a home when we love it, was surely exemplified by Mary. She was not so much a gardner, though, as that hearkened too much back to her village roots which she now had long left behind. Eventually, after a lifetime of world travels, their home was filled with timeless remembrances of places and people they had known and loved and thereby still felt a connections to.

All her long life Mary sought refuge in a book. When her daughters came home from school, they inevitably found their mom stretched out on a sofa in the den, book in hand, reading. It focused her mind, calmed her, took her outside of herself, was a deeply transporting experience in addition to expanding her knowledge, and probably began as an escape device when the pain of her mother's death became intolerable and ended with: "If I were a man, I would have been a lawyer because I like to read so much!" she would say.

Throughout Mary's lifetime, letter-writing was still in its heyday, so that most days when she went to the mailbox there was a hand-written, handsome, envelope of tangible heft addressed to her. This she would take to her desk, sit down, reach for an artful looking letter opener, slide it with an audible "zick" across the flap, and proceed to read, a smile slowly growing over her face. Usually, she knew before she had the letter opened who the writer was because of the handwriting, the stationery itself, or just because she knew who owed her a letter. Stationery stock came in every conceivable color besides white; some friends wrote using a pen with a signature color such as brown or green instead of black or blue; some had her name embossed or printed at the top with the second sheet clear; some friends, like Mary herself, had a hand embosser to press her name and address onto the paper and onto the flap of the envelope. Mary kept the letter awhile, re-reading it, reflecting on it, enjoying it, formulating her response or questions until within the requisite period of time she sat down to compose her reply.

A letter didn't offer the instant of gratification of a phone call; it was almost an exchange of gifts! There is a pace to letter writing and reading that comes from the person's own inner rhythm. Letters let us take turns, let us sit and mull and say exactly what we mean. A letter doesn't take one by surprise in the middle of dinner, or intrude when we are with other people or ambush us in the midst of other thoughts. It waits. There is a private space between the give and take for thinking. There is leisure and emotional luxury in letter writing. There are no obvious silences to anxiously fill. There are no interruptions to brook. There are no nuances and tones of voice to distract. One can hold a letter in her hands, can put it in a bundle, can show it to another, for there is something to show for it. One can take it out years later on a summer's night when she wants to remember.

It was a sad night for Mary in December of 1949, often described by her, when she got the phone call from her Uncle Ted of Bloomington telling her that her beloved Papa Doc had suffered a heart attack at home, was sped to the hospital, but didn't survive. The grateful villagers filled the church to crowded capacity and related story after story to Mary and Ada about the generosity, caring spirit, and lifesaving acts he had performed over the years as their village doctor. Above all, hundreds if not thousands avowed that he had brought them into this world. To their relief, the house and contents were willed to Mary and Ada, only one life insurance policy was designated to Marie forcing her immediate removal to Bloomington and a nursing job. Thus after many years banned from its door, the sisters reentered their paternal home to claim their rightful inheritance, a highly emotional experience for both young women not yet forty years old. Although Marie had tossed porcelain and belongings from an upper floor window, there were still treasures to be gleaned such as their father's microscope, Haviland china, shoe-shine stand, and photograph albums—all still lovingly held today in family possession. In due time, the sisters sold the home and auctioned off some the furnishings which had no meaning for them.

Yet again the sisterly love between Mary and Ada was on display, the envy of all who looked on. By letter, phone, or car, contact was frequent and deeply satisfying over their lifetimes. Ada had traveled with Bill and Mary to Yellowstone National Park the summer of her graduation from the University of Illinois; they had visited her in her first career apartment in Chicago at the Seranac Hotel, managed by Charley Tanner, father of her former teacher Dorene Tanner, and located near the Museum of Science and Industry; they had watched her progress first at Bell Labs and later as assistant director of Washington National Insurance Company's Personnel Department in Evanston, Illinois. There Ada served the majority of her career years and in the course of training new employees found herself actually training young men who occasionally became her superior, for such was the fate of women in her day.

Ever close, the sisters Mary and Ada traveled often to each other's homes. Ada and Chuck Seales were in the late 1940s living in Cleveland, Ohio, a long drive from Moline but possible in one day. Three year old Linda led them as they lugged their suitcases up the stairs and admonished, "You're not sus-posed to put your sticky fingers on the wallpaper!" Cute and endearing as Linda was, there was simply nothing that could draw their attention, could hold it and mesmerize them, or could compare with the stupendous, awe-inspiring, magical phenomenon which stood in its walnut case in the Seales' living room—a television! It was the first time that the Oehlers had ever seen a television set in a home! Before the month was out, a television set stood in the Oehler living room in Moline, of course.

To own a television in 1949 was beyond avant-garde—it was sensational! It was beyond new—it was revolutionary! A console set with a sixteen inch picture tube cost $695—half the price of a new car. Life was never the same; one's memories were sorted by before TV and after TV. Radio was ubiquitous by that time and thoroughly enjoyed, but the addition of visuals made a huge impression on one's experience. Although programming entered one's home only some hours of the day, leaving the would-be watchers to glue their eyes to the boring, stationery "test pattern." And did I mention that the picture was in a fuzzy black and white, no color? Still, Susie and Kathleen were begging to watch puppets "Kukla, Fran, and Ollie" and their silly antics or "Captain Video;" but really anything at all mesmerized them. At Susie's birthday party, Mary happily led the girls in games until one girl screamed and pointed, "Is that a television set?!" From that moment on Mary could not even lure the girls to the table set with cake and ice cream. Parents who came to pick up their daughters came in, sat down, and mutely stared at the flickering screen, much to the chagrin of the birthday girl and Mary too!

Quickly TV producers devised a line up of shows that fit right into family life: "What's My Line," a game show where a panel of celebrities tried to guess the guest's occupation; "The Perry Mason Show," a detective who solved all manner of crimes, especially murder; "The Millionaire," featuring an unidentified philanthropist who gave away a million dollars each week and then watched the recipient handle or mishandle it; "I Love Lucy," a comedy starring Lucille Ball and Desi Arnaz; "Bonanza," a rancher's story; "The Ed Sullivan Show," in which the host introduced entertaining acts much like vaudeville, most famously The Beatles. It was no exaggeration to say that life began to revolve around the television line up.

About that very same time, a very formidable fear was forcing itself into the psyches and clutching at the hearts of parents all over America: poliomyelitis. The dreaded disease of paralysis especially affected children, without known cause, cure, or mode of spread, and by 1950 was approaching epidemic proportions. In 1952, the worst year, 58,000 cases were diagnosed in the United States alone, 3145 people, mostly children died, while 21,269 victims were paralyzed to varying degrees from lameness to a life condemned to an "iron lung," the machine which moved the chest muscles so the stricken child could breathe. It was not until 1954 that Jonas Salk developed a vaccine to eradicate the terror. Like a plague, polio seemed to strike more in the summer months making parents like Mary and Bill associate polio with public swimming pools. Although the mode of infection was still not known, the Oehlers in their grasp at straws decided to deny their daughters swimming pool privileges. The concern was all the topic among their set with the solution finally selected to send their daughters to private camp in the northern wilds of Minnesota.

Thus it was that Susie and Kathleen, along with Moline girls, Steffy and Adeline Shevlin, Janie Wilson, Margaret and Nancy Neir, Sandy Bendle, traveled by train to Chicago, were met by chaperones, put on a sleeping-car train bound for Bimidji, Minnesota, and bussed to Camp Kamaji on Cass Lake near the headwaters of the Mississippi River. Six weeks away from home was a challenge for nine-year-old Kathleen but she survived thanks to the plethora of activities on water and shore, to the council fires where she sat in the gloaming with her fellow "tribe" members watching the flames, sparks, and smoke rise along with the voices of the girls in song, and thanks to the visit mid-session of Mary and Bill. At any rate, the sisters loved camp so much that they cried with their best friends when they had to go home and begged their parents to let them go again the next year. So sure enough, with the plague of polio still rampant, no prevention or cure yet discovered, two steamer trunks were packed in the Oehler home and shipped to Camp Kamaji for a second session in 1952.

That year there was a second reason to make shipping the girls away for a major part of their school vacation. With her inheritance of financial assets from her Dad's estate and the sale of their Cape Cod home for $18,500, Mary and Bill bought a lot in a new development at the southwest edge of Moline called Crestwood Hills. Mary and Bill were going to be occupied daily with the construction of a new "dream home." Lots there were large and because of the many rivulets and tributaries which over the eons had carved the land between the Mississippi and Rock rivers, were terraced by ravines making interesting home sites. The best possible house design was therefore the new style called "ranch" with an exposed basement. In other words, from the street the house appeared to be a one-story ranch, but from the ravine in the back it was a two-story with windows and entry doors on the lower level as well as on the street side. As evidence of the post World War II boom the house had a two-car garage, for Mary and Bill soon owned two automobiles. No street-car or bus cruised past this house; in fact, there was no sidewalk. Translation: Americans in the early 1950s stopped walking and drove their cars everywhere they went, no matter how short the distance! The price tag for the finished dream house at 2510—29th Avenue Court was $36,000. Later, an artist friend of Mary's, Mazel Case, memorialized the home on canvas, viewed from the ravine side rather than the street, still in family possession.

At the time of the move up the social ladder that this home implied, November of 1952, Bill was chief engineer of the John Deere Planter Works, the youngest in its history. Many of the new neighbors were themselves Deere and Company executives: Chief of the Legal Department Lewis Wilson and his family, corporate board member Robert Carlson, treasurer Kenneth Anderson and family, and eventually the president of Deere, Robert Hanson. "Pill Hill" was a name some Moliners gave to one part of the neighborhood because it was home to numerous doctors and dentists: Doctors: Fritz Eile, Bryce Ozanne, William Koivun, Louis Arp, and Stanley Servine. By that time, Mary too had achieved an admirable rung in the social milieu of Moline by her membership and leadership in women's organizations such as the Emma Kough Circle of King's Daughters, Mary Martha Guild at the First Congregational Church, Chapter HB of P.E.O., Moline Public

Hospital Grey Ladies Service Corps, alumni chapter of Gamma Phi Beta, and American Society of University Women.

There were two entry doors to the house just ten feet apart. From the driveway, the first door, a Dutch door meaning the top half could swing open while the lower half stayed in the closed position, led to the kitchen while the second door, more formal with two small upper windows and panels beneath, opened to the formal entry and living room. Mary and Bill chose their signature barn red for the exterior cedar shingles, but the front walkway for the two doors just described had vertical paneling painted white with grey trim and flagstones on the floor; the door was colonial grey. Indoors the floors were tongue and groove oak boards of a light finish with dark exposed pegs, designed to align with the new style of decor called "Early American" which the two espoused. Two wood-burning fireplaces graced the home, one in the living room bordered by wide bookshelves, and one directly beneath in the then newly conceptualized "recreation room." A bay window in the living room accommodated a small maple antique table and two antique Windsor chairs, a place perfect for sharing a cup of tea with a friend and offering a view to the mature trees which separated the home visually and physically from the house across the ravine on a parallel street.

Over the wood floors of the living and dining rooms, Mary and Bill chose to lay what looked like an Early American braided rug but was actually an off the bolt, bound-edges carpet. Their camel back sofa purchased at the time of their wedding fit perfectly in the new living room and their Eastlake bedroom set suited their bedroom, but their former dining room set was needed in the dinette or breakfast area of the new home requiring the purchase of a new round maple table with clever "lazy Susan" atop, eight chairs, and a hutch. A new cherry bedroom set consisting of a double bed with canopy atop, a dresser and mirror, a chest of drawers, and one nightstand was selected for their daughters' room. Twin occasional chairs were needed in front of the fireplace as was a davenport for the wood paneled bedroom they chose to use as a den/TV room. Mary's Grandpa's Morris chair fit in there just right too. Mary got a "bang" (her word) out of her discovery of John Deere motif drapery material so had a set whipped up for the window of the den to her everlasting smug satisfaction at being the first of her set to do that!

The new kitchen had knotty-pine cupboards, a white porcelain sink with a newly invented garbage disposal, and another brand new on the market automatic dishwasher. Having an engineer for a husband meant that Mary got all the latest gadgets and efficiencies as they came on the market. The disposal took some learning, however. No fingers were severed, but Gladys McKahin's chunky diamond ring (her father was a jeweler) slipped off the ring holder dish above the sink in the commotion of serving a P.E.O. luncheon when the disposal was running, and to Mary's horror and Gladys' furor they couldn't locate the on/off switch in time. The friendship endured unabated, but it was awhile before the story could be termed a funny one!

Flooring for the kitchen was an Armstrong hallmark, a Spanish tile-like deep red pattern which exists still today for nostalgia lovers and those passionate about the Early American look. A signature decoration in Mary's kitchen hung over the door to the connecting garage: two horseshoes, which themselves signified good luck, bonded together with Mary's name stamped on one and Bill's on the other in a rustic statement of solidarity. They liked the metaphor so much, in fact, they made it their wedding gift to many many couples over the years.

Decor throughout the home was given a decidedly aesthetic boost when Hjoesta Hellberg,long-time friend of Spud and Katharine and thus friend of Mary and Bill, came on the scene. One evening over dinner in the former's home, Hjoesta asked Bill how he planned to decorate his new home, and Bill replied "Well, I'll paint it of course." "Let me have a look first" countered the owner of Hellberg Decorating Company, the premier firm in the Tri-Cities and a classically trained artist in his original home country, Sweden. Mary and Bill knew they couldn't afford the Hellberg company but what could they say? When Mary walked Hjoesta through the house she was amazed at the ideas he came up with: a wall paint, he mixed himself, that wasn't pink or mauve or beige but a chimerical color that was perfect in her living room. Walking down the window-less hall to the bedrooms, he purred in his soft Swedish accent, "Here, we need to bring in a little sunshine! I know just the right wallpaper!" Moldings, crown and base, wainscoting in the dining room, eight-panel doors should be a special color of white which wasn't really white, according to the master. Mary loved his suggestions for wallpaper in the bedrooms and dining room as they completely complemented the antiques she had lately acquired at Youngberg Antique Shop through Corsie's introduction: a chestnut dry-sink, two Windsor chairs, several light cherry occasional tables, paintings, framed Currier and Ives lithographs, porcelain "Jenny Lind" and "Mary Todd Lincoln" dolls a flax-spinning wheel, and a walnut school bench.

When Bill, after several sleepless nights, approached Hjoesta about the price of all the non-budgeted decorating, the professional painters also originally from Sweden, the high-end Benjamin Moore brand paint, the only one Hjoesta used, the painstaking, several coatings manner of application, the master only replied: "Don't worry, you can afford it, I'll see to that!" As it turned out, he could, because this was one of the times, Hellberg Decorating took a job just for the love of excellence and perhaps for the advertising which would accrue when the Oehlers entertained Deere & Company executives in their home.

Though the Oehler's only lived in the home twelve years, Mary always deemed it her favorite "because that's where I raised my girls." It was there she taught them life skills like getting along as she directed that they share not only a bedroom but a bed, "training," she said "for marriage." "Let your conscience by your guide," "Remember, you represent the family when you are out and about," she admonished. Discretion was her guiding principle which led her to disdain gossip. She knew how to keep a secret, to keep her own council. Once when her daughters were still pre-teens they heard of the concept of marital infidelity and ask if she knew anyone who had been unfaithful? To their utter horror and shock, she answered "yes." "Was it someone, we know?" they asked. "Yes," she again shockingly replied. For months Susie and Kathleen begged her to reveal the name of the person, but she remained silent knowing it was knowledge they could not yet handle. Mary was wise enough to know it would be too much information for her daughters' tender psyches and would negatively affect their relationship with the woman. They were in their forties when another person told them, too late to ruin their opinion of her.

Mary did not teach her daughters any common frugalities of the day, however. She disparaged gardening, canning of vegetables once "Libby's" appeared on the grocery shelves, sewing, mending, reversing the collar of a man's shirt to renew its life, and ironing. Bill repaired his own clothes at a sewing machine he bought for himself. Corsie did the ironing using the huge mangle machine for bed and table linens. Still Mary was impressed when Pricilla Johnson sewed Susie a skirt and jacket suit from one of Bill's out of style worsted suits. A certain economy was displayed though in her habit of wearing a new dress first for social occasions or church, then for shopping or everyday, and finally for homewear. She saved the plastic bags, too, when In the 1960s grocery stores began packaging fresh foods in them for the first time; women like Mary actually washed and dried them to reuse before they were available for purchase a decade later. That's how valuable they were considered!

But she made up for all her extravagances with her culinary arts. As her close friend, Gladys McKahin, who had a degree in home economics from Iowa State University, marveled: "Mary, how can you season your cooking like you do when you have only your taste to go on?" Just for the fun of it, Mary loved to take a bite of some new preparation, close her eyes, savor it, and recite all the ingredients she could taste to the amazement of those at the table. She always joked: "It's because of my big nose that my sense of taste is so good!" Her aversion to milk and eggs meant she passed them over, but absolutely loved cheese, all kinds, the bluer and stinkier the better! In her day, many everyday dishes began with a white sauce—one tablespoon melted butter, one tablespoon flour, bit of salt and pepper, and one cup of milk, all cooked in a pan while stirring till thickened. To the white sauce she would add cheese, a starch like cooked rice or potatoes, a bit of chopped meat, and most anything she found in the fridge or pantry to make the new concoction known as a casserole. Seasoned by her just right, after tasting to assure the right flavor was achieved, was called by her: "Doctoring it up." Packaged puddings and jello were new on the market in the 1940s so dessert often incorporated one of them. A meal was not a meal to Bill without dessert, and Mary happily complied. She was a pie baker, par excellence, but that wasn't an everyday offering. "A pie has to be eaten on the day it's baked," she declared, "but a cake can sit for days."

Stewed tomatoes laced with her own choice of dried herbs made a frequent appearance on Mary's winter table, but her love of tomatoes went on throughout the year. Once fresh tomatoes came to market, and that was only in the summer in the early days before they were shipped from Florida or Georgia or Missouri, she fixed her favorite salad she had learned from her mother: into a pretty cut-glass oblong bowl, also from her mother, she placed carefully peeled, slices of tomatoes, then she placed a layer of peeled cucumber slices atop, and finally rings of onion atop all. Though some will pucker their lips or hold their noses to read this, Mary next poured a good half cup of white vinegar over all, placed some ice cubes atop which in the summer heat melted and diluted the vinegar a bit. Yes, Mary had a taste for things tart and tangy, learned at home in the German community where pickling, though no longer needed for food preservation, was still a favorite flavor.

She had a sweet tooth though as she freely admitted. When her Uncle Paul sent her a box of chocolates she vowed to "space it out, just have one piece," but hide it in the dry- sink as she may, like steel to a magnet she couldn't resist the pull. Her streusel-filled coffee cake was a popular coffee klatch offering: 1 1/2 cups flour, 3 teaspoons baking powder, 1/4 teaspoon salt, 3/4 cup sugar, 1/4 cup shortening, 1 egg, 1/2 cup milk, 1 teaspoon vanilla beaten. Half of the batter, she placed in a eight inch square pan and added half the streusel composed of one cup brown sugar, two tablespoons flour, half a cup chopped nuts, two teaspoons cinnamon, and two tablespoons melted butter. Then came the rest of the batter topped with the rest of the streusel, and into a 375 degree oven it went for twenty-five to thirty minutes. Vanity kept Mary from packing on the pounds though; she was always on a diet, it seemed!

As Mary approached her forty-second birthday, the age of her mother when she died, a tangible foreboding gripped Mary sending her to Dr. Gustafson. Sure enough, he discovered she had elevated blood pressure. At last doctors in the early 1950s had a remedy, new prescription drugs and diuretics which after a trial and error to find the correct type and dose succeeded in normalizing Mary's numbers. She was very young when the pills became necessary but they worked, and she never forgot to take them for the remaining fifty years of her life!

Also new on the market were earrings for pierced ears. Mary had always struggled with the pain and irritation of the screw-on or clamp-on types, so with money from her inheritance in hand she strode one day into Josephson's Jewelry store on 5th Avenue to buy diamond studs— some bling to go with her Revlon famously red "Fire and Ice" lipstick, also new on the market! Her dress or accent piece was also often a shade of red. "If its red, I like it," was her motto! Original, perhaps, but always the "lady," with a drawer full of gloves in every shade and length, hats to fill several shelves, dresses and skirts — but absolutely no slacks or jeans. Bill said: "they aren't 'lady-like,' so you better never wear them!" And she never did till after he left this earth. Her sister thought she carried the "lady" look a bit too far though and accused her of looking "always dressed as if you are going to have tea with the Queen!" Mary's voluptuous size D bust line, perhaps the envy of her girl friends, was always an issue of concern to her that she modestly kept in check by buttoning up her shirtwaist dress to the second button from the top and disdaining any show of cleavage or décolleté. She truly was a lady!

A lady, in Mary's day, wore nylon stockings even in the privacy of her own home, held up by a garter belt consisting of a four non-fail fasteners which hung from a lingerie belt around her waist. Her shoes were a delicate size five and a half and often with substantial heel height. Later in the mid-fifties when "straight skirts" were the fashion she wore a girdle to hold up her stockings and check the jiggle. Ladies and gentlemen of the day carried handkerchiefs of lovely, delicate, soft fabrics, highly embellished with lace and embroidery, sorted in their own drawer according to the occasion, provenance noted and long remembered. Folks addressed each other by the appellations: Miss, Mister, Missus, Sir, Madam, or Ma'am unless they were related or longtime friends and even then if there was an age difference, perhaps never by the first name. Children always addressed adults by title and surname; the use of first names did not come into common usage until well into the sixties or even later, at least in central Illinois.

But there was one ostensibly un-lady-like habit Mary did espouse that came to popularity in 1920's: chewing gum! Though an anomaly, Mary took up chewing Doublemint, Spearmint, or Chicklets when the flappers first introduced gum and continued chewing for a good part of her adult life, just a half stick at a time for she was a lady, after all. She never took so much as a puff from a cigarette, though the flappers launched that too, but she sure did like to chew! Tempering the gum-chewing impression was her decidedly intellectual appearance which the eyeglasses she constantly wore to correct her astigmatism, gave.

Mary, in that day before the environmentalists and animal protectionists, reveled in her assortment of furs, first acquired when she was in college, not all genuine but running the gamut over the years from Beaver, Muskrat, and Marten, to Mink, in full length, stoles, hip-length, and drapes of complete little animals connected to each other jaw to tail. She even sought out and found a white rabbit jacket like the one she and Ada had shared in high school, for her daughters. They tried to avoid wearing it because their friends didn't wear furs and their dates didn't appreciate the way it ferociously shedded onto their blue serge suits. But it was the 1950s so the girls did as they were told. Ada's daughter, Linda, wore it too.

Throughout the years after Bill's mother died and Mary's parents both departed God's great green Earth, the Oehlers continued their frequent week-end drives to Minier, always lodging in the Oehler family home with Bill's dad. A visit to Mary's uncle, her mother's brother Paul Charles Peine, at his upstairs apartment "uptown" or supper with him at Minier's only restaurant across the street, where Paul took all his meals, absent a kitchen in his apartment. He was now Mary's only connection to her parent's generation; he had no wife or children; he welcomed the closeness he felt with Mary and Ada; and his nieces derived sustenance from his avuncular role in their lives. Christmas, Paul customarily celebrated with his cousin, Irma Peine who lived from 1900 to 2000 in Minier, but birthdays on August 16 (1885), were often passed with Mary and Ada, memorably his 80th and 90th.

Paul's career began, after graduation from the University of Illinois, at a shoe store in Billings, Montana, but ultimately after a failed romance

STORIES MY FOLKS TOLD ME

there he returned to manage the clothing department of the Peine Store in Minier, spanning the years from 1926 to his retirement in 1956. From 1936 to 1976, he served on the board of directors of Minier State Bank including as its vice-president. For fifty of his ninety-one years he valued his membership in the Minier Masonic Lodge and the Knights Templar, participating fully in many philanthropic activities.

Winters in retirement found Paul driving to St. Petersburg, Florida, where he liked to gather with other baseball aficionados to watch the major league teams from all over the country practice and prepare for the upcoming favorite spring pastime of men and women alike. Throughout his life, Paul rewarded himself with visits to Chicago's musical and theatrical venues, kept current with the entertainment life of that city through his subscription to the Chicago Tribune or a travel magazine subscription he and Mary gave each other on birthdays. Lean with a shirt size of small, sober as a judge, his only vice an occasional gentleman's cigar, Paul lived a quiet, solitary life. It was as if the brief exchanges, among all the familiar folks he encountered on his short walk to the Coffee Cup Cafe and those he happened upon there, at church, or at the Masonic Lodge were all the society he required.

With advanced age Paul Peine moved to Hopedale House in nearby Hopedale, Illinois, taking with him naturally his beloved piano and home organ to entertain himself and his fellow residents, like Will Oehler and Charley Tanner, most days. He tried to rent the two second floor apartments in his building in Minier, but without a kitchen they mostly stood empty; the first floor commercial spaces easily rented to an insurance agent and a beauty shop. After his ninetieth birthday his health did begin to slip. When he was hospitalized at the adjoining Hopedale Hospital Mary, though she was living half way across Missouri in Kimberling City, and Ada, though she was still employed at Washington National Insurance Company in Evanston, alternated week-end visits to him over a period of months. Sometimes Bill accompanied her but on May 16, 1977, Mary was alone when she stepped out of the car, hot off the press magazines, fruit, and books in her arms, and walked briskly the familiar steps to her uncle's room only to find it empty, the bed freshly made, the blinds opened to let the sunshine stream in, the smell of disinfecting agents permeating the scene. Alarmed, she ran to the nurses station to implore: "Where is Mr. Peine?" "Oh Madam, he died just hours ago. We phoned you and told your husband." Indeed, Bill had taken the message and called the state police who tried unsuccessfully to locate her on the highway. A shaken Mary crumpled a bit, recovered, and called Ada to commiserate and make funeral plans. They left Paul's organ at Hopedale House thinking a bit of their uncle should remain there.

As a second result of their fear of their children contracting polio, or perhaps as an excuse for the extravagance, Bill and Mary joined Short Hills Country Club which offered their daughters a private swimming pool with instructions in the Red Cross Junior Lifesaving course and many social events. To Mary and Bill came an introduction to the game of golf and an entrée to another level of Moline society. The years of late afternoon golf outings with friends when the heat of the day was past, when the cumulous clouds were slowly and silently passing overhead, when the grass beneath their feet was lush and emerald, and when birdcalls punctuated the air mixed with competition and frivolity before the cocktails and dinner in the clubhouse were some they both recalled later as among the best of their lives. They spent their requisite monthly dues by dining there often, enjoyed Mother's Day and holiday brunches, Susie and Peter's wedding luncheon, and numerous dinner parties there. But perhaps the most sensational event they celebrated at their country club was their twenty-fifth wedding anniversary in May of 1962. The party began in their home's lower level recreation room with cocktails and elaborate horsdouvres, attended by close to fifty friends and relatives. The reverse side of a silver platter marking the occasion (still in family possession) is engraved with the names of the bestowers: Helen and Bob Carlson, Lydia and Bruce Connell, Louise and Hayes Murphy, and Jean and Bill Koivun. Just so the reality of the twenty minute drive to the country club would not curtail anyone's enjoyment at Bill's bar, the hosts arranged for a school bus to appear at the house to drive their guests to and from the dinner. It was a surprise not mentioned on the invitation, so there were squeals of laughter and general merriment as the cocktail hour continued aboard the bus en-route to the club!

With a laugh between a hoot and a howl, a sneeze between a whoop and an achoo, a frightening choke reflex inherited from the Peines, a quick and ready sense of humor, the high-spirited Mary was considered a very fun woman by those who knew her. Maybe that's why she had so many friends. "Out to lunch" was not yet a popular activity for Moline ladies, but a hallmark of the 1950s was the dinner party. Prepared by the housewife from scratch from a recipe perhaps gleaned from "Ladies Home Journal," "McCall's Magazine," or "Good Housekeeping." served on her heirloom china and sterling silver flatware, the dinner party was the apogee of women like Mary, university educated but out of the workforce. Planned over time, mentally rehearsed, discussed with confidants, seating arrangements agonized over, centerpieces carefully crafted, her dress specially purchased for the occasion, the dinner party was executed almost like a domestic version of a lunar landing! Whether entertaining Bill's boss and his wife, Harold and Edna White, or simply Spud and Katharine or Herman and Marge Gephardt, grandson of Anke's sister Katherine, Mary could make an event out of an evening. Both she and Bill were newspaper readers, au currant with politics and government, liked to talk, and kept a lively discourse peppering 'round their table especially after the cocktail hour then so new and "de rigeur."

Grasshopper Pie was one recipe of hers requested by guests: 1 1/2 cups crushed Nabisco chocolate wafers (18 cookies), 4 tablespoons melted butter, mix and put in 9 inch pie pan, chill. Using a double boiler, melt 24 marshmallows and 3/4 cup half and half cream, then chill. Whip 1/2 pint whole cream. Add 1 1/2 oz white cream de cocoa and 1 1/2 oz. green cream de menthe. Mix with marshmallows, place in pie shell and freeze. Add green food coloring if desired. Serve topped with whipped cream or shavings of a bitter chocolate bar. Serves six or eight persons.

A recipe she used for her many ladies dessert events was simply called "Frozen Dessert" and it served sixteen to twenty from a thirteen inch by nine inch pan: Spread two cups of vanilla wafer cookie crumbs in the bottom of the pan. Melt one stick margarine and 2 1/2 ounce squares of unsweetened chocolate. Gradually add one or two cups of powdered sugar while beating with an electric beater. Add three beaten egg yolks and beat till smooth. Fold in three beaten egg whites and spread over the crumbs. Over that spread one half gallon of an ice cream of your choice (she chose peppermint), then a half a cup or more of the cookie crumbs, and freeze. Top with whipped cream if desired.

Since she had no job, had a cleaning woman and every labor-saving device money could buy, Mary even in her active, middle years was able to spend a good deal of time reading books. Each month, the Book of the Month Club sent her her choice which she then languorously perused while reclining on the yellow sofa in the den. She liked all kinds of books from funny to mystery to instructional to classic. When she came upon a humorous passage as in "The Egg and I" of the 1940s, she whooped a belly laugh out loud, thoroughly enjoying the moment. It peeved her no end when Bill would give her a hostile look and observe: "What's the matter with you?"

The card game, "Bridge," fascinated Mary over many years, gathered her a couple of times a month to the homes of her friends Bertie Peterson, Dorothy Lundahl (both wives of Deere board members), Gladys Lasser, Maesel Case, and Jean Greenwald. Bridge and crossword puzzles kept her mind sharp but also served as an outlet for her competitive nature and love of fun and laughter.

In time, Mary realized that she had achieved a certain status as the wife of a Deere & Company executive. Deere paid the highest wages in town by far; a job, any job with benefits there was a ticket to a comfortable life and a secure retirement, both much sought after in the Quad-Cities. Whereas, she had been a big fish in a little pond, Minier, she was now a big fish in a medium-sized pond. By serving on philanthropic boards Mary had paid back, had put down roots, and felt "at home" there by the Mississippi River.

To Mary's immense satisfaction, Susie stifled her fear of attending a large university, the University of Illinois, and decided to follow in the footsteps of her parents' forbears: Adela Peine Rost graduated in 1907; John Wilken Rost, MD, graduated in 1909; Paul Peine graduated in 1911; Alvin William Oehler, 1923; and of course Mary and Bill in 1935; and Ada in 1939. Also to Mary's joy, Susie pledged Gamma Phi Beta sorority and lived all four years in the sorority house, the same where Ada had lived and presided over as president a generation before her.

STORIES MY FOLKS TOLD ME

Two years after Susie left home, Kathleen pleased her parents and kept to the family tradition by choosing the identical path.

Shortly after the school term ended in June of 1960, Mary stood on the tarmac at Chicago's O'Hare airfield and looked at Bill who shot her a look which said: "My God, what have we just done?" They had just put their two daughters on a propeller Super Constellation bound for London, England, by way of refueling stops in New York City and Reykjavik, Iceland. The girls were traveling on a University of Illinois—Berlin Technological University sponsored ten-week student tour of England, France, Holland, Germany, Switzerland, Italy, Austria, and Czechoslovakia led by a professor of architecture and a professor of art history from the German university. Worry and loneliness did not consume the parents, now in their mid-forties, though. Oh no! Mary and Bill seized an advertisement in the Daily Dispatch, drove straight to the Butterworth Travel Agency, and signed themselves up for a European tour that very same summer!

This was ground-breaking stuff in 1960, just fifteen years after the end of World War II, when rubble still rose in mounds on the outskirts of European cities, when cathedrals were still only a fraction of their former stateliness, when centuries old structures were still being replaced by hastily erected concrete apartment buildings. Art galleries, symphony halls, palaces, and elegant classic old hotels were just barely ready for tourists again, but Americans had by then experienced the post-war economic boom, had money burning a hole in their pockets, and responded like today's kids going to Disneyland to the brand new notion of a European tour. So new was the idea that the travel agency held several evening seminars covering subjects like: How to Pack a Suitcase for Three Weeks of Travel, What Kind of a Camera Works Best in Europe, What Food to Expect in the European Countries, What Kind of Clothes to Pack, and How to Use the American Express Office in Major Cities to Communicate with Family at Home. Mary and Bill avidly attended them all, even the suitcase packing demonstration!

Seen in quotes from Mary's own travel log, still in family possession, the impressions she absorbed were numerous: "In Stockholm we visited Europe oldest theater still in use, had dinner in a 17th Century cellar called the Golden Fleece." "Met the Herslows in Malmo, toured with them, drove with Carl and Anna through southern Sweden with luncheon at a smorgasbord on the Baltic Sea, a visit to their summer home, and back to their estate called Lindholmen." "Dinner in Cologne was at a Swiss restaurant with zither music and eight year old cheese!" "The Alps from the air are beautiful!" "Flew from Geneva to Paris and our girls were waiting for us at the hotel. Looked good and hadn't seen them since June 10th. Had lunch and all four Oehlers took our tour to see Notre Dame and the outside of the Louvre." "We took the girls and with Willie and Ken Anderson and their Sally, went to the Lido for dinner and show. Really quite a place with beautiful girls!" "In London took a double decker bus to Piccadilly Circus to see the lights and signs." "Visited Westminster Abby—this I liked best of all the churches we have seen!" And at the end: "A wonderful, wonderful trip!"

Some of the hotels where the Oehlers overnighted were: Palace Hotel in Stockholm, Sweden; Savoy in Malmo, Sweden; Carlton Hotel in Cologne, Germany; Taunus Hotel in Wiesbaden, Germany; Boston Hotel in Rome, Italy; Terminus St. Lazare Hotel in Paris; Hotel Plaza in Brussels, Belgium; and Eccleston Hotel near Victoria Station in London.

Both Mary and Bill were struck by the familiarity of the faces they saw in Germany, swearing that this person on the street looked just like Minnie Pleines or that one looked like John Kuhfuss, folks they knew in Minier, 100% Germans by blood too, of course. One of Bill's jokes after the trip was his amazement that: "Even the little children in Paris could speak perfect French!"

Especially meaningful for Mary and Bill were the opportunities they had to visit friends in their European homes. In Malmo, Sweden, they were entertained by Anna and Carl Herslow, a landed customer of John Deere, whom they had met on a visit to Moline and whose son, Bengt, was a Deere intern for one year in Moline and frequent visitor to the Oehler home. The Herslows drove them out to their country home, Lindholmen, near Svedala, Sweden. Mary and Bill saw Paris in sharper focus in the company of Moline neighbors, Ken and Willie Anderson, then billeted in Paris by Deere's purchase of the Lanz Farm Machinery

Company. Together they strolled the Bois de Boulogne, shopped, dined at Maxim's, and nabbed prized tickets to the Follies-Bergere. But the highlight of their Parisian sojourn was successful scheduling of the stay of their two daughters to coincide with their own. For four days and nights the four were inseparable. Bill rented a room next to theirs in the beautiful Parisian hotel, Terminus St. Lazare, an unforgettable experience for the girls who were accustomed to the simplicity, even privations, of Youth Hostel quarters. Together they saw the Louvre, Notre Dame, Versailles, the nightlife with the Andersons, and of course a requisite stop at a bank to replenish their daughter's American Express checks. On by tour bus to Brussels the four Oehlers together traveled; there, as on a mission, walking up and down the narrow, pedestrian-only lanes to locate the famous "mannequin piss," sampling the famous Belgian chocolate, and enjoying delicious waffles from street vendors, all the time strengthening their sense of family solidarity, building a memory bank of shared new impressions to last a long long time.

Back in Moline the four were glad to have each other to share the story of their eventful summer for they learned very quickly that their experience was too rare, almost too exotic, to engage their friends' extended interest. Friends would ask, but as soon as Mary began to speak in detail, eyes would glaze over and the subject changed. "You just had to be there to get it," she would conclude. But with Bill and her girls, she could always find common ground and that was profoundly satisfying. They, alone with her, had experienced a door, big as a barn door, open to reveal a hitherto unknown, wonderful, endlessly fascinating world.

Although it is impossible to say for sure, it seems likely that their European tour of 1960 which introduced them to the different lifestyles, cultural life, art, and history, like a seed sown, germinated, and grown to fruition, made possible the change which came into each of their lives within a mere four years: Kathleen flew off alone to Pirmisens, Germany, to marry Paul Beich, her college sweetheart living there as a US Army serviceman in October of 1961; Susie married Hans-Peter Keller, an immigrant to Illinois from southern Germany in August of 1963; and Bill accepted a transfer by Deere & Company to live and work in Heidelberg, Germany, in early 1964. Yes, the impressions each Oehler absorbed while traveling in Europe were favorable—and lasting!

Regarding Kathleen's announcement that she and Paul Beich planned to marry, Mary and Bill felt conflicted. Their younger daughter was just nineteen years old, had completed just two years of university, and had not known Paul very long. On the positive side of the scale, they were impressed that Paul was scion to the Beich Candy Company, oldest son of a leading family of Bloomington, Illinois; they had driven to Bloomington to introduce themselves to Paul's parents and as Mary said: "Get the lay of the land." Both couples "hit it off" but thought a wedding was premature. However, neither parent knew of divorce as an option in that day before society's acceptance of that possibility became a trend; in their experience, marriage was forever; and if happiness did not follow the wedding, "well, you just make it work." Paul was lonely in Germany and Kathleen wanted to marry him, so instead of returning to the Gamma Phi house in Urbana, Kathy as she preferred to be called, flew alone after a sendoff dinner and night near O'Hare field hosted by Mary, Bill, and attended by Susie, Ruth and Paul Beich, Sr., and Ada. A case of hives prevented Mary from taking her place on the tarmac, but the bride-to-be was stunning in her new "going away outfit" and full of confidence and conviction as she departed.

As soon as Kathy and Paul completed the bureaucratic paperwork required to marry in Germany, Mary and Bill flew to be at their side to host a wedding reception and dinner attended by their John Deere acquaintances living in nearby Mannheim and Heidelberg as part of Deere's vanguard of the fledgling tractor company there. As parents of the bride, still concerned with the welfare of their younger daughter, Mary and Bill observed that the Cadillac Paul had bought to welcome his bride was riddled with problems and tactlessly perhaps called them from the bridal suite to go shopping for a new Volkswagen "Beetle." That accomplished, a quick tour and approval of the rooms the bride and groom had rented in a private home in Pirmasens ensued and the Oehlers flew home to Moline.

"Empty Nesters" now at the age of forty-nine, for Susie had just graduated from university and moved to her Chicago job at the Chicago Tribune, Mary and Bill embarked on a new stage of life. Letter writing was still the accepted mode of communication, the cost of stamps low and the cost of telephone high, so Mary still expected a letter each week from her girls as did they in return. All her life, a certain amount of time in a week was given over to letter writing, greeting cards, even post-cards when the message was short and impersonal. Bill wrote to his Dad in Minier every week; Mary wrote the regular but succinct missives to their daughters.

It was not the mailman who brought the announcement that Kathleen was expecting a baby in August though; the thrilled parents telephoned the news to the grandparents-to-be. "Well, that's what happens when you get married!" Bill crowed. No sooner than a second phone call came to announce the arrival on August 19, 1962, of Kathryn Mary Beich, than Mary and Bill booked a flight to meet her. Kathryn for Paul's deceased mother and Mary for Mary but dubbed Kammy at Mary's impulse almost immediately. Spud and Katharine traveled early to meet the baby as did Susie at Christmas-time.

Almost "footloose and fancy-free" now, Mary and Bill traveled with Spud and Katharine to Chicago for an Agricultural Society conclave and stopped by Susie's and her roommates apartment where a Saturday night party was occurring. Susie introduced them to her friends, including Peter Keller, but they didn't know they should give him more than a cursory glance and regretted it later when Susie announced she wanted to bring him to Moline so they could get to know him! Suspecting this was a "sign," Mary and Bill met the plane (Peter was employed by Japan Airlines) from Chicago and wined and dined the young man from Germany as if there was a "von" before his last name! During the cocktail hour, after a grand tour of Moline, the young man mustered his courage to ask for Susie'a hand in marriage. Fearing their reaction might be negative due to their countries enemy status during World War II, Peter was visibly relieved when Bill observed: "Well, you know, we are German too!" Eight months later on August 31,1963, Mary and Bill saw their second daughter marry and drive off in the three-speed, manual Plymouth they bought the couple as a wedding gift.

As one exciting event seemed to follow another, Bill came home from the John Deere Planter Works with the news that he had been asked to join the cadre of Deere employees in Mannheim, Germany, converting the Lanz Tractor Company to manufacture the full line of Deere farm implements under that eponymous name. He was given the title, Technical Director, with the assignment to establish manufacturing plants for a full line of agricultural implements. Kathleen, Paul, and Kammy were back in the States living in Lawrence, Kansas, where Paul studied; Susie was married and worked at the Chicago Tribune in Chicago; Bill's Dad was comfortably ensconced at Hopedale House near Minier; and Mary was one hundred percent in agreement, so Bill felt free to accept the position in Research and Product Development.

So began four years, 1964—1968, of a virtual European vacation for Mary, headquartered in their rented apartment at 26 Wielandstrasse in Heidelberg, Germany. Though it cost $11,000, Deere packed and shipped all her furniture by air to her new home, and it actually took two identical apartments, one a floor above the other to accommodate all her furnishings; Katie and Chuck Frazee, colleague of Bill, lived in the ground floor unit of the brand new, never occupied, new construction. Together, while their husbands were working, Mary and Katie combed the Heidelberg and Mannheim cultural offerings, touring the castle many times, the gardens, and philosophers walk. Most week-ends took Mary and Bill on drives, in their new Mercedes-Benz, of exploration, first in Germany, but eventually to every European tourist destination and many obscure lesser known but no less significant sights such as the Arctic Circle in northern Sweden to see the land of the midnight sun.

"It's like being in a giant PX (army post exchange) living here in Germany," Mary excitedly crowed! For every dollar she got four Deutschmarks which made all goods look like a real bargain to her and therefore irresistible. The shopping began in earnest when one evening the clatter crash sound of dishes falling and breaking announced the collapse of a built-in shelf holding her entire set of Noritake china. With the insurance check, Mary chose an eight place setting of Rosenthal, Germany's fine porcelain, and like a horse at the gun, the shopping binge began. Meissen figurines, Dresden figurines, wood carvings, hand-carved wood wall paintings, Bing and Gruendal figurines and Christmas plates, an oak antique stand clock, Belgian table linens, sturdy leather club chairs and sofa, lamps, Wedgwood and Belleek pieces, wine and beer glasses for their new taste in beverages, specialty flatware for eating fish, plates for serving snails, Venetian glass objects, several "Leiterwagen" or German hand carts, and Italian intaglio or inlayed wood side tables, everything still in family possession.

And then there was the clothes shopping made mandatory by the extra pounds both she and Bill put on dining on the rich, gravy-laden, wurst-stacked, butter-filled, bread-piled dishes and pastries of Europe. A desire to avoid the American "look" and to fit in also prompted Mary's wardrobe changes to boiled wool capes, mannish hats, and woolen suits. She even bought a couple of dirndls, the traditional German dress consisting of a blouse trimmed in lace, a bodice, full skirt, and an apron, which worn with a blond wig of braids made a very fetching party getup.

Yes, with the ease of a spoon slipping into soft ice cream, Mary and Bill refined their palate to the German cuisine. Recipes for her favorites were obtained from her "kaffe klatch" neighborhood friends who met in each other's homes to improve their German and English and to eat. For instance: "rouladen," a thin slice of roast beef, slathered with a good German mustard, a dill pickle laid atop, grated cheddar cheese sprinkled over, rolled and secured with a toothpick, and quickly browned, became a standby at Mary's table. "Birne Helene" became her frequent dessert, simple and delicious: lay a canned or fresh pear half on a dish, place a ball of vanilla ice cream in the recession, and drizzle chocolate sauce over. Likewise, "Pfirsiche Melba" (peach Melba) was a dessert Mary brought back to the States: place two canned or fresh peach halves, recession side up, in a bowl, add two small balls of vanilla Ice cream over the peaches, and drizzle raspberry sauce over. From Señora de Pedro Pombo-Duran, who hosted Mary and Bill while they were on a business trip to Spain, she acquired this recipe for Gespatcho for six: Cover the blender blade with water, add four medium tomatoes, peeled, cored, and cut up; one clove garlic, one-fourth medium onion, one small cucumber, one-half green pepper, yolk of one hard boiled egg, and a handful of dried bread crumbs. Blend at medium speed till well mixed. Add two tablespoons salad oil, vinegar and salt to taste. Mix at high speed. Taste for salt. Chill. If too thick, add ice cubes. Garnish with minced white of the hard boiled egg and parsley.

It was also while living in Germany that Mary began collecting boxes. At first, the snuffbox-sized purchases were nothing more than a souvenir to remind her of a wonderful day of travel to a special place, a visit to a superb porcelain shop, a charming village, or a restaurant but soon the collection took on a life its own! Bill brought her boxes from his business travels throughout Europe, her friends eagerly seized on the novel collection gifting her with one at every opportunity. Not all boxes were precious though a couple came close; some were whimsical, some were hand-made, some were of wood or metal, some were like little jewels; none was priceless. For all the rest of her long life Mary treasured her box collection, always a conversation piece, with a prime location in her home, even adding to it long after its display cabinet was chock full.

Ada, widowed, her daughter, Linda, off to college, visited many times. Together they toured the sights around Heidelberg, then expanded to the British Isles, Switzerland, Austria, Italy, and France. Over many years of vacation weeks from her executive position at Washington National Insurance Company in Evanston, Illinois, Ada flew the Lufthansa flight from O'Hare so often that she knew the flight attendant, Maria, as friend.

Another visitor was Louise Murphy, next-door neighbor in Moline whose husband, Hayes, preferred other pursuits over travel. Together, Mary and Louise took a bus tour to Rome to see the Pope and to Belgium, Louise's heritage. Katharine and Spud visited numerous time; Jess visited; Kathleen, Kammy, and Paul visited; Susie, Peter, and Christopher visited; Deere executives were continuously passing through, but European travel was not yet a commonplace activity among Moline friends so Mary never felt like she was running a small hotel.

Besides European travel, the Oehlers visited Susie and Peter in their Central American homes at Avenida las Americas 15-79, Zona 14, Guatemala City, Guatemala, at Carretera King 6 Hatillo, Junto Casa Dr. Villa de Morales, Tegucigalpa, Honduras, and at Barrio La Guaria, Moravia, 125 Vs Oeste Entrada Principal, San Jose, Costa Rica, where they enjoyed playing grandparents to Christopher and Cynthia Keller.

As long as they lived in Heidelberg Mary and Bill attended classes in the German language, making limited progress. At the "kaffee klatches," the German women wanted to practice their English; at the office, the Germans all spoke English or at least better than Bill's German. A Cassell's German dictionary was at the ready in their home and a small version was in Mary's purse, if an emergency arose, but the two essentially got along with their limited vocabulary plus lots of hand motions and facial expressions. That pretty much describes the encounters of Mary and Bill when they met with Ruth and Alfred Keller once Peter and Susie had introduced their parents. Peter's brother and wife, Goetz-Dieter and Gisela Keller, came for an overnight and to deliver the draperies they sold from their firm in Rottweil, and though Gisela spoke good English, miscommunication still occurred. Days after Mary and Bill had served the young couple a huge steak dinner, they learned from friends who had also received a delivery of curtains just an hour before, that they too had served them a large dinner. Not knowing how to explain that they had just eaten or not wanting to spoil the Oehlers hospitality, they simply ate heartily at both tables!

A kind of a cloud began to appear from time to time over Mary's extended vacation in Heidelberg with the concern that Kathleen's marriage was disintegrating. Twice she and Bill made hasty trips to Moline, where the young couple were living while Paul worked at an East Moline candy company, to counsel them and eventually to help their daughter move into a rental home with her two small children, Kammy and Paul, to help her to secure a position at Deere, and to help her find the babysitter for the children, Mrs. Smith. The rest of the time back in Heidelberg they tried to contend with little needles of worry which sometimes pierced the sunshine of their happy, carefree days.

By 1968 Bill's career took another turn which sent them packing back to Moline. Even Mary was ready. One can't be forever on vacation, and she missed her daughters and grandchildren, though the Kellers were living in Central America at the time. The Oehlers had sold their Crestwood Hills home in Moline requiring a hurried house search this time with the stipulation that it be located near a home to be occupied by Kathleen and her children. Luckily, this turned out to be possible. In the new subdivision, Rock View Estates, they found a newly constructed home with split foyer at 3609-36th Street to their liking especially because directly across the street was a duplex which they could purchase and rent to Kathleen, now divorced, and to another family on the second half of the duplex. Such an arrangement, though crafted with the best of intentions, was not harmonious; the will to be helpful turned intrusive, tempers flared, invectives were slung, doors slammed, tears flowed.

Serious problems in their relationship with Susie and Peter crept into Mary and Bill's lives at that same time when disappointment with Susie's conversion, while living in Guatemala, to Peter's Catholicism boiled over into outright rage. Though Bill, himself, never attended any church at all, he carried the prejudicial bias learned in small town middle America against Catholics as well as Jews. After an ample cocktail hour and during a steak dinner when Susie, Peter, and Christopher were staying with them in anticipation of the imminent arrival of their second baby which they wanted to be born in the United States rather than in Central America, Mary and Bill began a previously unmentioned subject of their misery over the humiliation of Susie's wedding being held in a Moline Catholic Church, Sacred Heart, and later over Susie's conversion. Mary, as often in a case when her emotions were stimulated too much by rage, when her temper-filled angry words turned to tears, had to leave the table and take to her bed for a day or so, thoroughly sick. Bill, however, continued his rant against the young couple until the worthy meat literally stuck in everyone's throat.

On and on, even during Susie's requisite five day hospital stay birthing Cynthia Denise, they continued to assault the defenseless Peter. The attacks let up when Susie and the new baby came home from the hospital but resumed when the issue of baptism arose. A stalemate ended with the young family going without the grandparents to Sacred Heart Church for Cynthia's baptism and then stopping off at the home of Katharine and Spud to celebrate. Lately, Mary and Bill had begun to resent the closeness their daughters had long held with "the aunt and uncle," as the girls called them, so this too felt like a stab to their honor. As soon as possible, when Cynthia was only three weeks old, the young family literally flew off to their new assignment in Costa Rica to reside at Barrio La Guaria, Moravia, 125 Vs Oeste Entrada Principal, San Joe, Costa Rica.

The culmination, with Kathleen, came when she fled with her secretly married husband, Jim Ashby, Kammy, and Paul to Spud and Katharine's, and in the middle of the same night to Atlanta, Georgia, to start a new life. Five painful years of separation, no contact by letter or phone whatsoever, between them and their daughter and grandchildren followed. From Susie and others who had contact with Kathleen, they at least knew of their daughter's whereabouts from Atlanta to Florida cities, but they never succeeded in a reconciliation.

For Mary, this was the second trial of her life which she had to suffer alone, keep her own counsel, couldn't confide fully in others because of her pride, her sense of shame, and perhaps the suspicion that she and Bill were at fault. Like a family feud, embarrassing yet intractable, the stalemate just went on and on. She confided with those closest to her, Ada, Corsie; special friends, Margaret Hansen, Jean Koivun, Gladys McKahin, and Gladys Lasser, and Bill's siblings, but no one could offer the comfort and consolation she so desperately sought; that she was denied. No one could wave a magic wand to instantly return her to life before the big fight.

Perhaps Mary and Bill couldn't adjust to their daughters' growing up, couldn't accept the new young men into their immediate family life, couldn't compete for their daughters' affection, couldn't cope with their daughters' new opinions and tastes, couldn't handle their daughters' independent ways. Whatever the cause, they suffered but eventually emerged whole. As Mary said: "I know that when I speak of family, I include Susie and Kathleen, but when you two think of your family you don't mean Daddy and me!"

Some solace was achieved in the summer of 1970 when Peter Keller was transferred by Deere and Company to the Intercontinental Limited branch office in Moline bringing Susie and about to be three grandchildren to live right across the street from them. Knowing that they would soon depart for the Ozarks and retirement, Mary and Bill sold their home in Rock View Estates to the young family and moved across the street to Kathleen's former half of the duplex. Mary stayed in town to await the birth of Susie's baby, Ingrid, but Bill, a still vigorous fifty-eight year old anxious to work with the carpenters on the construction of their new home, loaded his tools and drove on down to the Ozarks. It was in the middle of the night, in the early hours of October 20 when Peter phoned Mary, just across the street, that Susie was in labor, and she was needed. In what seemed like a mere five minutes, Mary appeared at the door fully dressed and made-up, ready for the most auspicious social event though it was just to care for Christopher and Cynthia once the day dawned!

On Bill's fifty-eighth birthday in June of 1970, he accepted Deere's special retirement program which set Mary and Bill onto a new pathway and away from Moline. Their chosen destination, after vacations spent visiting localities popular with young retirees, was Kimberling City, in the Ozark Mountains of Missouri, near Table Rock Lake and the country music town, Branson. Among the many attractions, there was a mild climate, where snow was rare, allowing their houseboat to be in the water year 'round. But the move also offered a kind of escape from the reminders of their feud with their daughter. It was also there that for the first time in their nearly fifty years of married life, Bill began to attend church services with her to the point of inviting the pastor and his wife into their home and on houseboat excursions. To Mary's amazement and joy, he even regularly attended a men's prayer group. We will never know for sure but can presume this change of heart was another reaction to the feud.

The community of young retirees appealed to Mary a lot though she did shed copious tears at leaving her many Moline friends. She threw herself into decorating their new home high overlooking the lake, continued her enjoyment of golf and the accompanying social life, organized a new chapter of the P.E.O. sisterhood, threw dinner party after dinner party in her effort to supplant her old friends with new ones, of whom Mary and Mac MacCall, Leanna and Marsh Edinger turned out to be the dearest.

When friends from Moline and Germany came to visit, Mary found many local attractions to impress: Silver Dollar City, a theme park set in 1880 Ozark Mountain life; numerous country music hall's in nearby Branson; Eureka Springs just across the southern border in Arkansas; drives through the Ozark Mountains full of spring flowering

STORIES MY FOLKS TOLD ME

trees, rushing rivulets, and craft and curiosity shop-filled villages. The mountain scene was definitely a change from Moline but nonetheless captured the hearts of Mary and Bill with its plain speaking charm and down-to-earth simplicity. As well, it was a diversion from their agony over their separation from their daughter, as change of location usually is.

Barn red was again their choice of color for the exterior of their new home on Hillcrest Drive high on a bluff overlooking Table Rock Lake. The porch looking to the road had a decided Ozark Mountain cabin appearance but the deck on the lake view side of the house was typically American with picnic tables, grills, redwood chaise lounges, and a hanging swing for three. Inside on the main floor was a living room with a built in wet bar, a fireplace with sweeping hearth, the German club furniture, and Bill's Wurlitzer organ; a thoroughly modern kitchen with appliances in the avocado green of that day; and a guest bathroom featuring a toilet seat painted by a friend which when raised said: "It's so nice to have a man around the house!" Also on that level, a bedroom for Mary utilized the canopy bed suite, had shelves for all her books and her own bathroom; Bill's room across the hall used the Peine Eastlake furniture, and his own bathroom gave privacy. Downstairs was another bedroom with bath, another living room with sofa-bed for even more guests, a laundry room, and Bill's amazing wood-working shop. That lower level gave out to the back yard of lush green grass kept immaculately groomed as it sloped, eventually steeply, down through undeveloped property to a road. There was a home next door but on the other side were acres of meadow where Bluebirds nested, perched, and warbled to their hearts' content nearly the whole year 'round.

It was to this house that Kathleen and her children, now including toddler Jamie, came on an incredibly joyous day for Mary and Bill in 1972, to reconcile with her parents. In the ensuing weeks, Mary couldn't help but admire the way her daughter established a home for her children in their town and got a job to support them, then finished her college degree by commuting to Missouri State University in Springfield and subsequently earned a master's degree in social work.

A certain kind of profound happiness came over Mary when both her daughters, who each had three children, gathered under her roof in that home on the hill. She throve while helping her daughters care for their children. Once when Susie and Peter returned from a ten day trip leaving their children with Mary and Bill, Mary greeted their return with: "We got her ready for kindergarten!" meaning Ingrid had taken her first steps and uttered new words under her tutelage. Kammy was the oldest, Paul was two years younger, Christopher came fourteen months after him, Cynthia in two and a half years, Jamie and Ingrid, born just three weeks apart were the youngest by twenty-eight months. Oh, the noise! Oh, the laughter! Oh, the "shenanigans" (Mary's word)! "If my dad could only have known these boys! He would have loved it!" Mary often exclaimed.

In her own words which reflected the time and place where she grew to womanhood, Mary could utter some pretty idiosyncratic expressions that amused and caught the attention of her wondering daughters and grandchildren:

"That was slick!" meant something was easy to do, clever, or nice. She used the   expression a lot.

"By golly!" with the emphasis on "By" meant she was amazed.

"That's a new wrinkle!" described a new idea.

"A real pain in the neck" criticized someone for getting on her nerves.

"Oh, for Pete's sake!" told she was exasperated.

When folks collaborated in a way negative to her, they were "in cahoots." "Where (or how) in the dickens?" spoke of a mystery to her.

When chiding someone for dressing too fancy: "You sure got all dolled up!" or

"She sure was gussied up!"

When Susie announced she had given up drinking Manhattans: "Yeah, but it   sure was fun, wasn't it?!"

"Don't take any wooden nickels!" admonished one to be wary.

"And then she chimed in," said someone interrupted.

"Chewin' the fat" referred to friends or family sitting in comfortable conversation.

"There was a whole slew of them" meant many of them.

STORIES MY FOLKS TOLD ME

"How are you Folks?" Folks was a frequent address of hers.

"Her dad doled out the candy" meant distributed the candy.

"You hit the nail on the head!" meant you are exactly right.

"If I had my druthers" referred to her preference.

"She sure gets on her high horse!" referred to a pompous woman.

"Who's making all that racket?" asked about some noise.

"We were sure all tuckered out" told of being tired.

"He could call a spade a spade" meant the speaker was frank.

"Like a bat out of hell" connoted speed.

Mary and Bill's shared love of travel took them, early in their retirement, to Colombia and Turkey when Bill volunteered with the International Executive Service Corps on three month assignments. With their airfare and furnished apartment rental their only reimbursement, the two felt as they had in Europe, once again on an extended vacation. Mary, too, volunteered where she felt eminently comfortable: in the library. It was in Ibague, Colombia, the land of emeralds, that Mary could finally realize her lifelong lust after fine jewelry. Small jewelry stores showcasing locally-mined emeralds literally lined the streets of town after town, and she loved to explore as many as she could provided there was a sign in the window that someone within spoke English. How fortuitous, she thought, that the emerald was her May birthstone! Once awakened, her quest to scour jewelry stores wherever she found herself whether South America, Europe, Caribbean Islands, or Springfield, Missouri, was a favorite activity culminating in her nickname: "sparkle plenty" after the Lil Abner character of the 1940s.

Their months spent living at the Hilton Hotel in Mersin, Turkey, afforded Mary and Bill the proximity of many A-list travel destinations and lesser known exotic places too like Tarsus, Adana, Izmir, Antalya, Ankara, Tusan, Troy, Gaziantep, Konya, Antakya, Istanbul, Alayna, Cyprus, and Ephesus. A travel journal and souvenirs from those many travels remain as family treasures. Again, Mary volunteered in the town library where some patrons delighted to practice their English with her and where she was assured of an ample supply of books written in English to read. She simply liked to be nestled in a library, a beacon and a monumental tribute to learning and civic pride, surrounded by weighty tomes and lofty spaces. Ada's visit right after Christmas put all right in Mary's world as well.

Some flights back to Europe, especially Germany where they still retained contact with Nina and Dolf Calot, the Bachmeiers, Wilhelm (Bill) Graf von Scwerin, Claude Roach, and the Hausers, occupied their retirement years. The dollar to deutschmark was no longer 1:4, but good deals were still available in the 1970s. One in particular was an offer they seized to fly the supersonic Concorde from Paris back to New York City after first reaching the continent via ocean liner. At such momentous occasions, Mary felt particularly far from Minier!

Though their marriage had more than once looked shaky, those high points of life, those shared experiences happening so far from their common origin, the ensuing companionship and shared memories, and the pleasure which such sharing brings was enough to compensate for the times fraught with frustration and temper. It was a trial for Mary whenever a morose sullenness would come over Bill, when mean words would be hurled at her in a low, disrespectful growling manner or when at the lowest point he would refuse to speak to her. The gloomy moodiness could last for days. As always during those times, Mary retreated or escaped into a good book. Even then she could be heard to laugh out loud, thoroughly absorbed in some hilarious situation she was reading. Both she and Bill felt strongly, though, their common roots of their earliest years in Minier, their bond built on a lifetime of adventures together. It couldn't be lightly severed. "Besides, where would I go?" Mary would invariably query.

They tried a few winters in MacAllen, Texas, where Bill had field-tested John Deere planters in years past and where several of his colleagues from the Planter Works days wintered, but it proved too far from family in the middle west, so in 1985 they followed Kathleen to Florida. Not to Bradenton where she and her children lived but to the old south town of northern Florida, Gainesville. As was always their way, probably because Bill was an engineer at heart and always needed to customize their home, they moved into a brand new construction in the golf club sub-division. It was Mary's idea to choose a university town where she thought they might meet like-minded folks, and they did make acquaintances through her P.E.O. sisters there, but mostly they met traditional "southerners" who regarded them as "yankees" confirming philosophical differences between them. After only a few years, the Oehlers headed farther south where other mid-westerners clustered, to Inverness, where once again the grass looked greener to Bill.

There for the first time ever the couple settled for a house which had actually been lived in by others. They were not the first owners of the lakeside home in central Florida, but by the time they had it painted their signature barn red and Bill had donned his carpenter's belt to make his modifications which included reversing the direction of a staircase, the house on Cresco Lane looked completely theirs. Again they played golf, met new people, and especially relished the years when grandson Jamie, studying at a nearby college, lived in the boathouse which Bill converted to private quarters for him. Meals were taken in the big house with the old folks, of course!

Wanting to attend P.E.O. meetings, though there was not a chapter in Inverness, Mary and her new best friend, Mary Beth Miller, traveled to the next closest meeting place in Sugar Woods. Sure enough, the distance proved a negative and set the two women on track to form a chapter in Inverness. First they had to find out if there were any more P.E.O.s already living in their town, but how to do that? Simple! Ask the post mistress to give them the names of women receiving the P.E.O. Record magazine. It worked! Together the small clutch of women, working with Florida state officers of the sisterhood, succeeded in founding chapter HC, enjoying many a grand time in the project. Always the generous hostess, Mary held the celebratory luncheon in her home using nearly all of her six sets of china in the process.

By 1992 Mary and Bill were eighty years old. They had celebrated birthdays and their fiftieth wedding anniversary with their daughters and Ada gathered 'round; they had comforted Mary's Uncle Paul in his last years; they had seen their six grandchildren grow to maturity; they had seen granddaughter Kammy marry George Young; and they were at peace though Bill, especially, was slowing down and diagnosed with heart disease. Evidence of his previously unspoken love and perhaps as a token of his apology for his behavior over the years came in the form of a surprise gift he made to Mary though it was not her birthday nor Christmas: a gold medallion on which was inscribed in French the words "I love you more than yesterday and less than tomorrow" Set with a large diamond and hanging from a gold chain, it spoke volumes and wiped the slate clean! For the rest of her life, she wore it over her heart!

Both her daughters were present at the Inverness Hospital during Bill's last illness of kidney failure and heart disease. The end came on the day before his eighty-third birthday. Strong in the face of loss, Mary remained in the house and attempted to continue with her bridge games, P.E.O., church gatherings, and friends, but she felt like a fish out of water without a husband and was surprised at how lonely she felt, how difficult she found all the everyday household decisions which she had formerly balked at when Bill so unilaterally made them.

Much before the proverbial mourning year wait was over, therefore, she decided to move closer to a family member in Jacksonville, granddaughter Kammy and George Young with little Georgie and Lucy. The Carriage Club, a senior citizen residence, on the city's south side became her home. Right away she met another soul-mate, Margaret Jones, when they discovered they were both P.E.O.s and mid-westerners. As she said to her grandson-in-law, Jim Patti, "Well, it's not a home and husband, but it's the next best thing." She was contented. In Jacksonville, Mary was able to return to the Mayo Clinic for her annual physical which she and Bill had done in their Moline years. This time there was no long trek to Rochester, Minnesota, but a short drive to the Jacksonville Mayo campus. There officials marveled and she preened at her small registration number signifying she was a long time and early Mayo patient.

Then hard on the heels of the loss of her husband came the death of her beloved Ada the very next year. As the older sister, Mary never imagined she would survive Ada; they were making such plans for travel, even had purchased tickets for an Alaskan cruise in June; Mary had chosen an apartment with a second bedroom for Ada's extended visits; they had been through so much together over their lifetimes, understood each other like no one else; and now Mary desperately needed Ada. She was bereft!

STORIES MY FOLKS TOLD ME

In her attempt to restore meaning to her life, Mary stumbled into the Publishers' Clearing House sweepstakes. Filling out the forms, writing the checks for magazines and cheap items she didn't need or want until late in the night, occupied her time and distracted her mind as a sort of coping device in her bereavement. Every day cartloads of boxes of 8-track tapes, reconfigured old movies, music cassette tapes, glassware, cooking equipment, ill-fitting clothing, junk jewelry, and such arrived from the mailroom of the Club to her dismay. Letters and phone calls from the sweepstake shysters assured her she was a finalist nearing the big pay day of a million dollars. Unscrupulous as they were and true to their reputation for preying on the elderly, they kept Mary engaged for three years and thousands of dollars no matter her daughters attempts to thwart. Then one hallelujah day in conference with her banker and family, she finally saw the situation clearly, expressed her remorse, and like a reformed gambler addicted to the blackjack table never wrote another check to the clearing house.

For Mary's 90th birthday party, over thirty family members and friends filled the guest dining room of the Carriage Club. Ada's daughter, Linda, got the prize for traveling the farthest, but both daughters and husbands, Tom Washburn and Peter Keller; all her grandchildren, Kammy Beich Young and husband George, Paul Beich, Jamie Beich, Christopher Keller and wife Julia, Cynthia Keller Patti and husband Jim, and Ingrid Keller Conroy and husband Coleman; and six great-grandchildren, George and Lucy Young, Sophie Keller, Jane and John Patti, and Tommy Conroy were there for the happy occasion. (Yet to be born are great-grandchildren Greta and Erica Keller, Charlotte Mary Patti, Rory and Adeline Susanne Conroy) Tributes were made and Mary herself spoke about her life and the pleasure she felt to be so celebrated that day by her nearest and dearest. Ever the lady with a streak of vanity, she was gratified to see that the "portrait" cake was her university graduation portrait and not a more recent shot.

Just one more move remained for Mary. Kathleen and Tom retired to Fernandina Beach, an island north of Jacksonville, built a home there, located a small care-home walking distance away, the Jane Adams House, and installed Mary there for the few months remaining to her on this great green Earth.

Mary's ashes now lie beside Bill's in Minier cemetery just steps from those of her parents, John and Adela Rost; grandparents, Mary and George Peine; great-grandparents, Hennig and Caroline Buehrig; Uncle Paul Peine; parents-in-law, Emma and William Oehler; sisters-in-law, Lyla Oehler Johnson, Dorene Tanner Oehler, and Nelle Forsythe Oehler; brothers-in-law Delmer Oehler, Jess Oehler, and Delmer Johnson; and scores of aunts, uncles, and cousins.

Mary and Bill Oehler

Memories of their grandmother, Mary, were expressed at her Florida funeral and add another level to the understanding of her:

Jamie Beich: "I have fond memories of Grandma Mary. Some of my earliest memories are visiting her in Missouri. She loved to serve me coffee with a lot of sugar added, of course. She would always serve it in my favorite mug. The mug had a frog at the bottom that would slowly surface as I drank the coffee. I would eagerly drink my coffee served by Grandma Mary. I also value the memories of the last years of her life that I was able to be near her when she as living in a retirement community. She would be so excited to have someone bring her a hamburger and watch football with. Regardless of where I brought the hamburger from she would always remark how good it was. I also remember when she took me to a bookstore to buy a bible. I value it still today."

Paul Beich: "I liked my Grandma. We liked each other, and we each had our own ways of showing that. She had a certain way of saying to me, 'Well, it's good to see ya! I haven't seen ya in awhile—whaddya been up to?—staying outta trouble?—that's good' that delightfully revealed her rural Midwestern roots and seemed to come out all as one sentence. The way she said it let me know clearly how glad she was to see me.

"In her later years, when I'd come and visit her, it would typically take us about ten minutes to get caught up on all that we needed to talk about—what I was doing for work, news about her grandchildren or great-grandchildren, etc. Then we'd just sit. My favorite thing to do when I'd come see her was to sit next to her on the sofa. It was one of my favorite ways to let her know I liked her. She'd read, I'd read. Occasionally there was something to say, more often there wasn't. But it was always good just to sit next to each other.

"My relationship with Grandma taught me that love does not depend on understanding or agreeing about things. There was 53 years of difference in our age. We were from different eras. I frequently didn't know about her cultural references, and she rarely knew of mine. And we rarely agreed on 'important things.' Occasionally she'd ask me if I was 'still a Democrat' with a certain tone of disapproval in her voice, followed by another assertion of 'I'm a Republican' (as if that wasn't already clear to me). My typical answer to her question was 'It's worse than that, Grandma.' She never asked what I meant, and I didn't tell her, because we both knew it didn't matter all that much. As recently as last fall we got into an argument about whether it was alright to use a certain word to describe a certain type of college football player. We argued a little about that, but the argument quickly died down. I learned from Grandma that we didn't have to understand each other or each other's way of seeing things in order to love each other.

"Thank you, Grandma, for all the years of being my grandmother, and friend. Thanks for all your warm greetings, and for the long, slow afternoons of sitting next to each other. I love you and I'll miss you."

Ingrid Keller Conroy: "My Grandma was a wonderful conversationalist. She had an incredible memory and was knowledgeable when it came to many subjects. Two of my favorite topics were memories she had of her own family as well as my childhood visits to Kimberling City. She spoke so fondly of her family and her years growing up in Illinois. She had many humorous tales to tell and was a great storyteller. She also enjoyed reminiscing about her travels with Grandpa while working with Deere and afterwards. I always knew my Grandma loved me. Although she tended not to verbally express her love, she would always hold my hand. This was especially great, because when you are no longer a little girl, people think you are too old for something like this. This showed me that this type of contact can mean as much or even more than words. I will miss her very much."

Christopher Keller: "Yessir, if she were here right now with us (and of course she is), she would tell us to simmer down and not make a fuss. However, she would enjoy the part of this that relates to reminiscing. She always had a razor sharp mind and could replay moments from her memory like they were answers to a crossword puzzle. Grandma was also a great story teller. This is the one thing I'll miss most about her. She could take me far away to a time long ago. I am sure her childhood growing up in a small town in Illinois, of her lifelong closeness with her sis Ada, of her father who was a doctor, of Uncle Paul who ran the general store, of meeting her husband who grew up with her in the same small town, of time spent at the University of fIllinois, of her two daughters Kathy and Susie of her PEO chapter and friends, of her many travels around the world. of her six grandchildren, of her eight great-grandchildren, of many exciting football games, of her retirement in Kimberling City, of her time in Florida, and of her final days with her family near."

Cynthia Keller Patti: "When I think of Grandma in her prime, I think of how she surrounded herself with antiques, pretty collectibles and things from her rural upbringing in Minier. Grandma and Grandpa moved several times in retirement but she always artfully accommodated each piece of furniture as well as figurines, box collection, plates and multiple sets of china into each new home. This helped contribute to a sense of continuity for me at least and I suppose it did for her as well.

"As a kid and teenager I didn't really understand her interest in the things she had collected over time. I was just very aware that my grandmother had a sterling silver serving utensil for every possible food or beverage. There were also lots of delicate looking dishes holding candies and treats. It was fun to run around the house upon arrival and search for the bowls with my favorites.

"Now as a grownup, I can identify a bit with her desire to collect and surround herself with things filled with meaning to her. Inspected superficially I could say she liked to shop and had a penchant for Depression glass, all things porcelain, and antique furniture. On a deeper level, though, I think it helped create a comforting environment for her and Grandpa as well as shrug off some of the negative memories of the Depression.

"Things like the bedroom set from the Peine store and the camel back couch Grandma and Grandpa received as a wedding gift helped her connect to her Minier childhood. The box collection and other porcelain reminded her of their travels and life abroad. The other antiques represented her hobby and interest in history. In a way these things defined her.

"I admit to liking my things a bit too much sometimes as well. I prize my antique German china. I'm delighted to be the new owner of the camel back couch and feel fortunate to have it in my living room. The cherry silver cabinet, which Grandpa himself crafted, is another treasure from Grandma and Grandpa that reminds me of them each time I see and use it. When I tried on Grandma's wedding gown, I knew that was the only dress for me.

"Grandma was a real lady and by surrounding herself with pretty things and things from the past she was defining herself in a way and communicating to those whom she invited into her home about her past, her life and interests."

Kathryn Mary Beich Young: "My memories of Grandma are…the smell of Jean Nate cologne, sleeping in her big pretty bed with a ruffled cover, cocktail parties with exotic hors D'oeuvres like miniature corn on the cobs, "Guten Morgen!" when I stumbled into the kitchen for breakfast, my first car, postcards from around the world, birthday cards and presents, a big house that's fun to play in, football, magazines, history books, the Publisher's Clearinghouse sweepstakes, cracking up over her quick-witted retorts, how much she loved being with Aunty Ada, and how much she always missed her mother."

Ada Margaret Rost Seales and Charles Franklin Seales, Jr.— Generation 4 —1, 2, 3, 8—

Born, October 8, 1916, the result of her mother's visit to her father who was tending to wounded soldiers brought to New York City during World War I, Ada was welcomed into a loving household of parents, Adela and John Rost; sister, Mary; and grandfather, George Peine. Her young years have already been described as her life was very closely intertwined with Mary's and came out in Mary's story, but despite their tight bond their development did take them on differing though paralleling paths.

Immediately following graduation from the University of Illinois in Champaign, Ada who had been president of the Gamma Phi Beta sorority there, learned of an opportunity to earn a master's degree in psychology. The sorority wanted to charter a new chapter at the University of Nebraska in Lincoln and sought young Gamma Phis to live in the new sorority house there to guide and mentor the collegian members. When Ada and her friend, Phillis Armstrong (later Johnson), learned that room and board was included, they were convinced and on their way! Those two years became an extension of her college days which Ada always called "the best years of my life!" After family life, of course!

Ada had known Chuck Seales, from Springfield, Illinois, at the University of Illinois; he waited tables at her sorority house to support his education there. Friendly banter was all that was allowed in those days when dating between sorority girls and employees was forbidden, but though World War II service and study of the law required Chuck while a master's degree consumed Ada, their paths later crossed in

STORIES MY FOLKS TOLD ME

Chicago—at the courthouse! Ada's first job with Child and Family Services and Chuck's first job as an attorney demanded attendance there, causing their paths to cross, and the spark to ignite. When they married on May 1,1943, Chuck was in U.S. Army uniform and on matrimonial leave, so Ada returned alone to her studio apartment to await her husband's discharge.

That joyous day came with the war's end in June of 1945. Among the many stories which filled the talk of the day was the one told by Ada's cousin, Mose Peine, her cousin and son of Raymond, son of William (brother of Ada's grandfather, George): Mose had been left for dead on a battlefield of France, but a fellow infantryman stopped to pick him up and literally dragged him off the field. Weeks in a hospital ensued; miraculous healing resulted; shipment home to Minier for full recovery followed. For Mose's dad Raymond, gratitude knew no bounds! He made it his life's mission to find and thank the lad who had saved his boy from certain death! A letter writing campaign, complete with dead-ends and frustration, revealed his identity, communication was achieved, and reward money was dispatched.

Like Mary, Ada had suffered the death of their mother—at the tender age of nine and a half. With her, too, the loss was a part of her life always. She continued to think of her mother, though perhaps not every day or with the same intensity. Recollection was nevertheless evoked sometimes by a date on the calendar or a sight, sound, aroma, melody or place that elicited the missing person. For Ada, the most difficult day was always Mother's Day. Those personal moments, seemingly forever paused in time, were shared by the sisters. No matter how many years passed, the memories remained.

Amazingly, that early suffering did not suppress Ada's positive attitude, her glass half full outlook, her solution-oriented point of view. Her cheerful disposition, her outgoing personality, her loving expressions endeared her to all who came to know her throughout her eighty years. Mary often wistfully summed it up, "Ada is just like Dad!"

Her niece, Susie, spoke at the 80th birthday celebration Ada threw for her family and friends at a hotel private dining room: "Aunty Ada, it must have been a very sunny day on October 8, 1916, because you seem to have taken that as your cue and set out to spread sunshine every day all your life long. Your many friends are a testimony to your sunny, outgoing, generous personality. Friends from college days sixty years ago are still a part of your circle as are friends from church, neighborhood, Washington National Insurance Company, and volunteerism. You traveled alone on Travcoa tours, all over the world, but never once on those tours did you dine alone.

"I've tried to learn your secret to your happy, optimistic disposition. I've noticed the picture hanging in your home of a potted flower with the saying underneath: 'Bloom where you are planted.' That gives me a hint! You often uttered, 'No matter what, I always read the comic page everyday!' Your Christian faith which so obviously is embedded in you, must also be part of the mix!

"And then there's the telephone—specifically the long distance wires—your luxury, you say! They love you at ATT because you stayed with them even when other companies came luring with their tempting offers, and they love you because you constantly "reach out!" Probably it's a toss-up whom you phone oftener, your daughter or your sister, but one thing's for sure—there have been some funny stories ensuing. I hope you'll take it the right way if I tell one on you right now! Once several years ago your sister answered the phone, surprised that it was you. 'Why Ada, what is it? You just called me yesterday!' Your bright reply was, 'Oh, I know but I just called the plumber and there was no answer!'

"We all love your humor. You always find the funniest greeting card to send us, and you're quick with the witty rejoinder. When asked to what you attribute your long life you immediately replied: 'cigarettes and scotch!'"

When Ada was only thirty six years old she suffered a second unimaginable death of a loved one. Her husband of eleven years, Charles Franklin Seales, passed away from melanoma, spread from a mole on his back. For many women that would have caused a breakdown, a surcease in progress down life's path, but Ada packed her bags and flew with nine-year-old Linda to Midge and Dex Barrett in LaCanada, California.

When those two weeks of rest and restoration were completed, she returned to her home in Arlington Heights, Illinois, to begin her career anew. With a position at Washington National Insurance Company assured, she hired a live-in housekeeper and caretaker for Linda, Ann Gurney, later succeeded by Helen Parker. She did not have to give up the home she and Chuck had built; she did not have to make a latch key child of her daughter; she did not have to give up travel, a college education for Linda, nor an enviable wardrobe for them both. Without losing a beat, Ada picked up the hand she had been dealt and proceeded to bloom where she was planted. Nor was a grousing complaint about her lot ever heard to issue from her lips. A little plaque, "Footsteps in the Sand," hanging on her refrigerator pictured a person walking on the beach. In some places there are two sets of footprints behind but in another only one set. The observer questions why sometimes there is only one set of footprints. The answer: "When you saw that there was only one set of footprints it was during your worst travails, and that's when I carried you," the Lord said.

She instinctively knew that life doesn't always go according to one's plan. She understood that in joy, pain, and even in personal failure, God is close. Faith steadied her. She trusted God as in Isaiah 46:4—"I am He, I am He who will sustain you. I have made you and I will carry you. I will sustain you and I will rescue you." In her Presbyterian church, Ada was a loyal participant and volunteer serving as an Elder and on a pastoral search committee among many other duties. She requested that her cremated remains be interred in the memorial garden there and they were, beneath the Isabel Bloom sculpture of a smiling girl placed by Linda and Ada's friend, Donelda Schaible.

Each year, Ada rewarded herself with an exotic vacation of two weeks duration on a Travcoa tour: India for the Taj Mahal, Singapore, Australia, Thailand, Malaysia, Indonesia, Hong Kong, South Africa, and the Caribbean multiple times for Ada loved a beach. Besides those, she visited Linda and sons Josh and Zack Johns in LaConner, Washington; Susie and Peter in Guatemala, Costa Rica, and Torch Lake; Mary and Bill in their various homes in Moline, Heidelberg, Kimberling City, Gainesville, and Inverness. Contact with her sister-in-law, Elizabeth Seales Shoaf Benefiel, never wavered no matter how many years passed since Chuck's death, so phone calls and meetings with her, also, were frequent. Ada, too, had inherited the travel bug!

For a certified career woman, Ada could remarkably cook a mighty fine roast beef dinner! Her chest freezer in the basement was always stocked to the brim with her favorite steaks, ice creams, frozen dinners till Mary exclaimed, "Ada, you could live a month on the food in your freezer!" Decades after she had had a husband to share the details of a cocktail party or a lavish dinner party, Ada continued to hold them in her home, shouldering the load herself simply because she liked the fun and the conversations, especially with the men. Whole black pitted olives were a standard on Ada's table because she liked them. Some of her family members include them at their festive dinners to this day, just as a reminder of Ada!

After Linda left for college at Ohio Wesleyan University and the last housekeeper had retired, Ada hired a woman from her church to clean her house, somewhat developmentally disadvantaged though she was. Ada truly valued relationships more than anything else!

Becoming a grandmother at the age of sixty-six was surely a high point of Ada's life. Two little boys, Josh and Zack, were to her a revelation of energy and high spirits, luring her to many visits to LaConner, Washington, and never missing a Christmas there with them. Preferential fares from their mom's employer, United Airlines, enabled them to visit their Grandma every summer, too, of course.

In 1992, retired, seeing the housing market soar beyond belief and recognizing that a major part of her estate was in that real estate, Ada sold her home garnering an amazing sum for her two-story brick and batten home at 222 Drury Lane. She and Chuck had been right, back in 1952, that the Stonegate neighborhood of Arlington Heights was exceptionally desirable and would continue with its wide lots, winding tree-lined streets, and beautiful homes to be so. Dear to her, long-held friendships, and countless memories were anchored there but it wasn't as if she was moving far. She could continue her relationship with Chuck and Dotty Bobbinet and Helen and Don Smith. It just wouldn't be as spontaneous as when she went out for a stroll. The two-bedroom apartment she chose was comfortable, near that of her friend Donelda Schaible, and offered activities for the residents and communal meals. Volunteerism, like Meals on Wheels, P.E.O., walking with friends at the mall before the shops opened filled Ada's days but she always found time to read the Chicago Tribune, work the cross-word puzzle, read the "funnies" and make a few phone calls to friends and family. She was never sick a day.

She stated many times that she hoped to live to see in the new millennium, and she almost made it, but that was not meant to be. Though keeping a healthy and fit lifestyle since she gave up cigarettes in her early seventies, a three month bout of cancer took her on June 28, 1997. Testimony to the number of friends she had and their affection for her were the scores of flower arrangements delivered to her hospital room. Hopefully, she recognized then how many lives she had affected and influenced, because she had a gift for connecting with people, for saying just the right thing or sometimes for holding her opinion and just listening. She had all the best qualities one could wish for in a sister, sister-in-law, mother, daughter, aunty, or friend!

Chuck's remains lie in Oak Ridge Cemetery in Springfield, Illinois, just steps from the Lincoln Tomb. Ada's ashes were interred in the memorial garden of her church in Arlington Heights, Illinois, the First Presbyterian.

CONCLUSION OF THE STORIES

MORE THAN ONE hundred years after the arrival of our first ancestors, our folks, now into the third and fourth generation, identification with Germany was pretty much diffused. But the Tazewell County rich black soil still prevailed. It had changed with augmentation and new farming techniques, yet it still provided the highest yields imaginable year after year, still earned the moniker: "gift of the glacier."

I hope I have illustrated my belief that family is a fundamental building block of society, even of civilization. I wish my progeny to see that they are part of an ongoing tribe of living breathing people who made a life worth telling. Indeed, every life has a story! Every life matters! As Charles Lindbergh wrote, "Each of us stands at the narrow of an hourglass the product of all who went before, the foundation of all who follow." Each life, therefore, is crucial! I hope I have helped the reader feel a connection to the thirty-four folks whose lives I have described, those who blazed the trail before us. Perhaps the readers can even see themselves in the stories of past times, startled at the similarity of their own thoughts and desires with those of past lives, for every heart imagines itself the first to thrill to a myriad of sensations which once stirred the hearts of earlier folks, and will stir again in future men and women who walk the earth. That life repeats itself is a fundamental constant of the universal experience. That the evolution and continuity of the cycle of human life and love are forever fascinating, I believe deep in my heart.

I hope the reader will see that our folks have always experienced difficulties, challenges, and disappointment yet strove to overcome them, to look for and find joy, satisfaction, and even fulfillment in their lives. Life is not all a bowl of cherries, as folks used to say. I think that in the lives of our folks we can see the universal human experience unfolding as they concerned themselves with such basic and vital problems as man's quest for happiness, the problem of suffering, of good and evil in human conduct, of regrets, of death, and of the unknown which lies beyond the grave. We of today have those same universal concerns so hopefully the stories of their lives can serve as an aid to understanding and solving the problems which we, ourselves, confront.

Of course the world outside the lives of our individuals, like a parallel world, was one of almost continuous warfare, intolerance, enmity, envy, disease, anxiety, corruption, and cruelty some of which actually impacted their lives. But they knew a balance. There was family life, love, community, and faith, without which no human being can come out of this life sane. Our folks were real people, not heroes or heroines, who worked hard and made a difference step by step, evidence that the human spirit is very tough and resilient.

Finally, let me say that our folks incrementally, each in their own small way, helped make this country what it is today: a powerful, great, noble and good nation—the best in the history of mankind, and, yes, still an exceptional nation. For a successful life is the accumulation of many small parts, many small steps trodden forward. They add up to a life that is more than the sum of its parts, a life that makes a difference to society. We, today, have inherited a great legacy and with it a great duty to do the work to ensure its continuation. It's the least we owe our folks!

STORIES MY FOLKS TOLD ME

EPILOGUE

I WILL BRING my story to an end here with a quote from 2 Maccabees, 15: "If it is well written and to the point, that is what I wanted; if it is poorly done and mediocre, that is the best I could do…. Let this, then, be the end."

ACKNOWLEDGEMENTS

ALTHOUGH I HAVE spared myself the rigor of footnotes, I feel compelled to reveal that I gleaned the majority of historical information from the following books: "The Birth of the Modern" by Paul Johnson, "A History of the American People" by Paul Johnson, "News from the Land of Freedom" edited letters, "Enduring Vision" by Houghton Mifflin Company, "John Deere's Company" by Wayne Broehl, Jr., "Eyewitness Travel Germany" by Doring Kindersley, and "History of Minier, Illinois," E.J. Graber, editor.

For the genealogy work, I am indebted especially to Oren Imig for the Imig and Graff families, Margaret Buehrig for the Buehrig family, Irene Risser for the Oehler family, and to my parents, Mary Rost Oehler and William Oehler for their collections of newspaper clippings, letters and mementos, and especially their wealth of memories which they so generously shared in story form with me over the years. I must mention, of course, ancestry.com which I scoured with a fine-toothed comb over many long winter evenings. My sister, Kathy Washburn, cousins Linda Seales, Rita Johnson Witzgall, and John Johnson also shared many memories and photos to enliven the stories. My German-born husband, Hans-Peter Keller, provided many pertinent insights and historical details regarding the homeland of many of my subjects. My daughter, Cynthia Keller Patti, assisted me in scanning of photographs, in preparation for the electronic printer, Xlibris. My husband Peter, son Chris Keller, and daughter Ingrid Keller Conroy encouraged me at just the right moments over the years of writing. I am truly grateful to you all!

9 781524 506551